A Minitab Guide to Statistics

SECOND EDITION

Ruth Meyer • David Krueger

Prentice
Hall

Upper Saddle River, NJ 07458

Acquisitions Editor: Quincy McDonald
Supplement Editor: Joanne Wendelken
Assistant Managing Editor: John Matthews
Production Editor: Wendy A. Perez
Supplement Cover Manager: Paul Gourhan
Supplement Cover Designer: PM Workshop Inc.
Manufacturing Buyer: Lisa McDowell

© 2001 by Prentice Hall
Upper Saddle River, NJ 07458

Printed in the United States of America

10 9 8 7 6 5 4 3 2 1

ISBN 0-13-014156-9

Prentice-Hall International (UK) Limited, London
Prentice-Hall of Australia Pty. Limited, Sydney
Prentice-Hall Canada, Inc., Toronto
Prentice-Hall Hispanoamericana, S.A., Mexico
Prentice-Hall of India Private Limited, New Delhi
Pearson Education Asia Pte. Ltd., Singapore
Prentice-Hall of Japan, Inc., Tokyo
Editora Prentice-Hall do Brazil, Ltda., Rio de Janeiro

TABLE OF CONTENTS

Contents

PREFACE

A Minitab Guide to Statistics was written to introduce professionals and students to Minitab, a general purpose statistical computer system. This guide gives comprehensive information on the use of Minitab in statistics. Included are statistical concepts and techniques that are generally covered in a basic statistics course.

More About Minitab

Minitab was developed at Penn State in 1972 for students in introductory statistics courses. Since then, Minitab has evolved into a comprehensive statistical system that is also used by students in advanced data analysis courses, and by scientists, engineers, and managers in business, government, and industry. Minitab is the international standard for the teaching of statistics. It is used at more than 5,000 sites in 60 countries.

Minitab runs on PCs, Macintosh computers, workstations, minicomputers, and mainframes. Although there are some differences in Minitab across releases and computer platforms, the commands and worksheet are basically the same.

This guide was developed for use with Minitab Release 13 as well as prior releases. All dialog boxes, graphs, and other output are produced with Release 13. If you have a different Minitab release, most of the commands are compatible, but the output may differ. We also worked all examples with Minitab Student Release 12. Menu and session commands and output are quite similar to Release 13, but some simulations in Chapter 6 will have to be reduced in size because of available memory.

Features

This guide illustrates the use of Minitab in organizing and analyzing data. As statistical concepts are introduced in each chapter, we present appropriate Minitab commands, and provide step-by-step descriptions of how to effectively use Minitab. Interesting real world data sets are used throughout the guide in examples, and exercises which conclude each chapter. A computer diskette containing many of the data sets is available. The Appendix describes the large data sets. We have chosen examples and exercises from myriad professions, including business, education, government, health, medicine, and sports.

The chapters in this guide are designed to correspond to chapters of leading statistics texts. The final chapter of the supplement describes a survey sampling project. The objectives of the project are to illustrate the use of Minitab in questionnaire evaluation and to provide a review of statistical techniques.

How to Use this Guide

The only way to learn Minitab is by doing Minitab. Since this software is relatively easy to use, you will experience success very quickly as you produce professional graphs within a short time. We encourage you to redo the examples that we have included in this guide. Most of the data sets are on a disk; the menu path and session commands are provided for each example. After you have mastered our examples, try the exercises at the end of the chapters.

Minitab works with data in a worksheet of columns and rows, very much like a spreadsheet. The commands are available through menus or through a command language in the Session window. If you are using Windows, you probably will use menu commands more often; however, menu and session commands can be used interchangeably. We show menu paths and session commands side-by-side for each example.

Clicking on a menu usually opens a dialog box allowing you to select variables and choose options. You will find dialog boxes throughout the guide. To select variables, you need to have the cursor in the box in which you want to enter the variables. Then highlight the variable(s) in the list of variables box and press *Select* or double-click on the variables. You can also type the column number or name in the box. We indicate this step in the menu path with the word *Select* followed by the name of the column.

As we name new columns or constants in a dialog box, we indicate this in the menu path with the word *Enter* followed by a column name. Minitab automatically uses the next available column or constant. Since the commands are printed in the session window, you can follow the action.

If you are using only session commands, you can follow the step-by-step list of commands to the right of the menu paths. The success will depend on the version of Minitab that you are using. Check the *Help* facility if you get an error message.

Where to find More Information about Minitab

There are additional texts available for information on Minitab. We recommend the *Minitab User's Guides* from Minitab, Inc. You can also access Minitab information 24 hours a day on the World Wide Web at the address below. There you can download Minitab macros, find press releases, capabilities lists, and product information, and view graphical samples. Information about Minitab software and texts may be obtained from:

Minitab, Inc.
3081 Enterprise Drive
State College, PA 16801-3008

Telephone: 1-814-238-3280
Fax: 1-814-238-4383
Website: www.minitab.com

```
┌─────────────────────────────────────────────────────────┐
│  ┌───────────────────────────────────────────────────┐  │
│  │                                                     │  │
│  │                   CHAPTER 1                         │  │
│  │                                                     │  │
│  │            INTRODUCTION TO MINITAB                  │  │
│  │                                                     │  │
│  └───────────────────────────────────────────────────┘  │
└─────────────────────────────────────────────────────────┘
```

Minitab[1] is a computer software package that can increase your understanding of statistics and decrease your calculation time. It was originally designed to be an easy-to-use statistical system to help in the teaching of statistics. It has evolved into a powerful package for data analysis and graphics. In this chapter we give a general view of how Minitab works, and illustrate some menu and session commands to enter, print, and save data.

MINITAB COMMANDS INTRODUCED IN THIS CHAPTER

END   INSERT   NAME   PRINT   READ
SET   STOP

1.1   ACCESSING MINITAB

Minitab is available on PC and Macintosh computers, minicomputers, or mainframes. Although there are some differences in Minitab across releases and computer platforms, the commands and worksheet are basically the same.

MICROCOMPUTER ENVIRONMENT

If you use a microcomputer, you need to be familiar with the operating system, the directory and path names, disk drives, and diskettes. If you need more practice with these features, please refer to your system's user guide.

With the Minitab user interface, you can type commands and subcommands in the session window or you can execute them by choosing from menus and by completing dialog boxes. The commands and corresponding output are given in the session window. In addition, you can copy, edit, and execute previous commands.

To use a Windows version of Minitab, you need to know the basics of Windows. This includes moving and resizing windows, using menus, and using dialog boxes. If you are not familiar with these basics,

---

[1]   Minitab is a trademark name of Minitab, Inc.

please refer to documentation or the online help facility on Windows.

To start Minitab using Windows, double click the shortcut to Minitab icon on the desktop or choose the path:

Start ▸ Programs ▸ MINITAB 13 for Windows ▸ MINITAB

The screen that you will see is similar to that shown below. It contains the session and data windows, menu bar, standard and project manager toolbars, and status bar. These windows can be repositioned or resized.

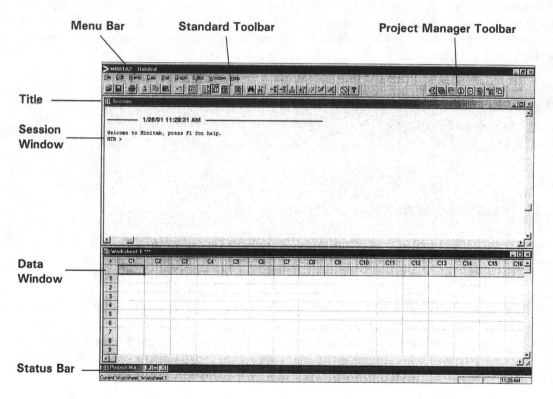

The **session window** lets you create a program by typing commands and subcommands. Typically menu and session commands, subcommands, and the corresponding output are displayed as they are executed. Data entered in the session window are also displayed. The **data window** allows you to enter data in a worksheet either by typing, generating, or importing data from a file.

Across the top is the **menu bar**, from which you can open menus and choose commands. Click on a menu item, then click again to open a submenu, execute a command, or open a dialog box. Menu items that are dimmed are not currently available for use.

For example, if you choose the path

Window ▸ Project Manager

the following screen is opened.

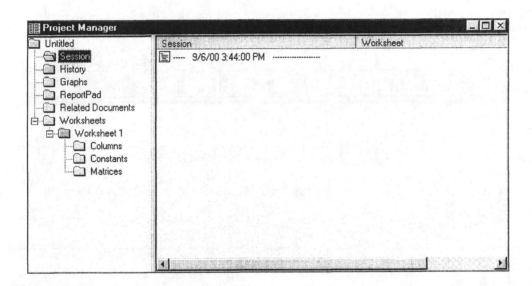

Minitab's **project manager** is new in Release 13. It allows you to better organize and manage your work. The following folders contain commands, data, output, graphs, and other related documents.

- **Session**   Use this folder to copy, delete, or print output and graphs from the session window. You can append contents of the session window to the ReportPad.

- **History**   This folder contains all the commands used during a project session. Use this folder to repeat a sequence of commands or to create a macro (described in Chapter 2).

- **Graph**   Use this folder to manage all graphs. You can delete, arrange, or append graphs to the ReportPad.

- **ReportPad**   This is Minitab's new word processor to create reports. Right-click output or graphs to add to the ReportPad. You can edit and print a report from the ReportPad, or copy to another word processor such as Microsoft Word.

- **Related Documents**   This gives a list of other related non-Minitab files, documents, or

Internet URLs for reference or other use.

- **Worksheet**   Use this folder for information on worksheets including columns, constants, counts of columns, missing values, and matrices.

The **project manager toolbar** provides shortcuts to these folders.

The **standard toolbar** displays buttons for commonly used functions; the buttons change depending on which window is active. Place your mouse pointer over the button to see its name. Here is the standard toolbar when the data window is active.

For example, the icons cut, copy, and paste cells in the data window.

The **status bar** at the bottom of the screen displays explanatory text for the menu item or toolbar button you are currently using.

NOTE

We use Release 13 for Windows to illustrate all examples in this guide. The session window commands and corresponding output are provided in each example. If you are using other releases of Minitab, most of the commands have the same arguments and subcommands; some of the output may differ slightly. Refer to the Minitab User's Guide for your Release or the HELP facility for specific information on commands that differ from the examples in this guide. We worked all examples with Minitab Student Release 12 and added notes in the simulation examples where you may have insufficient memory.

MAINFRAME VERSION

If you use a mainframe computer, you need to learn how to 'log on' to the system. Generally the log on procedure requires you to enter an account number, a user name or user identification, and a password.

If you are successful with the log on procedure, you are in the computer's operating system. The computer usually gives you information about the system, and then a system prompt. It expects you to respond with a system command. The procedure for accessing Minitab varies, but generally, you need to type the word **Minitab** following the system prompt. The system responds with the version of Minitab that it has in its library, some information on Minitab, and the MTB > prompt. You can then enter Minitab session commands.

1.2   MINITAB WORKSHEET

Minitab works with data in a worksheet of columns and rows. Usually, a column contains the data for one variable, with an observation in each row or a data point in each cell. Columns are denoted C1, C2, C3, . . . , and rows within columns are numbered 1, 2, 3, and so on. Most Minitab work is done in columns. The first row is reserved for column names.

↓	C1	C2	C3	C4	C5	C6
	Name					
1						
2						
3						
4						

Multiple worksheets are available with **Minitab Release 13** with each worksheet allowing up to 4,000 columns. The numbers of rows and cells depend on the memory allocation. You can control this if you choose

  Edit ▸ Preferences ▸ General

Move the slider in the memory usage section somewhere between the following endpoints:

- **Share nicely.** Minitab will share more memory with other programs currently running.
- **Use as much as necessary.** Minitab will use as much memory as necessary, sharing less memory with other programs currently running.

Multiple worksheets are also available with **Student Release 12** with each worksheet allowing up to 1,000 columns with 5,000 data points. The size is displayed on the screen when you start Minitab.

WORKING WITH THE WORKSHEET

This section gives more details on Minitab's worksheet. Usually a column contains the data for one variable, with an observation in each row or a data point in each cell.

Columns
- A column contains alpha or numeric data (date/time is a third type of data). The type of data can be assigned or changed.
- Minitab identifies a column as alpha or numeric by the first value entered in that column.

Rows
- Individual rows can be accessed by specifying the row number in parentheses following the column number or name; C1(9) denotes the ninth row of C1.
- The subscript can be any expression which produces a positive integer. C1(COUNT(C2)) denotes the row of C1 corresponding to the number of observations in C2.

Cells
- Cells in a data window contain values that you enter or generate with commands.
- Cells do not contain formulas as in Microsoft Excel and Lotus 1-2-3.

MINITAB CONSTANTS

Minitab can store individual numbers, such as an average or standard deviation, in constant locations denoted K1, K2, K3, . . . **Constants** are created by LET or by any command that produces a single number answer. An example is MEAN, the command that calculates the arithmetic average. The result of the command is automatically printed; you need to print the stored constant to view it. For example, if a column named Scores contains test results, the MEAN command below calculates, prints, and stores the mean in a constant K1. The PRINT command prints K1.

```
MTB > MEAN 'Scores' K1

Mean of Scores

   Mean of Scores = 76.600

MTB > PRINT K1

Data Display

   K1    76.600
```

For more advanced work, Minitab has **matrices** denoted M1, M2, M3, . . . Each matrix can store one table of numbers. The number of available matrices depends on your computer.

When you begin a Minitab session, the worksheet is blank. During the session, you enter data in the worksheet, work with the data, and then you can save to a file for future use. Minitab reminds you to save your work before you end a session.

1.3   MENU AND SESSION COMMANDS

Minitab commands are available through the menus or through a command language in the session window. These commands, called menu commands and session commands, can be used interchangeably.

USING MENU COMMANDS

To use menu commands, click on an item in the menu bar to open the menu, execute a command, open a submenu, or open a dialog box. If a menu item is dimmed, it is currently unavailable.

For example, to open the data window, click the **Window** menu, then click **Worksheet**. *This path is shown in this guide as*

Window ▸ Worksheet

Choosing a command from a menu usually opens a **dialog box** allowing you to select variables and choose options. To select variables, you need to have the cursor in the box in which you want to enter the variables. Then highlight the variable(s) in the list of variables box and press **Select**. The variable(s) will appear in the box with the cursor.

You can name new columns in a dialog box. For example, when you use the Calculator function, you can name a column or constant in which to store the results. Minitab will automatically use the next available column or constant.

NOTE

*The **OK** button in the dialog box is usually the last button to press to activate a command. Pressing the **Enter Key** is the same as the OK button. You want to be sure the dialog box is completed before you press OK or the Enter key. For all the exercises in this guide, we provide the steps and the variables to select, and use **OK** after the final step is complete.*

USING SESSION COMMANDS

Session commands are useful alternatives to menu commands, especially when you want to use macros to automatically repeat a series of commands. Most session commands are simple, easy to remember words, like PLOT, SAVE, or SORT.

You can execute session commands in either the session window, or by using the command line editor. To execute commands in the session window, type the commands at the MTB > prompt. If the MTB > prompt is not displayed in the session window, choose

Editor ▸ Enable Commands

The command line editor lets you edit a set of commands and data before you actually execute the commands. To execute commands using the command line editor, choose

Edit ▸ Command Line Editor

and type, paste, and edit commands in the command line editor window. Then click

Submit Commands

to execute the commands in the session window. For example, type the following lines in the command line editor:

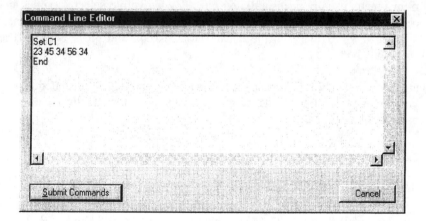

and click Submit Commands. The data will be entered in column C1.

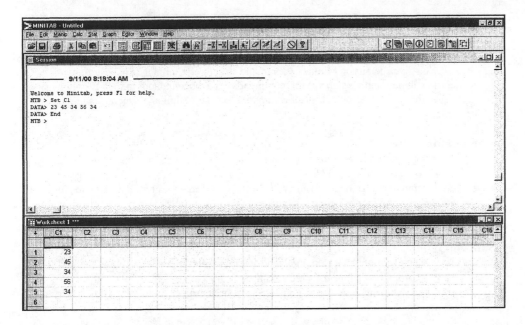

NOTE

Minitab has several hundred different commands, some of which have options and subcommands. Whenever we introduce a command or subcommand, we give a brief description, the Release 13 for Windows menu command in bold print, and the session commands with arguments and subcommands. Refer to the HELP facility for additional information concerning other Minitab versions.

MORE ON SESSION COMMANDS

This section gives details on Minitab's command structure. Commands have arguments to identify columns and constants. Most commands have subcommands to specify options or to provide additional output. Subcommands are very similar to menu command options.

Commands
- Type the command and arguments in proper order on the command line. *No extra text is allowed on the command line*
- Each command must begin on a new line. If a command does not fit on one line, use the **ampersand symbol &** or two plus ++ symbols at the end of the command line. Minitab responds with **CONT>**, and you can continue the command.

Subcommands
- To use one or more subcommands, end the command line with a semicolon and a **SUBC>** prompt will appear on the next line.
- Type the subcommands and arguments in proper order, ending each line with a semicolon.
- End the last subcommand line with a period. If you forget to place a period, you will get the **SUBC>** prompt; enter a period on that line.
- If you make a mistake, enter **ABORT** on a new subcommand line. This cancels the command and all subcommands.

Specifying Arguments
- An argument entered on a command or subcommand line can be a column, constant, text string, or a number.
- Enter column numbers (C1) or column names ('Sales'), stored constants (K5) or names ('Mean'), or a computer file ('Problem2.mtp').
- Enclose text strings such as titles or file names in double quotes ("Population of the Fifty States").
- Enclose a constant in double quotes if you want to use it as text ("1999").
- Abbreviate a set of consecutive columns or stored constants with a dash (PRINT C1-C5 is the same as PRINT C1 C2 C3 C4 C5.
- Abbreviate a sequence of numbers with a colon (1:5 is the same as 1 2 3 4 5).

1.4   ENTERING DATA FROM THE KEYBOARD

Minitab provides many ways to enter data in a worksheet. You can type data in the data or session windows, open a file, paste data from the clipboard, or generate data. This section shows you how to enter data from the keyboard in both the data and session windows and how to generate patterned data. Minitab uses alpha or text data, numeric data, and date/time data. Although some commands such as those for input, output, and editing work with alpha data, most Minitab commands work only with numeric data. Alpha data, for example the names of companies, are often used as row labels.

USING ALPHA DATA

This section gives some rules on alpha data. Minitab uses alpha or text data, numeric data, and date/time data.

- Alpha or text data may contain up to 80 characters, including letters, numbers, punctuation symbols, or blanks.
- Any number that appears in an alpha column is treated as alpha data, and cannot be used in calculations.
- Alpha and numeric data cannot be contained in the same column.
- Alpha data can be stored in columns and as constants.
- Alpha data can be converted to numeric data.

NOTE

*A **missing data value** is denoted by an * in a numeric column and by a blank in an alpha column. Most commands exclude missing values in calculations. A diagnostic is given if a command does not accept missing data.*

DATA WINDOW

You can enter data, view the worksheet, and edit data in the data window in Windows or the data screen in a PC version. To enter data, simply highlight the cell by using arrow keys or by clicking it with the mouse, and then entering data.

■ **Example 1**   **Data Window: Enter, View, Save, and Print the Data**

The number of seats that a state may have in the House of Representatives is based on the state's census. According to the 2000 census, eight states gained seats in the House over the previous ten years. The following table gives the 2000 census data, the ten-year percentage change in population, and the increase in the number of seats in the House of Representatives for each of the eight states. Enter the data in a Minitab worksheet, print, and save the data.

State	Population	Change	Increase
Arizona	5,130,632	40	+2
Georgia	8,186,453	26	+2
Florida	15,982,378	24	+2
Texas	20,851,820	23	+2
Nevada	1,998,257	66	+1
Colorado	4,301,261	31	+1
North Carolina	8,049,313	21	+1
California	33,871,648	14	+1

type. Add column names to the name row. Enter large numbers without commas, as commas will change a column to a text column and then it cannot be used in calculations. We save the data to drive A:\ as a portable file.

	C1-T	C2	C3	C4	C5	C6	C7	C8	C9	C10	C11
	States	Pop2000	Change	USReps							
1	Arizona	5130632	40	2							
2	Georgia	8186453	26	2							
3	Florida	15982378	24	2							
4	Texas	20851820	23	2							
5	Nevada	1998257	66	1							
6	Colorado	4301261	31	1							
7	North Carolina	8049313	21	1							
8	California	33871648	14	1							
9											
10											
11											

File ▸ Save Current Worksheet As
  Choose location in **Save in:**
  Enter name in **File name:**
  Choose Minitab Portable in **Save as type:** click **Save.**

MTB > Save 'A:\Census2000.mtp;
SUBC>   Portable.

Minitab responds to confirm that the data are saved.

```
Saving file as: A:\Census2000.MTP
```

You will notice that Minitab prints a subcommand *Replace* in the session window each time you save a data file. If you already have a file saved with the same name, Minitab will ask you whether you want to replace it.

To obtain a printed copy of the worksheet, activate the data window and open **File ▸ Print Worksheet**. The dialog box shown below will appear and you can choose printing options and add a title.

SESSION WINDOW

In the session window, you can use SET or READ to enter numeric and alpha data in columns, or use INSERT to add data to columns. The END statement marks the end of the data.

ENTERING DATA IN THE SESSION WINDOW

If a filename is given, data are read from the file into the worksheet. Otherwise the command is followed by a DATA> prompt. Numbers are usually entered free format, separated by commas or blanks, on one or more lines.

SET DATA IN C	Enters data in one column
READ DATA IN C ... C	Enters data row by row in specified columns
INSERT DATA (K AND K+1) C ... C	Adds data to the top (K=0), between rows (K and K+1), or bottom (omit K)
NOBS = K	Specifies number of observations
FORMAT (SPECIFICATION)	Enters alpha data
FILE 'FILENAME'	Reads from a file
END	Use on DATA> after all data are entered

NOTE

Several lines can be used to enter numerical data in a column. Just press the enter key when you get near the edge of the screen. Minitab responds with DATA; continue typing numbers following the prompt.

NAMING COLUMNS

This session only command assigns a name, in upper or lower case letters, to each specified column or stored constant. Anytime a name is used, it must be enclosed in single quotes (apostrophes). After a column or constant has been named, Minitab commands accept either the number or name.

NAME E 'NAME1' E 'NAME2' ...   Names a column, constant, or matrix

Some restrictions on the names are:
1. The name may be no longer than 31 characters.
2. The name may not begin or end with a blank.
3. The single quote (') and # symbols may not be used in a name.
4. Column and constant names must be different, but a name may be changed at any time.

Comment *We recommend that you always use column names. It makes the program and output easier to read and understand.*

VIEWING THE DATA

Use this command to display columns, constants, and matrices in the session window. If more than one column is given, the columns are printed vertically across the screen, and the row numbers are printed down the left side of the screen. If only one column is given, the data are printed horizontally across the screen.

Manip ▸ Display Data   Shows a dialog box for you to **Select** type

PRINT E ... E   Prints columns, constants, or matrices on the screen.

■ **Example 2**   **Session Commands: SET, NAME, and PRINT**

Refer to the data given in Example 1 on the number of seats that a state may have in the House of Representatives. Enter the data in a Minitab worksheet and print the data.

Solution To input the alpha data, use the FORMAT subcommand with SET. The SPECIFICATION option defines the spacing for the states' names on the DATA> lines. The simplest specification is to enter one name per line with (A10) specifying up to 10 characters. Numeric data are entered free format.

```
MTB > NAME C1 'States' C2 'Pop2000' C3 'Change' C4 'USReps'
MTB > SET 'States';
SUBC> FORMAT (A10).
DATA> Arizona
DATA> Georgia
DATA> Florida
DATA> Texas
DATA> Nevada
DATA> Colorado
DATA> N.Carolina
DATA> California
DATA> END
MTB > SET 'Pop2000'
DATA> 5130632 8186453  15982378  20851820
DATA> 1998257 4301261  8049313  33871648
DATA> END
MTB > SET 'Change'
DATA> 40 26 24 23 66 31 21 14
DATA> END
MTB > SET 'USReps'
DATA> 2 2 2 2 1 1 1 1
DATA> END
```

We use PRINT to display the data in the session window. Then we can copy the output to the Project Report Pad or to the Clipboard and paste it in a word processor to obtain a paper copy.

```
MTB > PRINT 'States'-'USReps'
```

Data Display

Row	States	Pop2000	Change	USReps
1	Arizona	5130632	40	2
2	Georgia	8186453	26	2
3	Florida	15982378	24	2
4	Texas	20851820	23	2
5	Nevada	1998257	66	1
6	Colorado	4301261	31	1
7	North Carolina	8049313	21	1
8	California	33871648	14	1

■ **Example 3**   **Session Commands: READ, SET, INSERT and SAVE**

Stocks traded on the U.S. stock exchanges are historically quoted in fractions. To make the U.S. markets more compatible with global markets, the Securities and Exchange Commission ordered a phased conversion from fractions to dollars and cents to begin in August 2000 and be completed in

April 2001. Consider the financial data reported in decimals on September 9, 2000 for four stocks traded on the New York Stock Exchange (NYSE). The column named Ticker gives the symbol used in trading. The High and Low are the 52-week highest and lowest selling prices, and Closing is the day's final selling price. The P/E ratio is the price of the stock divided by earnings and Dividend is the annual dividend rate.   Enter the alpha and numeric data in a Minitab worksheet.

Stocks	Ticker	High	Low	Closing	P/E	Dividend
AT&T	T	61.00	29.63	30.25	16	0.88
Home Depot	HD	70.00	41.75	52.94	47	0.16
Wal-Mart	WMT	70.25	43.44	52.00	40	0.24
McDonald's	MCD	49.56	29.06	28.81	20	0.20

Solution   If you are entering data in the session window, it's easier to use SET to enter names. The SPECIFICATIONS for the alpha data FORMAT (A10) and FORMAT (A3) say to use up to ten and three characters for each name.

```
MTB > NAME C1 'Stocks' C2 'Ticker' C3 'High' C4 'Low' C5 'Closing' &
CONT> C6 'P/E' C7 'Dividend'
MTB > SET 'Stocks';
SUBC> FORMAT (A10).
DATA> AT&T
DATA> Home Depot
DATA> Wal-Mart
DATA> McDonald's
DATA> END
MTB > SET 'Ticker';
SUBC> FORMAT (A3).
DATA> T
DATA> HD
DATA> WMT
DATA> MCD
DATA> END
```

A table of numeric data is easier to enter with READ. Data are entered, row by row, following the DATA> prompt.

```
MTB > READ C3-C7
DATA> 61 29.63 30.25 16 .88
DATA> 70 41.75 52.94 47 .16
DATA> 70.25 43.44 52.00 40 .24
DATA> 49.56 29.06 28.81 20 .20
DATA> END
   4 rows read.
MTB > PRINT C1-C7
```

Data Display

Row	Stocks	Ticker	High	Low	Closing	P/E	Dividend
1	AT&T	T	61.00	29.63	30.25	16	0.88
2	Home Depot	HD	70.00	41.75	52.94	47	0.16
3	Wal-Mart	WMT	70.25	43.44	52.00	40	0.24
4	McDonald's	MCD	49.56	29.06	28.81	20	0.20

Next let's add the following financial data to the table.

Stocks	Ticker	High	Low	Closing	P/E	Dividend
PepsiCo	PEP	47.06	29.69	42.56	32	0.56
Musicland	MLG	9.75	5.88	7.19	4	*

```
MTB > INSERT 'Stocks';
SUBC> FORMAT (A10).
DATA> PepsiCo
DATA> Musicland
DATA> END
MTB > INSERT 'Ticker';
SUBC> FORMAT(A3).
DATA> PEP
DATA> MLG
DATA> END
MTB > INSERT C3-C7
DATA> 47.06 29.69 42.56 32 .56
DATA> 9.75 5.88 7.19 4 *
DATA> END
MTB > PRINT C1-C7
```

Data Display

Row	Stocks	Ticker	High	Low	Closing	P/E	Dividend
1	AT&T	T	61.00	29.63	30.25	16	0.88
2	Home Depot	HD	70.00	41.75	52.94	47	0.16
3	Wal-Mart	WMT	70.25	43.44	52.00	40	0.24
4	McDonald's	MCD	49.56	29.06	28.81	20	0.20
5	PepsiCo	PEP	47.06	29.69	42.56	32	0.56
6	Musicland	MLG	9.75	5.88	7.19	4	*

The final step is to SAVE the data. We need single quotes for the drive A:\ and file name.

```
MTB > SAVE 'A:\NYSE.MTP'
Saving file as: A:\NYSE.MTP
```

ENTERING PATTERNED DATA

A sequence of numbers, repeated numbers, or repeated sequences of numbers can be entered very quickly in Minitab. If you are using the menu command, Minitab prompts you for the pattern in the dialog box. If you are using the session command, you need to enter the pattern.

Calc ▸ Make Patterned Data

SET C   Enter the pattern after the DATA> prompt

The following are examples of patterned data for the SET session command:

1. Sequence of numbers, where *a* is the starting number and *b* is the ending number: **a:b**
   DATA> 1:5 enters (1 2 3 4 5).

2. Sequence of numbers, where the step between the numbers is *c*: **a:b/c**
   DATA> 2:10/2 enters (2 4 6 8 10).

3. Repeated sequence of numbers, where *r* is the number of times the sequence *a:b* is repeated: **r(a:b)**
   DATA> 3(1:4) repeats the sequence 1, 2, 3, 4 three times (1 2 3 4 1 2 3 4 1 2 3 4).

4. Repeated numbers, where *r* is the number of times each number is repeated: **(a:b)r**
   DATA> (1970:1972)3 repeats each year between 1970 and 1972 three times: (1970 1970 1970 1971 1971 1971 1972 1972 1972).

5. Combinations of the above procedures can be used.

The following example illustrates combinations of patterns. The sequence we enter in C1 is 2 2 3 3 4 4 2 2 3 3 4 4 2 2 3 3 4 4.

Calc ▸ Make Patterned Data ▸ Simple Set of Numbers   MTB > Set C1
Enter C1 in **Store patterned data in:**   DATA> 3(2:4)2
Enter **From first value:** 2 and **To last value:** 4.   DATA> End
Enter 2 in **List each value** and 3 in **List the whole sequence. OK**

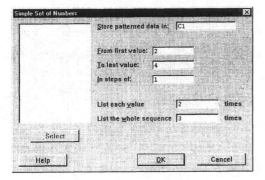

1.5 PRINTING YOUR WORK

To print the contents of the session, data, graph, report or history window, *activate the window* and use the menu command

File ▸ Print (*Active Window*)

This command gives different printing options depending on which window is active and whether or not you have highlighted a section of a window. There is no session command equivalent of Print Window.

You can also select and copy blocks of data, text, or graphs to the **Clipboard**. From the Clipboard, you can paste contents to a word processor. In Minitab, highlight the desired contents to print, and choose

Edit ▸ Copy

Use **Paste** in the word processor to bring the information into a document for editing and printing.

ENDING A SESSION

Use the menu item **Exit** or session command STOP to terminate a Minitab session and to put you back in the computer's operating system. After you have used these commands in recent releases, Minitab prompts you to save the current project if you have not already done so.

File ▸ Exit

STOP   Terminates a Minitab session

EXERCISES

1. Consider the following exam scores for 13 students. Enter the data in the data window. Obtain a paper copy of the worksheet.

Student	Exam 1	Exam 2	Exam 3
Brenda L.	75	62	88
John P.	66	78	73
Susan J.	92	96	98
Jason A.	86	77	79
Saleem A.	95	92	92
Justen P.	79	71	85
Fred K.	81	82	74
Shawn T.	63	80	80
Mike P.	76	73	64
Dwayne T.	45	59	69
Jim K.	85	86	78
Mary K.	77	79	81
Harold S.	57	68	70

2. In the book *Rating the Presidents* published by Citadel Press, the 41 U.S. presidents were rated based on a poll of 719 historians, political scientists, and others across the country. Abraham Lincoln was declared the nation's best president. Among recent presidents, Bush ranks 22nd, Clinton 23rd, and Reagan 26th. The following table lists the top ten presidents according to some leadership qualifications. Enter, print, and save the data in Minitab.

President	Leadership Qualities	Accomplishments Crisis Management	Political Skill	Appointments	Character Integrity
1. Lincoln	2	1	2	3	1
2. F. Roosevelt	1	2	1	2	15
3. Washington	3	3	7	1	2
4. Jefferson	6	5	5	4	7
5. T. Roosevelt	4	4	4	5	12
6. Wilson	7	7	13	6	8
7. Truman	9	6	8	9	9
8. Jackson	5	9	6	19	18
9. Eisenhower	10	10	14	16	10
10. Madison	14	14	15	11	6

3. The following table gives the 1999 quarterly sales in millions of dollars for five companies. Enter the table in a Minitab worksheet, print and save the data.

Company	Q1	Q2	Q3	Q4
Peters	45	78	65	81
Sinco	68	91	76	95
Mairo	33	45	43	52
Beck	59	76	88	74
Relle	49	73	67	80

4. The area of the world as a whole is 196.94 million square miles, of which 70.8% is water. The 1996 world population is 5.771 billion people, and the annual growth rate is 1.5%. Principal sources for world facts and statistics include the Central Intelligence Agency, Europa Publications, International Institute for Strategic Studies, International Monetary Fund, Population Reference Bureau, and Unesco. The following table gives some facts on 14 major countries.

Country	Population	Area	Currency	Capital
Bangladesh	119,800,000	55,598	taka	Dhaka
China	1,217,600,000	3,691,500	yuan	Beijing
Egypt	63,700,000	386,661	pound	Cairo
Ghana	18,000,000	92,098	cedi	Accra
Haiti	,300,000	10,714	gourde	Port-au-Prince
Indonesia	949,600,000	1,222,244	rupee	Jakarta
Netherlands	15,500,000	16,133	guilder	Amsterdam
Pakistan	133,500,000	307,374	rupee	Islamabad
Poland	38,600,000	120,728	zloty	Warsaw
Russia	147,700,000	6,592,850	ruble	Moscow
Sweden	8,800,000	170,250	krona	Stockholm
Taiwan	21,400,000	13,900	dollar	Taipei
United States	265,200,000	3,615,278	dollar	Washington, D.C.
Vietnam	76,600,000	128,066	dong	Hanoi

a. Enter the data; obtain a printed copy. Save the data.
b. How would you determine which countries are more heavily populated than others in this group? Explain.
c. Are there other countries of interest to you? Obtain information on these countries. Insert these in the data set.

5. Example 1 of this chapter entered data on the changes in population and the number of seats that a state may have in the House of Representatives based on the 2000 census. According to the 1990 census, eight states also gained one or more seats in the House over the previous ten years. The following table gives the 1990 census data, the ten-year percentage change in population, and the increase in the number of seats in the House of Representatives for each of the eight states. Enter the data in a Minitab worksheet, print, and save the data. How do the 2000 changes compare with the 1990 changes. Which states gained during both decades?

State	Population	Change	Increase
California	29,839,250	26.1	+7
Texas	17,059,805	19.9	+3
Florida	13,003,362	33.4	+4
North Carolina	6,657,630	13.2	+1
Georgia	6,508,419	19.1	+1
Virginia	6,216,568	16.3	+1
Washington	4,887,941	18.3	+1
Arizona	3,677,985	35.3	+1

CLASS DATA SET

This data set can be set up as a class project, and used for statistical analysis throughout the course. We refer to this data base in some chapter exercises.

After an introductory session on Minitab, ask each student to respond to the following suggested variables:

Gender
Number of credits earned prior to this quarter/semester
Number of credits this quarter/semester
Marital status
Age
Distance student lives from class
Number of hours student works
Grade point average
Type of car
Major program

The students can create the data base individually or as a class project. Each student can save the worksheet for later use.

The Appendix contains a data set obtained from a sample of 200 students. The data set is included on the data disk available with this guide. The SAVE command was used to save the class data set on the disk. To access the data, use the menu path

File ▸ Open Worksheet

or RETRIEVE the file from drive A (or B), by typing:

```
MTB > RETRIEVE 'A:\Classdata.mtp';
SUBC> PORTABLE.
```

This chapter covers more topics to help you feel comfortable with Minitab. In Chapter 1 we showed you how to enter data from the keyboard. This chapter shows you how to import data from other applications and how to manipulate data. You will also learn about Minitab character and professional graphs, mathematical calculations, and error correction.

MINITAB COMMANDS INTRODUCED IN THIS CHAPTER

CODE	COPY	DELETE	END	EXECUTE
HELP	INFORMATION	JOURNAL	LET	NOJOURNAL
NOOUTFILE	NOTE, #	OUTFILE	PARSUM	RANK
RETRIEVE	SAVE	SIGNS	SORT	STACK
UNSTACK	WRITE			

2.1   IMPORTING DATA FROM OTHER APPLICATIONS

In Chapter 1 we showed you how to enter data from the keyboard in the session window or the data window. You can also import data from different types of external files, or you can copy data to the Windows Clipboard from another application and paste data into Minitab.

EXTERNAL FILES

Data can be imported from Lotus 1-2-3, Lotus Symphony, Borland Quattro Pro, dBase, Microsoft Word and Excel, or from other Minitab files. Use the path

File ▸ Open Worksheet

and find the correct file type in the **List Files of Type** box in the dialog box; highlight the file you want to open.

For example, to input an Excel file that was saved on drive A:, select the file type in the dialog box: **Excel (*.xls)**, select a directory and file, click Preview, make changes in how Minitab should interpret the file, click **OK**, and click **Open**:

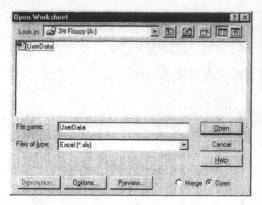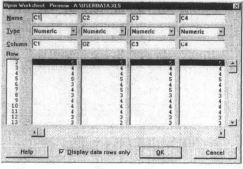

The following message in the session window and data in the data window shows successful import.

```
Retrieving worksheet from file: A:\UserData.XLS
# Worksheet was saved on Mon Oct 9 2000
```

To add data from a file to the current worksheet, use

File ▸ Open Worksheet

In the dialog box, click Merge, select a directory and file, and click **Open**. If you like, click Preview, make changes in how Minitab should interpret the file, and click OK.

In the Preview dialog box, you can make all the changes to the merge file that could normally be made only to a non-Minitab file.

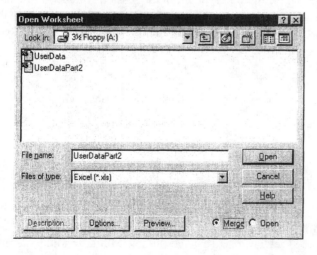

A standard ASCII file created by other software can be entered in a Minitab worksheet.

File ▸ Other Files ▸ Import Special Text

If you are in the session window, use the READ, SET, and INSERT commands that were described in Chapter 1 to enter data from files. Use READ if there are several columns, and INSERT if you are appending data to a worksheet. For example,

```
MTB > READ C1-C12;
SUBC> FILE 'MEDFILE'.
```

inputs data from the file called MEDFILE into columns C1 to C12 of the worksheet. When used in a Minitab command, filenames must be enclosed in single quotation marks.

NOTE

*Minitab has a **Dynamic Data Exchange** feature. This means that Minitab can receive data from other applications, or send data to other applications in a client/server environment. Refer to a Minitab manual or the HELP facility for more information.*

USING THE CLIPBOARD

Data from Lotus, Excel, other spreadsheet or word processing packages, can be copied to the Windows Clipboard from other applications and pasted in Minitab. When you cut or copy, the data are stored in the Windows Clipboard. Because the Clipboard is shared by all Windows programs, anything pasted in the Clipboard can be pasted in any other program.

To use the Clipboard, copy data to the Clipboard, then click the cell where you want to begin, and choose

Edit ▸ Paste Cells

In the dialog box, you can choose whether you want the data to be inserted above or to replace any existing data in the worksheet.

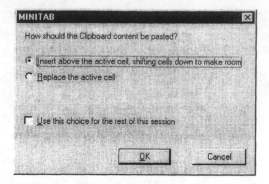

NOTE

*The **Windows Clipboard** can only hold one thing at a time. Data copied to the Windows Clipboard are only available until you cut or copy something else, or until you exit Windows.*

2.2   MANIPULATING DATA

In this section , you will become familiar with the power and flexibility of the data management feature of Minitab. We cover stacking and unstacking data, coding data, copying columns and constants to new locations, summarizing the signs of data, finding the cumulative counts, ranking and sorting data. Many of the data manipulation commands are found under the **Manip** menu.

In Minitab, usually a column contains the data for one variable, with an observation in each row or a data point in each cell. This is referred to as **unstacked data**.

The alternative is to organize data as **stacked data** where we have subsets of data points belonging to different categories or groups. For example, we may have data on the ages when employees were promoted in an industry, and we may want to study differences in ages of men and women. We can enter all ages in one column and codes identifying man or woman in another column.

Minitab allows us to stack and unstack data for ease in creating graphs and charts and in analyzing data. The following gives the commands and illustrations.

STACKING AND UNSTACKING DATA

Use STACK to combine corresponding columns and constants in a block or blocks. If each block contains more than one constant or column, you need to enclose the block in parentheses. Use SUBSCRIPT to create a column of subscripts: the first block is given the subscript 1, the second block 2, and so on. USENAMES, new in Release 13, creates subscripts based on variable names.

Use UNSTACK to separate one or more columns in blocks of columns or stored constants. The subcommand SUBSCRIPTS specifies the blocks. Rows with the smallest subscript are stored in the first block, second smallest in the second block, and so on.

Manip ▸ Stack
Manip ▸ Unstack Columns

STACK (E ... E) *on* ... (E ... E) *in* (C ... C)	Combines columns and constants
SUBSCRIPTS C	Creates a column of subscripts
USENAMES	Uses alpha or text names
UNSTACK (C ... C) *in* (E ... E) ... (E ... E)	Separates columns and constants
SUBSCRIPTS C	Specifies blocks to separate

Consider the following example.

	C1	C2	C3	C4
1	-2	23	-6	45
2	-6	37	-8	62
3	-3	41	-9	65

The first set of commands combines the data in C1 and C3 and stores the data in C5. The next set of commands combines the data in C2 with the data in C4 and stores variable names or subscripts denoting the two columns in C7.

Manip ▸ Stack ▸ Stack Columns   MTB > Stack C1 C3 C5
  Select C1 and C3 in **Stack the following columns:**
  Store stacked data in:
    Click **Column of current worksheet:** and enter C5. **OK**

Manip ▸ Stack ▸ Stack Columns   MTB > Stack C2 C4 C6;
  Select C2 and C4 in **Stack the following columns:**   SUBC> Subscripts C7;
  Store stacked data in: SUBC> UseNames.
    Click **Column of current worksheet:** and enter C6;
    Enter C7 in **Store subscripts in:**
  Click **Use variable names in subscript column. OK**

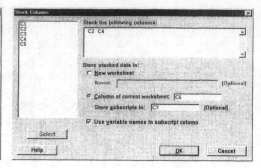

New Worksheet:

	C1	C2	C3	C4	C5	C6	C7-T
1	-2	23	-6	45	-2	23	C2
2	-6	37	-8	62	-6	37	C2
3	-3	41	-9	65	-3	41	C2
4					-6	45	C4
5					-8	62	C4
6					-9	65	C4

CODING DATA

The CODE command converts data to alpha or numeric data. It searches columns for the value and replaces them with a new value.

Manip ▸ Code

CODE (K ... K) *to* K ... (K ... K) *to* K *for* C ... C *put in* C ... C   Converts data type

For example, suppose C1 contains the following data: M, M, F, M, M, F, where M is male and F is female. The following converts M to a numeric value 1, and F to a 0.

Manip ▸ Code ▸ Text to Numeric   MTB> Code ("M") 1 ("F") 0 C1 C2
  Select C1 in **Code data from columns:**
  Enter C2 in **Into columns:**
  Enter M in **Original values** and 1 in **New:**
  Enter F in **Original values** and 0 in **New. OK**

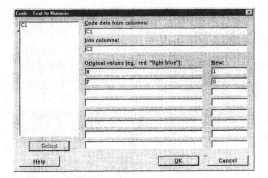

Old Worksheet:

	C1-T
1	M
2	M
3	F
4	M
5	M
6	F

New Worksheet:

	C1-T	C2
1	M	1
2	M	1
3	F	0
4	M	1
5	M	1
6	F	0

COPYING DATA

The COPY command copies data from columns and constants to new columns and constants.

Manip ▸ Copy Columns

COPY C ... C *to* C ... C	Copies columns to new columns
COPY K ... K *to* C	Copies constants to columns
COPY K ... K *to* K ... K	Copies constants to new constants
COPY C *to* K ... K	Copies columns to constants
USE *rows* K ... K	Specifies rows to copy
USE *rows where* C = K ... K	Specifies rows to copy
OMIT *rows* K ... K	Specifies rows not to copy
OMIT *rows where* C = K ,.. K	Specifies rows not to copy

For example, suppose we have gender data in C1 and test scores in C2, and want to copy the data for males only into C3 and C4.

Manip ▸ Copy Columns
  Select C1 and C2 in **Copy from columns:**
  Enter C3 and C4 in **To columns:**
  Click **Use rows**;
  Click **Use rows with text column**, enter C1;
    Enter M in **equal to. OK**

MTB > Copy C1 C2 C3 C4;
SUBC> Use C1 = 'M'.

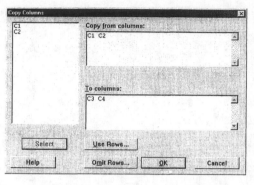 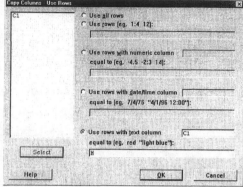

Old Worksheet:

	C1-T	C2
1	M	83
2	M	88
3	F	72
4	M	95
5	M	76
6	F	87

New Worksheet:

	C1-T	C2	C3-T	C4
1	M	83	M	83
2	M	88	M	88
3	F	72	M	95
4	M	95	M	76
5	M	76		
6	F	87		

SUMMARIZING THE SIGNS OF DATA

The SIGNS command gives a summary table of negative, zero, and positive values. The option converts negative, zero, and positive values to -1, 0, and +1, respectively.

Calc ▸ Calculator

SIGNS *of* E (*put in* E)   Gives a summary table of negative, zero, and positive values

For example, suppose C1 contains the numbers: 3, 9, -5, 0, -3, -5 and 7. The session command provides a summary of the negative, zero, and positive values, as follows.

```
MTB > SIGNS C1 C2
     3  Negative values     1  Zero values      3  Positive values
```

The menu command and LET function do not provide the summary table, but the column output is the same.

Calc ▸ Calculator   MTB > LET C2 = SIGNS(C1)
  Enter C2 in **Store result in variable:**
  Enter SIGNS(C1) in **Expression. OK**

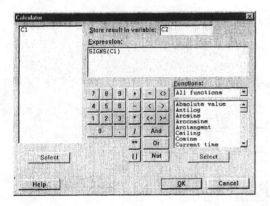

Old Worksheet:

	C1
1	3
2	9
3	-5
4	0
5	-3
6	-5
7	7

New Worksheet:

	C1	C2
1	3	1
2	9	1
3	-5	-1
4	0	0
5	-3	-1
6	-5	-1
7	7	1

FINDING CUMULATIVE COUNTS

This command calculates and stores partial sums. The partial sum for a specific row is equal to the sum of the rows up to and including that row.

Calc ▸ Calculator

PARSUM *of* C *put in* C   Calculates partial sums of data

Consider the following example.

Calc ▸ Calculator   MTB > LET C2 = PARSUM (C1)
　　Enter C2 in **Store result in variable:**
　　Enter PARSUM (C1) in **Expression. OK**

Old Worksheet: **New Worksheet:**

	C1
1	6
2	9
3	8
4	3
5	6
6	0
7	1

	C1	C2
1	6	6
2	9	15
3	8	23
4	3	26
5	6	32
6	0	32
7	1	33

RANKING THE DATA

The RANK command ranks the data values in order of magnitude, from least to greatest. If there are ties, the average rank is assigned. Many statistical procedures, such as nonparametric tests, use relative ranks of the data rather than actual numerical values.

Manip ▸ Rank
Calc ▸ Mathematical Expressions

RANK C *put ranks in* C   Ranks data in order of magnitude

In the following example, the data in C1 are ranked and stored in C2.

Manip ▸ Rank   MTB > Rank C1 C2
   Select C1 in **Rank data in:**
   Enter C2 in **Store ranks in**. **OK**

Old Worksheet: **New Worksheet:**

	C1
1	78
2	97
3	84
4	84
5	69
6	42
7	98
8	84
9	78

	C1	C2
1	78	3.5
2	97	8.0
3	84	6.0
4	84	6.0
5	69	2.0
6	42	1.0
7	98	9.0
8	84	6.0
9	78	3.5

The smallest value 42 receives a rank of 1; the next smallest 59 receives a rank of 2, and so on. The highest value 98 has a rank equal to the number of values in the data set. The value 78 appears twice and has a rank equal to the average of 3 and 4; the value 84 appears three times and has a rank equal to the average of 5, 6, and 7.

SORTING ALPHA OR NUMERIC DATA

This command orders alpha or numeric data in one or more columns, and carries along corresponding data in additional columns. The reordered data are stored in the last group of specified columns. Missing values are sorted last in numeric columns, and first in alpha columns.

Manip ▸ Sort

SORT C ... C *put in* C ... C	Sorts and stores sorted data
BY C C	Determines the order of sorting
DESCENDING C ... C	Sorts data in descending order

■ **Example 1**   **Sorting Alpha Data**

Example 1 of Chapter 1 gives data on the United States 2000 census, the ten-year percentage change in population, and the increase in the number of seats in the House of Representatives for eight states. Alphabetize the states, retaining the 2000 census for each state.

Solution   The census data are stored on the data disk in a file named **Census2000.mtp**. INFO gives the column information on the current worksheet.

File ▸ Open Worksheet   MTB > Retrieve 'A:\Census2000.mtp';
  Look in: choose 3½ Floppy (A:)   SUBC> Portable.
  Files of type: choose Minitab Portable(*.mtp)
  File name: choose Census2000. **Open**

```
Retrieving worksheet from file: A:\Census2000.MTP
Worksheet was saved on Wed Jan 10 2001
```

```
MTB > INFO
```

Information on the Worksheet

	Column	Count	Name
T	C1	8	States
	C2	8	Pop2000
	C3	8	Change
	C4	8	USReps

There are eight data points in each column. The column named States is a text column.

Choosing a command from a menu opens a dialog box such as the one shown below. You can highlight and/or click to choose variables and options. Click on **OK** or use Enter to execute the command.

Manip ▸ Sort   MTB > Sort 'States'-'USReps' C5-C8;
  Select States - USReps in **Sort column(s):**   SUBC> By 'States'.
  Enter C5-C8 in **Store sorted column(s) in:**
  Click **Sort by column**; **Select** States. **OK**

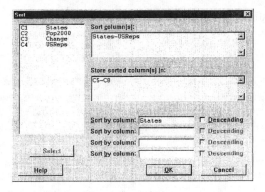

Manip ▸ Display Data
   Select C5-C8 in **Display. OK**

MTB > Print C5-C8

Data Display

Row	C5	C6	C7	C8
1	Arizona	5130632	40	2
2	California	33871648	14	1
3	Colorado	4301261	31	1
4	Florida	15982378	24	2
5	Georgia	8186453	26	2
6	Nevada	1998257	66	1
7	North Carolina	8049313	21	1
8	Texas	20851820	23	2

2.3   MINITAB GRAPHS

There are two types of graphs available with recent releases of Minitab: character (GSTD) and professional (GPRO) graphs. Character graphs are generally the same as those in previous Minitab releases, but are obsolete with the Windows versions of Minitab. These are simple character-style graphs which are displayed directly in the session window. Character graphs print on most any printer, and can easily be integrated with text and comments. When using session commands, you need to enter the command GSTD before you enter a character graph command, and GPRO after to return to professional graphics mode.

The Graph window displays professional or high-resolution graphics. These include a wide range of professional quality graphs that you can edit interactively. The default graphics mode is professional mode; however, if you have switched to GSTD during a Minitab session, you need to enter GPRO to switch back to professional graphics mode. We illustrate these graphs in the following example.

NOTE

Professional or high resolution graphs are not available on all versions of Minitab. Most of the graphs in this Guide are professional graphs; however, in most cases there are character graph counterparts with similar session commands and subcommands. Professional graphs can be constructed with Student Release 12.

■ **Example 2**   **Character and Professional Graphs**

The table gives rates of return on stocks and bonds, short term investments, and inflation rates for the years 1990 through 1999 for a retirement fund. The rate of return is a measure of the amount of money an investor makes on an investment. The inflation rate is the yearly change in the Consumer Price Index (CPI). Graphically compare the performance of stocks and bonds.

	Yearly Financial Rates									
	1990	**1991**	**1992**	**1993**	**1994**	**1995**	**1996**	**1997**	**1998**	**1999**
Wilshire 5000 Stock Index	12.8	7.0	13.9	16.3	1.2	24.7	26.2	29.3	28.9	19.6
Salomon Bros Bond Index	7.7	10.8	14.2	12.0	-1.3	12.5	5.0	8.2	10.5	3.1
91-Day U.S. Treasury Bills	8.2	6.9	4.6	3.1	3.4	5.4	5.4	5.3	5.3	4.7
Inflation Rate	4.7	4.7	3.1	3.0	2.5	3.0	2.8	2.3	1.7	2.0

Solution   This is an example of a time series, where data are collected at regular intervals over a time period. To enter the data, open the data window and enter the rates and names in columns C1 to C5 as shown below.

```
MINITAB - Untitled
File  Edit  Manip  Calc  Stat  Graph  Editor  Window  Help
```

RetirementFund.MTP ***

↓	C1	C2	C3	C4	C5	C6	C7	C8
	Year	Stocks	Bonds	T-Bills	InfRate			
1	1990	12.8	7.7	8.2	4.7			
2	1991	7.0	10.8	6.9	4.7			
3	1992	13.9	14.2	4.6	3.1			
4	1993	16.3	12.0	3.1	3.0			
5	1994	1.2	-1.3	3.4	2.5			
6	1995	24.7	12.5	5.4	3.0			
7	1996	26.2	5.0	5.4	2.8			
8	1997	29.3	8.2	5.3	2.3			
9	1998	28.9	10.5	5.3	1.7			
10	1999	19.6	3.1	4.7	2.0			
11								
12								
13								

If you save the worksheet as a portable file, you can use it on most other types of computers and operating systems. Minitab automatically adds the extension **.mtp**.

File ▸ Save Worksheet As
   Choose location 3½ Floppy (A:) in **Save in:**
   Enter 'RetirementFund' in **File name:**
   Choose Minitab Portable in **Save as type. OK.**

MTB > Save 'A:\RetirementFund.mtp';
SUBC>   Portable;
SUBC>   Replace.

```
Saving file as: A:\RetirementFund.MTP
```

The first graph we illustrate is a character graph of stock returns over the ten year time period.

Graph ▸ Character Graphs ▸ Time Series Plot
   Select Stocks in **Series:**
      Enter 1990 in **Origin. OK**

MTB> Gstd
MTB> MTSPlot 'Stocks';
SUBC> Origin 1990 'Stocks'.
MTB > Gpro.

* NOTE * Character graphs are obsolete.

Character Multiple Time Series Plot

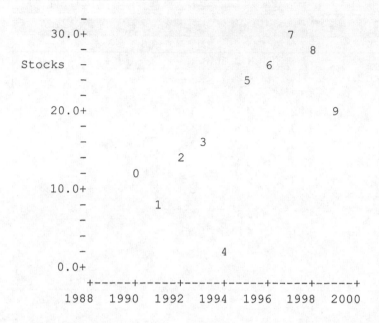

```
          -
  30.0+                                    7
          -                                     8
 Stocks   -                           6
          -                         5
          -
  20.0+                                        9
          -
          -                    3
          -                 2
          -           0
  10.0+
          -              1
          -
          -
          -                    4
   0.0+
          +-----+-----+-----+-----+-----+-----+
        1988  1990  1992  1994  1996  1998  2000
```

Minitab uses the year's last digit to plot each data point. You can manually connect the points on the character time series plot over time to show the volatility of stock returns. The lowest annual return was in 1994 and the highest was in 1997.

The next graph is a professional graph with the stocks and bonds time series on the same axes.

Graph ▸ Time Series Plot	MTB > TSPlot 'Stocks' 'Bonds';
Select Stocks in **Graph 1Y**	SUBC> Index 1990:1999;
and Bonds in **Graph 2 Y**;	SUBC> TDisplay 11;
In **Data Display**, choose Connect **For each** Graph;	SUBC> Connect;
Choose Symbol **For each** Graph;	SUBC> Symbol;
Click **Annotation** and **Title**; add a title;	SUBC> Title "Stocks and Bonds";
Click **Options**,	SUBC> Axis 11;
Enter 1990:1999 in **Index:**	SUBC> Label "Year";
Click **Frame**, choose **Axis**,	SUBC> Axis 2;
In row 1 of **Label**, enter Year,	SUBC> Label "Return";
In row 2 of **Label**, enter Return;	SUBC> Overlay.
Click **Frame**, choose **Multiple graphs**,	
Choose **Overlay graphs on the same page. OK**	

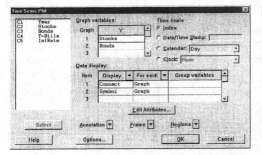

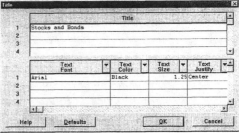

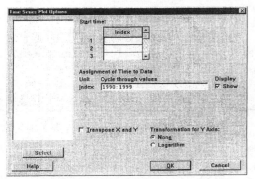

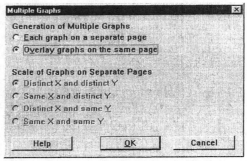

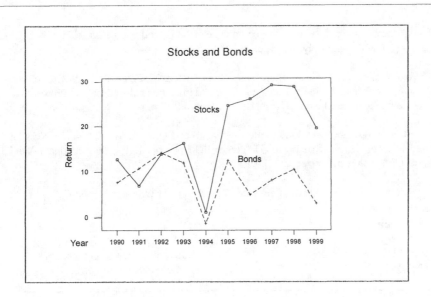

The time series plot shows the volatility in mean annual rates of return for stocks and bonds over the ten-year time period. Plotting both series on the same graph shows the differences between the rates of return for the two types of investments.

NOTE

*Most Minitab professional graphs can be edited interactively. For example, the names of the time series **Stocks** and **Bonds** were added to the previous graph. To add text, click on **Editor ► Show Tool Palette**; choose **T** for text; place the pointer on the graph where you want to add a text box for a name, and click. Enter the text in the dialog box. You can then click on the text box and move it anyplace on the graph. Click on **Editor ► View** to print or copy the graph.*

2.4   DOING ARITHMETIC

You can use the **Calculator** under the **Calc** menu or the session command LET to compute algebraic expressions, to do comparison or logical operations, and to correct errors.

CALCULATIONS

With the calculator function, you can enter the mathematical operation you want Minitab to perform, select variables, buttons, and functions to build your expression in the dialog box.

The arithmetic expression may use columns, constants, and the arithmetic symbols : + add; - subtract; * multiply; / divide; and ** to raise to a power.

The expression may also use column commands, such as MEAN and SUM. The column name or number following the column command must be enclosed in parentheses. No extra text may be used with LET unless it follows a # sign.

Comparison operations include the following: = or EQ(equal to); ~=, <>, or NE (not equal to); < or LT (less than); > or GT (greater than); <= or LE (less than or equal to) and >= or GE (greater than or equal to).

Logical operations include the following: & or AND; | or OR; and ~ or NOT.

Calc ► Calculator

LET E = *mathematical expression*	Use to do arithmetic and comparisons
LET C(K) = K	Use to enter values or to correct errors

The following are some examples of expressions that can be done with the **Calculator** or LET.

LET C1 = (C2 + C3)*10 - 60	Row by row calculations of data in C2 and C3
LET C2 = ABS(C1 - MEAN(C1))	Absolute value of data in C1 less the mean

```
LET K1 = 5.3                        Stores 5.3 as a constant K1
LET K2 = MEAN(C1)/STDEV(C1)         Divides mean by standard deviation of data in C1
LET C5 = (C1 < 5)                   Row by row, puts a 1 in C5 if C1 is less than 5,
                                    and a 0 otherwise
LET K2 = C1(6)                      Stores the value in row 6 of C1 as a constant
LET C1(28) = 3.14                   Enters 3.14 in row 28 of C1
LET C5(15) = "black"                Enters the alpha data 'black' in row 15 of C5 if it is a text
                                    column
```

2.5   MISCELLANEOUS TOPICS

This section gives information on some additional capabilities of Minitab. Topics include accessing help and information, annotating programs, correcting errors, and Minitab macros.

ACCESSING ONLINE HELP

The HELP facility contains a general overview as well as specific information about commands and subcommands. To access HELP, enter HELP on the command line, press F1, click the Help button in the lower left corner in any dialog box, or use the HELP menu command.

Help

HELP (COMMAND (SUBCOMMAND))   Most valuable Minitab command

OBTAINING INFORMATION

To obtain information on the columns and constants that are defined in the current worksheet, open Project Manager, click on the Information icon ⓘ in the Project Manager toolbar, or use the following session command. The output includes column names and counts of values and missing values, and constants used in the worksheet. Columns containing alpha data are labeled T.

Window ▸ Project Manager ▸ Worksheets

Project Manager Toolbar

INFORMATION © ... C)   Use for information on specific columns.

DOCUMENTING YOUR PROGRAM

You can include notes or comments in a Minitab program with the NOTE command or # symbol. NOTE can be used to display messages on the screen to a user during execution of a macro. These are session commands only.

NOTE	Command line beginning with NOTE is not executable
#	Used anywhere on a command, subcommand, or data line.

For example, to identify levels of a qualitative variable, use NOTE before data are entered.

```
MTB > NOTE 1 represents male, 0 represents female
```

CORRECTING ERRORS

This section covers some common errors and corrections. If you are using Execs in Minitab, all errors can be corrected with the computer system editor or a word processor.

1. Some menu commands to keep in mind include the following:

    *   To undo your most recent action, use **Edit ‣ Undo**
    *   The **Edit ‣ Edit Last Dialog** command lets you repeat your last command without having to fill in the dialog box.
    *   The **Manip** menu contains several commands for correcting or changing data in the worksheet.

2. A data value was entered incorrectly.

    From the Data window, you can move to the cell containing the error and enter the correct value. From the Session window, you can use LET to change a single number. The form is

    ```
    MTB > LET Cj(i) = correct number
    ```

    where j is the column number and i is the row number containing the error. For example,

    ```
    MTB > LET C1(5) = 87.3
    ```

    replaces the incorrect value in the fifth row of column C1 with 87.3.

3.   Too many data values have been entered.

In the data window, you can highlight the cell or cells to delete, and use **Edit ▸ Delete Cells.**

DELETING ROWS

The DELETE command deletes rows of data, and adjusts the remaining rows to fill in the deleted rows. Use a colon to delete a sequence of rows.

Manip ▸ Delete Rows

DELETE K ... K *from* C ... C   Deletes rows of data

For example, to omit $36.25 and $23.80 for days 2 and 5 from the data, use the command

```
MTB > DELETE 2 5 C1
```

Old Worksheet:

	C1
1	2.50
2	36.25
3	46.25
4	18.75
5	23.80
6	16.50

New Worksheet:

	C1
1	2.50
2	46.25
3	18.75
4	16.50

4.   An error message appears on the screen.

Often this is the result of choosing options or entering arguments incorrectly. The error message is usually self-explanatory, or the online HELP can provide details. For example, a colon is used to specify more than one row for DELETE; using a hyphen causes an error.

```
MTB > DELETE 1-5 C1
* ERROR * Specified rows are not in increasing order
      No rows deleted.
MTB > DELETE 1:5 C1
```

5.   One or more rows of data were accidentally omitted from one or more columns.

Adding data is easy to do in the data window. Move to the bottom of columns to add data, or use the cut and paste feature in the **Edit** menu to insert data at the top or in the middle of columns.

Commands such as the following are functional when the data window is active:

Editor ▸ Insert Rows
Editor ▸ Insert Cells

One or more empty rows or cells are inserted above the active row or cell, the remaining rows or cells are moved down, and you can type or paste missing data.

The session INSERT command adds data at the top, between two rows, or at the bottom of specified columns, but is more cumbersome especially if you are inserting alpha data. You need a FORMAT statement as illustrated in the following example.

```
MTB > INSERT 3 4 C1 C2;
SUBC> FORMAT (A4,X,F4).
DATA> Thur 36.50
DATA> END
```

The command inserts data, Thur and 36.50, between rows 3 and 4 of C1 and C2. The FORMAT subcommand says to insert the name given in the first four spaces (A4) into C1, skip the next space (X), then insert the four digit number (F4) into C2.

Old Worksheet: **New Worksheet:**

	C1-T	C2
1	Mon	2.50
2	Tues	36.25
3	Wed	46.25
4	Fri	18.75
5	Sat	23.80
6	Sun	16.50

	C1-T	C2
1	Mon	2.50
2	Tues	36.25
3	Wed	46.25
4	Thur	36.50
5	Fri	18.75
6	Sat	23.80
7	Sun	16.50

MINITAB MACROS

One of the advantages of session commands is when you want to repeat a set of commands. A Minitab **macro** is made up of a set of session commands saved in a file so you can automatically perform repetitive tasks. A macro is designed to extend the functionality of Minitab. For example, Release 13 has macros for process capability analysis, Pareto charts, response surface design and analysis, and others in subdirectories in the main Minitab directory. You can also create and execute your own macros using menu commands, session commands, or an editor.

Minitab has several types of macros: Exec, global macro, and local macro. An **Exec** is a file with the extension .MTB which allows you to repeat a set of commands many times, a useful feature for running simulations. Or you can write an interactive macro, which pauses and prompts the user for information during execution. In an Exec, the input data are always in the same columns, and the output data must always be assigned the same columns. We illustrate the use of an Exec to repeat a set of commands for random sampling in Chapter 6.

Global macros use Minitab as a programming language to perform operations that are not available as commands. For example, you can use DO-loops, IF statements, and subroutines. Local macros are the most complicated to create but allow you to specify columns of data in other worksheets.

A **%Macros** is a macro which has greater power and flexibility than an Exec. A %Macro is an ASCII text file with the extension MAC that contains commands you can execute as a macro. Please refer to a Minitab Reference Manual or HELP for more information. We illustrate %Macros for linear regression and analysis of variance in later chapters.

EXERCISES

1. Example 2 of this chapter contains time series data including stocks, bonds, and treasury bills. Retrieve the data from the saved file, and repeat the steps to construct the graphs. Experiment with the options for the graphs. Print the graphs and Session window. Would you have been better off investing in stocks, bonds, or treasury bills the past ten years? Discuss.   (File: **RetirementFund.mtp**)

2. Refer to the Appendix after this chapter. Describe the differences between the program file, outfile, and data file. Suppose as secretary of the local chapter of the Global Society for the Advancement of Leadership (GSAL), you are asked to give a weekly update of the members, including type and number of each member's activities for the week. How does knowledge of the different files available with Minitab aid you in this weekly task?

3. Forbes magazine ranks the 40 highest-paid entertainers and their estimated gross incomes. The following table gives the rankings and income in millions of dollars for 1995 and 1996 combined. (File: **Entertainers.mtp**)

	Name	Income		Name	Income
1.	Winfrey, Oprah	$171	21.	Stallone, Sylvester	$44
2.	Spielberg, Steven	150	22.	Grisham, John	43
3.	Beatles	130	23.	Williams, Robin	42
4.	Jackson, Michael	90	24.	Zemeckis, Robert	42
5.	Rolling Stones	77	25.	Roseanne	40
6.	Eagles	75	26.	Douglas, Michael	40
7.	Schwarzenegger, Arnold	74	27.	Willis, Bruce	36
8.	Copperfield, David	63	28.	Pavarotti, Luciano	36
9.	Carrey, Jim	63	29.	Kiss	35
10.	Crichton, Michael	59	30.	Schulz, Charles	33
11.	Seinfeld, Jerry	59	31.	Cosby, Bill	33
12.	King, Stephen	56	32.	Travolta, John	33
13.	Brooks, Garth	51	33.	Carey, Mariah	32
14.	Webber, Andrew Lloyd	50	34.	Clancy, Tom	31
15.	Hanks, Tom	50	35.	Costner, Kevin	31
16.	Siegfried and Roy	48	36.	Washington, Denzel	30
17.	Cruise, Tom	46	37.	Letterman, David	28
18.	Ford, Harrison	44	38.	Metallica	28
19.	Eastwood, Clint	44	39.	Gibson, Mel	28
20.	R.E.M.	44	40.	Bullock, Sandra	25

   a. Retrieve the data. Check the data for errors; correct any errors. Print the worksheet. Peruse the data. Are there any surprises in the data?

   b. The data are sorted by income. Sort the data in alphabetical order and save in new columns. Print the alphabetized data.

   c. Enter a code for male, female, and group entertainers. Copy the data for male entertainers; print. Report your findings on male entertainers.

4. The Bookshelf of the local public library sells used books at a semiannual book sale. The books sold at the most recent sale were classified as children, fiction, or nonfiction. The types of the first 30 books are given in the following table. Enter the data and print a paper copy. Save the data in a file for further analysis in later chapters.

Bookshelf Sale of Used books

Fiction	Fiction	Nonfiction	Children	Children
Fiction	Fiction	Fiction	Fiction	Fiction
Fiction	Children	Children	Children	Nonfiction
Children	Fiction	Nonfiction	Fiction	Fiction
Nonfiction	Children	Nonfiction	Fiction	Children
Children	Nonfiction	Children	Nonfiction	Nonfiction

5. The area of the world as a whole is 196.94 million square miles, of which 70.8% is water. The 1996 population is 5.771 billion people, and the annual growth rate is 1.5%. Principal sources for world facts and statistics include the Central Intelligence Agency, Europa Publications, International Institute for Strategic Studies, International Monetary Fund, Population Reference Bureau, and Unesco. The following table gives some facts on some major countries. Determine the population density of each country. How does each country compare with the world's population density? Discuss. You may have saved this data in a file in Chapter 1, Exercise 4.

Country	Population	Area	Currency	Capital
Bangladesh	119,800,000	55,598	taka	Dhaka
China	1,217,600,000	3,691,500	yuan	Beijing
Egypt	63,700,000	386,661	pound	Cairo
Ghana	18,000,000	92,098	cedi	Accra
Haiti	7,300,000	10,714	gourde	Port-au-Prince
Indonesia	201,400,000	741,000	rupee	Jakarta
Netherlands	15,500,000	16,133	guilder	Amsterdam
Pakistan	133,500,000	307,374	rupee	Islamabad
Poland	38,600,000	120,728	zloty	Warsaw
Russia	147,700,000	6,592,850	ruble	Moscow
Sweden	8,800,000	170,250	krona	Stockholm
Taiwan	21,400,000	13,900	dollar	Taipei
United States	265,200,000	3,615,278	dollar	Washington, D.C.
Vietnam	76,600,000	128,066	dong	Hanoi

6. Consider the data set on heart attack victims collected by an ambulance company that is given in the Appendix. Retrieve the file from the data disk available with this guide. Delete the data that do not pertain to victims in the metro area. Print the new data. (File: **Heart.mtp**)

APPENDIX: OTHER MINITAB FILES

Minitab uses several types of files to store data, commands, and output. You can save a copy of the program in a journal file, a part of a program in a macro or Exec, a session window in an outfile, and a worksheet. Each type of file has its own file extension. The default extension is a three-letter ending that describes the type of file; however, you have the option of adding your own file extension. For example, Minitab adds the extension .MTW to a file containing the data in the Minitab worksheet. In this section we describe a program file, macro, an outfile, and data file.

PROGRAM FILE

The session command JOURNAL can be used to document a Minitab session or to save a program or part of a program, called an Exec. All commands are saved in a standard ASCII text file, which can be printed and edited by any editor or word processor and can be run at any time with the EXECUTE command.

JOURNAL ('FILENAME')   Default filename extension is .MTJ, the default
                                     filename is MINITAB.MTJ

NOJOURNAL   Cancels JOURNAL command

For example, to save a program with the filename file EXAMPLE1, use

```
MTB > JOURNAL 'EXAMPLE1'
```

All lines in the program are saved in EXAMPLE1.MTJ. The file is a standard ASCII text file, which can be edited with your computer system editor or a word processor.

EXECUTE A PROGRAM FILE OR EXEC

Minitab executes all commands in a program or Exec file. The default extension for an Exec file is .MTB. Use the full filename to execute a program having a different extension. More than one EXECUTE statement can be used in a program.

File ▸ Other Files ▸ Run an Exec

EXECUTE ('FILENAME') (K *times*)   Default filename extension is .MTB

For example, the program file EXAMPLE1.MTJ can be executed by entering the command,

```
MTB > EXECUTE 'EXAMPLE1.MTJ'
```

Comment *We suggest that you use the filename extension .MTJ for a JOURNAL program file. The default extension used by EXECUTE is .MTB, the same extension used for a Minitab Exec.*

OUTPUT FILE

The session command OUTFILE saves the output in a standard ASCII text file. You can then edit the file with the system editor or a word processor and print it. The default filename extension is .LIS. If a filename is reused, the new output is appended to the end of the existing file.

OUTFILE 'FILENAME'   Saves the output from all subsequent commands

NOOUTFILE   Stops saving output

For example, to save the output in a file named EXAMPLE1.LIS, enter

```
MTB > OUTFILE 'EXAMPLE1'
```

prior to the program commands. Output from commands entered before OUTFILE or after NOOUTFILE is not saved.

NOTE

It is always an excellent idea to save the worksheet. Quite often you need to run more than one program using the same set of data, or you may need to correct errors at a later time. The file created by the SAVE command described below cannot be edited, printed, or used with other software; Minitab must be used to edit or print the data. When you use RETRIEVE, any data in the current Minitab worksheet is erased.

SAVING DATA FILES

The SAVE command stores the entire worksheet, including column names and constants. The file *cannot* be edited, printed, or used with other software; Minitab must be used to edit or print the data.

The top of the main Minitab window shows the title of your current worksheet. To save the current worksheet in the same file and format as the file name displayed in the window title, use the menu command:

File ▸ Save Current Worksheet

If the current worksheet is untitled, this command brings up a dialog box where you can specify a file type, file name and location in which to save your data. To rename your worksheet or save it to a new location, choose:

File ▸ Save Current Worksheet As

SAVE ('FILENAME')	Default name is MINITAB; Default extension .MTW
PORTABLE	Use to transfer to a different type of computer; Default extension is .MTB
LOTUS (*PC only*)	Saves as Lotus or Symphony spreadsheet file

RETRIEVING DATA FILES

To enter a saved file into the worksheet, use the menu path:

File ▸ Open Worksheet

RETRIEVE 'FILENAME'	Enters data saved by the SAVE command
PORTABLE	Use with .MTB filename extension
LOTUS (*PC only*)	Use with Lotus or Symphony spreadsheet file

For example, the following saves the worksheet on drive A:

```
MTB > SAVE 'A:\EXAMPLE1'
Saving file as: A:\EXAMPLE1.MTW
```

as EXAMPLE1.MTW. To retrieve the saved worksheet on the same type of computer, use.

```
MTB > RETRIEVE 'A:\EXAMPLE1'
Retrieving worksheet from file: A:\EXAMPLE1.MTW
# Worksheet was saved on Sat Sep 30 2000
```

The default filename extension .MTW is optional. If you use the PORTABLE subcommand, the extension is .MTP.

EXPORTING FILES

A Minitab data file can be saved as a standard ASCII text file and exported to other software programs or another Minitab application. For example, you may use the computer system editor or a word processor to edit the data. In Minitab, use READ, SET, or INSERT to input a standard ASCII text file created by the system editor or some other program.

File ▸ Other Files ▸ Export Special Text

WRITE 'FILENAME' C ... C   Default extension is .DAT
    FORMAT (SPECIFICATION)   Use for alpha data

For example, the command

```
MTB > WRITE 'EXAMPLE1' C1 C2 C3
```

saves the data from columns C1, C2, and C3 in a file called EXAMPLE1.DAT. The data in this file can be entered in a Minitab worksheet using the command

```
MTB > READ DATA IN C4 C5 C6;
SUBC> FILE 'EXAMPLE1'.
```

NOTE

Data can be read in different columns than those used in the WRITE command; but column names and stored constants are not saved. Minitab adds missing values if column lengths are not equal.

SAVING A PROJECT

Projects contain session window output, graphs, and worksheets. You can have multiple worksheets open in one project. When you open a project file, all the worksheets that were inside that project when you last saved are available to you. When you save a project, the worksheets are saved within that project file.

File ▸ Save Project   Default filename extension is .MPJ

CHAPTER 3

DESCRIBING QUALITATIVE DATA

An important role of statistics is to provide techniques to collect, describe, and analyze data for the decision making process. This chapter demonstrates some Minitab techniques for organizing and summarizing qualitative data sets in tables and graphs. We include frequency and percentage distributions, bar charts, pie charts, and Pareto charts.

NEW COMMANDS

CHART   %PARETO   %PIE   TABLE   TALLY

3.1   GRAPHS FOR QUALITATIVE DATA

Qualitative data include nominal data and ordinal data. **Nominal** or **categorical data** are measurements that identify the category of each unit in a sample or population. Some examples of nominal data are brands of microcomputers, planned majors of first year university students, types of bacteria found in swamp water samples, and opinions on a proposed change in the federal tax laws.

Ordinal data are measurements which represent some order or ranking of units in a sample or population. Ordinal data contain all the information of nominal data plus an ordering of the data. For example, the performance ratings of brands of microcomputers on a scale of 1(poor) to 5(excellent), severity of playground injuries from 1(serious) to 4(minor), letter grades on a statistics test from A to F, and daily stress level of college students categorized as minimal, moderate, and heavy. Since ordinal data are simply ranking or ordering of units, arithmetic calculations are usually meaningless.

NOTE

In the examples in this chapter and those that follow, we do not show data entry. Data sets for many examples and exercises are provided on the disk available with this Minitab guide. In each case, we give a filename to identify the data set. Please refer to Chapter 1 for a review of data entry from the keyboard or to Chapter 2 for importing data files from other applications.

FREQUENCY DISTRIBUTIONS

The TALLY command summarizes nominal and ordinal data. The output options include frequency, percent frequency, cumulative frequency and cumulative percent frequency distributions. Percent frequency is the percentage of observations in each category. Cumulative frequency cumulates the number of observations as categories are listed and cumulative percent frequency cumulates the percentages as categories are listed. The output can be saved with the session subcommand STORE.

Stat ▸ Tables ▸ Tally

TALLY C...C	Summarizes data in a table
COUNTS	Number of observations in each category
PERCENTS	Percent frequencies
CUMCOUNTS	Cumulative frequencies
CUMPERCENTS	Cumulative percentages
ALL	Calculates all of the above
STORE C...C	Saves output (Session command only)

NOTE

If you are using Minitab Version 9 on a mainframe, you will need to use a numerical code to enter qualitative data. For example, male may be coded 1 and female 2. Some of the charts and graphs will not be available with Version 9. Character graphs are generally available on the mainframe.

■ Example 1   Frequency Distributions

Consider the class data set provided in the Appendix. Students were asked to state whether they own a United States car, a foreign car, or whether they do not own a car. The following is a sample of types of cars for 30 students. Construct a frequency and a percent frequency distribution.

Types of Student Cars

US	Foreign	None	None	US	US	US
None	US	None	Foreign	Foreign	US	US
US	US	US	US	US	Foreign	US
US	None	Foreign	US	US	US	US
US	US					

Solution The 30 alpha data values are entered in column C1 named CarType. The TALLY command provides several distributions.

Stat ▸ Tables ▸ Tally
  Select CarType in **Variables:**
  Click **Counts** and **Percents**.

MTB > Tally 'CarType';
SUBC> Counts;
SUBC> Percents.

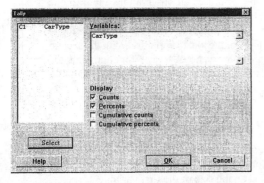

Tally for Discrete Variables: CarType

CarType	Count	Percent
Foreign	5	16.67
None	5	16.67
US	20	66.67
N=	30	

Percent frequency equals 100(frequency)/n where n is the number of observations. From the output we see that about 67% of the students have a United States model, 17% have a foreign model and 17% do not own a car.

NOTE

The following CHART, PIE CHART, and PARETO commands are not available with Minitab Version 9. You can use HISTOGRAM to graphically describe qualitative data. There also may be differences in the ordering of alpha data on the output of some tables and graphs with Minitab Release 13. Alpha data may be placed in alphabetical order.

CHART

CHART produces many kinds of charts, including bar charts, line charts, symbol charts, and area charts. CHART has two forms. One form uses all observations input in one column and gives a bar chart with the height of each bar showing the count of each unique observation. A second form uses two columns, one containing the observations for the *y*-axis variable and the other containing the groups for the *x*-axis variable. With the second form, the default height of a bar is the sum of observations. Other functions include COUNT, N (non-missing), NMISS (missing), MEAN, MEDIAN, MINIMUM, MAXIMUM, STDEV (standard deviation), and SSQ (sum of squares).

Graph ▸ Chart

CHART C	Use for the single variable form
CHART C*C	Use for the second form; second column is the grouping variable
INCREASING	Increasing order based on the size of the first variable
DECREASING	Decreasing order based on the size of the first variable
CPERCENT	Percent scale
CUMULATIVE	Cumulative frequency scale
Functions	SUM, COUNT, N, NMISS, MEAN, MEDIAN, MINIMUM, MAXIMUM, STDEV, SSQ

■ **Example 2**   **Bar Chart**

Consider the car ownership data given in Example 1 of this chapter. Construct and interpret a bar chart.

Solution   The data are in column C1 named CarType.

Graph ▸ Chart   MTB > Chart 'CarType';
  In **Graph** row 1,   SUBC > Bar;
    Select CarType in **X**;   SUBC>   Title "Student Cars".
  Click **Annotation**, choose **Title**, add a title. **OK.**

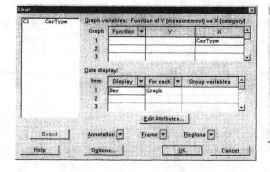
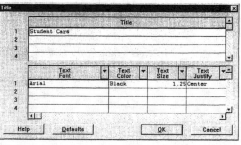

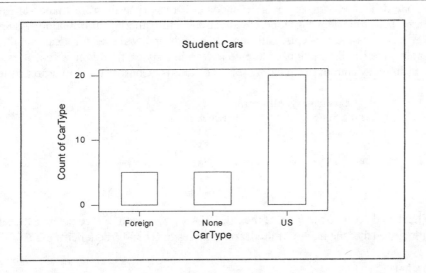

The height of the bars represents the number of cars of the three types owned by students. In this sample, four times as many students own U.S. cars as foreign cars.

PIE CHART

PIE CHART takes data in two forms. The first form uses all observations in one column; each slice of the pie chart corresponds to the frequencies of each unique observation. The second form uses two columns; one contains the names of unique observations and the other contains the frequencies of unique observations. Menu command options include ordering the categories, exploding slices of the pie, combining categories with low frequencies, and adding a title. The default output gives names, counts, and percent frequencies.

Graph ▸ Pie Chart

%PIE C   Use for the first form; column for names for the second form
   COUNTS C   Use for frequencies column for the second form

■ **Example 3**   **Pie Chart**

The Learning-Style Inventory (LSI) evaluates the way a person learns and deals with ideas and day-to-day situations. The test, based on several tested theories of thinking and creativity, indicates whether a person has one of four learning styles: Accomodator learns primarily from "hands-on" experience; Diverger learns best from viewing concrete situations and gathering information; Assimilator has interest in abstract ideas and concepts; and Converger finds practical uses for ideas and theories. The following table gives a distribution of the four learning styles found in a recent study of 324 information technology employees in Minnesota and Kansas. Construct and interpret a pie chart.

Learning Style Inventory

Learning Style	Frequency
Accomodator	53
Diverger	55
Assimilator	95
Converger	<u>121</u>
	324

Solution The data determine the form of the PIE CHART command. Since the data are summarized in a distribution, we enter the names of the learning styles in C1 and frequencies in C2.

Graph ▸ Pie Chart
  Click **Chart table**;
  Select LearningStyle in **Categories in:**
    Select Frequency in **Frequencies in:**
  Click **Options**,
    choose **Add lines connecting labels to slices**;
  Add a **Title. OK.**

MTB > %Pie 'Learning Style';
SUBC>　Counts 'Frequency';
SUBC>　Title "Learning Style Inventory";
SUBC>　Lines.

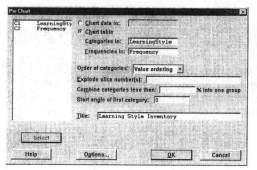
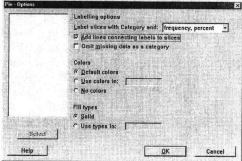

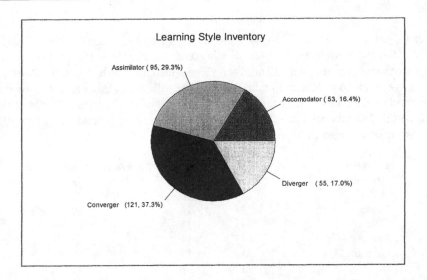

The pie chart indicates that most information technology employees are Convergers (about 37%) or Assimilators (about 29%). This is perhaps not surprising when one realizes the strengths of Convergers include problem solving and decision making, and strengths of Assimilators include planning and creating models. These are traits of qualified information technology employees.

PARETO CHARTS

A Pareto chart is a bar chart that orders the bars from largest to smallest along with a line that shows the cumulative percentage and count of the bars. This chart is often used with analyzing defects in a manufacturing process to help determine the types of defects which are most prevalent in a process. This helps a company focus its improvement efforts on areas where it can make the largest gains by eliminating causes of defects.

USING PARETO CHART

Pareto chart takes data in two forms. One form has all observations in one column. The second form uses two columns where one contains the names of unique observations and the other contains the frequencies of unique observations.

Stat ▸ Quality Tools ▸ Pareto Chart

%PARETO C   Observations column for one form; column for names for second

    COUNTS C   Frequencies column for second form

■ **Example 4**   **Pareto Chart**

The Summer Olympics were held in Sydney, Australia in September 2000. The 17 days of sports resulted in 80 of the 200 participating nations winning medals. The United States lead the medal count for the second consecutive games with 39 gold and 97 total medals. The host country Australia enjoyed its best games ever with 16 gold and 58 total metals. The following table gives the numbers of gold, silver, bronze and total medals won by the top 12 countries. These countries won 208 of the 301 gold medals; 178 of the 299 silver medals, 181 of the 328 bronze medals, and 567 of the 928 medals. Produce and interpret a Pareto chart for this data set.

Country	Gold	Silver	Bronze	Total
Australia	16	25	17	58
Britain	11	10	7	28
China	28	16	15	59
Cuba	11	11	7	29
France	13	14	11	38
Germany	14	17	26	57
Italy	13	8	13	34
Netherlands	12	9	4	25
Romania	11	6	9	26
Russia	32	28	28	88
South Korea	8	9	11	28
United States	39	25	33	97

Solution We enter the data in columns C1-C5 named as in the table above. The worksheet is stored in **Olympics.mtp**.

Stat ▸ Quality Tools ▸ Pareto Chart
  Click **Chart defects table**
    Select Country in **Labels in:**
    Select Total in **Frequencies in:**
  Enter 99% in **Combine defects after the first**;
  Add a **Title**. **OK**

MTB > %Pareto 'Country';
SUBC>   Counts 'Total';
SUBC>   Others 99;
SUBC>   Title "2000 Summer Olympics".

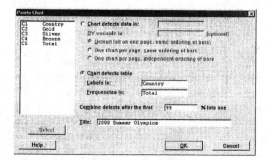

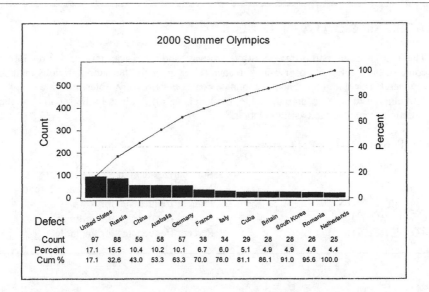

2000 Summer Olympics

Defect	United States	Russia	China	Australia	Germany	France	Italy	Cuba	Britain	South Korea	Romania	Netherlands
Count	97	88	59	58	57	38	34	29	28	28	26	25
Percent	17.1	15.5	10.4	10.2	10.1	6.7	6.0	5.1	4.9	4.9	4.6	4.4
Cum %	17.1	32.6	43.0	53.3	63.3	70.0	76.0	81.1	86.1	91.0	95.6	100.0

The Pareto chart orders the bars from largest to smallest and produces a line that shows the cumulative percentage and counts of the medals won by the 12 countries. The left vertical scale gives counts and the right vertical scales percentages. The table below the chart provides counts, percents, and cumulative percents. The chart shows that the US won about 17% of the medals of the top 12 winning countries, and the US and Russia won about a third of the medals.

3.2 CLASSIFYING QUALITATIVE DATA

Many times we collect data on the same qualitative variable for several groups. For example, we may want to classify the severity of playground injuries for girls and for boys, or the stress levels of students at different education levels. With Minitab, we can construct a table to tally the responses for each group.

CLASSIFYING DATA IN TABLES

The TABLE command prints one-way, two-way, and multi-way tables. By default, a count of the number of observations in each cell is given. Other output options include row percents, column percents, and total percents. For two-way tables, the values in the first entered column become the table row labels and the values in the second entered column become the table column labels.

Stat ▸ Tables ▸ Cross Tabulation

TABLE C ... C	Summarizes data in a table
COUNTS	Number of observations in each category
ROWPERCENTS	Percent frequencies for rows
COLPERCENTS	Percent frequencies for columns
TOTPERCENTS	Percent frequencies for the table

■ **Example 5**   **Two-way Classification Table**

Consider the following sample of 30 students randomly sampled from the class data set provided in the Appendix of this supplement. Students were asked to state their marital status and car type. Compare the types of cars that students own for each marital status group.

Student	Car Type	Status	Student	Car Type	Status
1	US	Single	16	US	Married
2	US	Single	17	US	Single
3	Foreign	Single	18	Foreign	Single
4	US	Single	19	Foreign	Married
5	US	Married	20	US	Other
6	US	Single	21	US	Other
7	None	Married	22	None	Other
8	US	Other	23	US	Single
9	US	Married	24	Foreign	Single
10	US	Single	25	US	Single
11	None	Single	26	US	Single
12	US	Other	27	Foreign	Married
13	US	Single	28	US	Married
14	US	Single	29	US	Married
15	None	Single	30	None	Other

Solution   In this example we show several tables and charts. Car data are entered in C1 'CarType' and marital status in C2 'Status'. The sample is saved in **30Students.mtp.**

First we construct a two-way table which shows the frequencies and percentages of car ownership types for the three marital status groups.

Stat ▸ Tables ▸ Cross Tabulation
  Select CarType and Status
   in **Classification variables:**
  Click **Counts** and **Column percents**. **OK**

MTB> Table 'CarType' 'Status';
SUBC> Counts;
SUBC> Colpercents.

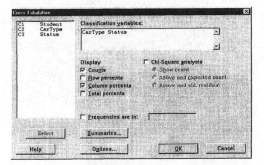

Tabulated Statistics: CarType, Status

Rows: CarType   Columns: Status

	Married	Other	Single	All
Foreign	2	0	3	5
	25.00	--	18.75	16.67
None	1	2	2	5
	12.50	33.33	12.50	16.67
US	5	4	11	20
	62.50	66.67	68.75	66.67
All	8	6	16	30
	100.00	100.00	100.00	100.00

Cell Contents --
                Count
                % of Col

The table classifies car ownership for the three marital status groups. The first row shows that of the five foreign cars in the sample, two are owned by married students and three by single students. Although many more single students (11) than either married (5) or other (4) students own US cars, about the same percent within each marital status group own US cars. This illustrates the importance of using percentages instead of frequencies when comparing groups.

A bar chart graphically compares car ownership for the three marital status groups. The first bar chart displays frequencies of car ownership for the marital status groups.

Graph ► Chart
  Select Status in **Graph 1 X**;
  Data display: choose **Bar** in **Display**;
   Click **For each**, choose **Group;**
   Select CarType in **Group variables**;
  Click **Annotation**, choose **Title**, add a title;
  Click **Frame**, click **Axis**,
   Enter Number of Students in **Label 2.**
  Click **Options**; click **Cluster**: **Select** CarType. **OK**

MTB > Chart 'Status';
SUBC>   Cluster 'CarType';
SUBC>   CPercent;
SUBC>   Bar 'CarType';
SUBC>   Title "Student Car Ownership";
SUBC>   Axis 1;
SUBC>   Axis 2;
SUBC>   Label "Number of Students".

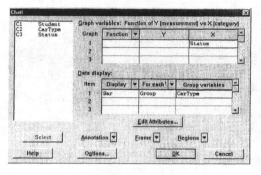
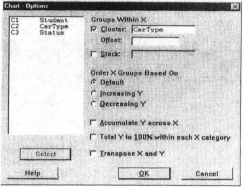

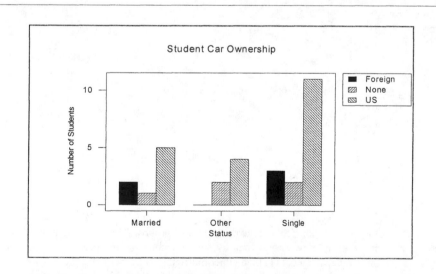

The greatest difference in car ownership is in the 'Other' category of marital status. No one in this group has a foreign car. As expected, most students in every category have U.S. cars.

The next bar chart displays percentages of car ownership for the marital status groups. The only difference in the dialog boxes is to change the *y-axis label* to Percent of Students and to change the *options* dialog box for percentages.

Graph ▸ Chart
  Select Status in **Graph 1 X**;
  Data display: choose **Bar** in **Display**;
   Click **For each**, choose **Group**;
   Select CarType in **Group variables**;
  Click **Annotation**, choose **Title**, add a title;
  Click **Frame**, click **Axis**,
   Enter Percent of Students in **Label 2**;
  Click **Options**; click **Cluster:**
   Select CarType in **Cluster:**
  Click **Total Y to 100% within each X category. OK**

MTB > Chart 'Status';
SUBC> Cluster 'CarType';
SUBC> CPercent;
SUBC> Bar 'CarType';
SUBC> Title "Student Car Ownership";
SUBC> Axis 1;
SUBC> Axis 2;
SUBC> Label "Percent of Students".

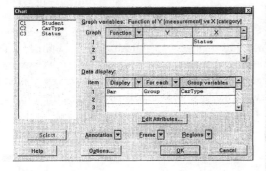
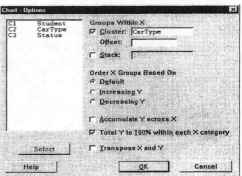

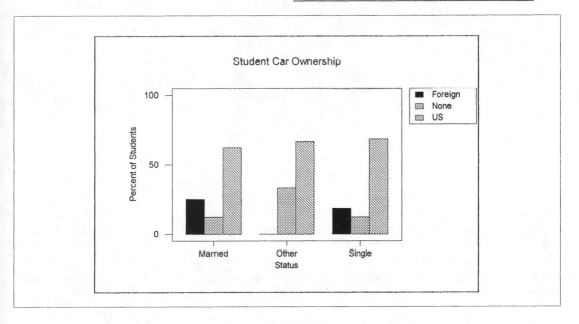

The bar charts point out the importance of using percentages instead of frequencies when comparing groups. The frequency bar chart seems to indicate differences in US car ownership for the three marital status groups, but the percentage bar chart indicates that the percentages of US car ownership is about the same for the three groups.

NOTE

Often qualitative variables in surveys are numerically coded, or need to be numerically coded for analysis. For example, Minitab Version 9 requires numeric data for analysis. With later versions of Minitab, the analysis can proceed with either alpha or numeric data. The next example shows how numeric data can be converted to alpha data. The CODE command was described in Chapter 2.

■ **Example 6**   **Comparing Groups**

This example considers responses of 200 employees on a survey in which employees of a large research and development corporation are classified according to gender and highest degree obtained. The corporation, wanting to provide an in-house continuing education program for its employees, surveyed the employees to determine the interest in such a program. Two questions on the survey related to gender and current educational level. The following table gives some of the responses for 200 employees. Compare the education levels of male and female employees.

Code for Table:

Gender: Male = 1   Female = 2
Highest Degree: High School = 1   Bachelor = 2
                    Master = 3   Ph.D. = 4

Gender	Degree	Gender	Degree	Gender	Degree	Gender	Degree
2	2	2	2	2	4	2	1
1	4	2	3	1	2	1	2
1	4	1	2	2	2	2	4
1	2	1	3	2	2	2	1
1	4	1	2	2	2	2	2
1	2	2	2	2	1	1	1
1	2	1	3	1	2	2	3
2	4	1	3	2	1	1	2
2	1	2	1	2	1	1	2
2	4	2	1	1	2	2	1
.	.						
.	.						
.	.						

Solution In the file named **Degree.mtp**, the data are saved in numeric form using the same codes as in the survey. We construct a two-way table and bar chart to compare the education levels of males and females.

For illustration purposes, we convert the data to alpha data; however, the analysis could proceed with numeric data as well. INFO assures us that the data have been coded to alpha data.

Manip ▸ Code ▸ Numeric to Text
  Select Gender in **Code data from columns:**
  Select Gender in **Into columns:**
  Enter **Original values** 1, 2 and **New** Male, Female. **OK**

MTB > Code (1) "Male" (2) "Female"   &
CONT>   'Gender' 'Gender'

Manip ▸ Code ▸ Numeric to Text
  Select Degree in **Code data from columns:**
  Select Degree in **Into columns:**
  Enter **Original values** 1,2, 3, 4
    and **New** HighSchool, Bachelor, Master, PhD. **OK**

MTB > Code (1)"HighSchool" (2)"Bachelor"   &
CONT>   (3) "Master" (4) "PhD"   &
CONT>   'Degree' 'Degree'

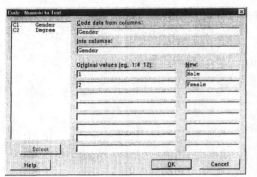 

MTB > INFO

Information on the Worksheet

```
      Column   Count   Name
   T  C1        200    Gender
   T  C2        200    Degree
```

The T before each column number indicates that alpha or text data are entered in each column. Both columns are of size 200.

We use a table and a bar chart to compare groups. The same information is provided with either numeric or alpha data.

Stat ▸ Tables ▸ Cross tabulation
  Select Degree and Gender
    in **Classification variables:**
  Click **Counts** and **Column percents**. **OK**

MTB > Table 'Degree' 'Gender';
SUBC>   Counts;
SUBC>   ColPercents.

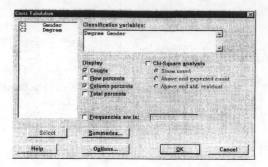

Tabulated Statistics: Degree, Gender

```
Rows: Degree      Columns: Gender

                Female      Male       All

Bachelor          43         41         84
                41.35      42.71      42.00

HighSchool        41          9         50
                39.42       9.38      25.00

Master            13         22         35
                12.50      22.92      17.50

PhD                7         24         31
                 6.73      25.00      15.50

All              104         96        200
               100.00     100.00     100.00

  Cell Contents --
                Count
                % of Col
```

Males tend to have higher levels of education than females. For example, about 40% of females and only 9% of males stated that high school was the highest degree; about 7% of females and 25% of males stated that Ph.D. was the highest degree.

Graph ▸ Chart
  Select Degree in **Graph 1 X**;
  In **Data display:**
    Click **For each**, choose **Group;**
    Select Gender in **Group variables**;
  Click **Annotation**, choose **Title**; add a title.
  Click **Options**, In **Groups Within X:**
    Click **Cluster, select** Gender;
    Click **Total Y to 100% within each X category. OK**

```
MTB > Chart 'Degree';
SUBC>   Title "Corporate Employees";
SUBC>   Cluster 'Gender';
SUBC>   CPercent;
SUBC>   Bar 'Gender'.
```

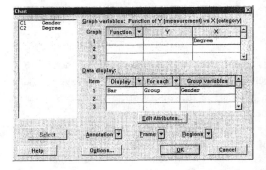
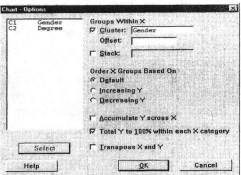

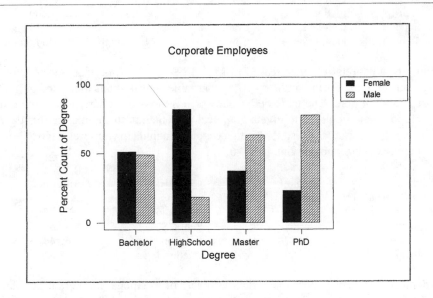

The graph shows that males tend to have higher levels of education than females. The highest percent frequency class for females is high school.

EXERCISES

1.   First year college students in an English class were asked about their computer experience using Windows. Levels of experience were given as None, Some, or Lots. The following table gives the responses for a random sample of 32 students. Describe the distribution of student window experience.

Windows Experience

Lots	Some	Lots	Some	Some	Lots	Lots	Some
Some	Some	Some	Some	Some	Lots	Lots	Some
Some	Some	Lots	None	Some	Some	Lots	Some
Some	Some	Some	Some	None	Some	None	Lots

2.   The Bookshelf of the local public library sells used books at a semiannual book sale. The books sold at the most recent sale were classified as children, fiction, or nonfiction. The types of the first 30 books are given in the following table. Describe the distribution of books sold at the Bookshelf. You may already have entered the data in Exercise 4 of Chapter 2.

Bookshelf Sale of Used books

Fiction	Fiction	Nonfiction	Children	Children
Fiction	Fiction	Fiction	Fiction	Fiction
Fiction	Children	Children	Children	Nonfiction
Children	Fiction	Nonfiction	Fiction	Fiction
Nonfiction	Children	Nonfiction	Fiction	Children
Children	Nonfiction	Children	Nonfiction	Nonfiction

3.   According to a national report released in May 1997 by the American Association of Fund-Raising Counsel Trust for Philanthropy, U.S. charitable contributions increased by 7.3% in 1996 to about $150.7 billion. The table below shows, in billions of dollars, where the gifts went in 1996. Suppose you are asked to give a graphical presentation to summarize this data. Prepare graphs using the techniques illustrated in this chapter. Include in your presentation some reasons for the increase in charitable giving in 1996.

Charities	Amount	Charities	Amount
Arts and Humanities	$10.92	Human Services	$12.16
Education	18.81	International Affairs	1.97
Environment/Wildlife	4.04	Public/Society	7.57
Foundations	8.27	Religion	69.44
Health	13.89	Unallocated	3.63

4.   The federal government reports the official estimate of the illegal immigrant population in the United States. The estimate, based largely on census data, covers illegal immigrants who have lived in this country at least a year. In 1992, the estimate was 3,900,000 and in 1996, the estimate was 5,000,000. The following table gives estimates for the top 1996 ten states. Produce and interpret a Pareto chart for the 1992 and for the 1996 estimates. Compare and discuss the differences.

State	1992 Estimate	1996 Estimate
Arizona	95,000	115,000
California	1,600,000	2,000,000
Florida	270,000	350,000
Illinois	220,000	290,000
Massachusetts	65,000	65,000
New Jersey	105,000	135,000
New York	410,000	540,000
Texas	530,000	700,000
Virginia	42,000	55,000
Washington	42,000	52,000

5. The following table gives the classification of students by gender for a sample of College of Education (COE) and College of Business (COB) majors. Use a table and bar chart to summarize the data. Do both colleges have about the same proportions of male and female students?

Gender	College	Gender	College	Gender	College
Female	COE	Male	COB	Male	COE
Female	COB	Male	COB	Male	COE
Male	COE	Female	COE	Female	COE
Male	COE	Male	COE	Male	COB
Female	COE	Male	COB	Male	COB
Female	COB	Female	COE	Female	COB
Female	COE	Male	COB	Female	COE
Male	COB	Male	COB	Female	COE
Male	COE	Male	COE	Male	COB
Female	COE	Female	COE	Male	COE
Male	COB	Female	COE	Male	COE
Male	COB	Female	COE	Female	COE
Male	COB	Male	COE	Male	COE
Male	COB	Male	COE	Female	COB
Male	COB	Male	COE	Male	COB
Male	COB	Male	COB	Male	COE
Male	COE	Female	COE	Male	COE
Female	COB	Male	COB	Male	COE
Male	COE	Male	COB	Male	COE
Female	COE	Male	COB	Male	COE
Male	COE	Male	COE	Male	COB
Male	COB	Male	COB	Female	COE
Female	COE	Female	COB	Male	COE
Male	COB	Female	COE	Female	COB
Female	COE	Female	COE	Male	COE
Male	COE	Female	COE		

6. Consider the campus crime statistics described in the Appendix. Summarize the type of crimes that have occurred on campus from Fall 1997 to Summer 1999. (File: **Crime.mtp**)

7. Consider the save rate statistics on heart attack victims described in the Appendix. What percent of the victims were saved? What percent of the victims lived in the Metro area? Does the save

rate for the metro and non-metro area seem to differ? Explain. (File: **Heart.mtp**)

8.   Consider the class data set given in the Appendix. Describe the distribution of majors. Which major has the highest number of students? (File: **Classdata.mtp**)

9.   An advertising agency is interested in whether a client's advertisement in the Minneapolis Tribune was noticed by the readers of the newspaper. The agency asked 50 subscribers if they read the advertisement and if they were less than 30 years old. The results are given in the table below.

Subscriber	Under 30?	Read Ad?	Subscriber	Under 30?	Read Ad?
1	yes	yes	26	yes	no
2	yes	no	27	no	no
3	no	no	28	yes	yes
4	no	no	29	no	no
5	no	yes	30	yes	no
6	no	no	31	yes	yes
7	yes	yes	32	yes	yes
8	yes	yes	33	no	yes
9	no	yes	34	no	no
10	yes	no	35	no	no
11	yes	yes	36	yes	no
12	yes	no	37	no	yes
13	no	no	38	no	yes
14	yes	no	39	yes	yes
15	no	yes	40	no	no
16	no	yes	41	yes	no
17	yes	yes	42	no	yes
18	no	no	43	no	yes
19	no	no	44	no	no
20	no	yes	45	yes	yes
21	yes	yes	46	yes	no
22	yes	yes	47	yes	yes
23	no	no	48	yes	yes
24	no	yes	49	no	no
25	no	no	50	no	no

a.   What proportion of the sample read the advertisement?

b.   Construct a two-way table. Does age seem to have an effect on the proportion of subscribers that read the ad? Explain.

CHAPTER 4

DESCRIBING QUANTITATIVE DATA

This chapter demonstrates Minitab commands for organizing and summarizing quantitative data sets. Graphs include stem-and-leaf displays, histograms, dot plots, and box plots. We include numerical measures that are typically used to describe data sets.

NEW COMMANDS

BOXPLOT	CENTER	COUNT	DESCRIBE	DOTPLOT
HISTOGRAM	MAXIMUM	MEAN	MEDIAN	MINIMUM
N	NMISS	RANGE	RCOUNT	RMAXIMUM
RMEAN	RMEDIAN	RMINIMUM	RN	RNMISS
RRANGE	RSSQ	RSTDEV	RSUM	SSQ
STDEV	STEM-AND-LEAF	SUM		

4.1 GRAPHS FOR QUANTITATIVE DATA

Quantitative data include interval and ratio data. **Interval data** are numerical data in which the difference between two possible values is meaningful, but the value of zero does not mean the absence of the variable of interest. Examples of interval data are daily high temperature and many standardized test scores such as the Scholastic Aptitude Test (SAT). To illustrate, temperatures measured on the Centigrade and Fahrenheit scales have different zero points, and values of zero do not mean the absence of temperature.

Ratio data, the highest level of data, are numeric measurements in which the ratio of two data values is meaningful, and a value of zero means the absence of the variable. The number of students absent from class, the daily returns of a mutual fund, and the age of a tissue culture are examples. Thus, zero students absent, a zero mutual fund return, and a zero age each means the absence of the variable of interest.

Graphical methods visually summarize relevant information contained in data sets. In this section we describe stem-and-leaf displays, histograms, and dot plots.

STEM-AND-LEAF DISPLAY

Stem-and-leaf is available only as a character graph. If you are working in the session window, you do not need to enter the command GSTD before using STEM-AND-LEAF. This display results in little loss of the original data. It partitions each observation in two parts: a stem and a leaf. The first column in the display gives a cumulative count of the observations beginning with the highest stem down to the stem containing the median, and a cumulative count of the observations beginning with the lowest stem up to the stem containing the median. The count for the stem containing the median is in parentheses. The second column contains the stems and the third column contains the leaves. Minitab uses 1, 2, or 5 lines per stem depending on the number of observations and range of the data.

Graph ▸ Stem-and-Leaf
Graph ▸ Character Graphs ▸ Stem-and-Leaf
Stat ▸ EDA ▸ Stem-and-Leaf

STEM-AND-LEAF C...C	Constructs a character graph
INCREMENT = K	Controls the scaling of the display, K is the distance between stems
TRIM *outliers*	Removes outliers from the display, labels outliers as low or high values
BY C	Use for stacked data, code in C

HISTOGRAM

A histogram is available both as a professional and character graph. It is a graph of a frequency, relative frequency, or percent frequency distribution. The frequency distribution for quantitative data consists of classes or intervals, and the frequencies or counts of the values that fall within each class. The relative frequency is the proportion of data values that fall in each class; the percent frequency is the percent of data values that fall in each class. Minitab determines the number of classes by the number of data values and the range of the data. You can change the output with subcommands.

Graph ▸ Histogram
Graph ▸ Character Graphs ▸ Histogram

HISTOGRAM C ... C	Constructs a histogram for each column
INCREMENT = K	Specifies the distance between midpoints
START *at* K (*end at* K)	Specifies midpoint of starting and last class
SAME	Use for same midpoints on all histograms
BY C	Use for stacked data, code in C

DOT PLOT

The dot plot is available as a character graph or a professional graph by executing a macro. If you are working in the session window, you do not need to enter the command GSTD before using DOTPLOT. The graph uses a horizontal axis and groups the data as little as possible. Observations are represented as dots on the horizontal axis.

Graph ▸ Dotplot
Graph ▸ Character Graphs ▸ Dotplot

%DOTPLOT	Executes a macro to construct a professional dot plot
DOTPLOT C ... C	Constructs a dot plot for each column
INCREMENT = K	Specifies the distance between tick marks
START *at* K (*end at* K)	Specifies first and last tick marks
SAME	Use same scale for each dot plot
BY C	Use for stacked data, code in C

■ **Example 1**   **Stem-and-Leaf Display, Histogram, and Dot Plot**

During spring semester 2000, a team of statistics students randomly sampled 50 university students to study their grade point averages (GPAs). The following table gives the GPAs for the 50 students in the study. Construct and interpret a stem-and-leaf display, a histogram, and dot plot.

Grade Point Averages

2.2	3.4	4.0	3.1	3.3	3.8	3.0	2.8	2.9	2.9
2.8	2.6	3.3	3.2	3.0	2.8	3.5	2.2	2.9	3.6
3.2	3.0	2.5	2.5	2.8	3.4	2.2	2.9	3.7	2.7
2.7	2.7	2.6	2.9	3.0	2.8	2.9	3.0	2.7	2.9
2.9	2.6	3.5	2.5	2.5	2.5	3.5	3.2	2.9	3.4

Solution   The grade point averages are saved in a file named **GPA.mtp**. The data are in column C1 named GPAs. Stem-and-leaf is available only as a character graph.

Graph ▸ Stem-and-Leaf   MTB > Stem-and-Leaf 'GPAs'
  Select GPAs in **Variables. OK**

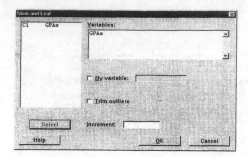

Stem-and-Leaf Display: GPAs

```
Stem-and-leaf of GPAs       N  = 50
Leaf Unit = 0.10

    3      2 222
    8      2 55555
   15      2 6667777
  (14)     2 88888999999999
   21      3 000001
   15      3 22233
   10      3 444555
    4      3 67
    2      3 8
    1      4 0
```

The N = 50 tells us that there are 50 values in the stem-and-leaf display. The leaf unit stated in the display is 0.10; which means the stem unit is 1. The smallest value, with a stem of 2 and a leaf of 2, is a 2.2 GPA, with three students having GPAs of 2.2. The largest value is 4.0, and the center of the distribution is about 2.9.

The column of numbers to the left of the display gives a cumulative count, beginning both from the smallest value at the top, and from the largest value at the bottom to the stem containing the median. Counting from the smallest, three observations are on the first stem, 8 on the first two stems, 15 on the first three stems, and so on. Counting from the largest value, 1 observation is on the last stem, 2 on the last two stems, 4 on the last three stems, and so on. The count of the class containing the median, 14 in this display, is placed in parentheses.

The HISTOGRAM command is available as a character and professional graph.

Graph ▸ Character Graphs ▸ Histogram
    Select GPAs in **Variables. OK**

MTB> Gstd
* NOTE * Character graphs are obsolete.
MTB > Histogram 'GPAs'
MTB> Gpro

Histogram

```
Histogram of GPAs    N = 50

    Midpoint          Count
        2.2               3    ***
        2.4               0
        2.6               8    ********
        2.8               9    *********
        3.0              14    **************
        3.2               4    ****
        3.4               5    *****
        3.6               4    ****
        3.8               2    **
        4.0               1    *
```

The character HISTOGRAM command gives a frequency distribution of the data and a pseudo-histogram with the asterisks (*) to the right of the count. The center is at approximately 3.0, and the distribution is slightly skewed to the right.

Graph ▸ Histogram
Select GPAs in **Graph 1 X**;
Click **Annotation**, choose **Title**; add a title. **OK.**

MTB > Histogram 'GPAs ';
SUBC> Title "Grade Point Average".

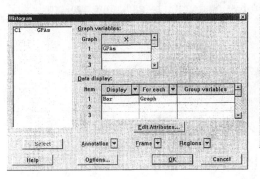

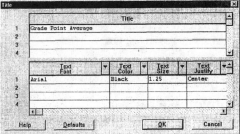

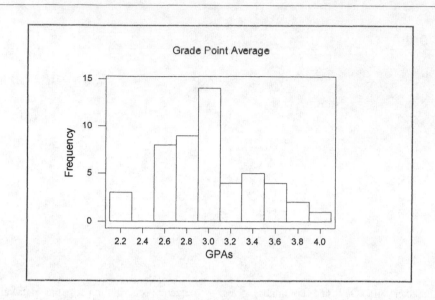

The histogram groups GPAs into classes of width 0.2. The first class is centered on 2.2 and runs from 2.1 to less than 2.3. The second class is centered on 2.4 and runs from 2.3 to less than 2.5, and so on. The second class is empty since no students have GPAs between 2.3 and less than 2.5. The distribution seems to be centered at about 3.0 and slightly skewed toward higher GPAs.

DOTPLOT is available as a character graph or a professional graph by executing a macro.

Graph ▸ Character Graphs ▸ Dotplot   MTB> DotPlot 'GPAs'
Select GPAs in **Variables. OK**

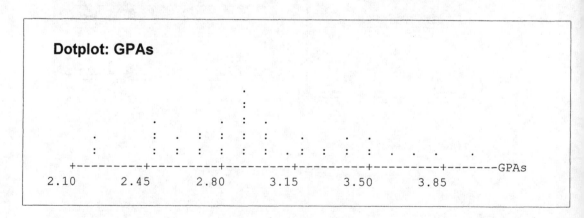

Graph ▸ Dotplot
  Select GPAs in **Variables;**
  Add Title. OK

MTB> %DotPlot 'GPAs';
SUBC> Title "Grade Point Average".

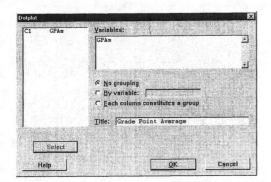

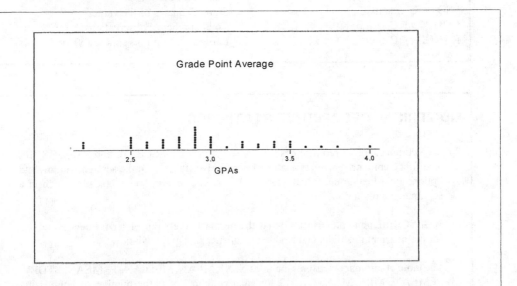

The output from the dot plot macro provides the same graphical information on the shape of the data as does the character dot plot. The dot plot shows the distribution centered at about 3.0 and skewed toward higher grade point averages.

4.2   NUMERICAL DESCRIPTIVE MEASURES

Numerical descriptive measures characterize or give information about a set of data. The mean and median are measures of the center of the data. Measures of spread include the standard deviation and range, and some measures of relative standing are the *z*-score and quartiles. Individual numerical measures can be calculated for columns or rows in a Minitab worksheet.

COMMANDS FOR DATA STORED IN COLUMNS

Each command described below calculates and prints a single number. The option stores the result as a constant.

Calc ▸ Column Statistics

N *of* C (*put in* K)	Number of nonmissing values
NMISS *of* C (*put in* K)	Number of missing values
MEAN *of* C (*put in* K)	Column average
MEDIAN *of* C (*put in* K)	Center value in ordered array
STDEV *of* C (*put in* K)	Sample standard deviation
MAXIMUM *of* C (*put in* K)	Largest value
MINIMUM *of* C (*put in* K)	Smallest value
SUM *of* C (*put in* K)	Sum of all the values
SSQ *of* C (*put in* K)	Sum of squares of the values
COUNT *of* C (*put in* K)	Total number of observations
RANGE *of* C (*put in* K)	Largest value minus smallest value

NUMERICAL DESCRIPTIVE STATISTICS

Two commands that produce descriptive statistics are DESCRIBE and %DESCRIBE. The first command generates a table of descriptive statistics in the session window and optionally, a histogram, a histogram with a normal curve, and a box plot, each in a separate graph window.

%DESCRIBE generates a histogram with a normal curve, a box plot, confidence intervals for the mean and median, and a table of statistics in a graph window.

The table of summary measures includes N, N*, MEAN, MEDIAN, TRMEAN, STDEV, SEMEAN, MIN, MAX, Q1, Q3 for each column. N is the number of nonmissing observations and N* is the number of missing observations. If there are no missing observations, N* is omitted on the output.

The 90% **trimmed mean** TRMEAN removes the smallest 5% and the largest 5% of the observations and averages the rest. The standard error of the mean, SEMEAN = STDEV/$\sqrt{n}$. Q1 is the first quartile and Q3 is the third quartile.

Stat ▸ Basic Statistics ▸ Display Descriptive Statistics

DESCRIBE C ... C	Calculates descriptive measures
BY C	Use for stacked data, code in C

■ Example 2   **Numerical Descriptive Statistics**

Refer to the study of grade point averages (GPAs) described in Example 1 of this chapter. Calculate the mean and standard deviation. Calculate and interpret the descriptive statistics.

Solution The data are retrieved from the GPA file saved in Example 1 (**GPA.mtp**). Mean and Standard Deviation calculate single numbers, which can be stored by adding the option. Each is a separate command.

Calc ▸ Column Statistics   MTB> Mean 'GPAs'
  Select GPAs in **Input variable:**
  Click **Mean. OK**

Calc ▸ Column Statistics   MTB> Stdev 'GPAs'
  Select GPAs in **Input variable:**
  Click **Standard deviation. OK**

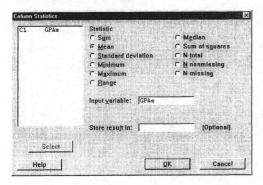
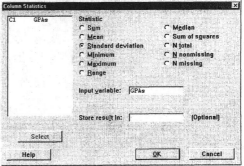

Mean of GPAs

```
Mean of GPAs = 2.9580
```

Standard Deviation of GPAs

```
Standard deviation of GPAs = 0.41012
```

The mean or arithmetic average grade point average of the 50 students is about 2.96 and the standard deviation is .410.

Stat ▸ Basic Statistics ▸ Display Descriptive Statistics   MTB> Describe 'GPAs'
  Select GPAs in **Variables. OK**

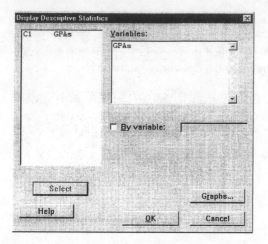

Descriptive Statistics: GPAs

Variable	N	Mean	Median	TrMean	StDev	SE Mean
GPAs	50	2.9580	2.9000	2.9500	0.4101	0.0580

Variable	Minimum	Maximum	Q1	Q3
GPAs	2.2000	4.0000	2.7000	3.2250

N	There are 50 observations in the data set.
Mean	The mean GPA is approximately 2.96.
Median	The median GPA is 2.9. The mean is larger than the median indicating the distribution may be skewed to the right
Tr Mean	This is a 90% trimmed mean. It is the average of the data values after removing the smallest 5% (rounded to the nearest integer) and the largest 5%. Since 5% of 50 is 2.5 or 3, the smallest 3 and the largest 3 grade point averages are removed and the mean of the remaining 44 grade point averages is calculated. The trimmed mean of 2.95 is slightly less than the untrimmed mean.
StDev	The sample standard deviation is 0.41.
SE Mean	The standard deviation of the mean is the sample standard deviation (0.4101) divided by the square root of the sample size (50). We use this measure to make inferences.
Min	The minimum grade point average is 2.2.
Max	The maximum grade point average is 4.0.
Q1	About 25% of the grade point averages are less than 2.7.
Q3	About 75% of the grade point averages are less than 3.2 and about 25% of the grade point averages are greater than 3.2.

4.3   INTERPRETING THE STANDARD DEVIATION

The standard deviation is a measure of the average deviation of the data values from the mean. There are two sets of guidelines for interpreting the standard deviation: Empirical Rule and Tchebysheff's Rule. Both rules consider the proportion of data values that fall within a certain number of standard deviations of the mean.

The **Empirical Rule** applies to data that have a symmetrical or mound-shaped distribution:

1. Approximately 68% of the measurements fall within $(\overline{x} - s, \overline{x} + s)$.
2. Approximately 95% of the measurements fall within $(\overline{x} - 2s, \overline{x} + 2s)$.
3. Nearly 100% of the measurements fall within $(\overline{x} - 3s, \overline{x} + 3s)$.

Tchebysheff's Rule applies to any data set regardless of the shape of the distribution. In general, the rule says that at least $(1 - 1/k^2)$ of the measurements fall within k standard deviations of the mean. For example, at least 8/9 or 89% of the measurements fall within 3 standard deviations of the mean.

■ **Example 3**   **Empirical Rule**

Refer to the study of grade point averages (GPAs) described in Example 1 of this chapter. Find the percentages of observations that fall within $\overline{x} \pm s$, $\overline{x} \pm 2s$, and $\overline{x} \pm 3s$. Compare these percentages with the Empirical Rule.

Solution   The grade point averages are saved in a file called **GPA.mtp**.

The CALCULATOR command (LET session command) is used to calculate the intervals, and to count the observations within each interval. To count, we use the less than (<) and greater than (>) comparisons, and the logical feature AND. If an observation falls within the interval, the result is set to 1; if not, the result is set to 0. A TALLY gives the resulting counts and percentages.

Calc ▸ Calculator
  Enter C2 in **Store results in variable:**
  Enter (C1>Mean(C1)-Stdev(C1)) And
  (C1<Mean(C1)+Stdev(C1)) in **Expression. OK**

MTB > Let C2 = (C1>Mean(C1)-Stdev(C1)) &
CONT>   And (C1<Mean(C1)+Stdev(C1))

Calc ▸ Calculator
  Enter C3 in **Store results in variable:**
  Enter (C1>Mean(C1)-2*Stdev(C1)) And
  (C1<Mean(C1)+2*Stdev(C1)) in **Expression. OK**

MTB >Let C3 = (C1>Mean(C1)-2*Stdev(C1)) &
CONT>   And (C1<Mean(C1)+2*Stdev(C1))

Calc ▸ Calculator
  Enter C4 in **Store results in variable:**
  Enter (C1 >(Mean(C1)-3*Stdev(C1)) And
  (C1<Mean(C1)+3*Stdev(C1)) in **Expression. OK**

MTB > Let C4 = (C4>Mean(C1)-3*Stdev(C1)) &
CONT>   And (C1<Mean(C1)+3*Stdev(C1))

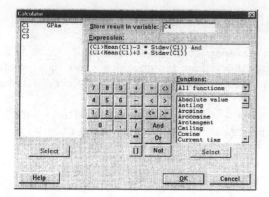

To summarize the frequencies and percent within each interval, we use TALLY.

Stat ▸ Tables ▸ Tally
Enter C2 C3 C4 in **Variables:**
Click **Counts** and **Percents. OK**

MTB > Tally C2 C3 C4;
SUBC > Counts;
SUBC > Percents.

Tally for Discrete Variables: C2, C3, C4

C2	Count	Percent	C3	Count	Percent	C4	Count	Percent
0	18	36.00	0	2	4.00	1	50	100.00
1	32	64.00	1	48	96.00	N=	50	
N=	50		N=	50				

There are 32 grade point averages or 64% of the observations within the interval $\bar{x} \pm s$; 48 grade point averages or 96% within the interval $\bar{x} \pm 2s$; and 50 or 100% within the interval $\bar{x} \pm 3s$. These percentages are close to those given in the Empirical Rule.

4.4   MEASURES OF RELATIVE STANDING

Measures describing the relationship of a measurement to the rest of the data are called measures of relative standing. Examples are the **standard score** or z-score and percentile rankings. The most commonly used measure is the z-score. It can be used to identify **outliers**, which are observations that are unusually large or small when compared with others in a data set. Outliers may be incorrect measurements or may be from a different population than the rest of the data set.

STANDARD SCORES OR *Z*-SCORES

The **z-score** represents the distance, in terms of standard deviations, that a measurement is from the mean of the data set. The sample *z*-score for a measurement x is $z = (x - \bar{x})/s$.

Calc ▸ Standardize

CENTER C...C *put in* C...C	Centers and scales each column independently
LOCATION (*subtracting* K...K)	Specifies means
SCALE (*dividing by* K...K)	Specifies standard deviations

For percentile rankings, Minitab provides the median and quartiles. The median is the 50th percentile or middle quartile, the lower quartile Q1 is the 25th percentile (the value that exceeds 25% of the data values), and the upper quartile Q3 is the 75th percentile. The interquartile range (IQR) is the distance between the upper and lower quartiles.

BOX PLOTS

A box plot is available both as a professional and character graph. The graph displays the main features of a set of data. The box represents the middle half of each data set. The ends of the box are approximately located at the quartiles, Q1 and Q3, and the median is marked with a '+' or a solid line. Special symbols on either side of the box indicate the extent of the data and the location of extreme values.

The interquartile range IQR is the distance between the upper and lower quartiles. Inner fences are located at a distance 1.5(IQR) below Q1 and above Q3. Outer fences are located at a distance 3(IQR) below Q1 and above Q3. Lines or dashed "whiskers" run from the edge of the box to the two most extreme values that are within the inner fences. A value between the inner and outer fence is plotted with an '*' and is a possible outlier. An extreme value beyond the outer fences is plotted with a '0' and is a probable outlier.

For symmetrical distributions, the median is located in the center of the box and the distances from the edges of the box to the smallest and largest values are approximately equal. A nonsymmetrical distribution tends to have longer whiskers and greater distance from the box edge to the median in the direction of the skewness.

Graph ▸ Boxplot
Graph ▸ Character Graphs ▸ Boxplot
Stat ▸ EDA ▸ Boxplot

BOXPLOT C	Use if data are in one column
BOXPLOT C*C	Use for stacked data; groups in second C

■ Example 4   **Calculate *z*-scores**

Refer to the study of grade point averages (GPAs) described in Example 1 of this chapter. Are there any outliers? Calculate and interpret *z*-scores. Construct and interpret a box plot.

Solution   We retrieve the **GPA.mtp** file saved in Example 1. Data are in a column named GPAs. The *z*-scores are calculated and put in numerical order for interpretation.

Calc ▸ Standardize   MTB > Name C2 'zscores'
  Select GPAs in **Input column(s):**   MTB > Center 'GPAs' 'zscores'
  Enter 'zscores' in **Store results in. OK**

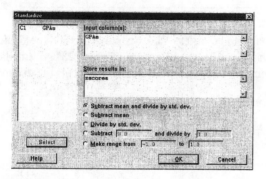

Manip ▸ Sort   MTB > Sort 'zscores' 'zscores';
  Select zscores in **Sort column(s):**   SUBC>   By 'zscores'.
  Select zscores in **Store sorted column(s) in:**
  Select zscores in **Sort by column. OK**

Manip ▸ Display Data
   Select zscores in the **display. OK**

MTB > Print 'zscores'

Data Display

```
zscores
-1.84823  -1.84823  -1.84823  -1.11674  -1.11674  -1.11674  -1.11674
-1.11674  -0.87291  -0.87291  -0.87291  -0.62908  -0.62908  -0.62908
-0.62908  -0.38525  -0.38525  -0.38525  -0.38525  -0.38525  -0.14142
-0.14142  -0.14142  -0.14142  -0.14142  -0.14142  -0.14142  -0.14142
-0.14142   0.10241   0.10241   0.10241   0.10241   0.10241   0.34624
 0.59007   0.59007   0.59007   0.83390   0.83390   1.07773   1.07773
 1.07773   1.32156   1.32156   1.32156   1.56539   1.80922   2.05305
 2.54071
```

The smallest and largest grade point averages have z-scores of -1.85 and 2.54 respectively. Neither of these values are outliers. Outliers are usually considered to be observations with z-scores less than -3 or greater than 3.

We use a box plot to graph the data and to detect outliers. We illustrate the character and professional box plots.

Graph ▸ Character Graphs ▸ Boxplot
   Select GPAs in **Variable. OK**

MTB> Gstd
* NOTE * Character graphs are obsolete.
MTB > Boxplot 'GPAs'
MTB> Gpro

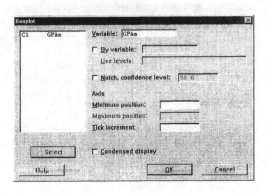

Boxplot

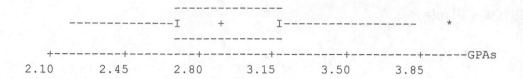

```
                             --------------
              ---------------I      +       I-------------------        *
                             --------------
             +---------+---------+---------+---------+---------+------GPAs
           2.10      2.45      2.80      3.15      3.50      3.85
```

The character BOXPLOT gives a horizontal view of the data. The box represents the middle half of the GPAs. The ends of the box are approximately located at the quartiles, Q1 and Q3, and the median is marked with a '+' or a solid line. We know these values from the descriptive statistics in Example 2. About 50% of the grade point averages are between 2.7 and 3.2; the median is about 2.9.

Lines or dashed "whiskers" run from the edge of the box to the two most extreme values that are within the inner fences. The value plotted with an '*' is a possible outlier (The maximum GPA of 4.0 was identified in Example 2).

The distribution is somewhat nonsymmetrical. It has longer whiskers and greater distance from the median to the box edge in the direction of higher GPAs.

Graph ▸ Boxplot
  Select GPAs in **Graph 1 Y**;
  Click **Annotation**, choose **Title**; add a title. **OK.**

MTB > Boxplot 'GPAs';
SUBC> Title "Grade Point Average".

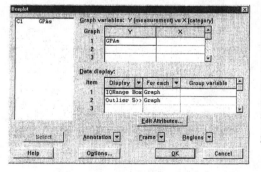

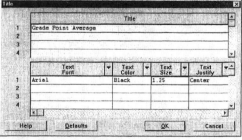

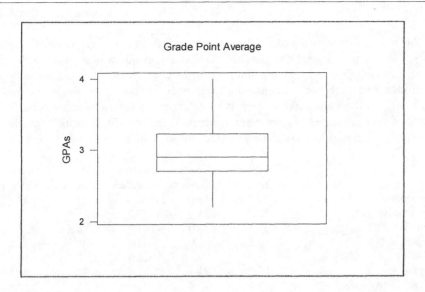

The professional box plot gives a vertical view of the data. More of the area of the box is located above the median; the upper whisker is longer than the lower whisker indicating the distribution is skewed toward higher grade point averages. This box plot did not detect any outliers.

COMMANDS FOR DATA STORED IN ROWS

The row statistics include sum, mean, sample standard deviation, minimum, maximum, range, median, sum of squares, number of values, and number of missing and nonmissing values. The statistic is calculated for each row in a set of columns and stored in the corresponding row of a new column.

Calc ▸ Row Statistics

RN E ... E *put in* C	Number of nonmissing values in rows
RNMISS E ... E C	Number of missing values in rows
RMEAN E ... E C	Mean of values in rows
RMEDIAN E ... E C	Median of values in rows
RSTDEV E ... E C	Standard deviation of values in rows
RMAXIMUM E ... E C	Maximum of values in rows
RMINIMUM E ... E C	Minimum of values in rows
RSUM E ... E C	Sum of values of values in rows
RSSQ E ... E C	Sum of squares
RCOUNT E ... E C	Number of columns
RRANGE E ... E C	Row range

■ **Example 5**   **Calculate Statistics Across Rows**

In 1998 the Postmaster General established the United States Postal Service Commission on a Safe and Secure Workplace. The charge to the commission was to develop a plan to make the 38,000 post offices and related facilities the safest environment for its employees. The commission subsequently conducted an intensive study which included a comprehensive survey of workplace violence. The following table gives the percentage of positive responses on several attitudes and psychological measures for different categories of employees in a certain local region. Calculate the mean, standard deviation, minimum and maximum of these measures for the employees in this region.

Measures	City Carriers	Rural Carriers	Mail Handlers	Post Masters	Other Managers
Autonomy	25.2	42.0	34.0	78.5	80.3
Pressure/Burden	55.0	21.3	37.7	29.6	47.2
Negative Attitude	30.5	17.9	42.3	8.3	28.7
Anger	5.3	2.0	4.4	1.3	2.5
Hostility	14.7	9.3	16.9	7.7	10.5
Coping	85.7	91.3	82.4	88.0	86.5
Distress and Anxiety	27.4	16.4	24.6	21.0	32.8
Verbal Aggressiveness	30.7	19.5	32.7	13.4	23.3

Solution   The survey data are saved in a file named **Attitudes.mtp.** Column names in the Minitab worksheet are similar to the headings in the table above.

Calc ▸ Row Statistics
  Click **Mean**;
  Select City-Other in **Input variables:**
  Enter 'Mean' in **Store results in. OK**

MTB > Name C7 'Mean'
MTB > RMean 'City'-'Other' 'Mean'

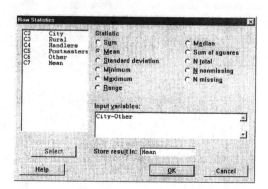

Calc ▸ Row Statistics
  Click **Standard deviation**;
  Select City-Other in **Input variables**:
  Enter 'StDev' in **Store result in. OK**

MTB > Name C8 'StDev'
MTB > RStDev 'City'-'Other' 'StDev'

Calc ▸ Row Statistics
  Click **Minimum**;
  Select City-Other in **Input variables**:
  Enter 'Minimum' in **Store result in. OK**

MTB > Name C9 'Minimum'
MTB > Rminimum 'City'-'Other' 'Minimum'

Calc ▸ Row Statistics
  Click **Maximum**;
  Select City-Other in **Input variables**:
  Enter 'Maximum' in **Store result in.OK**

MTB > Name C10 'Maximum'
MTB > RMaximum 'City'-'Other' 'Maximum'

Manip ▸ Display data
  Select Measures Mean- Maximum in **Display. OK**

MTB > Print C1 C7-C10

Data Display

Row	Measures	Mean	StDev	Minimum	Maximum
1	Autonomy	52.00	25.7166	25.2	80.3
2	Pressure/Burden	38.16	13.4448	21.3	55.0
3	Negative Attitude	25.54	12.9525	8.3	42.3
4	Anger	3.10	1.6837	1.3	5.3
5	Hostility	11.82	3.8460	7.7	16.9
6	Coping	86.78	3.2538	82.4	91.3
7	Distress and Anxiety	24.44	6.2280	16.4	32.8
8	Verbal Aggressiveness	23.92	7.9632	13.4	32.7

The row commands store the numerical measures in specified columns. For example, the measure on Anger ranged from 1.3 to 5.3 with a mean of 3.1 and standard deviation of 1.68.

EXERCISES

1. Minitab allows us to study the effects of a change in one or more data values on numerical descriptive measures. Consider the following data. Only the first data value in each column is different. Obtain a table of numerical descriptive measures for each column. Compare the means, medians, and standard deviations of the data sets.

C1	C2	C3
10	200	600
190	190	190
200	200	200
176	176	176
162	162	162
230	230	230
274	274	274
180	180	180

2. A large international corporation customarily rents homes for relocating employees in Phoenix, Arizona. The Personnel Division of the corporation is interested in studying the monthly rents of homes within the city. The following prices of 40 three bedroom homes were randomly selected. (File: **Phoenix.mtp**)

Rental Prices

$ 925	$1,095	$ 665	$ 895	$1,100
900	900	875	870	1,150
1,175	1,050	925	895	1,350
850	1,065	1,075	1,035	1,420
1,250	1,465	925	1,275	1,025
975	1,020	800	1,100	1,285
935	875	875	1,475	950
1,325	865	1,150	925	1,070

a. Numerically and graphically describe the rental prices. Write a short description of the data.
b. Find the percentages of observations that fall within $\bar{x} \pm s$, $\bar{x} \pm 2s$, and $\bar{x} \pm 3s$. Compare these with the Empirical Rule.
c. Calculate and sort the z-scores. Are there any outliers?

3. A service company is concerned about the length of time that customers had to wait before receiving the information they requested. The company randomly selected 40 customers and recorded the waiting time in minutes, as shown below. Numerically and graphically summarize waiting times. (File: **WaitingTime.mtp**)

Waiting Time for Service

9	11	12	13	13	14	14	15	15	16
16	16	17	17	17	17	18	18	18	19
19	19	19	20	20	20	21	21	21	21
21	22	22	22	24	24	25	27	29	38

4. Suppose a reference librarian selected a random sample of 30 customers before starting a new information retrieval system. The retrieval times in minutes are given below. Numerically and graphically summarize the data. Draw conclusions about the shape, center, and spread of the distribution of retrieval times. (File: **Retrieval.mtp**)

Information Retrieval Times

10	15	15	10	20	15	10	20	30	15
25	5	45	22	10	27	25	22	10	30
15	5	8	15	5	36	23	17	15	10

5. Brock and Brenda Lee, owners of Lee Produce Company, are studying the size of orders placed by customers in Stearns County. In the past week, they have received the following 30 orders, in dollars. Numerically and graphically summarize the size of customer orders. Discuss the results.

Lee Produce Company Orders

22	25	29	30	31	35	37	39	40	40
41	42	43	44	45	45	45	46	48	49
50	52	55	56	56	58	59	65	66	70

6. Forbes magazine ranks the 40 highest-paid entertainers and their estimated gross incomes. The following table gives the rankings and income in millions of dollars for 1995 and 1996 combined. (File: **Entertainers.mtp**)

	Name	Income		Name	Income
1.	Winfrey, Oprah	$171	21.	Stallone, Sylvester	$44
2.	Spielberg, Steven	150	22.	Grisham, John	43
3.	Beatles	130	23.	Williams, Robin	42
4.	Jackson, Michael	90	24.	Zemeckis, Robert	42
5.	Rolling Stones	77	25.	Roseanne	40
6.	Eagles	75	26.	Douglas, Michael	40
7.	Schwarzenegger, Arnold	74	27.	Willis, Bruce	36
8.	Copperfield, David	63	28.	Pavarotti, Luciano	36
9.	Carrey, Jim	63	29.	Kiss	35
10.	Crichton, Michael	59	30.	Schulz, Charles	33
11.	Seinfeld, Jerry	59	31.	Cosby, Bill	33
12.	King, Stephen	56	32.	Travolta, John	33
13.	Brooks, Garth	51	33.	Carey, Mariah	32
14.	Webber, Andrew Lloyd	50	34.	Clancy, Tom	31
15.	Hanks, Tom	50	35.	Costner, Kevin	31
16.	Siegfried and Roy	48	36.	Washington, Denzel	30
17.	Cruise, Tom	46	37.	Letterman, David	28
18.	Ford, Harrison	44	38.	Metallica	28
19.	Eastwood, Clint	44	39.	Gibson, Mel	28
20.	R.E.M.	44	40.	Bullock, Sandra	25

a. Graphically and numerically summarize the income for the top 40 entertainers.
b. Calculate separate numerical descriptive measures for the male entertainers, female entertainers, and groups. Discuss the differences between the three categories of entertainers.

7. The service manager at a quick oil and lube shop was concerned about the length and variability of time it was taking to service automobiles. The service system had one mechanic do everything. The service manager selects a random sample of 30 customers and records the service time for each customer. Numerically and graphically summarize the service times data.

Service Times

14	13	12	12	15	12
20	15	14	20	15	15
18	14	20	11	22	18
17	14	17	24	13	10
16	16	17	15	13	16

8. The President of a large company was concerned about the number of highly trained employees who might be retiring soon. If too many employees retire at the same time, replacing them might be difficult. This table provides the years of service of a random sample of 151 employees. **(ServiceYears.mtp)**

Years of Service

13	16	25	3	27	7	7	2	3	16	7	26	1	8
6	27	6	6	8	23	3	21	4	12	0	9	3	32
27	5	23	9	9	6	9	7	9	13	1	15	20	9
2	1	13	18	10	27	26	4	27	9	10	7	7	13
27	2	7	23	26	16	5	23	6	9	30	4	5	18
4	4	0	10	10	7	2	27	26	3	29	29	7	1
19	19	5	5	10	28	21	20	23	8	3	17	17	26
30	14	17	6	14	20	0	27	22	28	20	0	8	13
19	1	2	18	26	9	3	21	8	17	1	29	21	30
7	6	18	2	10	6	26	9	22	13	7	8	28	44
26	28	16	29	2	9	17	2	8	23	39			

a. Numerically and graphically describe the years of service. Do you think the presidents should be concerned about the retiring employees? Write a brief summary.
b. Find the percentages of observations that fall within $\bar{x} \pm s$, $\bar{x} \pm 2s$, and $\bar{x} \pm 3s$. Compare these with the Empirical Rule.
c. Calculate and sort the z-scores. Are there any outliers?

9. A dentist conducted an experiment to measure the effectiveness of a new type of dental anesthetic. Twenty-five patients receive the standard anesthetic while twenty-five others receive the new anesthetic. Each patient gave a measure of his or her discomfort on a scale from 0 to 100, higher scores indicating greater discomfort. Numerically and graphically compare the two samples. **(Dentist.mtp)**

Standard						New				
23	44	44	50	51		62	82	39	85	75
26	34	53	43	6		50	74	51	57	46
44	26	79	49	30		40	87	72	39	48
32	49	52	33	38		35	30	56	48	56
44	67	33	52	22		52	58	50	64	60

10. The service manager at a quick oil and lube shop was concerned about the length of time it was taking to service automobiles. The old system had one mechanic do everything. He proposed a new system where the mechanic would only change the oil. A second person would lubricate the car while doing a safety check. A random sample of 50 cars using the old system and 50 cars using the new system resulted in the following service times in minutes. Graphically and numerically compare the two systems. Do you think the new system is better than the old? Discuss. (**SystemTimes.mtp**)

Old System Times					New System Times				
6	10	10	11	11	6	6	7	7	7
11	12	12	12	12	7	8	8	8	8
12	12	13	13	13	8	9	9	9	10
13	13	13	13	13	11	11	11	11	11
13	14	14	14	14	11	11	12	12	12
14	14	14	15	15	12	12	12	12	13
15	15	15	16	16	13	13	14	14	14
16	16	17	17	17	14	14	14	15	15
17	18	19	19	19	15	15	15	15	15
20	20	21	22	28	16	16	19	19	23

11. During spring semester 2000 a team of statistics students compared grade point averages of university students who live on campus with students who live off campus. The team was interested in determining whether there are differences in grade point averages distributions for the two student groups. Random samples of grade point averages are given below: Numerically and graphically compare the two groups. (File: **CampusGPA.mtp**)

On-campus GPAs				Off-campus GPAs				
2.2	3.4	4.0	3.1	2.8	3.4	2.2	2.9	2.9
2.9	2.9	2.8	2.6	2.6	2.9	3.0	2.8	3.4
3.5	2.2	2.9	3.6	2.9	2.6	3.5	2.5	
3.3	3.8	3.0	2.8	3.7	2.7	2.7	2.7	
3.3	3.2	3.0	2.8	2.9	3.0	2.7	2.9	
3.2	3.0	2.5	2.5	2.5	2.5	3.5	3.2	

12. The yearly housing inventory index measures the number of months it takes to sell all available residential properties at the current yearly rate of sales. A low index indicates a strong market demand, shorter time on the market, and higher prices. A high index indicates a large supply of available homes and a decline in home prices. The *1995 Minnesota Housing Report* provides the 1993, 1994, and 1995 unsold housing inventory index for five Minnesota regions. Calculate and interpret the average and standard deviation of the yearly index for each region.

Region	1993	1994	1995
Range	17.3	9.8	7.7
Lakes	16.7	11.9	13.9
Metro	4.8	6.3	4.9
Southeast	10.3	8.1	6.9
Central	13.3	11.2	9.8

13. The Consumer Price Index (CPI) measures the change over time in the price of foods and services purchased by wage earners and clerical workers. The *Statistical Abstract of the United States 1989* reports the annual percent change in consumer prices for several countries for the years 1977 through 1987.   (File: **CountryCPI.mtp**)

Country	1978	1979	1980	1981	1982	1983	1984	1985	1986	1987
U.S.	7.6	11.3	13.5	10.3	6.1	3.2	4.3	3.5	1.9	3.7
Canada	8.9	9.2	10.2	12.5	10.8	5.8	4.3	4.0	4.2	4.4
Japan	3.8	3.6	8.0	4.9	2.7	1.9	2.2	2.1	0.4	-0.2
Austria	3.6	3.7	6.4	6.8	5.4	3.3	5.6	3.2	1.7	1.4
Belgium	4.5	4.5	6.6	7.6	8.7	7.7	6.3	4.9	1.3	1.6
Denmark	10.0	9.6	12.3	11.7	10.1	6.9	6.3	4.7	3.6	4.0
France	9.1	10.8	13.6	13.4	11.8	9.6	7.4	5.8	2.7	3.1
Italy	12.4	15.7	21.1	18.7	16.3	15.0	10.6	8.6	6.1	4.6
Spain	19.8	15.7	15.5	14.6	14.4	12.2	11.3	8.8	8.8	5.3
U.K.	8.3	13.4	18.0	11.9	8.6	4.6	5.0	6.1	3.4	4.2
W.Germ.	2.7	4.1	5.5	6.3	5.3	3.3	2.4	2.2	-0.2	0.2

For example, the 1978 number for the United States shows that the price of consumer goods increased 7.6% from 1977 to 1978.

   a. For each year, calculate the mean and standard deviation of the changes in consumer prices. Construct box plots for each year. What is the worldwide trend in consumer prices?
   b. For each country, calculate the mean, median, and standard deviation of the changes in consumer prices. Generally countries desire a low and constant growth in consumer prices. A low standard deviation indicates a constant growth. Which three countries have the lowest increases in consumer prices? Which three countries have the most constant growth?

14. A chemistry professor records lab project scores for each student. The following table gives the lab scores for each of 13 students.

Employee	1	2	3	4	5	6
Hodel, Lois	48	50	0	49	44	44
Eich, Peter	42	46	47	43	30	0
Zirbes, Tom	48	45	43	38	35	33
Notch, Mike	44	47	45	46	40	29
Barker, Hugh	44	32	42	50	38	43
Sakry, Carol	42	48	49	50	48	41
Fisher, Dean	44	44	49	43	44	41
Jurek, Roy	48	46	49	47	40	48
Wenz, Robin	50	38	47	43	35	28
Piehl, Gina	46	43	48	50	36	32
Coborn, Bob	42	46	49	50	45	39
Gohman, Lora	43	41	48	48	44	43
Theis, Mark	42	48	49	45	39	37

   a. Which three students had the highest average lab score? The lowest average lab score?
   b. Consistent performance is an important student characteristic. Are there any students who

are more consistent than others? Discuss.

c. Is there a change in the lab scores over time? Discuss.

d. Stack the lab scores in a column. Construct a histogram and a box plot of the stacked data. Describe the distribution of lab scores.

15. The Minnesota Real Estate Research Center compiles information on homes sold in several areas of Minnesota. The following table gives selling prices of 20 homes randomly selected from the homes sold in St. Cloud and Rochester in 1998.   (File: **MNHomes.mtp**)

St. Cloud		Rochester	
$105,000	$124,400	$123,925	$159,900
66,000	110,600	86,000	67,800
98,900	73,500	29,900	116,000
143,000	139,500	73,000	112,330
136,000	74,000	145,500	74,900
66,600	84,500	81,500	164,000
119,875	91,900	84,000	109,000
84,000	89,900	100,750	105,900
72,000	131,900	94,500	155,000
72,500	74,500	149,195	78,000

a. Numerically and graphically compare the selling prices in St. Cloud and Rochester. Does it appear that selling prices are higher and more variable in St. Cloud or Rochester?

b. Are there any outliers. What are the shapes of the selling price distributions?

16. The Census Bureau, Commerce Department Bureau of Economic Analysis, Department of Health and Human Services are among the organizations which collect data on the United States. The following table gives the 1995 budget including revenues and expenditures in billions of dollars for the 50 states and the District of Columbia. (File: **StateDept.mtp**)

State	Revenue	Expenditure	State	Revenue	Expenditure
Alabama	$ 11.389	$ 10.242	Montana	$ 3.023	$ 2.663
Alaska	7.358	5.423	Nebraska	3.890	3.823
Arizona	10.843	9.783	Nevada	4.500	4.051
Arkansas	6.446	5.915	New Hampshire	3.011	2.970
California	108.222	104.567	New Jersey	29.614	28.923
Colorado	10.028	8.673	New Mexico	6.303	5.599
Connecticut	12.744	12.507	New York	78.209	74.280
Delaware	2.876	2.557	North Carolina	19.377	19.916
Dist Columbia	3.376	3.391	North Dakota	2.288	2.129
Florida	33.216	30.103	Ohio	38.341	31.685
Georgia	16.585	15.308	Oklahoma	8.679	8.272
Hawaii	5.543	5.606	Oregon	10.826	9.013
Idaho	3.406	2.776	Pennsylvania	37.779	34.359
Illinois	30.351	28.132	Rhode Island	3.765	4.176
Indiana	14.653	14.136	South Carolina	10.637	10.386
Iowa	8.224	7.766	South Dakota	1.942	1.686
Kansas	6.730	5.742	Tennessee	11.864	11.028
Kentucky	11.011	10.543	Texas	42.019	39.091
Louisiana	13.348	12.893	Utah	5.348	4.833

Maine	3.926	3.889	Vermont	1.953	1.849
Maryland	14.842	13.537	Virginia	16.307	14.721
Massachusetts	21.493	21.557	Washington	19.930	18.003
Michigan	28.760	27.051	West Virginia	6.047	5.943
Minnesota	16.245	14.295	Wisconsin	18.677	14.621
Mississippi	7.205	6.235	Wyoming	2.181	1.887
Missouri	12.559	10.809			

   a. Obtain descriptive measures of the revenues and expenditures for the fifty states and the District of Columbia, and for the fifty states without the District of Columbia. Compare.

   b. Construct box plots for the budget items. Interpret.

   c. Calculate z-scores for the revenues. Rank the z-scores from largest to smallest. Are there any outliers?

17. Refer to the table in Exercise 16 which gives the 1995 budget including revenues and expenditures in billions of dollars for the 50 states and the District of Columbia.

   a. Calculate separate numerical measures for the revenues for the states and the District of Columbia east and west of the Mississippi River. Compare the measures.

   b. Are there any states which had greater expenditures than revenues in 1995? If there are, list these states and the amount overspent.

18. Consider the class data set given in the Appendix of this supplement and answer the following questions. (File: **Classdata.mtp**)

   a. Numerically and graphically summarize the distribution of ages of the students.

   b. Compare the ages of male and female students.

19. Consider the class data set given in the Appendix of this supplement and answer the following questions. (File: **Classdata.mtp**)

   a. Numerically and graphically summarize the distribution of the number of hours students work.

   b. Compare the hours worked for male and female students.

20. Consider the heart attack data set given in the Appendix. (File: **Heart.mtp**)

   a. Compare the ages of the saved and not saved victims of heart attacks.

   b. Compare the response time for victims in the metro and not in the metro area.

21. Results of surveys reporting the use of drugs, alcohol, and cigarettes among college students are given in the *Sourcebook of Criminal Justice Statistics* published by the Bureau of Justice Statistics. The following table gives the percentages of students' usage for the previous 30 days. The number of respondents to the survey ranged from 1,080 to 1,410 for the years 1984 through 1991. Calculate the mean, standard deviation, minimum and maximum of drug usage during these years. The data are saved in **Drug.mtp**.

Drug	1984	1985	1986	1987	1988	1989	1990	1991
Marihuana	23.0	23.6	22.3	20.3	16.8	16.3	14.0	14.1
Inhalants	0.7	1.0	1.1	0.9	1.3	0.8	1.0	0.9
Hallucinogens	2.6	2.0	3.6	3.4	2.8	3.7	2.5	2.0
Cocaine	7.6	6.9	7.0	5.0	4.7	3.0	2.3	2.3
Heroin	0.0	0.0	0.0	0.1	0.1	0.1	0.0	0.1
Other Opiates	1.4	0.7	0.6	0.8	0.8	0.7	0.5	0.6
Stimulants	5.5	4.2	3.7	2.3	1.8	1.3	1.4	1.0
Sedatives	2.2	1.4	1.3	1.3	1.2	0.4	0.2	0.3
Tranquilizers	1.1	1.4	1.9	1.0	1.1	0.8	0.5	0.6
Alcohol	79.1	80.3	79.7	78.4	77.0	76.2	74.5	74.7
Cigarettes	21.5	22.4	22.4	24.0	22.6	21.1	21.5	23.2

22. A concern of every American is the amount of taxes one pays to federal, state, and local governments. *Kiplinger's Personal Finance Magazine* reported in June, 1997, that tax bills in Washington, D.C. may not have as great an impact on Americans as taxes at the state and local level. The real significance of this statement is that tax rates in cities and states should be a primary consideration when one is looking for a place to relocate. For instance, one may wonder whether the overall tax burden is less in states with no income tax.

The following data comparing tax burdens of state and local income, sales, and property taxes, paid by a married couple with two kids and annual earnings of $65,000, were compiled by Right Choice, Inc. a South Hamilton, Mass., consulting company. The sales-tax numbers assume an average amount is spent on food, clothing, household goods, and gasoline. Property-tax numbers assume the family lives in a $225,000 home, with a 30-year mortgage.

Suppose you are thinking of relocating and you are concerned about taxes. Analyze the following tax burden data. Prepare a report of your analysis, including some regional comparisons. Include numerical measures and graphs. It's always a good idea to check data for accuracy. Verify that the totals are correct before you begin the analysis. (File: **CityTax.mtp**)

The South

City	State Income	Local Income	Property	Sales	Total
Birmingham, AL	$1,915	$975	$2,025	$1,096	$6,011
Montgomery, AL	1,915	0	1,125	1,096	4,136
Hot Springs, AR	3,072	0	2,250	840	6,162
Little Rock, AR	3,072	0	2,475	839	6,386
Miami, FL	0	0	4,050	553	4,603
St. Petersburg, FL	0	0	3,600	595	4,195
Tallahassee, FL	0	0	2,700	595	3,295
Atlanta, GA	2,416	0	2,700	666	5,782
Savannah, GA	2,416	0	3,375	666	6,457
Baton Rouge, LA	1,211	0	1,125	1,096	3,432
New Orleans, LA	1,211	0	2,025	1,233	4,469
Hattiesburg, MS	1,955	0	2,025	959	4,939
Jackson, MS	1,955	0	1,800	939	4,714
Charlotte, NC	2,994	0	2,700	822	6,516
Raleigh-Durham, NC	2,994	0	2,475	822	6,291
Oklahoma City, OK	2,556	0	2,025	1,284	5,865
Tulsa, OK	2,556	0	3,150	1,085	6,791
Charleston, SC	2,782	0	1,575	822	5,179

Columbia, SC	2,782	0	2,475	685	5,942
Memphis, TN	0	0	2,475	1,130	3,605
Nashville, TN	0	0	2,025	1,130	3,155
Austin, TX	0	0	5,175	701	5,876
Dallas, TX	0	0	4,500	701	5,201
Houston, TX	0	0	5,175	701	5,876
Richmond, VA	2,698	0	2,025	617	5,340
Roanoke, VA	2,698	0	4,500	617	7,815
Charleston, WV	2,595	0	2,250	822	5,667
Morgantown, WV	2,595	0	2,700	822	6,117

The Northeast

Greenwich, CT	$2,633	$ 0	$1,575	$510	$4,718
Hartford, CT	2,633	0	3,150	510	6,293
Washington, DC	4,166	0	1,800	489	6,456
Dover, DE	0	2,250	0	5,198	
Wilmington, DE	2,948	813	2,025	0	5,786
Boston, MA	3,162	0	3,150	425	6,737
Worcester, MA	3,162	0	2,025	425	5,612
Annapolis, MD	2,430	1,458	2,250	425	6,563
Baltimore, MD	2,430	1,215	3,600	425	7,670
Augusta, ME	2,813	0	4,275	510	7,598
Portland, ME	2,813	0	4,500	510	7,823
Concord, NH	0	0	6,075	0	6,075
Manchester, NH	0	0	5,850	0	5,850
Cherry Hill, NJ	1,050	0	5,400	510	6,960
Trenton, NJ	1,050	0	5,175	510	6,735
Albany, NY	3,225	0	6,300	680	10,205
Buffalo, NY	3,225	0	6,750	680	10,655
New York, NY	3,225	2,600	2,925	701	9,451
Harrisburg, PA	1,820	650	3,600	510	6,580
Philadelphia, PA	1,820	3,224	4,050	595	9,689
Pittsburgh, PA	1,820	1,869	5,400	595	9,684
Providence, RI	1,685	0	3,825	595	6,105
Wakefield, RI	1,685	0	3,375	595	5,655
Burlington, Vt	1,532	0	4,275	425	6,232
Montpelier, VT	1,532	0	4,275	425	6,232

The Midwest

Des Moines, IA	$3,330	$ 0	$6,075	$510	$9,915
Dubuque, IA	3,330	0	6,075	510	9,915
Chicago, IL	1,830	0	4,725	796	7,351
Springfield, IL	1,830	0	2,475	668	4,973
Fort Wayne, IN	2,074	244	4,950	425	7,693
Indianapolis, IN	2,074	427	2,250	425	5,176
Topeka, KS	2,088	0	2,925	843	5,856
Wichita, KS	2,088	0	2,700	809	5,597
Frankfort, KY	2,996	546	3,375	510	7,427
Louisville, KY	2,996	1,300	2,475	510	7,281
Detroit, MI	2,438	1,878	4,500	510	9,326
Lansing, MI	2,438	626	5,625	510	9,189
Duluth, MN	3,069	0	4,050	638	7,757
St. Paul, MN	3,069	0	4,950	595	8,614
Jefferson City, MO	2,193	0	1,350	853	4,396
Kansas City, MO	2,193	650	1,800	921	5,564
Bismarck, ND	858	0	4,050	510	5,418
Fargo, ND	858	0	3,150	510	4,518
Lincoln, NE	2,481	0	5,625	553	8,659
Omaha, NE	2,481	0	5,625	553	8,659

Cleveland, OH	2,391	1,300	3,600	595	7,886
Columbus, OH	2,391	1,300	3,375	510	7,576
Pierre, SD	0	0	4,275	822	5,097
Sioux Falls, SD	0	0	4,050	822	4,872
Madison, WI	3,664	0	4,950	468	9,082
Milwaukee, WI	3,664	0	5,850	468	9,982

The West

Anchorage, AK	$ 0	$0	$4,050	$ 0	$4,050
Juneau, AK	0	0	4,050	340	4,390
Phoenix, AZ	1,367	0	1,800	599	3,766
Tucson, AZ	1,367	0	2,025	595	3,987
Los Angeles, CA	1,824	0	2,700	701	5,225
Sacramento, CA	1,824	0	2,700	659	5,183
San Francisco, CA	1,824	0	2,700	723	5,247
Denver, CO	2,220	0	1,125	621	3,966
Pueblo, CO	2,220	0	2,250	638	5,108
Hilo, HI	3,729	0	1,125	548	5,402
Honolulu, HI	3,729	0	675	548	4,952
Boise, ID	3,137	0	3,150	685	6,972
Idaho Falls, ID	3,137	0	4,500	685	8,322
Billings, MT	3,056	0	3,375	0	6,431
Helena, MT	3,056	0	4,050	0	7,106
Albuquerque, NM	1,818	0	1,575	762	4,155
Santa Fe, NM	1,818	0	1,575	856	4,249
Carson City, NV	0	0	1,800	574	2,374
Las Vegas, NV	0	0	1,575	0	1,575
Portland, OR	3,852	0	2,700	383	6,935
Salem, OR	3,852	0	3,825	383	8,060
Provo, UT	2,951	0	2,025	839	5,815
Salt Lake City, UT	2,951	0	2,700	839	6,490
Olympia, WA	0	0	2,475	680	3,155
Seattle, WA	0	0	2,475	731	3,206
Casper, WY	0	0	1,800	685	2,485
Cheyenne, WY	0	0	1,800	685	2,485

CHAPTER 5

PROBABILITY DISTRIBUTIONS

Probability distributions of discrete and continuous random variables are discussed in this chapter. We demonstrate commands for calculating the mean and variance of a discrete probability distribution, and commands for the binomial, normal, Poisson, and exponential probability distributions.

NEW COMMANDS

CDF   INVCDF   PDF   PLOT

5.1 DISCRETE RANDOM VARIABLES

A variable x is a **random variable** if the value that x assumes is a chance event corresponding to the outcome of an experiment. There are two types of random variables, discrete and continuous. A **discrete random variable** can assume a countable number of values; a **continuous random variable** can assume a value corresponding to any point on some interval.

MEAN AND VARIANCE

The **mean** or **expected value** of a discrete random variable x is given by

$$\mu = \sum_{All\ x} xp(x).$$

The **variance**, a weighted average of the squared differences between the values of x and μ, is

$$\sigma^2 = \sum_{All\ x} (x - \mu)^2 p(x).$$

The square root of the variance is the **standard deviation**, denoted σ. You can use the calculator command (LET session command) to calculate the mean, variance and standard deviation of a discrete random variable.

For example, suppose you want to find the mean of x, the number of heads observed when two coins are tossed. The following is the distribution of x.

x	p(x)
0	.25
1	.50
2	.25

If the data are in columns as labeled above, commands to calculate the mean are as follows:

Calc ▸ Calculator
Enter 'Mean' in **Store results in variable:**
Enter SUM('x'*'p(x)') in **Expression. OK**

MTB > Name C3 'Mean'
MTB > Let 'Mean' = SUM('x'*'p(x)')

Manip ▸ Display Data
Select x, p(x), and Mean in **Display. OK**

MTB > Print 'x'-'Mean'

Data Display

```
 Row     x    p(x)    Mean

  1      0    0.25     1
  2      1    0.50
  3      2    0.25
```

The **probability distribution** of a discrete random variable gives all possible values of the random variable and the probability of observing each value. We can graph a probability distribution with the plot command.

PLOTTING TWO OR MORE VARIABLES

This graph shows the relationship between two columns of numbers. You can graph up to 100 pairs of columns. Methods to display the points include symbols, project lines, connect lines and areas. Project lines work well for displaying discrete distributions, and connect lines for continuous distributions. The default displays symbols at the points.

Graph ▸ Plot

PLOT C*C ... C*C	First column in a pair is the *y*-axis variable
CONNECT	Connects points
SYMBOL	Uses your choice of symbols
PROJECT	Displays projection lines from points
AREA	Fills the area beneath points
TITLE	Adds a title to the graph

■ **Example 1**   **Discrete Probability Distribution**

Consider the following probability distribution in which the random variable x is the number of consumers in a sample of $n = 5$ who favor shopping on the Internet.

x	$p(x)$
0	0.003
1	0.028
2	0.132
3	0.309
4	0.360
5	0.168
	1.000

Graph the probability distribution. Find the mean, variance, and standard deviation.

Solution   We enter the distribution in columns C1 and C2 named x and p(x). PLOT gives a graph of the probability distribution.

Graph ▸ Plot
  Select p(x) in **Graph 1 Y** and x in **Graph 1 X**;
  Click **Display**, choose **Project**;
  Click **Annotation**, click **Title**, add a title. **OK**

MTB > Plot 'p(x)' * 'x';
SUBC> Project;
SUBC> Title "Internet Shopping".

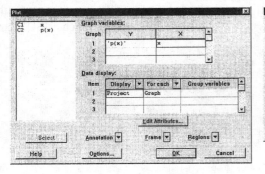
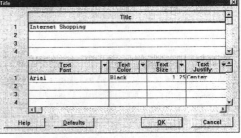

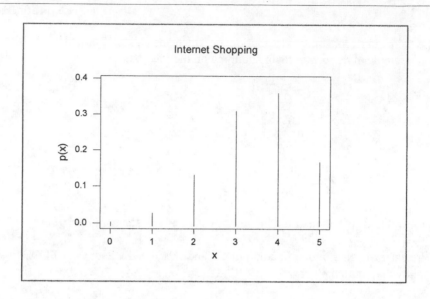

The graph shows that the distribution is skewed toward smaller values of *x*. There seems to be favorable response for shopping on the Internet.

To calculate the mean, variance, and standard deviation of the probability distribution, we evaluate the equations for μ, σ^2, and σ. Parentheses are required with mathematical functions, such as SUM and SQRT.

Calc ▸ Calculator
  Enter 'Mean' in **Store results in variable:**
  Enter SUM('x'*'p(x)') in **Expression. OK**

MTB > Name C3='Mean'
MTB > Let 'Mean' = SUM('x'*'p(x)')

Calc ▸ Calculator
  Enter 'Variance' in **Store results in variable:**
  Enter SUM(('x'-'Mean')**2*'p(x)') in **Expression. OK**

MTB > Name C4='Variance'
MTB > Let 'Variance'=SUM(('x'-'Mean')**2*'p(x)')

Calc ▸ Calculator
  Enter 'StDev' in **Store results in variable:**
  Enter SQRT('Variance') in **Expression. OK**

MTB > Name C5 = 'StDev'
MTB > Let 'StDev' = SQRT('Variance')

Manip ▸ Display Data
  Select x - StDev in **Display. OK**

MTB > Print 'x'-'StDev'

Data Display

Row	x	p(x)	Mean	Variance	StDev
1	0	0.003	3.499	1.05400	1.02664
2	1	0.028			
3	2	0.132			
4	3	0.309			
5	4	0.360			
6	5	0.168			

The mean of five consumers who favor Internet shopping is 3.5; the standard deviation is 1.0266.

5.2 SPECIAL DISCRETE RANDOM VARIABLES

This section illustrates the binomial and Poisson random variables and probability distributions. A binomial random variable describes the outcome of an experiment which results in one of two outcomes, generally termed success and failure. A Poisson random variable is one which describes the number of occurrences of an event during a given unit of time, or other measurement.

BINOMIAL RANDOM VARIABLE

The outcome of an experiment can often be described as falling in one of two categories. For example, a coin either is heads or tails, a newborn is either male or female, a memo is either correctly typed or not, an account is either paid up or is overdue, and a product is either preferred or not preferred by a customer. The categories are usually denoted success and failure.

The **binomial distribution** is the probability distribution of the number of successes on n identical and independent trials. The probability of success, denoted π (*pi*), is constant for each trial. The probability of failure is $1 - \pi$. The mean or expected value of the binomial random variable is defined $\mu = n\pi$, and the variance is $\sigma^2 = n\pi(1 - \pi)$.

Minitab calculates probabilities, cumulative probabilities, and inverse cumulative probabilities for a binomial random variable x. The **probability** option provides the probability for each specified value of x. The **cumulative probability** is the probability that a random variable x is less than or equal to a certain value. **Inverse cumulative probability** calculates the value x_0 associated with a specified probability p such that $P(x \le x_0) = p$. If no value gives the exact probability p, Minitab prints the two values that give probabilities that are just less than and just greater than p.

CALCULATING DISCRETE PROBABILITIES

This command calculates probabilities of specified values of x, cumulative probabilities, and inverse cumulative probabilities for a discrete random variable x. If calculations are to be done for one value of x, the value can be entered in the dialog box or on the command line. An input column is required if calculations are to be done for several values. The results can be stored or printed.

Calc ▸ Probability Distributions ▸ Binomial
Calc ▸ Probability Distributions ▸ Poisson

PDF (*values* E ... E) (*store in* E ... E)   Calculates the probability distribution
  BINOMIAL n = K pi = K   Use for the binomial probability distribution
  POISSON *mu* = K   Use for the Poisson probability distribution

CDF (*values* E ... E) (*store in* E ... E)   Calculates the cumulative distribution
  BINOMIAL n = K pi = K   Use for binomial probabilities
  POISSON *mu* = K   Use for Poisson probabilities

INVCDF *values* E (*store in* E)   Calculates inverse cumulative probabilities
  BINOMIAL n = K pi = K   Use for binomial probabilities
  POISSON *mu* = K   Use for Poisson probabilities

■ **Example 2**   **Binomial Probability Tables**

Tables of binomial probabilities or cumulative binomial probabilities are given in most statistics textbooks. With Minitab, you can generate these probability tables. Use Minitab to obtain the binomial probability and cumulative probability distributions for $\pi = .1$ and $\pi = .9$, with $n = 10$. Graph both probability distributions.

Solution   We enter the values $(0, 1, \ldots, 10)$ of the binomial random variable in a column named 'x'.

Calc ▸ Make Patterned Data ▸ Simple Set of Numbers   MTB > Name C1 = 'x'
  Enter 'x' in **Store patterned data in:**   MTB > Set 'x'
  Enter **From first value:** 0 and **To last value:** 10. **OK**   DATA> 0/10
                                      DATA> End.

Calc ▸ Probability Distributions ▸ Binomial   MTB > Name C2 'p(x)'
  Click **Probability**;   MTB > PDF 'x' 'p(x)';
  Enter 10 in **Number of trials:**   SUBC> Binomial 10 .1.
   and .1 in **Probability of success:**
  Select x in **Input column:**
   Enter 'p(x)' in **Optional storage**. **OK**

Calc ▸ Probability Distributions ▸ Binomial
  Click **Cumulative probability**;
  Enter 10 in **Number of trials:**
  and .1 in **Probability of success:**
Select x in **Input column:**
  Enter 'cum p(x)' in **Optional storage**. **OK**

MTB > Name C3 = 'cum p(x)'
MTB > CDF 'x' 'cum p(x)';
SUBC> Binomial 10 .1.

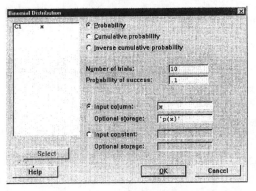
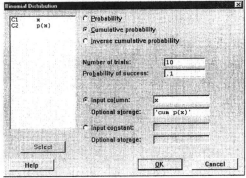

Manip ▸ Display Data
  Select x, p(x), and cum p(x) in **Display**. **OK**

MTB > Print 'x'-'cum p(x)'

Data Display

Row	x	p(x)	cum p(x)
1	0	0.348678	0.34868
2	1	0.387420	0.73610
3	2	0.193710	0.92981
4	3	0.057396	0.98720
5	4	0.011160	0.99837
6	5	0.001488	0.99985
7	6	0.000138	0.99999
8	7	0.000009	1.00000
9	8	0.000000	1.00000
10	9	0.000000	1.00000
11	10	0.000000	1.00000

The probability option gives the probability for each specified value of x. The cumulative probability gives the probability that a random variable x is less than or equal to a certain value. For any x value, the cumulative probability is equal to the sum of the probabilities up to and including the probability for that x value.

Graph ▸ Plot
   Select p(x) in **Graph 1 Y** and x in **Graph 1 X**;
   Click **Display**, choose **Project**;
   Click **Annotation**, click **Title**, add a title. **OK**

MTB > Plot 'p(x)' * 'x';
SUBC>   Project;
SUBC>   Title "Binomial Probability Distribution".

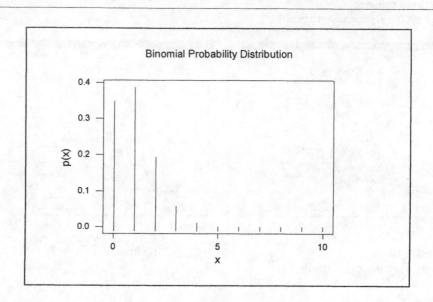

The probability distribution with $\pi = .1$ is skewed to the right; that is, the probabilities are high for low values of x.

We use the same values (0, 1, . . . , 10) in the column named 'x' for the binomial random variable when $\pi = .9$ and $n = 10$. The columns 'p(x)' and 'cum p(x)' are already named.

Calc ▸ Probability Distributions ▸ Binomial
  Click **Probability**; enter 10 in **Number of trials:**
  Enter .9 in **Probability of success:**
  Select x in **Input column:**
  Select p(x) in **Optional storage. OK**

MTB > PDF 'x' 'p(x)';
SUBC>   Binomial 10 .9.

Calc ▸ Probability Distributions ▸ Binomial
  Click **Cumulative probability**;
  Enter 10 in **Number of trials:**
  and .9 in **Probability of success:**
  Select x in **Input column:**
  Select cum p(x) in **Optional storage. OK**

MTB > CDF 'x' 'cum p(x)';
SUBC>   Binomial 10 .9.

Manip ▸ Display Data
  Select x, p(x), and cum p(x) in **Display. OK**

MTB > Print 'x'-'cum p(x)'

Data Display

Row	x	p(x)	cum p(x)
1	0	0.000000	0.00000
2	1	0.000000	0.00000
3	2	0.000000	0.00000
4	3	0.000009	0.00001
5	4	0.000138	0.00015
6	5	0.001488	0.00163
7	6	0.011160	0.01280
8	7	0.057396	0.07019
9	8	0.193710	0.26390
10	9	0.387420	0.65132
11	10	0.348678	1.00000

Graph ▸ Plot
  Select p(x) in **Graph 1 Y** and x in **Graph 1 X**;
  Click **Display**, choose **Project**;
  Click **Annotation**, click **Title**, add a title. **OK**

MTB > Plot 'p(x)' * 'x';
SUBC>   Project;
SUBC>   Title "Binomial Probability Distribution".

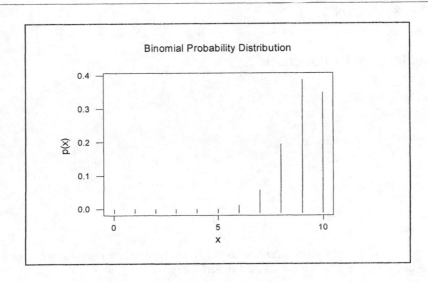

Binomial Probability Distribution

This probability distribution with $\pi = .9$ is skewed to the left; that is, the probabilities are high for large values of x.

■ **Example 3**   **A Binomial Probability Distribution**

Suppose that 70% of all consumers favor Internet shopping. Five consumers are randomly sampled, and the number who favor Internet shopping is recorded. Let x be the number of consumers who favor this concept.

    a.   Obtain and describe the probability distribution. Find the mean and standard deviation.
    b.   What is the probability that no one favors Internet shopping? That 4 do?
    c.   What is the probability that 3 or more do?
    d.   Find the number of consumers such that the probability of being less than or equal to this number is about 0.5.

Solution   Since each consumer either favors Internet shopping or doesn't, there are two possible outcomes. The number of consumers x who favor Internet shopping is a binomial random variable, with $n = 5$ and $\pi = .7$. The possible values of x are from 0 to 5 consumers.

a.   First we obtain the binomial distribution table. The possible values of x (0,1, ..., 5) are placed in column C1 named 'x'.

Calc ▸ Probability Distributions ▸ Binomial   MTB > PDF 'x';
   Click **Probability**;   SUBC> Binomial 5 .7.
   Enter 5 in **Number of trials:**
    and .7 in **Probability of success:**
   Select x in **Input column. OK**

Probability Density Function

Binomial with n = 5 and p = 0.700000

x	P(X = x)
0.00	0.0024
1.00	0.0284
2.00	0.1323
3.00	0.3087
4.00	0.3602
5.00	0.1681

Note this distribution is approximately the same as that given in Example 1. The number of consumers who favor Internet shopping is a binomial random variable.

To calculate the mean and standard deviation, we use the formulas. Since $n = 5$ and $\pi = .7$, the mean is $\mu = n\pi = 3.5$ and the standard deviation is $\sigma = \sqrt{n\pi(1-\pi)} = 1.0247$. Because of rounding the probabilities in Example 1, these results differ slightly from μ and σ calculated in that example.

b. From the distribution, we find the probability that no one favors Internet shopping is .0024; the probability that four consumers favor is .3602.

c. To find the probability that three or more consumers favor Internet shopping, we find $P(x \geq 3)$ = $1 - P(x \leq 2)$. The latter part is a cumulative probability.

Calc ▸ Probability Distributions ▸ Binomial
  Click **Cumulative probability**;
  Enter 5 in **Number of trials:**
   and .7 in **Probability of success:**
  Enter 2 in **Input constant. OK**

MTB > CDF 2;
SUBC> Binomial 5 .7.

Cumulative Distribution Function

Binomial with n = 5 and p = 0.700000

```
    x      P( X <= x )
  2.00        0.1631
```

The cumulative probability command gives $P(x \leq 2)$. The probability that three or more consumers favor Internet shopping is $P(x \geq 3) = 1 - P(x \leq 2) = 1 - 0.1631 = .8369$.

---

d. To find a value of x_0 such that the probability that x is less than or equal to this value is about 0.5, we find the inverse cumulative probability: $P(x \leq x_0) = .5$.

Calc ▸ Probability Distributions ▸ Binomial
  Click **Inverse cumulative probability**;
  Enter 5 in **Number of trials:**
   and .7 in **Probability of success:**
  Enter 0.5 in **Input constant. OK**

MTB > InvCDF .5;
SUBC> Binomial 5 .7.

Inverse Cumulative Distribution Function

Binomial with n = 5 and p = 0.700000

```
    x      P( X <= x )          x      P( X <= x )
    3        0.4718             4        0.8319
```

Minitab gives the cumulative probabilities for x equal to 3 and 4. The value of 3 has a cumulative probability of about 0.5; the probability that the number of consumers is less than or equal to 3 is about 0.5.

POISSON RANDOM VARIABLE

The Poisson probability distribution is useful for describing the number of occurrences of an event during a given unit of time, or other measurement. Applications include the number of arrivals per hour at an emergency ward of a large hospital, the number of computer breakdowns per month, the number of typing errors per page, and the number of accidents per year at a production facility.

The Poisson distribution is specified by one parameter μ, the average number of events that occur in a given unit of measurement. The variance of the Poisson distribution is the same as the mean. The commands are defined earlier in this chapter.

■ **Example 4**   **Poisson Probability Tables**

Tables for Poisson probabilities or cumulative Poisson probabilities are given in most statistics textbooks. With Minitab, you can generate similar tables of Poisson probabilities. Use Minitab to obtain the Poisson probability and cumulative probability distributions for $\mu = 2.2$.

Solution To calculate the distributions, we need to enter values for x. Since x cannot be negative, we use values from 0 to more than 3 standard deviations above the mean. The standard deviation is the square root of 2.2, $\sigma = 1.48$. Sometimes we need to use trial and error to find the highest value of x to get a cumulative probability of 1.0000, accurate to four decimal places. In this problem, we enter (0, 1, ..., 10) in a column named 'x'.

Calc ▸ Probability Distributions ▸ Poisson
    Click **Probability**;
    Enter 2.2 in **Mean:**
    Select x in **Input column:**
       Enter 'p(x)' in **Optional storage. OK**

MTB > Name C2 'p(x)'
MTB > PDF 'x' 'p(x)';
SUBC> Poisson 2.2.

Calc ▸ Probability Distributions ▸ Poisson
    Click **Cumulative probability**;
    Enter 2.2 in **Mean:**
    Select x in **Input column.**
       Enter 'cum p(x)' in **Optional storage. OK**

MTB > Name C3 = 'cum p(x)'
MTB > CDF 'x' 'cum p(x)';
SUBC> Poisson 2.2.

Manip ▸ Display Data
    Select x, p(x), and cum p(x) in **Display. OK**

MTB > Print 'x' - 'cum p(x)'

Data Display

Row	x	p(x)	cum p(x)
1	0	0.110803	0.11080
2	1	0.243767	0.35457
3	2	0.268144	0.62271
4	3	0.196639	0.81935
5	4	0.108151	0.92750
6	5	0.047587	0.97509
7	6	0.017448	0.99254
8	7	0.005484	0.99802
9	8	0.001508	0.99953
10	9	0.000369	0.99990
11	10	0.000081	0.99998

Graph ▸ Plot
  Select p(x) in **Graph 1 Y** and x in **Graph 1 X**;
  Click **Display**, choose **Project**;
  Click **Annotation**, click **Title**, add a title. **OK**

MTB > Plot 'p(x)' * 'x';
SUBC>   Project;
SUBC>   Title "Poisson Probability Distribution".

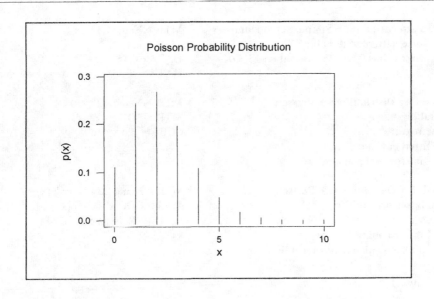

The Poisson probability distribution with $\mu = 2.2$ is skewed to the right.

■ **Example 5**   **Poisson Probabilities**

In a large Midwestern city, there is a residential area near a car and train intersection. To alert traffic of an oncoming train, a whistle blows as often as 80 times a day. A resident has requested a change in the city ordinance to stop the blowing of the whistle during nighttime hours. Data on the accident rate without a whistle has been collected at a similar intersection. It was found that the mean number of accidents without the whistle was 5.5 per year. Assume the number of accidents per year x is described by a Poisson distribution.

    a. What is the mean and standard deviation of x?
    b. Find the probability distribution and cumulative probability distribution of the number of accidents per year. Graph the probability distribution.
    c. Find the probability that there is one accident. One or fewer accidents.

Solution

a.   The mean and variance of a Poisson random variable are both equal to 5.5, the mean number of number of accidents without the whistle. The standard deviation is the square root of the variance: $\sigma = 2.3452$.

b.   To calculate the distributions, we need to enter values for x. Since x cannot be negative, we use values from 0 to more than 3 standard deviations above the mean. We enter the values 0 to 15 in a column named 'x'. PLOT gives a graph of the probability distribution.

Calc ▸ Make Patterned Data ▸ Simple Set of Numbers Enter 'x' in **Store patterned data in:** Enter **From first value:** 0 and **To last value:** 15. **OK**	MTB > Name C1 = 'x' MTB > Set 'x' DATA> 0/15 DATA> End.
Calc ▸ Probability Distributions ▸ Poisson Click **Probability**; Enter 5.5 in **Mean:** **Select** x in **Input column:** Enter 'p(x)' in **Optional storage**. **OK**	MTB > Name C2 'p(x)' MTB > PDF 'x' 'p(x)'; SUBC> Poisson 5.5.
Calc ▸ Probability Distributions ▸ Poisson Click **Cumulative probability**; Enter 5.5 in **Mean:** **Select** x in **Input column**. Enter 'cum p(x)' in **Optional storage**. **OK**	MTB > Name C3 = 'cum p(x)' MTB > CDF 'x' 'cum p(x)'; SUBC> Poisson 5.5.

Manip ▸ Display Data
  Select x, p(x), and cum p(x) in **Display. OK**

MTB > Print 'x' - 'cum p(x)'

Data Display

Row	x	p(x)	cum p(x)
1	0	0.004087	0.004087
2	1	0.022477	0.026564
3	2	0.061812	0.088376
4	3	0.113323	0.201699
5	4	0.155819	0.357518
6	5	0.171401	0.528919
7	6	0.157117	0.686036
8	7	0.123449	0.809485
9	8	0.084871	0.894357
10	9	0.051866	0.946223
11	10	0.028526	0.974749
12	11	0.014263	0.989012
13	12	0.006537	0.995549
14	13	0.002766	0.998315
15	14	0.001087	0.999401
16	15	0.000398	0.999800

The probability option provides the probability for each specified value of *x*. The values of *x* with the highest probabilities are those near $\mu = 5.5$.

Graph ▸ Plot
  Select p(x) in **Graph 1 Y** and x in **Graph 1 X**;
  Click **Display**, choose **Project**;
  Click **Annotation**, Click **Title**, add a title. **OK**

MTB > Plot 'p(x)' * 'x';
SUBC> Project;
SUBC> Title "Poisson Probability Distribution";
SUBC> Title "Number of Accidents".

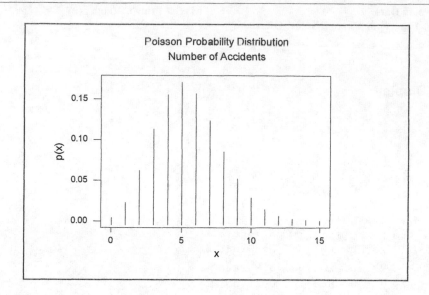

The probability distribution is slightly skewed to the right; the high probabilities are for x values near the mean $\mu = 5.5$.

c.   To find the probability that there is one accident at an intersection without a train whistle, we can look in the table above or enter a constant as follows. The cumulative probability gives the probability of one or fewer accidents.

Calc ▸ Probability Distributions ▸ Poisson
  Click **Probability**;
  Enter 5.5 in **Mean:**
  Click **Input constant** and enter 1. **OK**

MTB > PDF 1;
SUBC>   Poisson 5.5.

Probability Density Function

```
Poisson with mu = 5.50000


      x        P( X = x )
   1.00           0.0225
```

The probability that there is one accident is $P(x = 1) = .0225$.

Calc ▸ Probability Distributions ▸ Poisson
  Click **Cumulative probability**; enter 5.5 in **Mean:**
  Click **Input constant** and enter 1. **OK**

MTB > CDF 1;
SUBC> Poisson 5.5.

Cumulative Distribution Function

```
Poisson with mu = 5.50000

     x      P( X <= x )
  1.00         0.0266
```

The probability that there is one or fewer accidents is P($x \leq 1$) = .0266.

5.3 CONTINUOUS RANDOM VARIABLES

A **continuous random variable** x can assume any value within an interval. Examples include the length of time for a drug to be effective, the daily percent change in stock prices, and the weight of newborn babies.

The graph of a continuous probability distribution is a smooth curve called the **probability density function**, denoted $f(x)$. The **density function** is a rule that determines how the probability is distributed over the range of the possible values of x. To graphically describe a probability distribution, the total area under the smooth curve must equal 1. The probability of a continuous random variable x having a value within a given interval is represented by the corresponding area under the curve. Since the area over any point is zero, the probability at a point is zero; thus, P($z \leq a$) = P($z < a$).

NORMAL RANDOM VARIABLE

The **normal probability distribution** is one of the most useful distributions in statistics. This mound-shaped distribution is completely specified by the mean μ and standard deviation σ. Some random variables that might be normal include weight of one-year-olds, the monthly rate of return of a stock, the time to access the Internet, and the time required to complete an experiment.

The **standard normal random variable**, denoted z, has mean $\mu = 0$ and standard deviation $\sigma = 1$. Calculating the z-score can standardize any random variable x:

$$z = (x - \mu)/\sigma.$$

The **z-score** gives the number of standard deviations between the observation x and the mean μ.

With Minitab you can calculate probability densities, cumulative probabilities, and inverse cumulative probabilities for a normal random variable. The **probability density** is the value of $f(x)$, the height of the normal curve at the specified x. The **cumulative probability** is the probability that a random variable x is less than or equal to a certain value. **Inverse cumulative probability** calculates the value x_0 associated with a specified probability p such that $P(x \le x_0) = p$.

CALCULATING PROBABILITIES

This command calculates probability densities, cumulative probabilities, and inverses of cumulative probabilities. An input column is required if you want probabilities for more than one value. The results can be stored or printed. The default normal distribution is the standard normal distribution with $\mu = 0$ and $\sigma = 1$.

Calc ▸ Probability Distributions ▸ Normal
Calc ▸ Probability Distributions ▸ Exponential

PDF E ... E (*store in* E ... E)	Calculates probability densities
NORMAL (*mu* = K *sigma* = K)	Use for normal distributions
EXPONENTIAL *mu* = K	Use for exponential probabilities
CDF E ... E (*store in* E ... E)	Calculates cumulative probability densities
NORMAL (*mu* = K *sigma* = K)	Use for normal distributions
EXPONENTIAL *mu* = K	Use for exponential distributions
INVCDF E ... E (*store in* E ... E)	Calculates inverse cumulative probability
NORMAL (*mu* = K *sigma* = K)	Use for normal random variable
EXPONENTIAL *mu* = K	Use for exponential random variable

■ **Example 6**   **Standard Normal Probabilities**

The standard normal distribution has a mean $\mu = 0$ and standard deviation $\sigma = 1$. Graph the standard normal probability distribution.

Solution According to the Empirical Rule, nearly all of the observations fall within three standard deviations of the mean. Using a slightly larger interval, we graph the distribution for some z values: -4.0, -3.9, -3.8, . . . , 4.0.

Calc ▸ Make Patterned Data ▸ Simple Set of Numbers	MTB > Name C1 = 'z'
Enter 'z' in **Store patterned data in:**	MTB > Set 'z'
Enter **From first value:**-4 and **To last value:** 4;	DATA> -4:4/.1
Enter **In steps of:** .1. **OK**	DATA> End.
Calc ▸ Probability Distributions ▸ Normal	MTB > Name C2 = 'f(z)'
Click **Probability density**;	MTB > PDF 'z' 'f(z)';
Enter **Input column:** z	SUBC> Normal 0.0 1.0.
and **Optional storage:** 'f(z)'. **OK**	

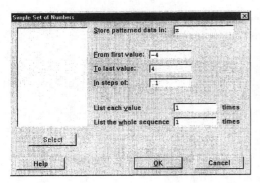

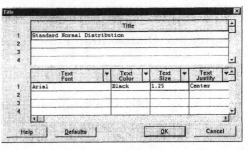

Graph ▸ Plot
  Enter f(z) in **Graph 1 Y** and z in **Graph 1 X**;
  Click **Display** and choose **Connect**;
  Click **Annotation**, choose**Title**, add a title. **OK**

MTB > Plot 'f(z)' * 'z';
SUBC>   Connect;
SUBC>   Title "Standard Normal Distribution".

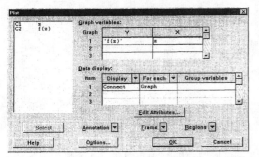

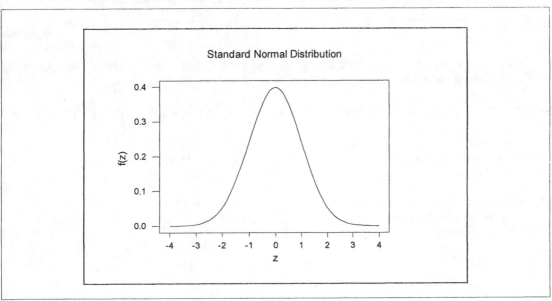

The standard normal distribution has $\mu = 0$ and $\sigma = 1$. We know from the Empirical Rule that nearly 100% of the area is within three standard deviations of the mean.

■ **Example 7**   **Normal Probabilities**

The following is a series of normal probability problems. Use Minitab to solve each.

a.   Find the probability that the standard normal random variable is less than or equal to -1.5.

Solution   We use the cumulative probability function to find P($z \leq$ -1.5).

Calc ▸ Probability Distributions ▸ Normal	MTB > CDF -1.5;
Click **Cumulative probability**;	SUBC> Normal 0.0 1.0.
Click **Input constant:** and enter -1.5. **OK**	

Cumulative Distribution Function

```
Normal with mean = 0 and standard deviation = 1.00000

        x     P( X <= x )
  -1.5000        0.0668
```

The probability that the standard normal random variable is less than or equal to -1.5 is .0668.

---

b.   Find the probability that a normally distributed random variable lies within two standard deviations of the mean.

Solution   We find the probability that z is between -2 and 2: P(-2 $\leq z \leq$ 2) = P($z \leq$ 2) - P($z <$ -2).

Calc ▸ Probability Distributions ▸ Normal	MTB > CDF 2;
Click **Cumulative probability**;	SUBC> Normal 0.0 1.0.
Click **Input constant:** and enter 2. **OK**	
Calc ▸ Probability Distributions ▸ Normal	MTB > CDF -2;
Click **Cumulative probability**;	SUBC> Normal 0.0 1.0.
Click **Input constant:** and enter -2. OK	

Cumulative Distribution Function

```
Normal with mean = 0 and standard deviation = 1.00000

       x      P( X <= x )
   2.0000         0.9772
```

Cumulative Distribution Function

```
Normal with mean = 0 and standard deviation = 1.00000

       x      P( X <= x )
  -2.0000         0.0228
```

From the output, we find P(-2 ≤ z ≤ 2) = P(z ≤ 2) - P(z < -2) = .9772 - .0228 = .9544.

c.   Find the probability that a standard normal random variable is greater than 1.8.

Solution   The probability that *z* is greater than 1.8 is P(*z* > 1.8) = 1 - P(*z* ≤ 1.8).

Calc ▶ Probability Distributions ▶ Normal
  Click **Cumulative probability**;
  Click **Input constant:** and enter 1.8. **OK**

MTB > CDF 1.8;
SUBC> Normal 0.0 1.0.

Cumulative Distribution Function

```
Normal with mean = 0 and standard deviation = 1.00000

       x      P( X <= x )
   1.8000         0.9641
```

The probability that *z* is greater than 1.8 is 1 - .9641 = .0359.

d.   Find z_0 such that the probability of obtaining a value less than z_0 is 0.10.

Solution   In this problem, we use the inverse cumulative probability function to find the value z_0 such that $P(z \leq z_0) = 0.1$.

Calc ▶ Probability Distributions ▶ Normal
  Click **Inverse cumulative probability**;
  Click **Input constant:** and enter 0.1. **OK**

MTB > InvCDF .1;
SUBC> Normal 0.0 1.0.

Inverse Cumulative Distribution Function

```
Normal with mean = 0 and standard deviation = 1.00000

P( X <= x )            x
    0.1000       -1.2816
```

The probability of getting a *z* value less than -1.28 is 0.10.

■ **Example 8**   **A Normal Distribution**

The average amount of time it takes a student to complete a certain task is approximately normally distributed with μ = 50 minutes and σ = 5 minutes.

    a. Obtain a graph of the normal distribution.
    b. What proportion of all students take between 40 and 55 minutes?
    c. What proportion of all students take longer than one hour?
    d. Seventy-five percent of all students take less than what time to complete the task?

Solution   According to the Empirical Rule, most of the observations fall within three standard deviations of the mean.

a.   Using a slightly larger interval, we graph the distribution for integer values of *x* within the interval, $\mu \pm 4\sigma$, or (30, 70).

Calc ▸ Make Patterned Data ▸ Simple Set of Numbers	MTB > Name C1 = 'x'
Enter 'x'; in **Store patterned data in:**	MTB > Set 'x'
Enter **From first value:** 30 and **To last value:** 70. **OK**	DATA> 30:70
	DATA> End
Calc ▸ Probability Distributions ▸ Normal	MTB > Name C2 = 'f(x)'
Click **Probability density**;	MTB > PDF 'x' 'f(x)';
Enter **Mean:** 50, **Standard deviation:** 5;	SUBC> Normal 50 5.
Enter **Input column:** x	
and **Optional storage:** 'f(x)'. **OK**	
Graph ▸ Plot	MTB > Plot 'f(x)' * 'x';
Enter f(x) in **Graph 1 Y** and x in **Graph 1 X**;	SUBC> Connect;
Click **Display** and choose **Connect**;	SUBC> Title "Normal Probability Distribution";
Click **Annotation**, choose **Title**, Add title. **OK**	SUBC> Title "Student Task Time".

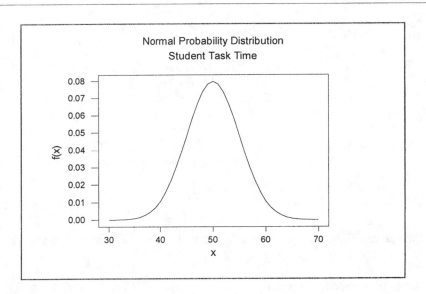

The graph shows a very small probability of a certain task taking less than 35 minutes or greater than 65 minutes. Nearly all task times will be between 35 and 65 minutes — the range of task times within three standard deviations of the mean.

b. To find the proportion of students that take between 40 and 55 minutes, we use the cumulative probability function to find $P(40 \leq x \leq 55) = P(x \leq 55) - P(x < 40)$.

Calc ▸ Probability Distributions ▸ Normal
  Click **Cumulative probability**;
  Enter **Mean: 50, Standard deviation: 5**;
  Click **Input constant:** and enter 55. **OK**

MTB > CDF 55;
SUBC> Normal 50 5.

Calc ▸ Probability Distributions ▸ Normal
  Click **Cumulative probability**;
  Enter **Mean: 50, Standard deviation: 5**;
  Click **Input constant:** and enter 40. **OK**

MTB > CDF 40;
SUBC> Normal 50 5.

Cumulative Distribution Function

```
Normal with mean = 50.0000 and standard deviation = 5.00000

        x      P( X <= x )
  55.0000         0.8413
```

Cumulative Distribution Function

```
Normal with mean = 50.0000 and standard deviation = 5.00000

       x      P( X <= x )
  40.0000         0.0228
```

The probability that a student has a task time between 40 and 55 minutes is 0.8413 - .0228 = .8185. This is the equivalent to saying that about 82% of all students take between 40 and 55 minutes for a certain task.

c.   To find the probability that a randomly selected student takes longer than one hour, we find $P(x > 60) = 1 - P(x \leq 60)$.

Calc ▸ Probability Distributions ▸ Normal
  Click **Cumulative probability**;
  Enter **Mean: 50, Standard deviation: 5**;
  Click **Input constant:** and enter 60. **OK**

MTB > CDF 60;
SUBC> Normal 50 5.

Cumulative Distribution Function

```
Normal with mean = 50.0000 and standard deviation = 5.00000

       x      P( X <= x )
  60.0000         0.9772
```

The probability that a randomly selected student takes longer than one hour is 1 - .9772 = .0228. This means that about 2 students out of every 100 take more than an hour to complete a certain task.

d.   To find the time such that 75% of all students take less than that to complete the task, we use the inverse cumulative probability function to find the value x_0 such that $P(x \leq x_0) = 0.75$.

Calc ▸ Probability Distributions ▸ Normal
  Click **Inverse cumulative probability**;
  Enter **Mean: 50, Standard deviation: 5**;
  Click **Input constant:** and enter .75. **OK**

MTB > InvCDF .75;
SUBC> Normal 50 5.

Inverse Cumulative Distribution Function

```
Normal with mean = 50.0000 and standard deviation = 5.00000

P( X <= x )           x
    0.7500       53.3724
```

Seventy-five percent of all students take less than about 53 minutes to complete the task.

EXPONENTIAL RANDOM VARIABLE

The **exponential distribution** is useful for describing the length of time between arrivals and other events. For example, the exponential distribution may approximate the length of time between arrivals of an airport shuttle bus and the length of time between breakdowns of a mainframe computer.

An **exponential random variable** can take on any value greater than zero. The distribution is specified by one parameter μ; the standard deviation σ is the same as the mean. The commands to calculate probabilities are described earlier in the chapter.

■ **Example 9**   **An Exponential Probability Distribution**

Waiting line or queuing theory is concerned with modeling the characteristics of a service system. Both the time between arrivals of customers (inter arrival time) and the time to service a customer (service time) are reasonably approximated by an exponential distribution. Suppose the length of time between arrival of customers at a hair stylist salon can be described by an exponential distribution, with mean equal to 10 minutes.

   a. Find the mean and standard deviation of x, the time between arrivals. Graph the probability distribution.
   b. What is the probability that the inter arrival time is more than 15 minutes?
   c. Find the probability that the length of time between arrivals is within two standard deviations of the mean.

Solution

a. The mean and standard deviation of the exponential random variable are $\mu = 10$ and $\sigma = 10$. To determine likely values of x, we calculate the interval, $\mu \pm 3\sigma$, or (-20, 40). Since x must be greater than 0, we use integer values of x from 0 to 40.

Calc ▸ Make Patterned Data ▸ Simple Set of Numbers
  Enter 'x' in **Store patterned data in:**
  Enter **From first value:** 0 and **To last value:** 40. **OK**

MTB > Name C1 = 'x'
MTB > Set 'x'
DATA> 0:40
DATA> End

Calc ▸ Probability Distributions ▸ Exponential
  Click **Probability density**;
  Enter **Mean:** 10;
  Enter **Input column:** x
  and **Optional storage:** 'f(x)'. **OK**

MTB > Name C2 = 'f(x)'
MTB > PDF 'x' 'f(x)';
SUBC> Exponential 10.

Graph ▸ Plot
  Enter f(x) in **Graph 1 Y** and x in **Graph 1 X**;
  Click **Display** and choose **Connect**;
  Click **Annotation**, click **Title**, add a title. **OK**

MTB > Plot 'f(x)' * 'x';
SUBC> Connect;
SUBC> Title "Exponential Distribution";
SUBC> Title "Customer Arrival Time".

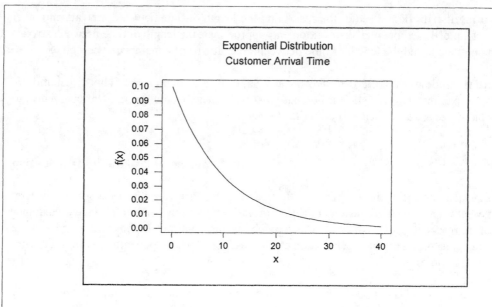

The graph shows that this exponential distribution is highly skewed to the right or skewed toward high inter arrival times.

b.   To find the probability that the inter arrival time is more than 15 minutes, we find $P(x > 15) = 1 - P(x \le 15)$.

Calc ▸ Probability Distributions ▸ Exponential
  Click **Cumulative probability**;
  Enter **Mean:** 10;
  Click **Input constant:** and enter 15. **OK**

MTB > CDF 15;
SUBC> Exponential 10.

Cumulative Distribution Function

```
Exponential with mean = 10.0000

       x      P( X <= x )
  15.0000        0.7769
```

The probability that the inter arrival time is more than fifteen minutes is approximately 1 - .78 = 0.22.

c. To find the probability that the length of time between arrivals is within two standard deviations of the mean, we find $P(\mu - 2\sigma \le x \le \mu + 2\sigma) = P(-10 \le x \le 30)$. Since time must be greater than 0, we find $P(0 < x \le 30) = P(x \le 30)$.

Calc ▸ Probability Distributions ▸ Exponential
  Click **Cumulative probability**;
  Enter **Mean:** 10;
  Click **Input constant:** and enter 30. **OK**

MTB > CDF 30;
SUBC> Exponential 10.

Cumulative Distribution Function

```
Exponential with mean = 10.0000

       x      P( X <= x )
  30.0000        0.9502
```

The probability that the time between arrivals is within two standard deviations of the mean is .95. This agrees very closely with the Empirical Rule, even through the distribution is highly skewed to the right.

5.4   OTHER PROBABILITY DISTRIBUTIONS

This chapter illustrated the binomial, Poisson, normal, and exponential probability distributions. Minitab has many other probability distributions available with the menu path **Calc ▸ Probability Distributions** or the session PDF, CDF, and InvCDF commands. We can calculate probabilities or probability densities, cumulative probabilities, and inverse cumulative probabilities for each of the following distributions:

Chisquare	Normal	t	Logistic	Beta
Poisson	Hypergeometric	F	Uniform	Binomial
Discrete	Integer	Lognormal	Cauchy	Exponential
Gamma	Laplace	Weibull		

EXERCISES

1. Let x equal the number of blemishes on a shirt produced by the Shirt Factory. Suppose the random variable x has the following distribution. Use Minitab to present the probability distribution in graphical form. Calculate the mean, variance, and standard deviation of the probability distribution.

    Shirt Factory Blemishes

x	$p(x)$
0	.85
1	.1
2	.05

2. The New Edition Bookstore very frequently needs to order recently published books. The manager uses the following probability distribution for x, the number of copies demanded in the first week the book is available.

    Bookstore Demand

x	$p(x)$
5	.1
6	.3
7	.3
8	.2
9	.1

    a. Use Minitab to present the probability distribution in graphical form.
    b. Calculate the mean, variance, and standard deviation of the probability distribution.

3. Suppose x is a binomial random variable with $n = 10$.

    a. For $\pi = .01, .1, .5, .8$, and $.9$, obtain the binomial probability distribution and a graph of each distribution.
    b. How does the shape of the graph change as π increases?
    c. For what values of π are the binomial probability distributions symmetric or nearly symmetric?

4. Suppose x is a binomial random variable with $\pi = .2$.

    a. Obtain the probability distribution and graph of each distribution for the following values of n: 2, 5, 10, 20, and 40.
    b. What happens to the shape of the graph as n increases?

5. Suppose x is a binomial random variable with $\pi = .2$. For $n = 40$, calculate the probability that x is within one standard deviation of the mean. Within two standard deviations of the mean. How do these probabilities compare with the Empirical Rule?

6.   A company samples 200 parts from a large shipment. They accept the shipment if there are 10 or fewer defectives in the sample, and reject the shipment if there are more than 10 defects in the sample.

    a.   What is the probability of accepting the shipment if the shipment is 3% ($\pi = .03$) defective?
    b.   What is the probability of rejecting the shipment if the shipment is 10% defective?

7.   An advertising agency was hired to introduce a new product. It claimed that after its campaign, 40% of all customers were familiar with the product. Let x be the number of customers familiar with the product in a random sample of 25 customers.

    a.   Calculate the mean and standard deviation of x. Graph the probability distribution.
    b.   What is the probability that more than one-half the customers (13 or more) in the sample were familiar with the product?

8.   Let x equal the number of people over age 65 who still work in a random sample of 50 selected from all people over age 65. According to a recent article, about 30% of all people over age 65 world wide still work.

    a.   Calculate the mean and standard deviation of x. Graph the probability distribution.
    b.   Obtain the intervals $\mu \pm \sigma$, $\mu \pm 2\sigma$, and $\mu \pm 3\sigma$. Find the probability that x falls in each interval. Compare these probabilities with the Empirical Rule.

9.   The Internet Society recently reported that 82.3% of the home pages are developed using the English language. Suppose we randomly select 100 home pages. Let x be the number of home pages developed in English.

    a.   How many home pages should we expect to view in a non English language?
    b.   What is the probability that we view more than 10 non English home pages? That we view no non English home pages?

10.   A quality control inspector at an automobile assembly plant has found that the number of discernible paint defects on a car has a Poisson distribution with a mean of two defects per car.

    a.   Calculate the mean and standard deviation of x, the number of paint defects per car.
    b.   Graph the probability distribution.
    c.   What is the probability that there are no paint defects? Five or more defects?

11.   Suppose the number of blemishes produced by a Shirt Factory follows a Poisson distribution with a mean $\mu = 0.2$.

    a.   Find the mean and standard deviation of x, the number of blemishes per shirt. Graph the probability distribution.
    b.   Find the probability that a shirt has no blemishes.
    c.   If a shirt has one or more blemishes, the company classifies it as a second. Determine the

proportion of all shirts that are classified as seconds.

12. The number of customers arriving at a bank drive-up service has a Poisson probability distribution with a mean of one customer per minute.

   a. Use Minitab to present the probability distribution as both a table and a graph. Find the variance and standard deviation.
   b. Find the probability that there are more than two arrivals in a given minute at the drive-up service.
   c. The bank would like to have enough service capability so that the probability of servicing all customers arriving in a given minute is at least 0.99. How many customers should the bank be able to service?

13. Statistics from the Internal Revenue Service disclose that the chance of a tax return audit is about .009 for taxpayers with income less than $50,000. Let x be the number of tax return audits in a random sample of 100 such tax payers.

   a. Graph the binomial probability distribution of x.
   b. Find the probability that no one will be audited, assuming the IRS's disclosure is accurate.

14. Suppose the number of spreadsheet errors per hour for an accountant's assistant follows a Poisson distribution with a mean $\mu = 1.2$.

   a. Find the mean and standard deviation of x, the number of spreadsheet errors per hour. Graph the probability distribution.
   b. Find the probability that an hour goes by without an error.
   c. Find the probability that the assistant will have between 1 and 4 errors in a given hour.

15. Compute and plot the probability density function for a normal random variable with $\mu = 100$ and $\sigma = 10$. Use values of x from approximately three standard deviations below the mean to three above the mean.

16. The Cloverhills Dairy uses a filling machine to fill one quart (32 ounces) bottles of milk. The net weight of milk placed in the bottles is normally distributed with a standard deviation of 0.5 ounces. Adjusting a setting on the filling machine controls the average amount of milk placed in the bottles.

   a. Assume the filling machine is adjusted to fill bottles with an average of 32.2 ounces. What proportion of the bottles are filled with less than 32 ounces?
   b. Companies must meet certain standards. Assume Cloverhills Dairy is required to fill no more than 1% of the bottles with less than 32 ounces. At what level should the machine be set so they meet the requirement with the least amount of average fill?

17. A quality control inspector believes that the machine used to fill bottles of mineral water is set to dispense an average of 12 ounces. Assume that the amount dispensed has a normal distribution

with a standard deviation of 0.5 ounces.

    a. Graph the probability distribution of x.
    b. Suppose that amounts less than 11.9 ounces have to be refilled. Calculate the fraction that must be refilled.

18. The time x to boot a microcomputer is approximately normally distributed with a mean of 70 seconds and standard deviation of 15 seconds.

    a. Graph the probability distribution of x.
    b. Find the probability that the time is within two standard deviations of the mean.
    c. What is the probability the time is less than one minute?

19. The following data are the recorded minutes between the arrivals of visitors at the South Hampton Zoo. (File **ZooArrival.mtp**)

Time Between Arrivals

.2	.4	.5	.9	1.2	1.9	3.2	1.2	.2
8.0	10.5	7.1	13.5	.5	.5	5.5	2.2	.7
9.0	1.4	5.7	7.2	2.2	3.2	.5	5.0	.5
.4	6.4	.1	3.8	18.2	5.8	.4	.3	.7
13.2	.3	14.9	5.3	15.5	2.1	1.9	8.1	1.0
7.2	2.4	.3	.6	1.3	8.3	1.9	3.1	.3
.7	6.6	4.4	10.8	4.3	3.5	1.0	11.4	1.1
1.2	18.4							

    a. Graph the data. Does the exponential distribution reasonably describe the data?
    b. If the exponential distribution describes the data, estimate μ and σ.

20. Suppose the length of time that an individual has to wait in line to be served at a fast food franchise is exponentially distributed with $\mu = 1.5$ minutes.

    a. Graph the exponential distribution. Find the mean and standard deviation.
    b. Find the probability that a customer will wait more than 3 minutes before being served.
    c. What is the probability that an individual will be served within 30 seconds?
    d. Find the length of time x such that 80% of all customers wait longer than x.

CHAPTER 6

SAMPLING AND SAMPLING DISTRIBUTIONS

A primary objective of statistics is to use sample data to make inferences about population parameters. Sample statistics, such as the mean and standard deviation of a sample, are used to estimate corresponding population parameters. Since a sample statistic is computed from random variables, it is random, and has a probability distribution called a sampling distribution. Sampling distributions are used to make a probability statement about the error in estimation. This chapter illustrates some sampling techniques and the sampling distribution of the sample mean.

NEW COMMANDS

BASE	ECHO	EXECUTE	NOECHO	RANDOM
SAMPLE	STORE			

6.1 STATISTICAL SAMPLING TECHNIQUES

Oftentimes, decisions must be made on the basis of a subset of the population of data, called a **sample**. Time and cost constraints, and the unavailability of data, preclude a study of the entire population. The statistical technique of selecting a sample of data from the population is called sampling.

The most fundamental sampling technique is **simple random sampling**, which is a method of selecting a sample from a population such that every sample of size n has an equal chance of being selected. We can use a random number generator in Minitab to select a simple random sample from a finite or infinite population.

A **finite population** consists of a countable number of observations. For example, if we have collected data on cholesterol levels of heart patients over a period of several years and want a preliminary study of a subset of the data, we would randomly sample from the finite population of heart patients. Or we may want to randomly select a sample of starting salaries of the finite population of 1999 graduates.

An **infinite population** consists of an undefined number of observations. If a production process continues indefinitely under the same conditions, the process output can be considered an infinite population. For example, the manufacturing of computer chips results in an infinite population.

SAMPLING FROM A FINITE POPULATION

A finite population consists of a countable number of observations. The SAMPLE command generates a simple random sample from a finite population. You can sample with replacement, where the same values can be selected more than once, or without replacement, where each value can be selected once.

Calc ▸ Random Data ▸ Sample from Columns

SAMPLE K *rows from* C ... C, *put in* C ... C   Randomly sample K rows
   REPLACE   Sample with replacement

■ **Example 1**   **Random Sampling: Finite Population**

The Appendix of this manual contains a data set compiled by the Minnesota Real Estate Research Center on homes sold in 1999 in St. Cloud, Minnesota. Consider the selling prices of homes. Select three random samples of size five from the 200 selling prices. Calculate the mean of each sample.

Solution The selling prices of 200 homes are saved in the file **Homes.mtp**. Of the eight data columns in this file, this example uses the column named SellingPrice.

We use SAMPLE to select and store the three random samples, and calculate the mean of each sample.

Calc ▸ Random Data ▸ Sample From Columns   MTB > Name C9 'Sample1'
  Enter 5 in **Sample rows from column(s):**   MTB > Sample 5 'SellingPrice' 'Sample1'
  Select SellingPrice in **Columns:**
  Enter 'Sample1' in **Store samples in. OK**

Calc ▸ Random Data ▸ Sample From Columns   MTB > Name C10 'Sample2'
  Enter 5 in **Sample rows from column(s):**   MTB > Sample 5 'SellingPrice' 'Sample2'
  Select SellingPrice in **Columns:**
  Enter 'Sample2' in **Store samples in. OK**

Calc ▸ Random Data ▸ Sample From Columns   MTB > Name C11 'Sample3'
  Enter 5 in **Sample rows from column(s):**   MTB > Sample 5 'SellingPrice' 'Sample3'
  Select SellingPrice in **Columns:**
  Enter 'Sample3' in **Store samples in. OK**

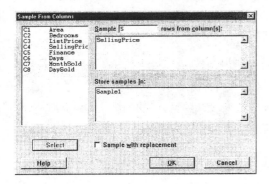

Calc ▸ Calculator
  Enter 'Mean1' in **Store results in:**
    and Mean(Sample1) in **Expression. OK**

MTB > Name C12 'Mean1'
MTB > Let 'Mean1' = Mean(Sample1)

Calc ▸ Calculator
  Enter 'Mean2' in **Store results in:**
    and Mean(Sample2) in **Expression. OK**

MTB > Name C13 'Mean2'
MTB > Let 'Mean2' = Mean(Sample2)

Calc ▸ Calculator
  Enter 'Mean3' in **Store results in:**
    and Mean(Sample3) in **Expression. OK**

MTB > Name C14 'Mean3'
MTB > Let 'Mean3' = Mean(Sample3)

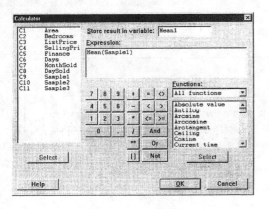

Manip ▸ Display Data
  Select Sample1 - Mean3 in **Display. OK**

MTB > Print 'Sample1'-'Mean3'

Data Display

Row	Sample1	Sample2	Sample3	Mean1	Mean2	Mean3
1	98900	50400	82700	90820	76380	99980
2	95200	86900	122300			
3	106900	108500	106900			
4	65400	84000	105700			
5	87700	52100	82300			

The sample means are estimates of the mean selling price of the population of 200 homes in St. Cloud, Minnesota. The sample values and, therefore, the sample means, vary from sample to sample.

USING EXECS

The sampling process, as illustrated in the previous example, is repetitive. You can reduce the time and the amount of typing by creating the simplest type of macro called an Exec. An **Exec** is a set of commands which is stored and then reused many times. In Minitab Release 13 and Student Release 12, an Exec is stored as a text file using a word processor. In prior releases, the STORE command saves the set of commands in an Exec file.

CREATING AN EXEC

Execs can be created and saved as a text file with a word processor or in Minitab with a set of stored commands. If you are working in Release 13, use the following to create an Exec:

1. In Minitab, enter session or menu commands to perform your analysis.
2. Open the history folder, select the session commands you wish to repeat, and choose **Edit ▸ Copy**
3. Paste the copied text into a word processor, such as Windows Notepad.
4. Save the file as a text file with the extension .MTB.

Some prior Minitab releases support STORE...END to save a set of commands. The option with STORE names an Exec with the default file extension .MTB. If the option is not used, the default name is MINITAB.MTB.

STORE ('FILENAME')   Enter commands after the STOR> prompt;
END   Use END for last statement

EXECUTING AN EXEC

The following menu and session commands repeat the commands stored in an Exec file K number of times. If the number K is not specified, the set of commands is executed once.

File ▸ Other Files ▸ Run an Exec

Run an Exec	✕
Number of times to execute:	1
Help	**S**elect File	Cancel

EXECUTE *the stored commands* ('FILENAME') (K *times*)

ECHOING THE COMMANDS

When using STORE and EXECUTE commands, you can control whether or not the set of stored commands is printed each time the set is executed. ECHO prints the set of commands and the command results; NOECHO, the default, prints only the results. There is no menu form for this command.

ECHO   Prints the commands and output of an Exec

NOECHO   Prints only the output of an Exec

NOTE

We recommend that you ECHO all commands of a macro until you are familiar with the STORE and EXECUTE commands. If the commands are printed each time they are executed, you can directly observe the execution of the stored commands. Usually this makes it easier to locate errors. The default is NOECHO.

■ **Example 2**   **Random Sampling: Using an Exec**

Refer to the data set compiled by the Minnesota Real Estate Research Center on homes sold in 1999. Use an Exec to repeat the sampling process described in Example 1. Select three random samples of size five from the 200 selling prices of homes, and calculate the sample means.

Solution The selling prices of 200 homes are saved in the file **Homes.mtp** with data saved in columns C1-C8. This example uses the column named SellingPrice.

The Exec can store the three sample means in one column. In Minitab, a number in parenthesis following a column number or name indicates a row. For example, Means(1) indicates the first row or cell of the column named Means. In this example, we store the three sample means in Means(1), Means(2), and Means(3).

We use a constant K1 as a pointer to specify the sample number and the row of a column named Means in which we enter the corresponding sample mean. K1 is initially set at 1, and then increased by 1 each time the set of stored commands is executed.

Each time we execute the Exec, a sample of five selling prices is selected and the mean is calculated and stored in the column named Means.

First, set up the columns and pointer:

```
MTB> NAME C9 'Sample'  C10 'Means'  K1 'Sample Number'
MTB > LET K1 = 1
```

Second, if you are using Minitab Release 13 or Student Release 12, enter the session or menu commands that you want to repeat.

```
SAMPLE 5 'SellingPrice' 'Sample'
Print K1 'Sample'
LET 'Means'(K1)=Mean(Sample)
LET K1=K1+1
```

Third, open the history folder, select the commands in the session window, and choose **Edit ▸ Copy**. Paste the text in a word processor, edit, and save as a text file with the extension .MTB. We saved the Exec in SamplingExec.MTB. In Student Release 12, use **File ▸ Save History Window As**.

Using STORE and END

Some prior releases of Minitab use the following to store and execute a set of commands. Set up the columns and pointer as above, and use the following to store the Exec.

```
MTB > STORE 'SamplingExec'
Storing in File: SamplingExec.MTB
STOR> Sample 5 'SellingPrice' 'Sample'
STOR> Print K1 'Sample'
STOR> LET 'Means'(K1) = Mean(Sample)
STOR> LET K1 = K1 + 1
STOR> END
```

Fourth, run the Exec.

File ▸ Other Files ▸ Run an Exec   MTB > EXEC 'SamplingExec' 3
  Enter 3 in **Number of times to execute:**
  Click **Select file** and enter SamplingExec in **File name:**
  Click **Open. OK**

```
Executing from file: A:\SamplingExec.mtb
```

Data Display

```
Sample Number    1.00000

Sample
    104700     105700      84400     106700      78200
```

Data Display

```
Sample Number    2.00000

Sample
     97300      93600      97200     115400      84400
```

Data Display

```
Sample Number    3.00000

Sample
    104700      70700     119600      81900      88800
```

Because we did not use the ECHO command, only the output is printed each time the macro is executed.

Manip ▸ Display Data   MTB> Print 'Means'
  Select Means in **Display. OK**

Data Display

```
Means
     95940      97580      93140
```

The sample means are estimates of the mean selling price of the population of 200 homes in St. Cloud, Minnesota with sample size 5. The sample means vary from sample to sample.

We repeat the program using ECHO. This command prints all commands and output. Every time we execute the Exec, we need to reset the pointer.

```
MTB> ECHO
MTB> LET K1 = 1
```

File ▸ Other Files ▸ Run an Exec   MTB > EXEC 'SamplingExec' 3
  Enter 3 in **Number of times to execute**.
  Click **Select file** and enter SamplingExec in **File name**.
  Click **Open**. **OK**

```
Executing from file: A:\SamplingExec.mtb
```

```
MTB > SAMPLE 5 'SellingPrice' 'Sample'
MTB > Print K1 'Sample'
```

Data Display

```
Sample Number     1.00000

Sample
    242000      50400     106700      76000     119100
```

```
MTB > LET 'Means'(K1)=Mean(Sample)
MTB > LET K1=K1+1
MTB > SAMPLE 5 'SellingPrice' 'Sample'
MTB > Print K1 'Sample'
```

Data Display

```
Sample Number     2.00000

Sample
    111000     104700      99300     112800      88800
```

```
MTB > LET 'Means'(K1)=Mean(Sample)
MTB > LET K1=K1+1
MTB > SAMPLE 5 'SellingPrice' 'Sample'
MTB > Print K1 'Sample'
```

Data Display

```
Sample Number     3.00000
```

```
Sample
     145100     120700      81900      68500      75000

MTB > LET 'Means'(K1)=Mean(Sample)
MTB > LET K1=K1+1
```

Manip ▸ Display Data
  Select Means in **Display. OK**

MTB> PRINT 'Means'

Data Display

```
Means
     118840     103320      98240
```

Again, we see the variability in the sample means produced by the sampling processes.

SAMPLING FROM AN INFINITE POPULATION

This command generates simple random samples of *n* observations from an infinite population with a specified probability distribution. Some distributions are given below. If you do not use a subcommand, Minitab generates data from a standard normal distribution.

Calc ▸ Random Data ▸ *Distribution*

RANDOM K *obs* C ... C	Default is a standard normal distribution
NORMAL *mu* = K *sigma* = K	Uses a normal distribution
BERNOULLI *pi* = K	Uses a Bernoulli distribution
BINOMIAL *n* = K *pi* = K	Uses a binomial distribution
EXPONENTIAL *mu* = K	Uses an exponential distribution
INTEGER *min* A *max* B	Uses an integer distribution
POISSON *mu* = K	Uses a Poisson distribution

Each time RANDOM is used, Minitab uses a different random starting point, generally based on the time of the day. If you wish to generate the same set of numbers, or specify the starting point of a sequence, use the BASE command.

Calc ▸ Set Base

BASE = K	Specifies starting point for random numbers

■ **Example 3**   **Random Sampling: Integer Distribution**

A random number table found in many statistics textbooks is constructed such that every digit occurs with equal probability. Use Minitab to generate a random number table. Construct a histogram of the random numbers. Comment on the randomness of the generated numbers.

Solution For a random number table, we generate 1,000 digits from the INTEGER distribution with a minimum value of 0 and a maximum value of 9.

Calc ▸ Random Data ▸ Integer   MTB> Name C1 'Digits'
  Enter 1000 in **Generate**;   MTB > Random 1000 'Digits';
  Enter Digits in **Store in column(s):**   SUBC>   Integer 0 9.
  Enter **Minimum Value** 0; **Maximum value** 9. **OK**

Integer Distribution		×
	Generate [1000] rows of data	
	Store in column(s):	
	[Digits ▲]	
	[▼]	
	Minimum value: [0]	
	Maximum value: [9]	
Select		
Help	**OK** **Cancel**	

Stat ▸ Tables ▸ Tally   MTB > Tally 'Digits';
  Select Digits in **Variables:**   SUBC>   Counts;
  Click **Counts** and **Percents**. **OK**   SUBC>   Percents.

Tally for Discrete Variables: Digits

Digits	Count	Percent
0	114	11.40
1	110	11.00
2	105	10.50
3	98	9.80
4	100	10.00
5	90	9.00
6	98	9.80
7	91	9.10
8	86	8.60
9	108	10.80
N=	1000	

The table gives the numbers of generated random digits. For example, there are 114 '0s' or 11.4% of the 1000 numbers, 110 '1s' or 11.0%, and so on. Each digit should appear approximately 10% of the time.

Graph ► Histogram	MTB > Histogram C1;
Select Digits in **Graph 1 X**;	SUBC> MidPoint;
Click **Annotation**, choose **Title**, add a title. **OK**	SUBC> Bar;
	SUBC> Title "Random Digits".

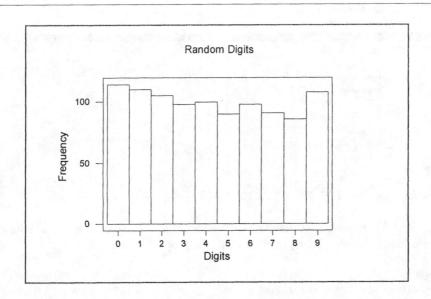

Both the distribution and histogram show that the random numbers occur with about the same frequencies. Since the probability of each digit occurring is .1, each should appear approximately 10% of the time, or 100 times.

■ **Example 4**   **Random Sampling: Coin Toss Experiment**

Consider an experiment in which fair coins are tossed and the number of heads is recorded. Suppose you are asked to observe the proportion of heads as you toss from 1 to 50 coins. Simulate this using Minitab. Plot the proportion of heads versus the number of tosses from $n = 1$ to 50.

Solution   A Bernoulli process is characterized by a series of independent trials, each of which results in one of two outcomes, success or failure. The probability of success, denoted π, remains constant from trial to trial. The probability of failure is $(1 - \pi)$. We can simulate the coin tossing experiment by a Bernoulli process with $\pi = .5$. A head, viewed as a success, is assigned 1, and a failure 0.

First, set the coin toss number in C1, and simulate 50 tosses of a fair coin.

Calc ▸ Make Patterned Data ▸ Simple Set of Numbers
    Enter 'Toss' in **Store patterned data in:**
    Enter **From first value:** 1; **To last value:** 50. **OK**

MTB > Name C1 = 'Toss'
MTB > Set 'Toss'
DATA> 1:50
DATA> End

Calc ▸ Random Data ▸ Bernoulli
    Enter 50 in **Generate rows of data:**
    Enter 'Heads' in **Store in column(s):**
    Enter .5 in **Probability of success. OK**

MTB > Name C2 = 'Heads'
MTB > Random 50 'Heads';
SUBC> Bernoulli .5.

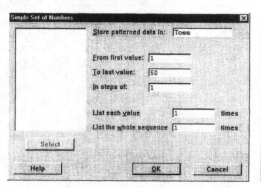 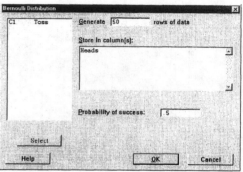

The next step is to find a cumulative count of the number of heads. To do this, we use the PARSUM command described in Chapter 2, and then calculate the proportion of heads.

Calc ▸ Calculator
    Enter 'SumHeads' in **Store result in variable:**
    Enter PARSUM(Heads) in **Expression. OK**

MTB > Name C3 = 'SumHeads'
MTB > Let 'SumHeads' = PARSUM('Heads')

Calc ▸ Calculator
    Enter 'P(Heads)' in **Store result in variable:**
    Enter SumHeads /Toss in **Expression. OK**

MTB > Name C4 = 'P(Heads)'
MTB > Let 'P(Heads)' = 'SumHeads'/'Toss'

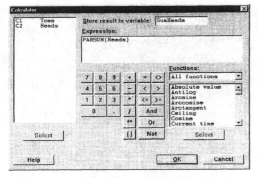 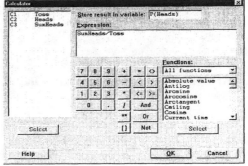

Manip ▸ **Display Data**
Select Toss - P(Heads) in **Display**. **OK**

MTB> Print 'Toss'-'P(Heads)'

Data Display

Toss	Heads	SumHeads	P(Heads)	Toss	Heads	SumHeads	P(Heads)
1	0	0	0.000000	26	0	12	0.461538
2	0	0	0.000000	27	1	13	0.481481
3	0	0	0.000000	28	1	14	0.500000
4	1	1	0.250000	29	0	14	0.482759
5	1	2	0.400000	30	0	14	0.466667
6	1	3	0.500000	31	1	15	0.483871
7	1	4	0.571429	32	1	16	0.500000
8	0	4	0.500000	33	1	17	0.515152
9	1	5	0.555556	34	1	18	0.529412
10	0	5	0.500000	35	0	18	0.514286
11	0	5	0.454545	36	0	18	0.500000
12	0	5	0.416667	37	0	18	0.486486
13	0	5	0.384615	38	0	18	0.473684
14	0	5	0.357143	39	1	19	0.487179
15	0	5	0.333333	40	1	20	0.500000
16	1	6	0.375000	41	1	21	0.512195
17	1	7	0.411765	42	0	21	0.500000
18	0	7	0.388889	43	0	21	0.488372
19	1	8	0.421053	44	0	21	0.477273
20	1	9	0.450000	45	0	21	0.466667
21	1	10	0.476190	46	1	22	0.478261
22	0	10	0.454545	47	0	22	0.468085
23	0	10	0.434783	48	0	22	0.458333
24	1	11	0.458333	49	1	23	0.469388
25	1	12	0.480000	50	0	23	0.460000

A graph shows how the proportion of heads changes as we toss more coins.

Graph ▸ Plot
  Select P(Heads) in **Graph 1 Y**
    and Toss in **Graph 1 X**;
  Click **Annotation**, choose **Title**, add a title. **OK**

MTB > Plot 'P(Heads)' * 'Toss';
SUBC>   Symbol;
SUBC>   Title "Coin Toss Experiment".

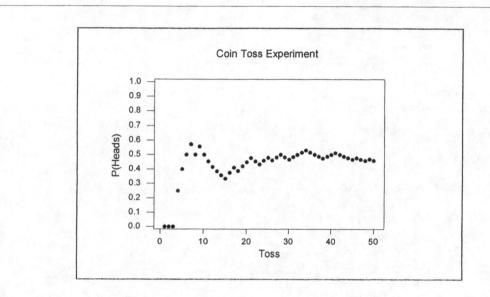

As the number of tosses increases, the proportion of heads approaches .5. We expect the process to stabilize at $\pi = .5$ as the number of tosses becomes very large.

■ **Example 5**   **Random Sampling: Dice Experiment**

Consider the experiment in which two fair dice are rolled, and the sum shown on the dice is observed. Simulate this experiment using Minitab. What is the approximate probability of observing a sum of 7? Compare this result with the exact probability of 1/6.

Solution The distribution to generate a random whole numbers from 1 to 6 for fair dice is the integer distribution, where each number is equally likely to occur. Each row of the columns named First and Second represents one trial. If you are using Student Release 12, you need to reduce the numbers generated to perhaps 1,000 tosses.

Calc ▸ Random Data ▸ Integer
  Enter 10000 in **Generate**;
  Enter 'First' 'Second' in **Store in column(s):**
  Enter **Minimum Value** 1; **Maximum value** 6. **OK**

MTB> Name C1 'First' C2 'Second'
MTB > Random 10000 'First' 'Second';
SUBC>   Integer 1 6.

Calc ▸ Row statistics
  Click **Sum**;
  Select First and Second in **Input variables:**
  Enter 'Sum' in **Store results in**. **OK**
	MTB > Name C3 = 'Sum'
	MTB > RSum 'First' 'Second' 'Sum'.

Stat ▸ Tables ▸ Tally
  Enter 'Sum' in **Variables:**
  Click **Counts** and **Percents**. **OK**
	MTB > Tally 'Sum';
	SUBC> Counts;
	SUBC> Percents.

Tally for Discrete Variables: Sum

Sum	Count	Percent
2	285	2.85
3	560	5.60
4	848	8.48
5	1127	11.27
6	1413	14.13
7	1614	16.14
8	1387	13.87
9	1095	10.95
10	829	8.29
11	564	5.64
12	278	2.78
N=	10000	

In this simulation, we observe a sum of 7 in 1,614 of the 10,000 tosses, or 16.14% of the time. This is close to the exact probability, $1/6 = .167$.

■ **Example 6**   **Random Sampling: Normal Distribution**

Suppose the amount of time it takes subjects in an experiment to complete a task is approximately normally distributed with $\mu = 50$ minutes and $\sigma = 5$ minutes. Simulate the experiment. Numerically and graphically describe the results.

Solution   We use the random command and the normal distribution to generate 100 observations.

Calc ▸ Random Data ▸ Normal
  Enter 100 in **Generate**;
  Enter 'Tasktime' in **Store in column(s)**;
  Enter Mean 50, Standard deviation 5. **OK**
	MTB > Name C1 = 'Tasktime'
	MTB > Random 100 'Tasktime';
	SUBC> Normal 50.0 5.0.

Stat ▸ Basic Statistics ▸ Display Descriptive Statistics
  Select Tasktime in **Variables:**
  Click **Graphs** and
    choose **Histogram of data, with normal curve. OK**

MTB > Describe 'Tasktime';
SUBC> GNHist.

Descriptive Statistics: Tasktime

Variable	N	Mean	Median	TrMean	StDev	SE Mean
Tasktime	100	49.058	48.992	49.140	4.740	0.474

Variable	Minimum	Maximum	Q1	Q3
Tasktime	34.646	59.505	46.244	52.042

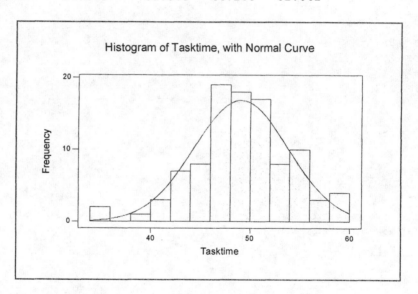

Histogram of Tasktime, with Normal Curve

The histogram shows that the simulated distribution of 100 task times is approximately normal. The sample mean, $\bar{x} = 49.1$ minutes, is close to $\mu = 50$ minutes. The sample standard deviation, $s = 4.740$ minutes, is close to $\sigma = 5$ minutes.

Let's increase the number of task times we simulate to 1,000 times.

Calc ▸ Random Data ▸ Normal
  Enter 1000 in **Generate;**
  Select Tasktime in **Store in column(s):**
  Enter **Mean** 50; **Standard deviation** 5. **OK**

MTB > Random 1000 'Tasktime';
SUBC> Normal 50.0 5.0.

Stat ▸ Basic Statistics ▸ Display Descriptive Statistics   MTB > Describe 'Tasktime';
   Select Tasktime in **Display:**   SUBC> GNHist.
   Click **Graphs** and
   choose **Histogram of data, with normal curve. OK**

Descriptive Statistics: Tasktime

Variable	N	Mean	Median	TrMean	StDev	SE Mean
Tasktime	1000	50.147	50.124	50.165	5.050	0.160

Variable	Minimum	Maximum	Q1	Q3
Tasktime	35.774	65.929	46.850	53.528

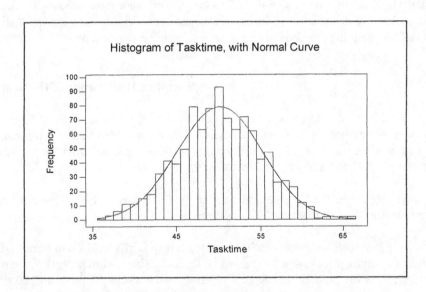

Histogram of Tasktime, with Normal Curve

The simulated distribution of 1000 task times looks more like a normal distribution than the simulated distribution of 100 task times. The sample mean, $\bar{x}$ = 50.1 minutes, is very close to μ = 50 minutes and the sample standard deviation, s = 5.050 minutes is very close to σ = 5 minutes.

In summary, the larger the sample size, the better the sample will reflect the population characteristics.

6.2 THE SAMPLING DISTRIBUTION OF THE SAMPLE MEAN

A sample statistic is used to estimate a population parameter. For example, the sample mean $\bar{x}$ is a point estimator of μ. Since $\bar{x}$ is computed from random variables, it is random, and has a probability distribution called the sampling distribution of $\bar{x}$.

The exact **sampling distribution of** $\bar{x}$ is the probability distribution of means of all possible samples of n observations from a population. If the number of possible samples is small, you can list all the samples and calculate the sample means. For example, consider a population of five stocks purchased in equal amounts by an investor. Define the population mean μ as the mean rate of return of the stocks. If we consider samples of $n = 3$ stocks, there are 10 possible samples (the combinations of 5 stocks taken 3 at a time). The 10 samples can be listed and the sample mean $\bar{x}$ calculated for each sample.

Most of the time, however, the possible number of samples is too large to list. For example, if the investor had purchased 10 stocks and is interested in samples of $n = 5$ stocks, there would be 252 possible samples. When the number of possible samples is large, the sampling distribution of $\bar{x}$ can be approximated by generating many simple random samples of size n and computing the mean of each sample. The probability distribution of the sample means approximates the sampling distribution of $\bar{x}$. The mean of the sampling distribution of $\bar{x}$ is $\mu_{\bar{x}} = \mu$, and the standard deviation is $\sigma_{\bar{x}} = \sigma/\sqrt{n}$.

■ **Example 7**   **Sampling Distribution of the Sample Mean**

The Appendix of this manual contains a data set compiled by the Minnesota Real Estate Research Center on homes sold in 1999 in St. Cloud, Minnesota. Find the approximate sampling distribution of the mean of a random sample of $n = 5$ observations randomly selected from the population. The population mean $\mu = \$97,854$ and standard deviation $\sigma = \$30,226$.

Solution   The selling prices of 200 homes are saved in the file **Homes.mtp**. Of the eight columns of data, this example uses the column named SellingPrice.

In Example 2 of this chapter we created an Exec named **SamplingExec.MTB** to sample five selling prices from the 200 selling prices in the file named HOMES. Using a word processor, we remove the PRINT statement from the program to suppress printing, and execute the program 100 times. The constant K1 specifies the sample number and the row of the column named Means used to store the sample mean. The following is the modified Exec.

The first step is to set up the columns and pointer.

```
MTB> NAME C9 'Sample'  C10 'Means'  K1 'Sample Number'
MTB> LET K1 = 1
```

The session or menu commands that we want to repeat are:

```
SAMPLE 5 'SellingPrice' 'Sample'
LET 'Means'(K1)=Mean(Sample)
LET K1=K1+1
```

File ▸ Other Files ▸ Run an Exec
Enter 100 in **Number of times to execute:**
Click **Select file** and enter SamplingExec in **File name:**
Click **Open. OK**

MTB > EXEC 'SamplingExec' 100

Manip ▸ Display Data
Select Means in **Display. OK**

MTB> PRINT 'Means'

Data Display

```
Means
   86160    109080     99200     96620    111640     74980     86220
   97160    109360     97540     82980     92460     96500    106920
   97860    118500     79340     86260     82200     99960    108760
   88400    104440     87440     78040     86620    100500     90060
   96160     94020    128460     90780     89840     77080    106060
   91640     92720     90640    110180     99800     89720    110780
   91520     84060     90220     70960     90660     90020     99980
  106920     92680    100540     85100     85180     92860    100940
  103960     95460     98780     97620     83440     96280     90700
   83380    120640     90180     90800     85740    128220    118540
   77960     88740     97960    106440    106520     96300     88960
   74520     88800     79660     95680    103580     82240     96440
  110340     90800     86280    102500    104380    128480     92940
  100160     98900     90560     82620     85080    106040     90440
   87240    108540
```

These means are calculated from samples of size 5 generated from a finite population of 200 home selling prices. This gives an approximate sampling distribution of the sample mean.

Stat ▸ Basic Statistics ▸ Display Descriptive Statistics
Select SellingPrice and Means in **Display. OK**

MTB > Describe 'SellingPrice' 'Means'.

Descriptive Statistics: Means

Variable	N	Mean	Median	TrMean	StDev	SE Mean
SellingPrice	200	97854	92500	95042	30226	2137
Means	100	95376	92900	94864	11679	1168

Variable	Minimum	Maximum	Q1	Q3
SellingPrice	48400	242000	80125	106875
Means	70960	128480	87290	102110

The mean, $95,376 of the approximate sampling distribution of $\bar{x}$ is somewhat less than the population mean μ = $97,854. The standard deviation of the sampling distribution $11,679 is an estimate of $\sigma_{\bar{x}}$.

Graph ▸ Histogram
  Select SellingPrice in **Graph 1 X**, Means in **Graph 2 X**;
  Click **Options**, Choose **Percent**;
  Click **Frame**, Choose **Multiple Graphs**,
   Choose **Same X and same Y. OK**

MTB > Histogram 'SellingPrice' 'Means';
SUBC>   MidPoint;
SUBC>   Bar;
SUBC>   Percents;
SUBC>   Same 1 2.

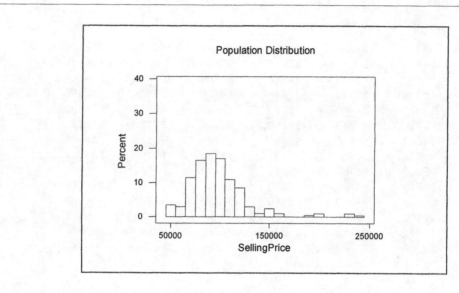

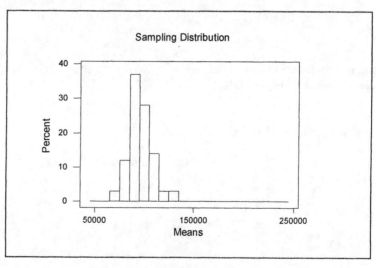

The first histogram is the population distribution of selling prices and the second is the simulated sampling distribution of $\bar{x}$. The population of selling prices is more variable than distribution of sample means.

NOTE

You may need to change the worksheet size to run some of these simulations. This depends on the Minitab release that you are using. To change this in Release 13, open the menu Edit ▸ Preferences ▸ General, move the slider in the memory usage section to use as much memory as necessary, and restart Minitab. In some releases, you can enter the size of the worksheet, restart Minitab, and the changed worksheet size will be displayed when the session window opens. Since Student Release 12 has a maximum worksheet size 5,000, the following simulations will have to be reduced in size.

■ **Example 8**   **Approximating Sampling Distributions**

Generate 1,000 random samples of 11 measurements from a **continuous uniform distribution**, with lower limit 0 and upper limit 1. Calculate the sample mean $\bar{x}$ and the sample median m for each sample. Compare the two sampling distributions.

Solution   We enter the samples across 1,000 rows rather than columns in order to use the row commands and store results. For instance, RMEAN and RMEDIAN compute means and medians across rows and store the results in columns. We can then construct histograms or other graphs of the means and medians.

First we show you how to graph the uniform distribution for values between 0 and 1 so that we can compare the simulated sampling distributions with the population distribution. Since all values of x have the same density, only the lower and upper values are entered in column C1 named 'x'.

Data Window
  Name C1 'x',
  Enter 0 and 1 in C1. **OK**

MTB > Name C1 = 'x'
MTB > Set 'x'
DATA> 0 1
DATA> End

Calc ▸ Probability Distributions ▸ Uniform
  Click **Probability Density**;
  Select 'x' in **Input column**:
    and enter 'f(x)' in **Optional storage. OK**

MTB > Name C2 = 'f(x)'
MTB > PDF 'x' 'f(x)';
SUBC> Uniform 0.0 1.0.

Graph ▸ Plot
  Select f(x) in **Graph 1 Y** and x in **Graph 1 X**
  Click **Display** and choose **Connect**;
  Click **Annotation**; choose**Title**, add a title. **OK**

MTB > Plot 'f(x)' * 'x';
SUBC> Connect;
SUBC> Title "Uniform Distribution".

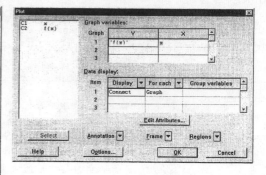

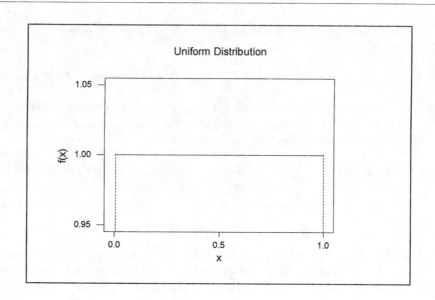

Uniform Distribution

The uniform probability distribution has a rectangular shape, with $\mu = (a + b)/2 = .5$, $\sigma^2 = (b - a)^2/12 = .0833$, and $\sigma = .2887$.

Calc ▸ Random Data ▸Uniform
  Enter 1000 **Generate**;
  Enter C1-C11 in **Store in column(s). OK**

Calc ▸Row Statistics
  Click **Mean**;
  Enter C1-C11 in **Input variables:**
  Enter 'Means' in **Store results in. OK**

MTB > Random 1000 C1-C11;
SUBC>   Uniform 0.0 1.0.

MTB > Name C12 = 'Means'
MTB > RMean C1-C11 'Means'

Calc ▸ Row Statistics
  Click **Median**.
  Enter C1-C11 in **Input variables:**
  Enter 'Medians' in **Store results in**. **OK**

Stat ▸ Basic Statistics ▸ Display Descriptive Statistics
  Select Means and Medians in **Variables**. **OK**

MTB > Name C13 = 'Medians'
MTB > RMedian C1-C11 'Medians'

MTB > Describe 'Means' 'Medians'

Descriptive Statistics: Means, Medians

Variable	N	Mean	Median	TrMean	StDev	SE Mean
Means	1000	0.50248	0.50206	0.50305	0.08436	0.00267
Medians	1000	0.50469	0.51125	0.50511	0.13588	0.00430

Variable	Minimum	Maximum	Q1	Q3
Means	0.24611	0.75357	0.44367	0.56276
Medians	0.08875	0.85276	0.40534	0.60025

The mean of the sample means is 0.50248; this is close to the mean of the sample medians, 0.50469. The standard deviation of the sampling distribution of the sample mean is 0.08436, somewhat less than that of the sample median, 0.13588.

Graph ▸ Histogram
  Select Means in **Graph 1 X**
   and Medians in **Graph 2 X**;
  Click **Frame, Multiple Graphs,**
   Choose **Same X and same Y**;
  Click **Options**, Choose **Density**;
  Click **Annotation**, choose **Title**; add a title. **OK**

MTB > Histogram 'Means' 'Medians';
SUBC> Density;
SUBC> MidPoint;
SUBC> Bar;
SUBC> Title "Sampling Distribution";
SUBC> Same 1 2.

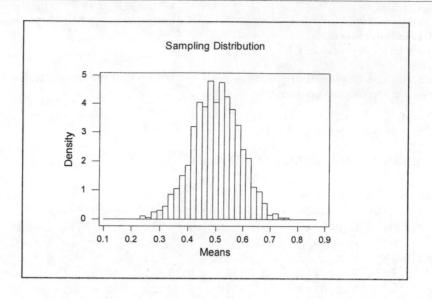

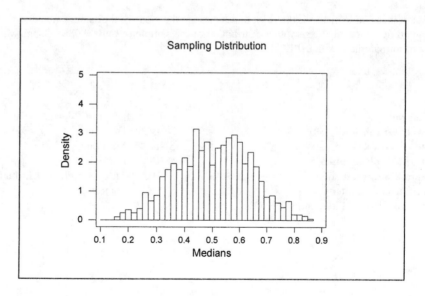

The histograms show that the sampling distributions of $\bar{x}$ and m are approximately normal, and that the sampling distribution of $\bar{x}$ is less variable than that of m. For these samples from the continuous uniform distribution, we conclude that the sample mean $\bar{x}$ contains more information about μ than the sample median m.

6.3   THE CENTRAL LIMIT THEOREM

Suppose random samples are selected from a population. The **Central Limit Theorem** states that the sampling distribution of $\bar{x}$ is approximately normal if n is sufficiently large.   The normal approximation is better for larger sample sizes.   When a random sample is selected from a normal population distribution, the sampling distribution of $\bar{x}$ is normal regardless of sample size.

■ **Example 9**   **Sampling Distributions of the Sample Mean**

For each of the following population distributions, graph the distribution and simulate the sampling distribution of the sample mean by generating 1,000 samples of sizes 5, 15, 25, 50 and 100. Describe the sampling distributions and tell how they illustrate the Central Limit Theorem.

Solution   **Uniform distribution with lower limit $a = 0$ and upper limit $b = 1$.**

Data Window
  Name C1 'x';
  Enter 0 and 1 in C1. **OK**

Calc ▸ Probability Distributions ▸ Uniform
  Click **Probability Density**; **Select** x **Input column**;
  Enter 'f(x)' **Optional storage**. **OK**

Graph ▸ Plot
  Select f(x) in **Graph 1 Y** and x in **Graph 1 X**
  Click **Display** and choose **Area**;
  Click **Annotation**; choose **Title**, add a title. **OK**

MTB > Name C1 = 'x'
MTB > Set 'x'
DATA> 0 1
DATA> End

MTB > Name C2 = 'f(x)'
MTB > PDF 'x' 'f(x)';
SUBC>   Uniform 0.0 1.0.

MTB > Plot 'f(x)' * 'x';
SUBC>   Area;
SUBC>   Title "Uniform Distribution".

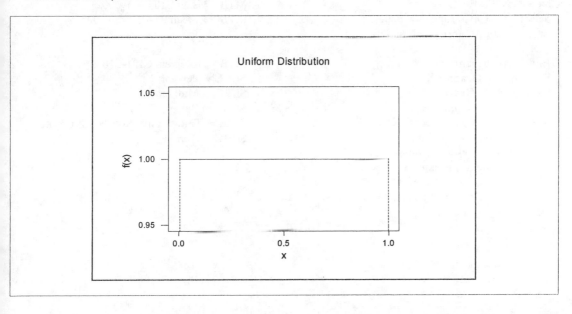

The uniform distribution has a rectangular shape, with $\mu = (a + b)/2 = .5$; $\sigma^2 = (b - a)^2/12 = .0833$; and $\sigma = .2887$.

The samples are generated in 1,000 rows of 100 columns (Some releases of Minitab have a limitation on the number of arguments available with a command). To calculate the sample means, we use the number of columns corresponding to each desired sample size.

Calc ▸ Random Data ▸ Uniform	MTB > Random 1000 C1-C100;
Enter 1000 in **Generate**;	SUBC> Uniform 0.0 1.0.
Enter C1-C100 in **Store in column(s)**. **OK**	
Calc ▸ Row Statistics	MTB > Name C101 = 'n=5'
Choose **Mean**;	MTB > RMean C1-C5 'n=5'.
Select C1-C5 in **Input Variables:**	
Enter 'n=5' in **Store result in OK**	
Calc ▸ Row Statistics	MTB > Name C102 = 'n=15'
Select C1-C15 in **Input Variables:**	MTB > RMean C1-C15 'n=15'
Enter 'n=15' in **Store result in**. **OK**	
Calc ▸ Row Statistics	MTB > Name C103 = 'n=25'
Select C1-C25 in **Input Variables:**	MTB > RMean C1-C25 'n=25'
Enter 'n=25' in **Store result in**. **OK**	
Calc ▸ Row Statistics	MTB > Name C104 = 'n=50'
Select C1-C50 in **Input Variables:**	MTB > RMean C1-C50 'n=50'
Enter 'n=50' in **Store result in**. **OK**	
Calc ▸ Row Statistics	MTB > Name C105 = 'n=100'
Select C1-C100 in **Input Variables:**	MTB > RMean C1-C100 'n=100'
Enter 'n=100' in **Store result in**. **OK**	
Graph ▸ Histogram	MTB > Histogram C101-C105;
Select n=5 in **Graph 1 X,**	SUBC> Percent;
Select n=15 in **Graph 2 X,**	SUBC> MidPoint;
Select n=25 in **Graph 3 X,**	SUBC> Bar;
Select n=50 in **Graph 4 X,**	SUBC> Title "SAMPLING DISTRIBUTION";
Select n=100 in **Graph 5 X;**	SUBC> Same 1 2.
Click **Frame, Multiple Graphs,**	
Choose **Same X and same Y**;	
Click **Options**, choose **Percent**;	
Click **Annotation,** choose **Title**, add a title. **OK**	

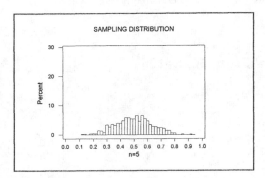

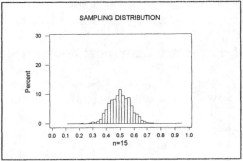

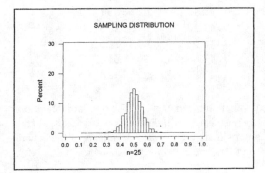

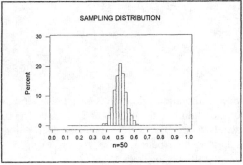

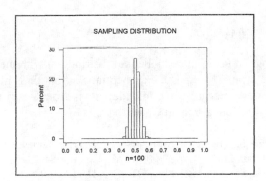

The histograms illustrate the sampling distributions of $\bar{x}$ when sampling from a uniform distribution. The distributions are approximately normal even for small sample sizes. This is generally the case with symmetrical population distributions. The distributions are centered at about the population mean $\mu = .5$; there is a decrease in the variation of the sampling distributions of $\bar{x}$ as the sample size is increased.

Stat ▸ Basic Statistics ▸ Display Descriptive Statistics   MTB > Describe 'n=5'-'n=100'
  Select 'n=5'-'n=100' in **Variables**. OK

Descriptive Statistics: n=5, n=15, n=25, n=50, n=100

Variable	N	Mean	Median	TrMean	StDev	SE Mean
n=5	1000	0.50035	0.50052	0.50036	0.13144	0.00416
n=15	1000	0.49988	0.49945	0.49978	0.07526	0.00238
n=25	1000	0.50127	0.50108	0.50143	0.05817	0.00184
n=50	1000	0.50009	0.50070	0.50003	0.04122	0.00130
n=100	1000	0.50045	0.50137	0.50041	0.02914	0.00092

Variable	Minimum	Maximum	Q1	Q3
n=5	0.11125	0.92499	0.40972	0.58881
n=15	0.21490	0.73849	0.44720	0.55115
n=25	0.28124	0.69855	0.46466	0.54106
n=50	0.37143	0.62290	0.47293	0.52646
n=100	0.42234	0.60988	0.48132	0.51990

Each sampling distribution is centered around the population mean, $\mu = .5$. The standard deviation of the sampling distribution of $\bar{x}$ is defined as $\sigma/\sqrt{n}$; for this uniform distribution, $\sigma = .2887$. The standard deviations of the simulated distributions approximate the standard deviations of the actual sampling distribution, which, for $n = 5, 15, 25, 50$ and 100, are equal to .1291, .0745, .0577, .0408 and .0289, respectively.

Exponential distribution with $\mu = 1$.

We repeat the Minitab program using the exponential distribution with mean $\mu = 1$. The standard deviation is the same as the mean, $\sigma = 1$. The exponential distribution is highly skewed to the right. Since the values of x are never negative, we include values from $x = 0$ to more than 3 standard deviations above the mean to obtain a smooth curve.

Calc ▸ Make Patterned Data ▸ Simple Set of Numbers   MTB > Name C1 = 'x'
  Enter 'x' in **Store patterned data in**.   MTB > Set 'x'
  Enter 0 in **From first value** and 5 in **To last value**. OK   DATA> 0:5/.1
  Enter **In steps of**: .1. OK   DATA> End

Calc ▸ Probability Distributions ▸ Exponential   MTB > Name C2 = 'f(x)'
  Click **Probability Density**;   MTB > PDF 'x' 'f(x)';
  Select 'x' in **Input column**   SUBC> Exponential 1.0.
    Enter 'f(x)' in **Optional storage**. OK

Graph ▸ Plot
    Enter 'f(x)' in **Graph 1 Y** and x in **Graph 1 X**.
    Click **Display**, choose **Connect**;
    Click **Annotation**, choose **Title**, add a title. **OK**

MTB > Plot 'f(x)' * 'x';
SUBC>   Connect;
SUBC>   Title "Exponential Distribution".

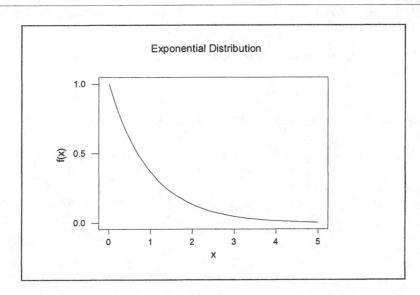

Exponential Distribution

The exponential distribution is skewed to the right. The curve crosses the *y*-axis at the mean $\mu = 1$.

The samples of 1,000 are generated in 100 columns. To calculate the sample means, we use the number of columns corresponding to each desired sample size.

Calc ▸ Random Data ▸ Exponential
    Enter 1000 in **Generate**;
    Enter C1-C100 in **Store in column(s). OK**

MTB > Random 1000 C1-C100;
SUBC>   Exponential 0.0 1.0.

Calc ▸ Row Statistics
    Choose **Mean**;
    Select C1-C5 in **Input Variables:**
    Enter 'n=5' in **Store result in OK**

MTB > Name C101 = 'n=5'
MTB > RMean C1-C5 'n=5'.

Calc ▸ Row Statistics
    Select C1-C15 in **Input Variables:**
    Enter 'n=15' in **Store result in. OK**

MTB > Name C102 = 'n=15'
MTB > RMean C1-C15 'n=15'

Calc ▸ Row Statistics
    Select C1-C25 in **Input Variables:**
    Enter 'n=25' in **Store result in. OK**

MTB > Name C103 = 'n=25'
MTB > RMean C1-C25 'n=25'

Calc ▸ Row Statistics
  Select C1-C50 in **Input Variables:**
  Enter 'n=50' in **Store result in. OK**

MTB > Name C104 = 'n=50'
MTB > RMean C1-C50 'n=50'

Calc ▸ Row Statistics
  Select C1-C100 in **Input Variables:**
  Enter 'n=100' in **Store result in. OK**

MTB > Name C105 = 'n=100'
MTB > RMean C1-C100 'n=100'

Stat ▸ Basic Statistics ▸ Display Descriptive Statistics
  Select 'n=5'-'n=100' in **Variable. OK**

MTB > Describe 'n=5'-'n=100'

Descriptive Statistics: n=5, n=15, n=25, n=50, n=100

Variable	N	Mean	Median	TrMean	StDev	SE Mean
n=5	1000	1.0089	0.9382	0.9837	0.4540	0.0144
n=15	1000	0.98551	0.96040	0.97472	0.26021	0.00823
n=25	1000	0.98412	0.97518	0.97812	0.19912	0.00630
n=50	1000	0.99241	0.98972	0.98987	0.14403	0.00455
n=100	1000	0.99705	0.99493	0.99567	0.10251	0.00324

Variable	Minimum	Maximum	Q1	Q3
n=5	0.0681	2.9037	0.6773	1.2722
n=15	0.41288	1.97882	0.79892	1.13193
n=25	0.47024	2.01744	0.85043	1.09487
n=50	0.56535	1.48204	0.89416	1.08347
n=100	0.64773	1.37716	0.92365	1.06131

The means of the simulated sampling distributions approximate the population mean $\mu = 1$. Since the standard deviation of an exponential distribution equals the mean, $\sigma = 1$, the standard deviations of the sampling distributions of $\bar{x}$ equal $\sigma/\sqrt{n} = 1/\sqrt{n}$, or .4472, .2582, .2000, .1414, and .1000 for $n = 5, 15, 25, 50,$ and 100, respectively. The standard deviations from the simulated distributions are close approximations.

Graph ▸ Histogram
  Select n=5 in **Graph 1 X,**
      Select n=15 in **Graph 2 X,**
  Select n=25 in **Graph 3 X,**
  Select n=50 in **Graph 4 X,**
  Select n=100 in **Graph 5 X;**
  Click **Frame, Multiple Graphs,**
   Choose **Same X and same Y;**
  Click **Options,** choose **Percent;**
  Click **Annotation,** choose **Title,** add a title. **OK**

MTB > Histogram C101-C105;
SUBC> Percent;
SUBC> MidPoint;
SUBC> Bar;
SUBC> Title "SAMPLING DISTRIBUTION";
SUBC> Same 1 2.

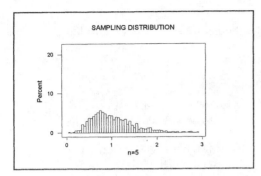

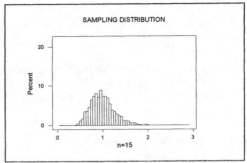

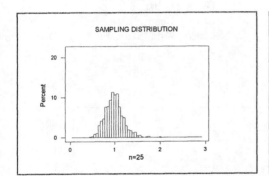

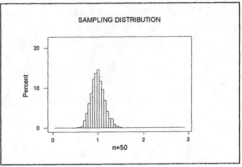

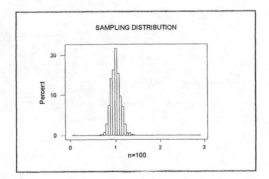

The histograms illustrate the sampling distributions of $\bar{x}$ when sampling from an exponential distribution. When distributions are highly skewed, the sampling distributions are approximately normal only for large sample sizes. The distributions are centered at about the population mean $\mu = 1.0$; there is a decrease in the variation of the sampling distributions of $\bar{x}$ as the sample size is increased.

Standard normal distribution with $\mu = 0$ and $\sigma = 1$.

To construct a graph of the standard normal distribution, we use values of z within four standard deviations of the mean.

Calc ▸ Make Patterned Data ▸ Simple Set of Numbers
   Enter 'z' in **Store patterned data in:**
   Enter **From first value:** -4 and **To last value:** 4;
   Enter **In steps of:** .1. **OK**

                   MTB > Name C1 = 'z'
                   MTB > Set 'z'
                   DATA> -4:4/.1
                   DATA> End.

Calc ▸ Probability Distributions ▸ Normal
   Select 'z' Input column:
     Enter 'f(z)' in **Optional storage. OK**

                   MTB > Name C2 = 'f(z)'
                   MTB > PDF 'z' 'f(z)';
                   SUBC> Normal 0.0 1.0.

Graph ▸ Plot
   Enter f(z) in **Graph 1 Y** and z in **Graph 1 X**;
   Click **Display** and choose **Connect**;
   Click **Annotation**, choose **Title**; add a title. **OK**

                   MTB > Plot 'f(z)' * 'z';
                   SUBC> Connect;
                   SUBC> Title "Standard Normal Distribution".

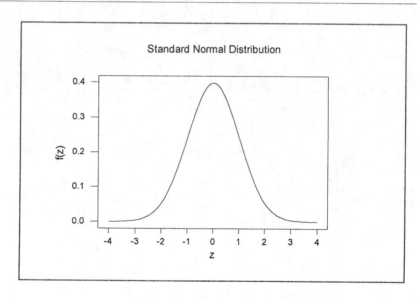

The standard normal distribution has $\mu = 0$ and $\sigma = 1$. We know from the Empirical Rule that nearly 100% of the area is within three standard deviations of the mean.

To calculate the sample means, we use the number of columns corresponding to each desired sample size.

Calc ▸ Random Data ▸ Normal
 Enter 1000 in **Generate**;
 Enter C1-C100 in **Store in column(s)**. **OK**

MTB > Random 1000 C1-C100;
SUBC>   Normal 0.0 1.0.

Calc ▸ Row Statistics
 Choose **Mean**;
 Select C1-C5 in **Input Variables:**
 Enter 'n=5' in **Store result in OK**

MTB > Name C101 = 'n=5'
MTB > RMean C1-C5 'n=5'.

Calc ▸ Row Statistics
 Select C1-C15 in **Input Variables:**
 Enter 'n=15' in **Store result in**. **OK**

MTB > Name C102 = 'n=15'
MTB > RMean C1-C15 'n=15'

Calc ▸ Row Statistics
 Select C1-C25 in **Input Variables:**
 Enter 'n=25' in **Store result in**. **OK**

MTB > Name C103 = 'n=25'
MTB > RMean C1-C25 'n=25'

Calc ▸ Row Statistics
 Select C1-C50 in **Input Variables:**
 Enter 'n=50' in **Store result in**. **OK**

MTB > Name C104 = 'n=50'
MTB > RMean C1-C50 'n=50'

Calc ▸ Row Statistics
 Select C1-C100 in **Input Variables:**
 Enter 'n=100' in **Store result in**. **OK**

MTB > Name C105 = 'n=100'
MTB > RMean C1-C100 'n=100'

Graph ▸ Histogram
 Select n=5 in **Graph 1 X,**
 Select n=15 in **Graph 2 X,**
 Select n=25 in **Graph 3 X,**
 Select n=50 in **Graph 4 X,**
 Select n=100 in **Graph 5 X;**
 Click **Frame, Multiple Graphs,**
  Choose **Same X and same Y;**
 Click **Options**, choose **Percent;**
 Click **Annotation,** choose **Title,** add a title. **OK**

MTB > Histogram C101-C105;
SUBC>   Percent;
SUBC>   MidPoint;
SUBC>   Bar;
SUBC>   Title "SAMPLING DISTRIBUTION";
SUBC>   Same 1 2.

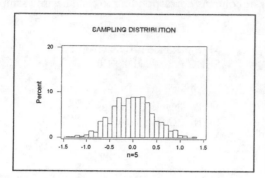

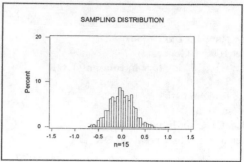

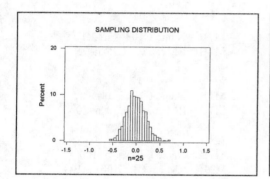

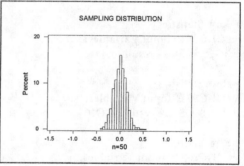

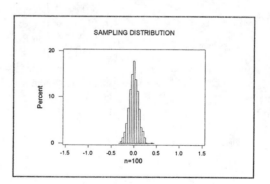

When sampling from a normal population, the sampling distribution of $\bar{x}$ is normal for any sample size. Again, we see all the distributions centered at the population mean $\mu = 0$ and the variation of the distributions decrease as the sample size increases.

Stat ▸ Basic Statistics ▸ Display Descriptive Statistics
Select 'n=5'-'n=100' in Variables. OK

MTB > Describe 'n=5'-'n=100'

Descriptive Statistics: n=5, n=15, n=25, n=50, n=100

Variable	N	Mean	Median	TrMean	StDev	SE Mean
n=5	1000	-0.0100	-0.0058	-0.0099	0.4375	0.0138
n=15	1000	-0.00894	-0.00998	-0.01166	0.25029	0.00791
n=25	1000	-0.00626	-0.00955	-0.00794	0.19548	0.00618
n=50	1000	-0.00293	-0.00390	-0.00341	0.13613	0.00430
n=100	1000	-0.00261	-0.00355	-0.00283	0.09920	0.00314

Variable	Minimum	Maximum	Q1	Q3
n=5	-1.5536	1.3219	-0.3077	0.2859
n=15	-0.67566	0.99246	-0.19154	0.16933
n=25	-0.55367	0.69935	-0.13689	0.12475
n=50	-0.41854	0.54055	-0.09025	0.08770
n=100	-0.28952	0.41420	-0.06711	0.06369

The means of the simulated sampling distributions approximate the population mean $\mu = 0$. The exact standard deviations of the sampling distributions of $\bar{x}$ equal $\sigma/\sqrt{n} = 1/\sqrt{n}$, or .4472, .2582, .2000, .1414, and .1000, for $n = 5, 15, 25, 50,$ and 100, respectively. The standard deviations of the simulated sampling distributions are close approximations.

In Summary

These simulated sampling distributions of $\bar{x}$ illustrate the Central Limit Theorem. If n is sufficiently large, the sampling distribution of $\bar{x}$ is approximately normal. The normal approximation is better as n is increased.

The mean of each simulated sampling distribution approximates the mean of the population from which the sample was selected. The standard deviation approximates $\sigma/\sqrt{n}$. As the sample size increases, the standard deviation decreases; that is, the sampling distribution becomes more concentrated around the population mean.

■ **Example 10**   **Sampling Distributions: Discrete Distribution**

A binomial random variable is a Bernoulli random variable if $n = 1$. A Bernoulli random variable can assume the value 1 with probability π, and the value 0 with probability $1 - \pi$. Success is generally associated with 1, and failure with 0. Suppose $\pi = .8$. The distribution has mean $\mu = \pi = .8$ and standard deviation $\sigma = \sqrt{\pi(1-\pi)} = .4$.

Simulate the sampling distribution of the mean by generating 1,000 samples of sizes 2, 10, 25, 50, and 100 from a Bernoulli distribution with $\pi = .8$. Construct a histogram and calculate the mean and standard deviation of each distribution. Summarize.

Solution The samples are generated in 1,000 rows of 100 columns.

Calc ▸ Random Data ▸ Bernoulli   MTB > Random 1000 C1-C100;
   Enter 1000 in **Generate**;   SUBC> Bernoulli .8.
   Enter .8 in **Probability of success**:
   Enter C1-C100 in **Store in column(s)**. **OK**

Calc ▸ Row Statistics   MTB > Name C101 = 'n=2'
   Choose **Mean**;   MTB > RMean C1-C2 'n=2'.
   Select C1-C2 in **Input Variables**:
   Enter 'n=2' in **Store result in OK**

Calc ▸ Row Statistics   MTB > Name C102 = 'n=10'
   Select C1-C10 in **Input Variables**:   MTB > RMean C1-C10 'n=10'
   Enter 'n=10' in **Store result in**. **OK**

Calc ▸ Row Statistics   MTB > Name C103 = 'n=25'
   Select C1-C25 in **Input Variables**:   MTB > RMean C1-C25 'n=25'
   Enter 'n=25' in **Store result in**. **OK**

Calc ▸ Row Statistics   MTB > Name C104 = 'n=50'
   Select C1-C50 in **Input Variables**:   MTB > RMean C1-C50 'n=50'
   Enter 'n=50' in **Store result in**. **OK**

Calc ▸ Row Statistics   MTB > Name C105 = 'n=100'
   Select C1-C100 in **Input Variables**:   MTB > RMean C1-C100 'n=100'
   Enter 'n=100' in **Store result in**. **OK**

The exact values of the mean and standard deviation of the sampling distribution of $\bar{x}$ are $\mu_{\bar{x}} = .8$ and $\sigma_{\bar{x}} = .4/\sqrt{n}$ or .2828, .1265, .0800, .0566 and .0400 for $n = 2, 10, 25, 50,$ and 100 respectively. The following command gives the results for the simulated sampling distributions.

Stat ▸ Basic Statistics ▸ Display Descriptive Statistics   MTB > Describe 'n=2'-'n=100'
Select 'n=2'-'n=100' in **Variables. OK**

Descriptive Statistics: n=2, n=10, n=25, n=50, n=100

Variable	N	Mean	Median	TrMean	StDev	SE Mean
n=2	1000	0.81650	1.00000	0.83833	0.26674	0.00843
n=10	1000	0.80210	0.80000	0.80500	0.12149	0.00384
n=25	1000	0.80304	0.80000	0.80467	0.07851	0.00248
n=50	1000	0.80276	0.80000	0.80364	0.05536	0.00175
n=100	1000	0.80224	0.80000	0.80244	0.03849	0.00122

Variable	Minimum	Maximum	Q1	Q3
n=2	0.00000	1.00000	0.50000	1.00000
n=10	0.40000	1.00000	0.70000	0.90000
n=25	0.52000	1.00000	0.76000	0.84000
n=50	0.62000	0.96000	0.76000	0.84000
n=100	0.67000	0.91000	0.78000	0.83000

The mean of each simulated sampling distribution closely approximates $\mu_{\bar{x}} = .8$. The standard deviations of the simulated sampling distributions are close approximations of the exact values.

Graph ▸ Histogram
  Select n=2 in **Graph 1 X,**
  Select n=10 in **Graph 2 X,**
  Select n=25 in **Graph 3 X,**
  Select n=50 in **Graph 4 X,**
  Select n=100 in **Graph 5 X,**
Click **Options**, choose **Percent**;
Click **Frame, Multiple Graphs,**
  Choose **Same X and same Y**;
Click **Annotation**, choose **Title**, add a title. **OK**

MTB > Histogram C101-C105;
SUBC> Percent;
SUBC> MidPoint;
SUBC> Bar;
SUBC> Title "SAMPLING DISTRIBUTION";
SUBC> Same 1 2.

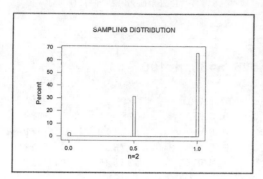

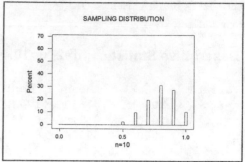

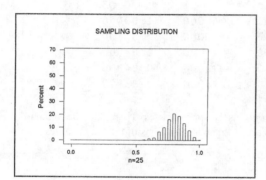

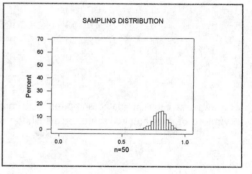

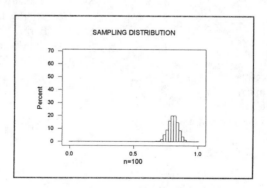

As n increases, the sampling distribution of $\bar{x}$ more closely approximates the normal distribution. These simulated sampling distributions of $\bar{x}$ for a discrete probability distribution illustrate the Central Limit Theorem.

EXERCISES

1. Preschool assertiveness measures for $n = 101$ children at a prestart program are given in the table. We expect the characteristics of a sample to be similar to the corresponding characteristics of the underlying population. Sample 30 measures from the following population. Summarize the population and the sample. Discuss similar characteristics. (File: **Preschool.mtp**)

Preschool Assertiveness Measures

98	76	89	65	58	77	90	92	83	83	96	78
94	93	84	78	74	70	68	54	68	79	77	75
72	83	89	90	93	78	96	82	87	86	94	59
71	89	90	99	74	77	78	65	68	98	73	85
89	69	72	78	65	97	94	89	67	58	40	84
78	77	78	89	66	70	72	89	73	75	84	86
89	74	95	83	74	55	77	82	98	89	65	78
77	90	93	99	52	89	85	89	76	74	89	67
66	89	76	89	93							

2. Consider the exponential distribution with $\mu = 2$. Obtain a graph of the probability distribution. Generate a random sample of 200 observations from the distribution and construct a histogram of the 200 observations. Compare the simulated distribution with the exact exponential distribution.

3. Estimate the probability that two or more people in a group of 25 have the same birthday. Use RANDOM with the INTEGER distribution to simulate 50 samples of $n = 25$ birthdays. Assume the 365 days of the year are equally likely to be birthdays. How many samples of 25 had matching birthdays? How does this compare with what you may expect?

4. Suppose the random variable x has a continuous uniform distribution with a lower boundary of 0 and an upper boundary of 10.

   a. Generate 100 samples of size $n = 9$. Calculate the means of the 100 samples and construct a histogram of the sample means. This is an approximation of the sampling distribution of $\bar{x}$. Comment on the shape of the distribution.
   b. Calculate the mean and standard deviation of the 100 sample means. Compare with $\mu = 5$ and $\sigma_{\bar{x}} = .962$.
   c. Repeat parts a and b for $n = 18$: $\mu = 5$ and $\sigma_{\bar{x}} = .680$. Summarize.

5. If a random sample is selected from a normal population distribution, the sampling distribution of $\bar{x}$ is normal for any sample size. Generate 100 samples from a normal probability distribution with $\mu = 300$ and $\sigma = 20$ for sample sizes 4, 8 and 16. For each sample size, construct a histogram of the sample means, and calculate the mean and the standard deviation of the 100 sample means. Summarize the results.

6. Consider the list price data on homes sold in St. Cloud, Minnesota given in the Appendix. Use

100 random samples of $n = 5$ to find the approximate sampling distribution of the mean. Find the estimates of μ and $\sigma_{\bar{x}}$. How do these compare with the actual values?

7. Suppose the distribution of scores on a real estate brokers' examination in a certain state is normal with $\mu = 435$ and $\sigma = 172$.

   a. Use 100 samples to approximate the sampling distribution of $\bar{x}$ for $n = 30$. What is the approximate mean and standard deviation of $\bar{x}$? How do these compare with the exact values of μ and $\sigma_{\bar{x}}$?
   b. Use 100 samples to approximate the sampling distribution of $\bar{x}$ for $n = 50$. Compare with the distribution in part a.
   c. Calculate $P(400 < \bar{x} < 470)$ for $n = 30$ and $n = 50$. Which probability is greater? Why?

8. Suppose the weight distribution of newborns at a large medical center is normal with $\mu = 6$ pounds and $\sigma = 2.5$ pounds.

   a. Use 100 samples of $n = 50$ to approximate the sampling distribution of $\bar{x}$.
   b. Use 100 samples of $n = 100$ to approximate the sampling distribution of $\bar{x}$. Compare with the distribution in part a.
   c. Calculate $P(5.75 < \bar{x} < 6.25)$ for $n = 50$ and for $n = 100$. Which probability is greater? Why?

9. Refer to the class data set given in the Appendix. Generate a random sample of 40 students. (File: **Classdata.mtp**)

   a. Numerically and graphically describe the grade point averages of the 40 students. Compare with the set of 200 students.
   b. Repeat part a for the ages of students.

CHAPTER 7

INFERENCES BASED ON A SINGLE SAMPLE

This chapter describes statistical procedures to make inferences about population parameters using a single sample. Estimation consists of a point estimate of the parameter and a measure of reliability based on the sampling distribution of the estimate. Hypothesis testing is used to make a decision or test a claim about the value of a parameter. This chapter presents procedures for making inferences about a population mean, proportion, and variance, and a nonparametric test about a population median.

NEW COMMANDS

%NORMPLOT	PONE	SINTERVAL	STEST
TINTERVAL	TTEST	ZINTERVAL	ZTEST

7.1 ESTIMATING A POPULATION MEAN

A **confidence interval** is an interval used to estimate a population parameter from sample data. The interval is composed of two basic parts: a point estimate of the parameter of interest and a measure of the margin of error. The error measure determines the width of the confidence interval. The confidence interval thus provides a range of possible parameter values.

One of the most important parameters characterizing a population is the mean. The estimation of the mean assertiveness training score, the estimation of the mean number of airline ticket cancellations per flight, and the estimation of the mean time for a pain medication to take effect are situations in which we want to make an inference about a population mean.

To estimate the mean μ, we select a sample from a population and calculate the sample mean. The sample mean $\bar{x}$ is a point estimator of μ. The previous chapter illustrated that the sample mean has certain characteristics even though it varies from sample to sample. Specifically, the sampling distribution of $\bar{x}$ is approximately normal if the sample size is large, or if the population distribution is approximately normal regardless of sample size. The mean of the sampling distribution is the same as the population mean, $\mu_{\bar{x}} = \mu$, and the standard deviation is $\sigma_{\bar{x}} = \sigma/\sqrt{n}$.

The appropriate Minitab command used to estimate a population mean depends on the sample size and whether or not the population standard deviation is known.

- When σ is known, use **1-Sample Z** if the population has an approximately normal distribution or if the sample size is large.
- When σ is unknown, you can use the **1-Sample t** if the population has an approximately normal distribution or if the sample size is large.

CONFIDENCE INTERVAL ESTIMATION

The first command below calculates a confidence interval for the mean. Graphical options include histogram, dot plot, and box plot displays. You need the population standard deviation σ to calculate this interval. The value for $z_{\alpha/2}$ is from the standard normal distribution corresponding to a K% confidence level, where K = $(1 - \alpha)*100\%$. The formula is

$$\bar{x} \pm z_{\alpha/2}\, \sigma/\sqrt{n}$$

Stat ▸ Basic Statistics ▸ 1-Sample Z

ZINTERVAL (K%) *sigma* K *data* C ... C	Calculates a confidence interval for the mean
GHISTOGRAM	Displays a histogram for each variable
GDOTPLOT	Displays a dot plot for each variable
GBOXPLOT	Displays a box plot for each variable

When σ is unknown, you can use **1-Sample t** if the population has an approximately normal distribution or if the sample size is large. The $t_{\alpha/2}$ value is from the *t* distribution corresponding to $(n - 1)$ degrees of freedom and K% confidence level. The formula is

$$\bar{x} \pm t_{\alpha/2}\, s/\sqrt{n}$$

Stat ▸ Basic Statistics ▸ 1-Sample t

TINTERVAL (K%) *data* C ... C	Calculates a confidence interval for the mean
GHISTOGRAM	Displays a histogram for each variable
GDOTPLOT	Displays a dot plot for each variable
GBOXPLOT	Displays a box plot for each variable

■ **Example 1**   **Confidence Interval for μ**

Murphy Ambulance Service recorded the following random sample of heart attack victim ages during the summer of 1999. Numerically and graphically summarize the ages. Construct and interpret a 90% confidence interval for μ, the population mean age.

Age of Heart Attack Victims

53	65	75	71	58	77	84	93	80
71	87	62	79	72	64	68	75	78
88	62	62	72	86	73	85	82	73
62	63	69	79	57	55	68	60	78
73	83	86	74	82				

Solution   The data are found in the column named Age in the file named **Heart.mtp**. Since the population standard deviation is unknown, we use the **1-Sample t** command. The histogram display provides a good graphical summary of the sample data.

Stat ▸ Basic Statistics ▸ 1-Sample t
  Select Age in **Variables:**
  Click **Options**, Enter 90 in **Confidence level:**
  Click **Graphs**, Check **Histogram of data**. **OK**

MTB > OneT 'Age';
SUBC>   Confidence 90.0;
SUBC>   GHistogram.

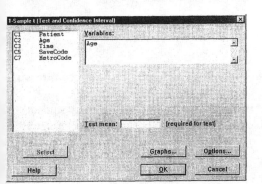

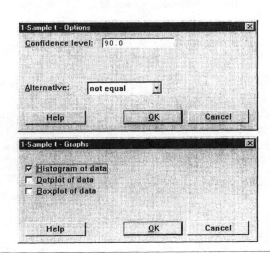

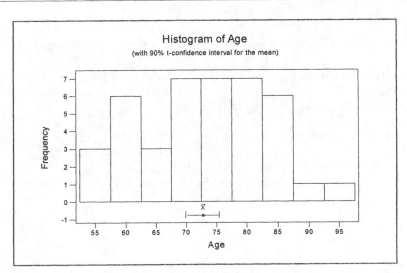

The histogram shows that most heart attack victims are in the 70 to 85 age range; it also shows the location of the sample mean and 90% confidence interval relative to all the sample observations.

One-Sample T: Age

Variable	N	Mean	StDev	SE Mean	90.0% CI
Age	41	72.78	10.07	1.57	(70.13, 75.43)

The sample mean age of about 73 years is a point estimate of the population mean age. We are 90% confident that the true mean age of all heart attack victims is between 70 and 75 years.

■ **Example 2**   **Comparing 90% and 95% Confidence Intervals**

During spring semester 2000 a team of statistics students randomly sampled 50 university students to study grade point averages (GPAs). The following table gives the data. Construct and interpret 90% and 95% confidence intervals for μ, the population mean grade point average. Interpret the confidence intervals. Compare the widths of the two intervals.

Grade Point Average

2.2	3.4	4.0	3.1	3.3	3.8	3.0	2.8	2.9	2.9
2.8	2.6	3.3	3.2	3.0	2.8	3.5	2.2	2.9	3.6
3.2	3.0	2.5	2.5	2.8	3.4	2.2	2.9	3.7	2.7
2.7	2.7	2.6	2.9	3.0	2.8	2.9	3.0	2.7	2.9
2.9	2.6	3.5	2.5	2.5	2.5	3.5	3.2	2.9	3.4

Solution The data are in the column named GPAs saved in a file named **GPA.mtp**.

Stat ▸ Basic Statistics ▸ 1-Sample t   MTB > OneT 'GPAs';
  Select GPAs in **Variables:**   SUBC> Confidence 90.0.
  Click **Options**, Enter 90 in **Confidence level. OK**

Stat ▸ Basic Statistics ▸ 1-Sample t   MTB > OneT 'GPAs';
  Select GPAs in **Variables:**   SUBC> Confidence 95.0.
  Click **Options**, Enter 95 in **Confidence level. OK**

One-Sample T: GPAs

Variable	N	Mean	StDev	SE Mean	90.0% CI
GPAs	50	2.9580	0.4101	0.0580	(2.8608, 3.0552)

One-Sample T: GPAs

```
Variable      N      Mean     StDev   SE Mean        95.0% CI
GPAs         50    2.9580    0.4101    0.0580   ( 2.8414,  3.0746)
```

The point estimate of μ, the population mean grade point average, is $\bar{x} = 2.96$. We are 90% confident that μ is between 2.86 and 3.06, and 95% confident that μ is between 2.84 and 3.07. The 95% confidence interval has a greater width than the 90% confidence interval. The larger the confidence coefficient, the greater the confidence interval width.

SIMULATING CONFIDENCE INTERVALS

Suppose we select many random samples from a population with mean μ and standard deviation σ, and construct a confidence interval for μ using each sample. We expect that the percent of intervals containing μ would approximately equal the confidence level. For example, if the confidence level is 90%, we expect that about 90% of the confidence intervals would contain μ and about 10% would not contain μ.

■ **Example 3**   **Simulating 90% Confidence Intervals**

Simulate 30 samples of size 50 from a normal distribution with $\mu = 70$ and $\sigma = 10$. Use **1-Sample Z** to construct 90% confidence intervals for the 30 samples. How many intervals contain the population mean μ? How does this compare with what you would expect?

Solution   Because Minitab constructs confidence intervals on column data, we generate the samples in 30 columns.

Calc ▸ Random Data ▸ Normal   MTB > Random 50 C1-C30;
  Enter 50 in **Generate**;   SUBC> Normal 70.0 10.0.
  Enter C1-C30 in **Store in column(s):**
  Enter 70 in **Mean** and 10 in **Standard deviation. OK**

Stat ▸ **Basic Statistics** ▸ **1-Sample Z**
  Enter C1-C30 in **Variables**, Enter 10 in **Sigma:**
  Click **Options**, Enter 90 in **Confidence level**. **OK**

MTB > OneZ C1-C30;
SUBC> Sigma 10;
SUBC> Confidence 90.0.

One-Sample Z:

The assumed sigma = 10

Variable	N	Mean	StDev	SE Mean	90.0% CI	
C1	50	70.30	11.21	1.41	(67.98,	72.63)
C2	50	71.18	11.50	1.41	(68.85,	73.50)
C3	50	69.10	8.23	1.41	(66.78,	71.43)
C4	50	72.46	9.45	1.41	(70.14,	74.79)
C5	50	70.98	10.74	1.41	(68.66,	73.31)
C6	50	69.02	8.08	1.41	(66.69,	71.34)
C7	50	72.06	9.74	1.41	(69.73,	74.38)
C8	50	67.81	10.15	1.41	(65.49,	70.14)
C9	50	70.51	8.68	1.41	(68.19,	72.84)
C10	50	68.42	12.01	1.41	(66.09,	70.74)
C11	50	71.35	9.93	1.41	(69.03,	73.68)
C12	50	70.88	8.90	1.41	(68.56,	73.21)
C13	50	69.23	7.62	1.41	(66.90,	71.56)
C14	50	70.56	11.04	1.41	(68.23,	72.88)
C15	50	72.17	9.87	1.41	(69.85,	74.50)
C16	50	68.23	9.02	1.41	(65.90,	70.55)
C17	50	70.35	9.73	1.41	(68.02,	72.67)
C18	50	69.11	10.45	1.41	(66.78,	71.44)
C19	50	70.35	10.28	1.41	(68.02,	72.67)
C20	50	72.79	10.24	1.41	(70.46,	75.11)
C21	50	70.91	9.39	1.41	(68.59,	73.24)
C22	50	70.04	11.55	1.41	(67.71,	72.36)
C23	50	69.58	7.36	1.41	(67.26,	71.91)
C24	50	69.37	8.77	1.41	(67.05,	71.70)
C25	50	69.78	10.55	1.41	(67.45,	72.11)
C26	50	66.95	9.73	1.41	(64.63,	69.28)
C27	50	71.60	9.98	1.41	(69.28,	73.93)
C28	50	70.05	10.68	1.41	(67.73,	72.38)
C29	50	68.68	9.12	1.41	(66.36,	71.01)
C30	50	67.08	11.74	1.41	(64.76,	69.41)

We expect that about 27 (90% of 30) confidence intervals would contain μ. In this simulation, 26 intervals contain $\mu = 70$; the samples in C4, C20, C26, and C30 fail to include the true mean. The simulated results agree closely with the expected results.

CHOOSING THE SAMPLE SIZE TO ESTIMATE μ

Increasing the **sample size** provides more information about the population, resulting in more reliable estimates of population parameters. The sample size formula for constructing a confidence interval for μ is $n = (z_{\alpha/2}\sigma/d)^2$, where $z_{\alpha/2}$ is the positive z-score corresponding to a $(1 - \alpha)100\%$ confidence coefficient, σ is the known or estimated population standard deviation, and d is the maximum desired distance that $\bar{x}$ is from μ. Since d is in the denominator, the sample size decreases as the distance d increases.

■ **Example 4**   **Sample Size to Estimate μ**

Example 2 of this chapter describes a study in which grade point averages were collected on 50 university students. Use 99% confidence intervals for μ, the true mean grade point average, to study the relationship between the sample size and the distance d. Assume the standard deviation of the grade point averages is $\sigma = .41$. Plot sample size versus distance. What is the relationship between sample size and distance?

Solution The formula to calculate the sample size for a given confidence coefficient, standard deviation, and distance is $n = (z_{\alpha/2}\sigma/d)^2$. We set some distances, $d = .05, .06, ..., .20$, in Distance, and evaluate the formula. The inverse probability distribution command provides the value of $z_{\alpha/2}$ for a 99% confidence interval.

Calc ▸ Make Patterned Data ▸ Simple Set of Numbers
  Enter 'Distance' in **Store patterned data in:**
  Enter .05 in **From first value:** .20 in **To last value:**
  Enter .01 in **In steps of. OK**

```
MTB > Name C1 = 'Distance'
MTB > Set 'Distance'
DATA>  .05:.20/.01
DATA>  End
```

Calc ▸ Probability Distributions ▸ Normal
  Click **Inverse cumulative probability**;
  Click **Input constant:** enter .995,
    and 'z' in **Optional storage. OK**

```
MTB > Name K1 = 'z'
MTB > InvCDF .995 'z';
SUBC>  Normal 0.0 1.0.
```

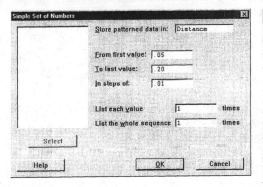

Calc ▸ Calculator
  Enter 'Size' in **Store result in variable:**
  Enter (z * .41 / Distance)**2 in **Expression. OK**

MTB > Name C2 = 'Size'
MTB > Let 'Size'=('z' * .41/'Distance')**2

Manip ▸ Display Data
  Select Distance Size and z in **Display. OK**

MTB > Print 'Distance' 'Size' 'z'

Data Display

Z   2.57583

Row	Distance	Size
1	0.05	446.130
2	0.06	309.813
3	0.07	227.618
4	0.08	174.270
5	0.09	137.695
6	0.10	111.533
7	0.11	92.176
8	0.12	77.453
9	0.13	65.996
10	0.14	56.904
11	0.15	49.570
12	0.16	43.567
13	0.17	38.593
14	0.18	34.424
15	0.19	30.895
16	0.20	27.883

The sample size decreases as the maximum desired distance that $\bar{x}$ is from μ increases. Note the value of $z_{\alpha/2}$ for a 99% confidence interval is about 2.58.

Graph ▸ Plot
  Select Size in **Graph 1 Y;**
  and Distance in **Graph 1 X;**
  Click **Display** and choose **Connect;**
  Click **Annotation**, choose **Title**, add a title. **OK**

MTB > Plot 'Size' * 'Distance';
SUBC>   Connect;
SUBC>   Title "Sample Size".

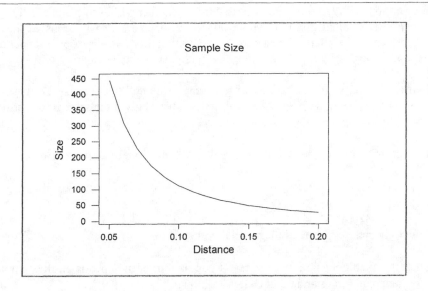

The graph illustrates a nonlinear relationship between sample size and distance. The sample size changes quickly with changes in smaller distances, and at a slower rate with larger distances. For example, as d increases from .05 to .06, the sample size decreases from 446 to 310 and as d increases from .19 to .20, the sample size decreases from 31 to 28.

With the table we can answer questions such as:

1. By what factor must a sample size be increased to reduce the distance by 50%?

To reduce the distance by 50%, the sample size has to be increased by a factor of four. For example, as we decrease d from .10 to .05, the sample size increases from 112 to 446.

2. What is the sample size that will provide a distance of about .10?

We estimate that a sample size of about $n = 112$ gives a distance of .10.

7.2   TESTING A HYPOTHESIS ABOUT A POPULATION MEAN

A **hypothesis test** is used to test a claim or to make a decision about the value of a population mean. For example, a bank manager may want to test the claim that the mean time spent waiting in line for banking services is less than five minutes, or the Environmental Protection Agency may want to test the claim that an automobile averages 35 miles per gallon in city driving. In either situation, a sample provides information to test a hypothesis about a population mean μ.

184   *Chapter 7*

The alternative hypothesis H_a is the hypothesis that the researcher wishes to establish. It is paired with an opposite hypothesis called the null hypothesis H_0. Both are stated in terms of the population parameter of interest. The alternative may be one-directional or two-directional, depending on the problem. By convention, we write the H_0 statement with an equality (=) sign.

The **significance level** α is the probability of rejecting a true null hypothesis. To make a decision about a population parameter, a $(1-\alpha)100\%$ confidence interval gives the same information as a two-tailed hypothesis test using an α level of significance.

The null and alternative hypotheses for a two-tailed test about a population mean are

$$H_0: \mu = \mu_0$$
$$H_a: \mu \neq \mu_0$$

where μ_0 is the hypothesized value of the population mean.

The appropriate Minitab command used to test a population mean depends on the sample size and whether or not the population standard deviation is known.

- When σ is known, use **1-sample Z** if the population has an approximately normal distribution or if the sample size is large.
- When σ is unknown, use **1-sample t** if the population has an approximately normal distribution or if the sample size is large.

THE P-VALUE

We can make a decision to reject the null hypothesis if the value of the test statistic falls in the rejection region. An alternative way to make a decision about the value of a population mean is to calculate the p-value, or observed significance level. The **p-value** is the probability of obtaining a value of the test statistic as extreme as that which is observed, assuming the null hypothesis is true. The p-value is very useful if the researcher prefers not to select an α level for the test. The reader can then determine whether to reject the null hypothesis based on the p-value. The null hypothesis is rejected if the p-value is less than the selected α value.

NOTE

In this Minitab manual, we illustrate two-sided confidence intervals. With Minitab Release 13, the output of a hypothesis test with 1-Sample Z and 1-Sample t includes the corresponding confidence interval. If the hypothesis test is one-tailed, the confidence interval is one-sided as well, and the lower or upper bound of the interval is printed. With Student Release 12, the confidence interval is separate from the hypothesis test.

HYPOTHESIS TEST ON μ

These commands perform a one sample *z*-test or *t*-test for the mean. Graphical options include histogram, dot plot, and box plot displays. Use ALTERNATIVE = +1 to test H_a: μ > K and ALTERNATIVE = −1 to test H_a: μ < K. You need the population σ to use **1-Sample Z**. The formula for the test statistic is

$$z = \frac{\bar{x} - \mu_0}{\sigma/\sqrt{n}}$$

Stat ▸ Basic Statistics ▸ 1-Sample Z

ZTEST (*mu* K) *sigma* K *data* C ... C	Does a hypothesis test for the mean
ALTERNATIVE K	Use for one-tailed test
GHISTOGRAM	Displays a histogram for each variable
GDOTPLOT	Displays a dot plot for each variable
GBOXPLOT	Displays a box plot for each variable

If σ is unknown, use **1-Sample t** if the population has an approximately normal distribution or if the sample size is large. The value of the test statistic is

$$t = \frac{\bar{x} - \mu_0}{s/\sqrt{n}}$$

Stat ▸ Basic Statistics ▸ 1-Sample t

TTEST (*mu* K) *data* C ... C	Does a hypothesis test for the mean
ALTERNATIVE K	Use for one-tailed test
GHISTOGRAM	Displays a histogram for each variable
GDOTPLOT	Displays a dot plot for each variable
GBOXPLOT	Displays a box plot for each variable

■ **Example 5**   **Hypothesis Test on μ**

Consider the grade point averages of a sample of 50 university students given in Example 2 of this chapter. Test whether the mean grade point average is less than 3.00. Use α = .05.

Solution The grade point averages are in a file named **GPA.mtp**; data are in the column named GPAs. To test whether the mean GPA is less than 3.00, the hypotheses are

H_0: μ = 3.00
H_a: μ < 3.00

Stat ▸ Basic Statistics ▸ 1-Sample t
   Select GPAs in **Variables:**
   Enter 3.0 in **Test mean:**
   Click **Options** and choose **less than** in **Alternative. OK**

MTB > OneT 'GPAs';
SUBC> Test 3.0;
SUBC> Alternative -1.

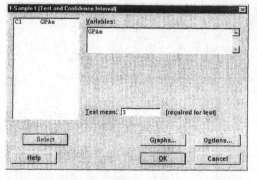
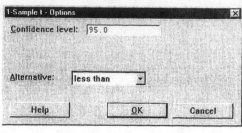

One-Sample T: GPAs

Test of mu = 3 vs mu < 3

Variable	N	Mean	StDev	SE Mean
GPAs	50	2.9580	0.4101	0.0580

Variable	95.0% Upper Bound	T	P
GPAs	3.0552	-0.72	0.236

The output provides the null and alternative hypotheses, the sample size, sample mean and standard deviation, standard error of the mean, test statistic, and *p*-value.

The test statistic, $t = -0.72$, is the number of standard deviations that the sample mean 2.958 is from the hypothesized mean, $\mu = 3.00$. Since $n = 50$ is considered a large sample, the t distribution approximates the z distribution. The rejection region consists of all test statistic values less than $-z_{.05}$ = -1.645. Since the test statistic does not fall in the rejection region, there is not sufficient evidence in the sample to conclude that the true mean grade point average is less than 3.00.

We also use the *p*-value to make a decision. The *p*-value is the probability that a random sample mean is less than or equal to 2.958 when H_0: $\mu = 3.00$ is true. The rejection region consists of all *p*-values less than α. Since the *p*-value = 0.24 is not less than $\alpha = .05$, there is not sufficient evidence in the sample to conclude that the true mean grade point average is less than 3.00.

◄ Example 6   **Small Sample Hypothesis Test About μ**

The changes in housing prices over short time periods are in part determined by supply and demand. The real estate board in a Minnesota community projected an increase in selling prices of homes in 1999 over the mean 1998 selling price of $101,800. The reason for the projection was an increase in demand due to some expansions of several area businesses and the subsequent increase in labor. To test the accuracy of the projection, a random sample of 16 homes sold in 1999 was selected, and the following selling prices recorded. Test whether the average home price increased from 1998 to 1999. Use $\alpha = .01$. Interpret the *p*-value.

Housing Prices

135,000	171,900	83,300	103,000	82,900	125,500	89,000	114,200
137,900	133,500	117,000	130,400	102,950	116,500	109,900	145,500

Solution The 1999 housing data for the Minnesota community are saved in a file named **HPrice.mtp**; prices are in a column named Price.

We use a one sample *t* test to determine whether the 1999 average home price has increased from the 1998 average price, and a box plot to graphically view the data. The hypotheses are

H_0: $\mu = \$101,800$
H_a: $\mu > \$101,800$

Stat ▸ Basic Statistics ▸ 1-Sample t	MTB > OneT 101800 'Price';
Select Price in **Variables:**	SUBC> Test 101800;
Enter 101800 in **Test mean:**	SUBC> Alternative 1;
Click **Options** and choose **greater than** in **Alternative:**	SUBC> GBoxplot.
Click **Graphs**, choose **Boxplot of data. OK**	

One-Sample T: Price

```
Test of mu = 101800 vs mu > 101800

Variable          N          Mean      StDev     SE Mean
Price            16        118653      23947        5987


Variable     95.0% Lower Bound         T          P
Price                    108158      2.82      0.007
```

The *p*-value of 0.007 is the probability of obtaining a *t* value as large as 2.82 assuming the H_0: $\mu = \$101,800$ is true. Since it is less than the significance level, $\alpha = 0.01$, there is sufficient evidence in the sample to conclude that the 1999 mean selling price is greater than the 1998 mean selling price; that is, there is enough sample evidence to support the real estate board's projection.

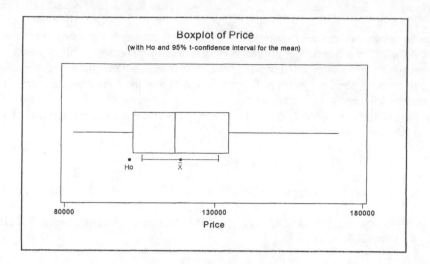

The box plot shows that the distribution of selling prices is slightly skewed, but does not have any outliers. There is not a serious departure from normality, a condition for using the *t* distribution for small sample sizes. Below the box is a 95% confidence interval on the true population mean selling price and the location of the hypothesized and sample mean. The hypothesized mean $101,800 is less than the confidence interval values. This also is an indicator that the mean selling price has increased.

TYPE I ERROR

When testing a hypothesis, α (**alpha**) is the probability of making a **Type I error**; that is, α is the probability of rejecting a true H_0. If we select many random samples from a population, we would expect to reject a true H_0 in about $(\alpha)100\%$ of the tests, and fail to reject a true H_0 in about $(1 - \alpha)100\%$. For example, if $\alpha = .05$, the probability of rejecting a true H_0 is 0.05. This means that the test procedure in repeated sampling leads to the rejection of a true H_0 about 5% of the time. The interpretation is similar to the repeated sampling interpretation of a confidence interval.

■ **Example 7**   **Simulating Type I Error**

Simulate 30 samples of size $n = 50$ from a normal distribution with $\mu = 70$ and $\sigma = 10$. For each sample, test the null hypothesis that the population mean is 70. Use $\alpha = .10$. How many times did you reject the true null hypothesis? How many times would you expect to reject the true null hypothesis?

Solution   We randomly generate the samples of 50 observations in 30 columns, and test

H_0: $\mu = 70$
H_a: $\mu \neq 70$

Calc ▸ Random Data ▸ Normal
  Enter **Generate** 50 and **Store in column(s):**C1-C30;
  Enter **Mean:** 70 and **Standard deviation:** 10. **OK**

Stat ▸ Basic Statistics ▸ 1-Sample Z
  Enter C1-C30 in **Variables:** and 10 in **Sigma:**
  Enter 70 in **Test mean. OK**

MTB > Random 50 C1-C30;
SUBC> Normal 70.0 10.0.

MTB > OneZ C1-C30;
SUBC> Sigma 10;
SUBC> Test 70.

One-Sample Z:

Test of mu = 70 vs mu not = 70
The assumed sigma = 10
SE Mean = 1.41

Variable	N	Mean	StDev	95.0% CI		Z	P
C1	50	71.11	10.18	(68.34,	73.89)	0.79	0.431
C2	50	70.21	9.35	(67.44,	72.98)	0.15	0.884
C3	50	68.11	9.51	(65.34,	70.88)	-1.34	0.181
C4	50	68.08	9.87	(65.31,	70.85)	-1.36	0.175
C5	50	69.73	10.93	(66.95,	72.50)	-0.19	0.846
C6	50	73.34	11.24	(70.57,	76.11)	2.36	0.018
C7	50	69.88	9.83	(67.11,	72.65)	-0.08	0.934
C8	50	68.26	10.92	(65.49,	71.04)	-1.23	0.220
C9	50	68.11	10.63	(65.34,	70.89)	-1.33	0.182
C10	50	70.31	12.03	(67.54,	73.09)	0.22	0.824
C11	50	72.55	9.01	(69.78,	75.32)	1.81	0.071
C12	50	69.47	10.16	(66.70,	72.25)	-0.37	0.710
C13	50	69.41	11.15	(66.64,	72.18)	-0.42	0.678
C14	50	68.92	10.12	(66.15,	71.69)	-0.76	0.446
C15	50	72.89	9.47	(70.12,	75.66)	2.04	0.041
C16	50	71.45	10.21	(68.68,	74.22)	1.03	0.304
C17	50	68.92	10.78	(66.14,	71.69)	-0.77	0.443
C18	50	74.00	8.74	(71.23,	76.78)	2.83	0.005
C19	50	69.80	10.50	(67.03,	72.57)	-0.14	0.886
C20	50	69.97	10.95	(67.20,	72.75)	-0.02	0.986
C21	50	68.70	7.80	(65.93,	71.47)	-0.92	0.359
C22	50	69.14	11.18	(66.36,	71.91)	-0.61	0.541
C23	50	72.00	9.49	(69.23,	74.77)	1.41	0.157
C24	50	70.12	10.43	(67.35,	72.89)	0.08	0.932
C25	50	68.50	8.95	(65.73,	71.27)	-1.06	0.289
C26	50	69.97	10.81	(67.19,	72.74)	-0.02	0.981
C27	50	67.93	10.90	(65.16,	70.70)	-1.47	0.143
C28	50	71.40	9.91	(68.72,	74.27)	1.06	0.291
C29	50	71.09	8.65	(68.31,	73.86)	0.77	0.443
C30	50	71.23	8.85	(68.46,	74.00)	0.87	0.385

Since the samples were randomly selected from a normal population distribution with a mean of 70, we know the null hypothesis is true. Using $\alpha = .10$, we reject the true null hypothesis in four of the 30 samples (C6, C11, C15 and C18). We would expect to reject the true null hypothesis in 3 (10% of 30) samples. Note: the form of the Minitab output has been modified to fit the page format of this manual. Specifically, the column containing the SE Mean of 1.41 has been deleted as it is the same for every sample, and is printed before the table.

TYPE II ERROR AND POWER

The probability of making a **Type II error** or the probability of accepting a false H_0 is called ß (**beta**). In any given test, ß depends on the true value of μ and is difficult to specify. For this reason, we generally conclude that we fail to reject H_0 rather than risk a Type II error.

Power, the probability of rejecting a false null hypothesis, equals 1 - ß. Suppose we select many random samples from a population and test a false H_0. Then we should accept a false H_0 in about (ß)100% of the tests, and reject the false H_0 in about (1 - ß)100% of the tests. For example, if ß = .05, in repeated sampling we should accept the false H_0 about 5% of the time.

■ **Example 8**   **Simulating Type II Error**

Simulate 30 samples of size $n = 50$ from a normal distribution with $\mu = 73$ and $\sigma = 10$. For each sample, test the null hypothesis that $\mu = 70$. Use $\alpha = .10$. How many tests result in the acceptance of the false null hypothesis? Estimate ß and the power of the test.

Solution For each of the 30 samples, we test

H_0: $\mu = 70$
H_a: $\mu \neq 70$

Calc ▸ Random Data ▸ Normal   MTB > Random 50 C1-C30;
    Enter 50 in **Generate**;   SUBC> Normal 73.0 10.0.
    Enter C1-C30 in **Store in column(s):**
    Enter **Mean:** 73 and **Standard deviation:** 10. **OK**

Stat ▸ Basic Statistics ▸ 1-Sample Z   MTB > OneZ C1-C30;
    Enter C1-C30 in **Variables:** and 10 in **Sigma:**   SUBC> Sigma 10;
    Enter 70 in **Test mean. OK**   SUBC> Test 70.

One-Sample Z:

```
Test of mu = 70 vs mu not = 70
The assumed sigma = 10
SE Mean = 1.41
```

Variable	N	Mean	StDev	95.0% CI		Z	P
C1	50	74.03	10.29	(71.26,	76.80)	2.85	0.004
C2	50	70.11	10.17	(67.34,	72.88)	0.08	0.939
C3	50	75.60	9.62	(72.83,	78.37)	3.96	0.000
C4	50	70.55	9.84	(67.78,	73.32)	0.39	0.699
C5	50	74.78	10.96	(72.01,	77.55)	3.38	0.001
C6	50	74.01	9.32	(71.23,	76.78)	2.83	0.005
C7	50	73.08	10.55	(70.31,	75.85)	2.18	0.030
C8	50	73.45	9.45	(70.68,	76.22)	2.44	0.015
C9	50	73.52	11.26	(70.75,	76.29)	2.49	0.013
C10	50	73.72	8.04	(70.95,	76.49)	2.63	0.009
C11	50	74.24	9.75	(71.47,	77.01)	3.00	0.003
C12	50	73.21	11.80	(70.44,	75.98)	2.27	0.023
C13	50	75.32	10.80	(72.55,	78.09)	3.76	0.000
C14	50	74.84	9.16	(72.06,	77.61)	3.42	0.001
C15	50	71.03	10.84	(68.26,	73.81)	0.73	0.465
C16	50	73.07	8.06	(70.30,	75.84)	2.17	0.030
C17	50	72.10	9.78	(69.33,	74.88)	1.49	0.137
C18	50	72.64	10.48	(69.87,	75.41)	1.87	0.062
C19	50	73.37	11.57	(70.59,	76.14)	2.38	0.017
C20	50	72.30	11.06	(69.53,	75.07)	1.63	0.104
C21	50	73.01	7.78	(70.24,	75.78)	2.13	0.033
C22	50	74.48	10.42	(71.71,	77.25)	3.17	0.002
C23	50	74.17	10.04	(71.40,	76.94)	2.95	0.003
C24	50	73.13	10.84	(70.36,	75.90)	2.21	0.027
C25	50	73.23	9.39	(70.46,	76.00)	2.28	0.022
C26	50	72.31	9.28	(69.54,	75.08)	1.63	0.103
C27	50	74.21	10.84	(71.44,	76.99)	2.98	0.003
C28	50	73.21	10.72	(70.44,	75.98)	2.27	0.023
C29	50	74.16	12.22	(71.39,	76.93)	2.94	0.003
C30	50	72.78	8.24	(70.00,	75.55)	1.96	0.050

Since the samples were randomly selected from a normal distribution with a mean of 73, we know the null hypothesis is false. We select the false H_0 if the *p*-value is greater than $\alpha = .10$. In this example, we have accepted the false H_0 in 6 of the 30 samples. Thus, we estimate ß to be 6/30 or .20, and Power = 1 - ß to be .80. Note: the form of the Minitab output has been modified to fit the page format of this manual; specifically, the column containing the SE Mean of 1.41 has been deleted as it is the same for every sample, and is printed before the table.

■ **Example 9**   **Calculating Power of a Test**

A random sample of $n = 20$ observations is selected from a normal distribution with an unknown mean and a standard deviation $\sigma = 10$.   Calculate the power of the test,

$$H_0: \ \mu = 70$$
$$H_a: \ \mu > 70$$

assuming the following values of the true mean 70.01 and the sequence 71, 72, 73, ..., 85. Use $\alpha = .05$. Obtain a power curve for the test. Describe the plot.

Solution   First, we need some definitions.

Since the population standard deviation $\sigma = 10$, the standard error $\sigma_{\bar{x}} = 10/\sqrt{20} = 2.236$. The value $\bar{x}_c$ on the border of the rejection region for the test is such that

$$P[\ \bar{x} \geq \ \bar{x}_c] = P[z \geq (\bar{x}_c - 70)/2.236] = \alpha = .05 \ \text{ when } H_0 \text{ is true.}$$

Since $P[z \geq 1.645] = .05$, we equate the terms within the two probability statements to get
   $(\bar{x}_c - 70)/2.236 = 1.645$ and $\bar{x}_c = 73.68$.

$\beta = P[\text{accept a false } H_0] = P[\bar{x}_c < 73.68] = \ P[z < (73.68 - \mu_a)/2.236]$
   where μ_a is the true population mean.

And finally, Power $= 1 - \beta$

Calc ▸ Make Patterned Data ▸ Arbitrary Set of Numbers   MTB > Name C1 = 'Mu'
   Enter 'Mu' in **Store patterned data in:**   MTB > Set 'Mu'
   Enter 70.01 and 71:85   DATA>   70.01 71:85
    in **Arbitrary set of numbers. OK**   DATA>   End

Calc ▸ Calculator   MTB > Name C2 = 'z'
   Enter 'z' in **Store result in variable:**   MTB > Let 'z' = (73.68 - Mu)/2.236
   Enter (73.68 - Mu)/2.236 **in Expression. OK**

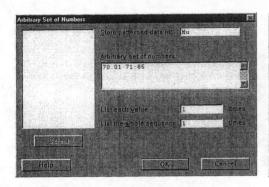
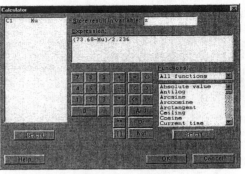

Calc ▸ Probability Distributions ▸ Normal
  Click **Cumulative probability**;
  Select z in **Input column:**
  Enter 'Beta' in **Optional storage. OK**

MTB > Name C3 = 'Beta'
MTB > CDF 'z' 'Beta';
SUBC>   Normal 0.0 1.0.

Calc ▸ Calculator
  Enter 'Power' in **Store result in variable:**
  Enter 1 - Beta in **Expression. OK**

MTB > Name C4 = 'Power'
MTB > Let 'Power' = 1 - Beta

Manip ▸ Display Data
  Select Mu, z, Beta, and Power in **Display. OK**

MTB > Print 'Mu'-'Power'

Data Display

Row	Mu	z	Beta	Power
1	70.01	1.64132	0.949635	0.05037
2	71.00	1.19857	0.884652	0.11535
3	72.00	0.75134	0.773776	0.22622
4	73.00	0.30411	0.619480	0.38052
5	74.00	-0.14311	0.443101	0.55690
6	75.00	-0.59034	0.277481	0.72252
7	76.00	-1.03757	0.149736	0.85026
8	77.00	-1.48479	0.068799	0.93120
9	78.00	-1.93202	0.026678	0.97332
10	79.00	-2.37925	0.008674	0.99133
11	80.00	-2.82648	0.002353	0.99765
12	81.00	-3.27370	0.000531	0.99947
13	82.00	-3.72093	0.000099	0.99990
14	03.00	-4.16816	0.000015	0.99998
15	84.00	-4.61538	0.000002	1.00000
16	85.00	-5.06261	0.000000	1.00000

Graph ▸ Plot
  Select Power in **Graph 1 Y**
   and Mu in **Graph 1 X**;
  Click **Display**, choose **Connect**;
  Click **Annotation**, choose **Title**, add a title;
  Click **Annotation**, choose **Footnote**, add a footnote. **OK**

MTB > Plot 'Power' * 'Mu';
SUBC> Connect;
SUBC> Title "Power Curve";
SUBC> Footnote "Hypothesis Test: &
CONT> Mu = 70 vs. Mu > 70".

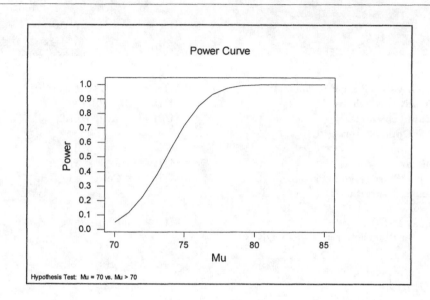

The power of the test is low for values of the mean close to $\mu_0 = 70$. The power of the test increases the further μ_a is from $\mu_0 = 70$. The probability of correctly rejecting a false null hypothesis increases as the distance between the true mean and μ_0 increases.

7.3   INFERENCES ABOUT A POPULATION PROPORTION

We introduced the binomial probability distribution, characterized by two outcomes, termed success and failure, in Chapter 5. The probability of success is π and the probability of failure is $1 - \pi$. This section describes statistical estimation and testing of π.

The point estimate is p, the proportion of successes in a random sample of n trials. If x is the number of successes in n trials, $p = x/n$. From the Central Limit Theorem, the sampling distribution of p is approximately normal for large sample sizes. A sample size is often considered large if 0 or 1 is not included in the interval $p \pm 2\sigma_p$. The mean of the sampling distribution of p is π and the standard deviation is $\sqrt{\pi(1-\pi)/n}$.

POPULATION PROPORTION ESTIMATION

Use the following commands to compute a confidence interval and perform a hypothesis test of the population proportion. The $(1 - \alpha)100\%$ confidence interval estimate for π is

$$p \pm z_{\alpha/2} \sqrt{p(1-p)/n}$$

The formula for the z test statistic is

$$z = \frac{p - \pi_0}{\sigma_p}$$

where π_0 is the hypothesized population proportion and $\sigma_p = \sqrt{\pi_0(1-\pi_0)/n}$

Stat ▸ Basic Statistics ▸ 1 Proportion

PONE C ... C *or* K K ... K	Inference on population proportion
CONFIDENCE *level* K	Default is 95% confidence
TEST K	Null hypothesis value of K
ALTERNATIVE = K	Displays a dot plot for each variable
USEZ	Use for large sample sizes

NOTE

Minitab Release 13 and Student Release 12 include this test on proportions. If your release does not have this test, you can use the Calculator function to determine the confidence interval, test statistic, and p-value.

■ **Example 10**   **Inferences about π**

In a sample of $n = 120$ business students, $x = 21$ responded that they did not own a computer. Construct and interpret a 95% confidence interval for π, the proportion of students who do not own a computer. Does this sample provide sufficient evidence that the proportion of all students who do not have a computer is less than .25? Test using $\alpha = .05$. Interpret the p-value.

Solution We assume a sample size of 120 is sufficiently large for the sampling distribution of p to be approximately normal, and use the subcommand UseZ.

Stat ▸ Basic Statistics ▸ 1 Proportion
  Click **Summarized data**, enter 120 in **Number of trials:**
   Enter 21 in **Number of successes:**
  Click Options, enter .25 in **Test proportion:**
  Click **Use test and interval based on normal distribution. OK**

MTB > POne 120 21;
SUBC>   Test .25;
SUBC>   UseZ.

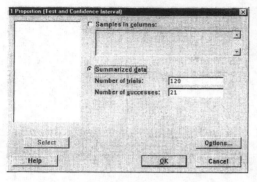

Test and CI for One Proportion

Test of p = 0.25 vs p not = 0.25

Sample	X	N	Sample p	95.0% CI	Z-Value	P-Value
1	21	120	0.175000	(0.107017, 0.242983)	-1.90	0.058

A point estimate of the population proportion of all students not owning computers is .175. We are 95% confident that the population proportion of students is between .11 and .24.

If we drop the assumption of sufficiently large sample size, there is only a slight change in the confidence interval.

Test and CI for One Proportion

Test of p = 0.25 vs p not = 0.25

Sample	X	N	Sample p	95.0% CI	Exact P-Value
1	21	120	0.175000	(0.111714, 0.254980)	0.058

The null and alternative hypotheses to test whether the proportion of all students who do not have a computer is less than .25 are

H_0: $\pi = .25$
H_a: $\pi < .25$

Stat ▸ Basic Statistics ▸ 1 Proportion
  Click **Summarized data**, enter 120 in **Number of trials:**
   Enter 21 in **Number of successes:**
  Click **Options** and enter .25 in **Test proportion:**
   Choose **less than** in **Alternative:**
  Click **Use test and interval based on normal distribution. OK**

MTB > POne 120 21;
SUBC> Test .25;
SUBC> Alternative -1;
SUBC> UseZ.

Test and CI for One Proportion

```
Test of p = 0.25 vs p < 0.25

Sample     X      N   Sample p   95.0% Upper Bound   Z-Value   P-Value
1         21    120   0.175000             0.232054     -1.90     0.029
```

The *p*-value = .029 is less than $\alpha = .05$. There is sufficient evidence in the sample to conclude that the proportion of all students who do not have a computer is less than .25.

CHOOSING THE SAMPLE SIZE TO ESTIMATE π

Determining the sample size for estimating a population proportion requires a prior estimate of π. If you do not have an estimate for π, you obtain the most conservative sample size for a given confidence level and a desired width with $\pi = .5$. To estimate a proportion within d units, the formula for the sample size is

$$n = (z_{\alpha/2}/d)^2 \pi(1 - \pi)$$

■ **Example 11**   **Determining Sample Size to Estimate π**

Example 10 of this chapter describes a study to estimate the proportion of all students not owning a computer. Suppose we want to estimate the proportion within $d = .01$ with 90% confidence. Determine the sample sizes required to estimate π using values of $\pi = .05, .10, .15, ..., .95$. Graph the sample size versus π. Summarize the results.

Solution The inverse probability distribution command gives the *z*-score for 90% confidence intervals which we need to evaluate the formula for *n*.

Calc ▸ Make Patterned Data ▸ Simple Set of Numbers
  Enter 'Pi' in **Store patterned data in:**
  Enter .05 in **From first value** and .95 in **To last value**;
  Enter .05 in **In steps of. OK**

MTB > Name C1 = 'Pi'
MTB > Set 'Pi'
DATA> .05 : .95 / .05
DATA> End

Calc ▸ Probability Distributions ▸ Normal
  Click **Inverse cumulative probability**;
  Click **Input constant: .95**;
  Enter 'z' in **Optional storage. OK**

MTB > Name K1 = 'Z'
MTB > InvCDF .95 'z';
SUBC> Normal 0.0 1.0.

Calc ▸ Calculator
  Enter 'Size' in **Store results in variable:**
  Enter ('z'/.01)**2 * Pi * (1-Pi) in **Expression. OK**

MTB > Name C2 = 'Size'
MTB > Let 'Size' = ('z'/.01)**2*Pi * (1-Pi)

Manip ▸ Display Data
  Select Pi, Size and z in **Display. OK**

MTB > Print 'Pi' 'Size' 'z'

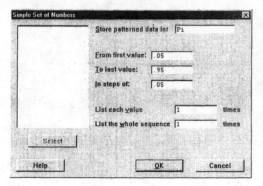
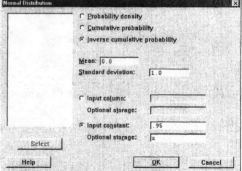

Data Display

Z   1.64485

Row	Pi	Size	Row	Pi	Size
1	0.05	1285.13	11	0.55	6696.22
2	0.10	2434.99	12	0.60	6493.30
3	0.15	3449.57	13	0.65	6155.11
4	0.20	4328.87	14	0.70	5681.64
5	0.25	5072.89	15	0.75	5072.89
6	0.30	5681.64	16	0.80	4328.87
7	0.35	6155.11	17	0.85	3449.57
8	0.40	6493.30	18	0.90	2434.99
9	0.45	6696.22	19	0.95	1285.13
10	0.50	6763.86			

Graph ▸ Plot
  Select Size in **Graph 1 Y**
   and Pi in **Graph 1 X**;
  Click **Display**, choose **Connect**;
  Click **Annotation**, choose **Title**; add a title. **OK**

MTB > Plot 'Size' * 'Pi';
SUBC> Connect;
SUBC> Title "Sample Size".

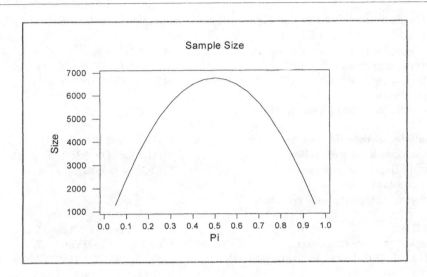

To estimate π, the table and graph show that we need the largest sample sizes when π is close to .5. This result is consistent with the fact that you obtain conservatively large samples by using $\pi = .5$. For example, the sample size for $\pi = .5$ is 6,764 students and the sample size for $\pi = .2$ or .8 is 4,329 students. This demonstrates the importance of having an approximate value of π; the further π is from .5, the smaller the necessary sample size needed to estimate π within a desired distance. A smaller sample size usually results in lower sampling costs.

7.4 ESTIMATING A POPULATION VARIANCE

The point estimate of a population variance σ^2 is the sample variance s^2. If the population has a normal distribution, the sampling distribution of s^2 has an approximate chi-square distribution with $(n - 1)$ degrees of freedom. There is not a Minitab command to construct a confidence interval for the population variance. For a $(1 - \alpha)100\%$ confidence interval, we can evaluate the formula,

$$\frac{(n - 1)\,s^2}{\chi^2_{1-\alpha/2}} \leq \sigma^2 \leq \frac{(n - 1)\,s^2}{\chi^2_{\alpha/2}}$$

where $\chi^2_{1-\alpha/2}$ and $\chi^2_{\alpha/2}$ are the respective right and left tail values of a chi-square distribution with $(n - 1)$ degrees of freedom.

■ **Example 12**   **Estimating the Population Variance**

A random sample of 50 university students has a mean grade point average of 2.96 and a standard deviation of $s = .41$. Construct a 95% confidence interval for the true variance of grade point averages, and a 95% confidence interval for the true standard deviation.

Solution   The degrees of freedom for this sample of 50 university students are $n - 1 = 49$.

Calc ▸ Probability Distributions ▸ Chi-square
  Click **Inverse cumulative probability**;
    Enter 49 **Degrees of freedom:**
  Click **Input constant**: .975;
    Enter 'ChiLower' in **Optional storage. OK**

MTB > Name K1 = 'ChiLower'
MTB > InvCDF .975 'ChiLower';
SUBC>   Chisquare 49.

Calc ▸ Probability Distributions ▸ Chi-square
  Click **Inverse cumulative probability**;
        Enter 49 **Degrees of freedom:**
  Click **Input constant**: .025;
    Enter 'ChiUpper' in **Optional storage. OK**

MTB > Name K2 = 'ChiUpper'
MTB > InvCDF .025 'ChiUpper';
SUBC>   Chisquare 49.

Calc ▸ Calculator
  Enter 'LowerVar' in **Store results in:**
  Enter (50-1) * .41**2/ChiLower in **Expression. OK**

MTB > Name C1 = 'LowerVar'
MTB > Let 'LowerVar' = &
CONT>   (50 - 1)*.41**2/ChiLower

Calc ▸ Calculator
  Enter 'UpperVar' in **Store results in:**
  Enter (50-1) * .41**2/ChiUpper in **Expression. OK**

MTB > Name C2 = 'UpperVar'
MTB > Let 'UpperVar' = &
CONT>   (50 - 1)*.41**2/ChiUpper

Calc ▸ Calculator
  Enter 'LowerSD' in **Store results in:**
  Enter SQRT(LowerVar) in **Expression. OK**

MTB > Name C3 = 'LowerSD'
MTB > Let 'LowerSD' = SQRT(LowerVar)

Calc ▸ Calculator
  Enter 'UpperSD' in **Store results in:**
  Enter SQRT(UpperVar) in **Expression. OK**

MTB > Name C4 = 'UpperSD'
MTB > Let 'UpperSD' = SQRT(UpperVar)

Manip ▸ Display Data
  Select LowerVar - UpperSD in **Display. OK**

MTB > Print 'LowerVar'-'UpperSD'

Data Display

Row	LowerVar	UpperVar	LowerSD	UpperSD
1	0.117297	0.261034	0.342487	0.510915

We are 95% confident that the population variance of university grade point averages is from .12 to .26., and 95% confident that the population standard deviation of university grade point averages is from .34 to .51.

7.5 TEST FOR NORMALITY

Several statistical procedures presented in this chapter are parametric procedures which assume that the sampled populations have approximately normal distributions. If the normality condition is not satisfied, than a nonparametric procedure may be appropriate to analyze the data. Minitab has a normality test for determining whether a set of data is randomly selected from a normal population.

The null and alternative hypotheses for a normality test are

H_0: Population has a normal distribution.
H_a: Population does not have a normal distribution.

TESTING FOR NORMALITY

The output includes summary statistics, the results of the test for normality, and a normal probability plot of the data. The data points on the graph fall close to a straight line for a normal distribution.

Stat ▸ Basic Statistics ▸ Normality Test

%NORMPLOT C	Uses Anderson-Darling test as default
SWTEST	Ryan-Joiner test
KSTEST	Kolmogorov-Smirnov goodness-of-fit test
TITLE	Adds a title to the normal plot

■ **Example 13**   **Testing for Normality**

Murphy Ambulance Service recorded the following random sample of heart attack victim ages during the summer of 1999. In Example 1 of this chapter, we constructed a confidence interval for μ, the population mean age. Is there significant evidence in the sample that the population of ages does not have a normal distribution?

Ages of Heart Attack Victims

53	65	75	71	58	77	84	93	80
71	87	62	79	72	64	68	75	78
88	62	62	72	86	73	85	82	73
62	63	69	79	57	55	68	60	78
73	83	86	74	82				

Solution   The data are saved in a file named **Heart.mtp**, and the ages are in a column named Age. The null and alternative hypotheses are

H_0: Population of patient ages has a normal distribution.

H_a: Population of patient ages does not have a normal distribution.

Stat ▸ Basic Statistics ▸ Normality Test   MTB > %NormPlot 'Age'
   Select Age in **Variable. OK**

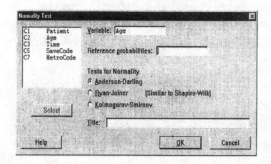

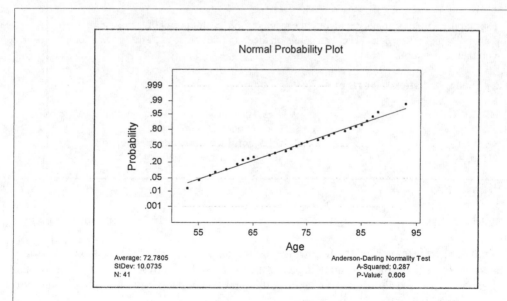

Normal Probability Plot

Average: 72.7805
StDev: 10.0735
N: 41

Anderson-Darling Normality Test
A-Squared: 0.287
P-Value: 0.606

The points on the graph fall close to a straight line. The *p*-value of 0.606 is not less than $\alpha = .05$. The sample does not provide significant evidence that the age distribution differs from normality.

■ **Example 14**   **Testing for Normality**

Several studies have shown that more students are working longer hours to pay for their college education. The hours worked per week for a random sample of 15 college students are given below. Is there significant evidence that the population of hours worked per week does not have a normal distribution?

Hours at Work per Week

23	25	28	30	0	20	0	35
22	15	0	0	0	0	15	

Solution We enter the data in a column named WorkHrs and construct a histogram of the data. The null and alternative hypotheses for a normal distribution of student work hours per week are

H_0: Population of work hours has a normal distribution.

H_a: Population of work hours does not have a normal distribution.

Graph ▸ Histogram
  Select WorkHrs in **Graph 1 X**;
  Click **Annotation**, choose **Title**, add a title. **OK**

MTB > Histogram 'WorkHrs';
SUBC>   MidPoint;
SUBC>   Bar;
SUBC>   Title "Hours Worked by Students".

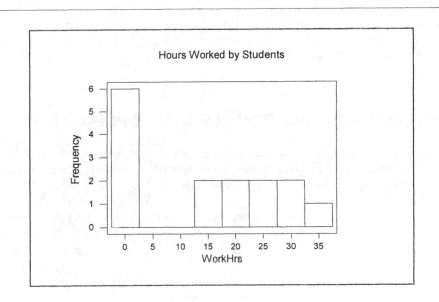

Six students do not work, resulting in the highly skewed distribution. Based on this sample, the distribution of work hours per week does not appear to be normal.

Stat ▸ Basic Statistics ▸ Normality Test   MTB > %NormPlot 'Workhrs'
  Select Workhrs in **Variable. OK**

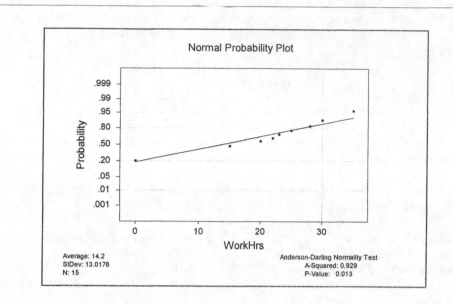

The *p*-value of 0.013 is less than $\alpha = .05$. There is significant evidence that the distribution differs from normality. The parametric test procedures assuming a normal population are not appropriate for making inferences about this population.

7.6   SIGN TEST FOR LOCATION OF A SINGLE POPULATION

The parametric test based on the *t* test statistic for testing a hypothesis about a population mean assumes that the sampled population is approximately normal. If this condition is not satisfied, a nonparametric procedure, such as the sign test, can be used.

The **sign test**, or test of location, is a nonparametric procedure designed to test a hypothesis about the median η of a continuous population. The test statistic is S, the number of observations out of a sample of size *n* exceeding the hypothesized median. The null and alternative hypotheses for a two-tailed test are

$$H_0: \ \eta = \eta_0$$
$$H_a: \ \eta \neq \eta_0$$

Under H_0, S has a binomial distribution with parameters *n* and $\pi = .5$.

MAKING INFERENCES ABOUT A POPULATION MEDIAN

This command does a nonparametric sign test for the median for one or more columns, or a sign confidence interval for the median. The sign test output includes the number of observations below, equal to, and above the hypothesized median, the p-value, and the sample median. If the median is not specified, a median of $K = 0$ is used.

Stat ▸ Nonparametrics ▸ 1-Sample Sign

STEST (*median* K) *data* C ... C	Does a test for population median
ALTERNATIVE = K	Use for a one-tailed test
SINTERVAL (K%) *data* C ... C	Confidence interval for the median

---

■ **Example 15**   **Test on Median**

Consider the data in Example 14. Several studies have shown that more students are working longer hours to pay for their college education. The hours worked per week for a random sample of 15 college students are given below. Do the data provide sufficient evidence to indicate that the median hours worked per week η for all college students is less than 20 hours? Use $\alpha = .05$.

Hours Worked per Week

23	25	28	30	0	20	0	35
22	15	0	0	0	0	15	

Solution The data are in a column named WorkHrs. The hypothesis test is

H_0: $\eta = 20$
H_a: $\eta < 20$

Stat ▸ Nonparametrics ▸ 1-Sample Sign   MTB > STest 20 'WorkHrs';
  Select WorkHrs in **Variables:**   SUBC> Alternative -1.
  Click **Test Median:** Enter 20;
  Click **Alternative**, choose **less than**. **OK**

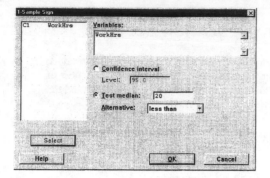

Sign Test for Median: WorkHrs

Sign test of median = 20.00 versus < 20.00

	N	Below	Equal	Above	P	Median
WorkHrs	15	8	1	6	0.3953	15.00

The sample median is 15 work hours per week. The *p*-value of .3953 is not less than the α level of 0.05. There is not sufficient evidence in the sample to conclude that the median work hours is less than 20.

EXERCISES

1. Simulate 50 samples of size $n = 15$ from a normal distribution with $\mu = 300$ and $\sigma = 50$. Construct 90% confidence intervals for the 50 samples. How many intervals included $\mu = 300$? How many would you expect to include μ?

2. Simulate 50 samples of size $n = 15$ from a normal distribution with $\mu = 100$ and $\sigma = 10$. For each sample, use $\alpha = .10$ to test the true null hypothesis, $\mu = 100$. How many times did you reject the true null hypothesis? How many times would you expect to reject the true null hypothesis?

3. Simulate 50 samples of size $n = 15$ from a normal distribution with $\mu = 105$ and $\sigma = 10$. For each sample, use $\alpha = .10$ to test the false null hypothesis, $\mu = 100$. How many times did you accept the false null hypothesis? Estimate ß and the power of the test.

4. The U.S. Department of Labor compiles data on the average state unemployment benefits. The following table gives the mean unemployment benefits per claim for a random sample of 20 states.

State	Benefit	State	Benefit
Arkansas	$1,557.25	Michigan	$2,862.24
California	1,844.25	Minnesota	2,615.84
Connecticut	1,915.88	Missouri	1,565.76
Delaware	2,113.76	New Jersey	2,653.50
Florida	1,851.08	New York	2,438.09
Idaho	1,705.86	North Carolina	1,071.17
Illinois	2,656.91	Ohio	2,205.94
Kentucky	1,476.99	Pennsylvania	2,434.81
Maine	1,538.05	Vermont	1,608.16
Massachusetts	2,869.55	Wyoming	2,549.71

    a. Determine whether the data are from an approximate normal distribution. Why is this important? Test for normality.
    b. Construct a 90% confidence interval to estimate μ, the mean state unemployment benefit. Interpret the interval.
    c. Construct a 90% confidence interval to estimate σ, the standard deviation of the state unemployment benefits. Interpret the interval.

5. A large grocery store has a packaging machine to weigh and package turkey. An adjustment on the machine allows the operator to fill packages of different weights. Suppose the store adjusts the filling machine to fill one pound packages. All packages do not contain exactly one pound because of either random variability in the weighing process, or an incorrect adjustment setting. To check if the machine is adjusted correctly, the following weights of a random sample of 40 packages were recorded. (File: **Weights.mtp**)

Packaging Weights

0.97	1.05	0.96	1.00	1.03	0.98	1.03	0.98	1.09	1.01
1.05	1.05	1.05	1.00	0.96	1.02	1.02	1.07	1.01	1.06
1.09	0.94	1.08	1.07	1.03	1.00	1.05	1.05	0.98	1.10
1.05	0.98	1.12	1.04	1.05	1.06	1.07	1.09	1.00	1.09

a. Construct a 95% confidence interval to estimate the mean weight of all packages filled by the machine. Graphically summarize the data. Interpret the confidence interval.

b. Do the data provide sufficient evidence to conclude that the population mean differs from one pound? Use a significance level of $\alpha = .05$. Interpret the *p*-value.

c. Compare the results of the hypothesis test with a 95% confidence interval for the population mean weight per package.

d. Construct a 95% confidence interval to estimate the population standard deviation of the package weight. Interpret the interval.

6. A large international corporation customarily rents several homes for relocating employees in Phoenix. The Personnel Division of the corporation is interested in studying the monthly rents of homes within the city. The following prices of 40 three-bedroom homes were randomly selected from Phoenix. (File: **Phoenix.mtp**)

Rental Prices

$ 925	$1,095	$ 665	$ 895	$1,100
900	900	875	870	1,150
1,175	1,050	925	895	1,350
850	1,065	1,075	1,035	1,420
1,250	1,465	925	1,275	1,025
975	1,020	800	1,100	1,285
935	875	875	1,475	950
1,325	865	1,150	925	1,070

a. Construct a 95% confidence interval to estimate the mean monthly rent of homes within the city. Graphically summarize the rental prices. Interpret the interval and graph.

b. Does the sample of rental prices provide sufficient evidence to conclude that mean rental price for three bedroom homes in Phoenix exceeds $900? Use $\alpha = .05$. Interpret the *p*-value.

c. Construct a 95% confidence interval for the population variance of rental prices. Can we conclude that the standard deviation of the rental prices for three bedroom homes in Phoenix exceeds $175? Discuss.

7. Consider the class data set that is given in the Appendix. The administrator of the college wants to estimate μ, the mean grade point average. (File: **Classdata.mtp**)

a. Construct and interpret 90% and 95% confidence intervals for μ. Do the confidence intervals suggest that the mean grade point average for all students differs from 2.75?

b. Does the sample provide sufficient evidence that the mean grade point average differs from 2.75? Use a significance level of $\alpha = .05$.

8. Refer to the homes data base given in the Appendix. The variable DAYS is the number of days a home is on the market before it is sold. (File: **Homes.mtp**)

   a. Graphically and numerically summarize the distribution of the number of days for all homes in the data set.
   b. Randomly generate a sample of 30 homes from the population of all homes in the data set. Use the sample to construct a 90% confidence interval for the mean number of days a home is on the market before it is sold.
   c. Does the 90% confidence interval include the population mean calculated in part a? If each of 50 students selected a random sample and constructed a 90% confidence interval, how many intervals would you expect to include the population mean? Why?

9. Consider the class data set given in the Appendix. Suppose we want to estimate π, the proportion of male majors. Construct and interpret a 90% confidence interval for π. Does the confidence interval suggest that the majority of students are male? (File: **Classdata.mtp**)

10. Consider the class data set given in the Appendix. The Women's Studies Director is interested in π, the proportion of female majors. Test whether the proportion of female majors differs from .50. Use $\alpha = .10$. Calculate and interpret the p-value. (File: **Classdata.mtp**)

11. Increasing the sample size can decrease the width of confidence intervals. If the sample size is changed by a factor of k, the width decreases by a factor of approximately $1/\sqrt{k}$. For example, if the sample size is increased by a factor of $k = 4$, the width is about one half of what it was before.

    a. Simulate a sample of 30 observations from a normal distribution with $\mu = 300$ and $\sigma = 50$. Construct a 95% confidence interval on the population mean.
    b. Repeat part a using samples of 120 and 480 observations.
    c. Calculate the width of each interval. Do the results agree with the relationship between sample size and the width of a confidence interval stated above? Discuss.

12. Determine the sample sizes required to estimate π, the proportion of successes in a population to within .10 with 95% confidence. Use values of $\pi = .05, .10, .15, ..., .95$. Graph the sample size versus π. Summarize the results.

13. A service company is concerned about the length of time that customers had to wait before receiving the help they requested. The company randomly selected 40 customers and recorded the wait time in minutes. The times are shown below.(File: **WaitingTime.mtp**)

Waiting Times for Service

9	11	12	13	13	14	14	15	15	16
16	16	17	17	17	17	18	18	18	19
19	19	19	20	20	20	21	21	21	21
21	22	22	22	24	24	25	27	29	38

a. Construct a 95% confidence interval to estimate the mean length of time that customers had to wait for service. Graphically summarize the wait times. Interpret the interval and graph.
b. Does the sample provide sufficient evidence to conclude that mean wait time exceeds 15 minutes? Use $\alpha = .05$. Interpret the p-value of the test.

14. The table in this problem gives the foreign revenue, expressed as a percentage of total revenue, for 20 U.S. multinational firms. Graphically analyze the percentages. Test for normality. Is the parametric test based on the t test statistic appropriate for testing a hypothesis about a population mean? Comment. Use the appropriate test to determine whether the mean U.S. foreign revenue percentage differs from 50%.

Firm	Foreign Revenue	Firm	Foreign Revenue
Exxon	73.2	Procter & Gamble	39.9
IBM	58.9	Philip Morris	19.6
GM	26.6	Eastman Kodak	40.9
Mobil	64.7	Digital	54.1
Ford	33.2	GE	12.4
Citicorp	52.3	United Technologies	32.9
EI DuPont	39.8	Amoco	26.1
Texaco	42.3	Hewlett-Packard	53.3
ITT	43.3	Xerox	34.6
Dow Chemical	54.1	Chevron	20.5

15. Suppose a reference librarian selected a random sample of 30 customers before starting a new information retrieval system. The retrieval times in minutes are given below. (File: **Retrieval.mtp**)

Information Retrieval Times

10	15	15	10	20	15	10	20	30	15
25	5	45	22	10	27	25	22	10	30
15	5	8	15	5	36	23	17	15	10

a. Graphically summarize the retrieval times. Test for normality.
b. Construct a 95% confidence interval to estimate the mean retrieval time.
c. Does the sample provide sufficient evidence to conclude that mean retrieval time is less than 20 minutes? Use $\alpha = .05$. Interpret the p-value of the test.

16. Many universities have implemented programs to increase the retention rate of students. One factor that causes students to leave a university is a feeling of loneliness. A sample of 40 students at a Midwestern university had the following scores on a standardized loneliness survey. Higher scores indicate greater loneliness. The national average score on the survey is 50. Is there sufficient evidence in the sample that the average score at this university is less than the national average? Use $\alpha = .05$. (File: **Loneliness.mtp**)

Loneliness Scores

69	39	64	49	37	17	39	54	61	48
32	16	38	63	19	33	49	21	49	47
52	83	58	57	36	24	40	49	42	59
41	40	19	52	36	44	48	30	54	25

17. Brock and Brenda Lee, owners of Lee Produce Company, are studying the size of orders placed by customers in Stearns County. In the past week, they have received the following 30 orders, in dollars. The owners have a goal this year of averaging at least $50 dollars per order. Comment on their attainment of this goal.

Lee Produce Company Orders

22	25	29	30	31	35	37	39	40	40
41	42	43	44	45	45	45	46	48	49
50	52	55	56	56	58	59	65	66	70

18. The service manager at a quick oil and lube shop was concerned about the length and variability of time it was taking to service automobiles. The service system had one mechanic do everything. The service manager selects a random sample of 30 customers and records the service time for each customer.

Service Times

14	13	12	12	15	12
20	15	14	20	15	15
18	14	20	11	22	18
17	14	17	24	13	10
16	16	17	15	13	16

a. Comment on the shape of the distribution of service times. Test for normality.
b. Estimate the mean and standard deviation of service time using 95% confidence intervals.
c. Does the manager seem to be meeting his goal of averaging less than 15 minutes per automobile with a standard deviation less than 5 minutes? Explain.

19. A recent math department study showed that the drop rate from College Algebra at a state university last year was about 40%. The department is trying a new plan for assigning students to math classes this year to decrease this drop rate. A random sample of 100 students taking College Algebra this year has been selected, and the proportion p of students that drop the class is recorded.

a. Graph the sampling distribution of p assuming that the drop rate this year has not changed from last year.
b. In this year's sample of 100 students, the proportion that dropped is $p = .35$. Does this sample provide sufficient evidence that the College Algebra drop rate this year has decreased from the drop rate last year? Use $\alpha = .10$.
c. Would you recommend that the math department continue using this plan to decrease the drop rate, or should they search for a new solution to the drop rate problem?

20. The President of a large company was concerned about the number of highly trained employees who might be retiring soon. If too many employees retire at the same time, replacing them might be difficult. The following table provides the years of service of a random sample of 151 employees. (File: **ServiceYears.mtp**)

Years of Service

13	16	25	3	27	7	7	2	3	16	7	26	1	8
6	27	6	6	8	23	3	21	4	12	0	9	3	32
27	5	23	9	9	6	9	7	9	13	1	15	20	9
2	1	13	18	10	27	26	4	27	9	10	7	7	13
27	2	7	23	26	16	5	23	6	9	30	4	5	18
4	4	0	10	10	7	2	27	26	3	29	29	7	1
19	19	5	5	10	28	21	20	23	8	3	17	17	26
30	14	17	6	14	20	0	27	22	28	20	0	8	13
19	1	2	18	26	9	3	21	8	17	1	29	21	30
7	6	18	2	10	6	26	9	22	13	7	8	28	44
26	28	16	29	2	9	17	2	8	23	39			

a. Comment on the shape of the distribution of years with the company.
b. The employees can retire after 25 years of service with the company. Estimate using a 90% confidence interval the proportion of employees who are eligible for retirement.
c. Does the sample provide sufficient evidence to conclude that mean years of service is more than 10 years? Use $\alpha = .05$. Interpret the *p*-value.

21. During the summer of 1999, a nursing home measured the quality of administering medication to the residents. Quality was divided into three categories: excellent - medication received within 15 minutes of scheduled time; acceptable - medication received between 15 and 30 minutes of scheduled time; and poor - medication not received within 30 minutes of scheduled time. A random sample of 200 medication administrations resulted in 128 classified as excellent, 46 as acceptable, and 26 as poor.

a. Use a 90% confidence interval to estimate the proportion of all medications that are of excellent quality.
b. The nursing home has set a quality standard that at least 75% of all medications should be of excellent quality. Is there significant evidence in the sample that the standard is not being met? Use $\alpha = .10$.

22. Consider the save rate statistics on heart attack victims given in the Appendix. Use a 95% confidence interval to estimate the mean age of heart attack victims. (File: **Heart.mtp**)

CHAPTER 8

INFERENCES BASED ON TWO SAMPLES

This chapter describes some statistical methods for comparing two populations. We describe estimation and hypothesis tests about the difference between two population means for independent and dependent sampling, the difference between two proportions, and the difference between two variances. We also include a nonparametric test, the Mann-Whitney test for comparing medians.

NEW COMMANDS

MANN-WHITNEY   PTWO   TWOSAMPLE-T   TWOT
%VARTEST

8.1   MAKING INFERENCES ABOUT $\mu_1 - \mu_2$: INDEPENDENT SAMPLING

The objective in this section is to make inferences about the difference between population means using two independent samples. For example, experimenters may want to compare the mean yields in a chemical laboratory using two different processes. Samples of daily yield are recorded for each process, the mean is calculated for each process, and an inference is made on the difference between mean yields. Or a professional golfer may want to assess the difference between mean distances a golf ball travels using two different types of drivers.

Suppose one population has mean μ_1 and variance σ_1^2, and the other population has mean μ_2 and variance σ_2^2. Independent samples are obtained if the random selection of n_1 measurements from the first population is unrelated to the random selection of n_2 measurements from the other population. The statistic $(\bar{x}_1 - \bar{x}_2)$ is a point estimate of the population parameter $(\mu_1 - \mu_2)$.

A $(1 - \alpha)100\%$ confidence interval for $(\mu_1 - \mu_2)$ is defined $(\bar{x}_1 - \bar{x}_2) \pm t_{\alpha/2} \sqrt{s_1^2/n_1 + s_2^2/n_2}$.

The null and alternative hypotheses for a two-tailed test are

$$H_0: \ \mu_1 - \mu_2 = D_0$$
$$H_a: \ \mu_1 - \mu_2 \neq D_0$$

where D_0 is the hypothesized difference between the means. Often D_0 equals 0.

The test statistic is defined

$$t = \frac{(\overline{x}_1 - \overline{x}_2) - D_0}{\sqrt{s_1^2/n_1 + s_2^2/n_2}}$$

If the two populations have approximately equal variances, the variances in the test statistic calculation are replaced by the pooled variance s_p^2, which is a weighted average of the sample variances. The formula for the pooled variance is

$$s_p^2 = \frac{(n_1 - 1)s_1^2 + (n_2 - 1)s_2^2}{n_1 + n_2 - 2}$$

MAKING INFERENCES: TWO INDEPENDENT SAMPLES

The following commands perform an independent two-sample t-test and calculate a confidence interval, with a default confidence level of 95%. If the data are unstacked, where data are entered in separate columns, use TWOSAMPLE-T. If the data are stacked data, where data are entered in one column and code identifying the group in a second column, use TWOT. Graphical display options include a dot plot and box plot.

If the two populations have approximately equal variances, the POOLED subcommand is used to obtain an estimate of the pooled variance s_p^2. Use ALTERNATIVE = +1 for H_a: $\mu_1 - \mu_2 > 0$ and ALTERNATIVE = -1 for H_a: $\mu_1 - \mu_2 < 0$.

Stat ▸ Basic Statistics ▸ 2-Sample t

TWOSAMPLE-T (K%) *data* C C	Use for unstacked data
POOLED	Uses pooled variance estimate s_p^2
ALTERNATIVE K	Specifies a one-tailed test
GDOTPLOT	Displays dot plots
GBOXPLOT	Displays box plots
TWOT (K%) *data* C *groups* C	Use for stacked data
POOLED	Uses pooled variance estimate s_p^2
ALTERNATIVE K	Specifies a one-tailed test
GDOTPLOT	Displays dot plots
GBOXPLOT	Displays box plots

NOTE

The assumptions for using the t distribution for small independent samples are that both sampled populations are normally distributed and have equal variances. If there is serious departure from these assumptions, a nonparametric test such as that described later in this chapter should be used to make inferences about the difference between means.

■ **Example 1**   **Comparing Two Population Means: Stacked Data**

Data on home prices for existing single-family homes are compiled by the WEFA Group, an economics consulting firm in Bala Cynwyd, Pa. The following table provides indicators for 1995 home prices, 1995 percentage changes, and the projected 1996 percentage changes, for a sample of cities in the eastern and western parts of the United States. Is there a difference in mean home prices in the eastern and western parts of the United States?

City	Price	1995%	1996%
Albany, NY	$108,607	-3.1	1.2
Allentown, Pa	85,250	-0.6	2.3
Bakersfield, Ca	137,171	-3.5	1.1
Baltimore, Md	112,747	-1.8	2.7
Bergen, NJ	195,232	1.6	3.9
Boston, Ma	180,865	1.1	4.5
Buffalo, NY	83,122	0.8	2.1
Charleston, SC	92,840	1.4	0.8
Charlotte, NC	104,433	-1.9	2.7
Fresno, Ca	107,627	0.7	2.0
Greensboro, NC	97,638	1.0	4.6
Greenville, SC	88,355	1.4	3.7
Harrisburg, Pa	79,846	-0.7	2.4
Hartford, Cn	129,130	-3.1	0.7
Middlesex, NJ	169,543	0.0	5.4
Monmouth, NJ	137,859	0.9	2.8
New Haven, Cn	134,856	-3.4	1.8
New York City	170,830	-1.1	0.8
Newark, NJ	187,128	0.3	3.7
Orange County, Ca	204,862	-2.8	0.6
Philadelphia, Pa	114,553	-3.8	2.2
Portland, Or	123,605	5.8	3.9
Raleigh/Durham, NC	119,355	3.1	7.3
Riverside, Ca	123,836	-4.1	0.2
Rochester, NY	85,043	-0.6	3.1
Sacramento, Ca	120,232	-3.2	0.5
San Diego, Ca	172,601	-1.7	0.9
San Francisco, Ca	220,067	-1.9	1.5
San Jose, Ca	224,828	-3.5	0.8
Seattle, WA	147,854	0.2	0.5
Springfield, Ma	102,678	-4.1	2.7
Stockton, Ca	98,440	-0.3	1.1
Syracuse, NY	82,372	-0.7	1.7
Tacoma, WA	119,884	1.0	2.3
Vallejo, Ca	110,441	0.2	1.1
Ventura, Ca	149,135	-3.4	-0.7
Washington, D.C.	155,176	-1.5	0.7

Solution The data are saved in **Cityhomes.mtp**. Columns are named City, HPrice, 1995 Change and 1996 Change.

This is an example of stacked data; all home prices are entered in one column. Before we can statistically compare home prices in the eastern and western United States, we need to enter a code to identify the different locations. *With recent versions of Minitab, alpha data can be used to identify groups; in older versions numerical codes must be used.* In this example, we enter East and West in a column named Location corresponding to the areas of the country where each city is located.

Manip ▸ Display Data   MTB > Print 'City' 'Location'
   Select City and Location in **Display. OK**

Data Display

Row	City	Location	Row	City	Location
1	Albany,NY	East	20	OrangeCounty,CA	West
2	Allentown,PA	East	21	Philadelphia,PA	East
3	Bakersfield,CA	West	22	Portland,OR	West
4	Baltimore	East	23	Raleigh/Durham,NC	East
5	Bergen,NJ	East	24	Riverside,CA	West
6	Boston,MA	East	25	Rochester,NY	East
7	Buffalo,NY	East	26	Sacramento,CA	West
8	Charleston,SC	East	27	SanDiego,CA	West
9	Charlotte,NC	East	28	SanFrancisco,CA	West
10	Fresno,CA	West	29	SanJose,CA	West
11	Greensboro,NC	East	30	Seattle,WA	West
12	Greenville,SC	East	31	Springfield,MA	East
13	Harrisburg,PA	East	32	Stockton,CA	West
14	Hartford,CN	East	33	Syracuse,NY	East
15	Middlesex,NJ	East	34	Tacoma,WA	West
16	Monmouth,NJ	East	35	Vallejo,CA	West
17	NewHaven,CN	East	36	Ventura,CA	West
18	NewYorkCity	East	37	Washington,D.C.	East
19	Newark,NJ	East			

TWOT is the session command for stacked data. We calculate a 90% confidence interval and use α = .10. To test whether the mean home prices differ, the two-tailed hypothesis test is

H_0: $\mu_1 - \mu_2 = 0$
H_a: $\mu_1 - \mu_2 \neq 0$

Stat ▸ Basic Statistics ▸ 2-Sample t   MTB > TwoT 90.0 'HPrice' 'Location';
   Click **Samples in one columns:**   SUBC>   Alternative 0;
   Select HPrice in **Samples**   SUBC>   GBoxplot.
     and Location in **Subscripts:**
   Click **Options** and enter 90% **Confidence level:**
   Click **Graphs** and choose **Boxplots of data. OK**

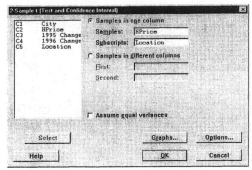

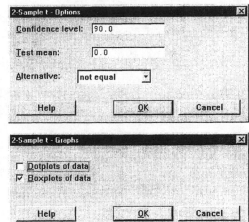

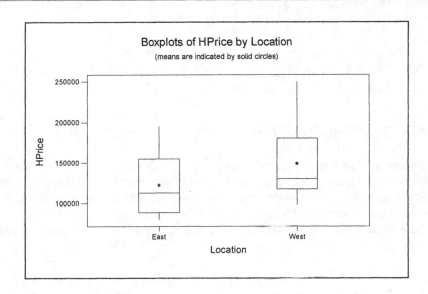

The box plots indicate that the home prices in the eastern part of the United States tend to be lower than in the west. The sample of eastern home prices has a lower mean and lower quartiles (Q1, median, and Q3), and lower standard deviation than the sample of western home prices.

Two-Sample T-Test and CI: HPrice, Location

```
Two-sample T for HPrice

Location     N      Mean      StDev    SE Mean
East        23     122498     37196      7756
West        14     149327     46814     12512


Difference = mu (East) - mu (West)
Estimate for difference:  -26829
90% CI for difference: (-52106, -1552)
T-Test of difference = 0 (vs not =):
             T-Value = -1.82   P-Value = 0.082   DF = 22
```

The output includes a table of statistics. The point estimator for the difference in mean home prices is $149,327 - 122,498 = $26,829. We are 95% confident that home prices average from $1,552 to $52,106 lower in the eastern than the western area of the United States.

The test statistic $t = -1.82$ has a *p*-value of .082. Since the *p*-value is less than $\alpha = .10$, we have sufficient evidence in the sample to conclude that there is a difference in mean home prices.

8.2   MAKING INFERENCES ABOUT μ_d: MATCHED PAIRS

A **paired difference experiment** is one in which the sample data consist of matched or paired observations randomly selected from a population of paired observations. For example, each pair may correspond to the same city, the same week, the same person, or the same sporting event. Frequently, a paired difference experiment provides more meaningful information about the difference between two means than independent sampling procedures. By pairing the observations when possible, some sampling variability is removed.

For example, suppose we want to compare the number of visitors to two city museums. If we collect admissions to both museums for 16 random weeks of the year, there may be a similar pattern of variation in mean admissions at both museums. This week-to-week variability in admissions is removed from the analysis by looking at the differences between weekly admissions to the museums.

The parameter of interest is the mean μ_d of the population differences. The point estimate of μ_d is $\overline{d}$, the mean of the sample differences. The estimated standard deviation is $s_d/\sqrt{n}$. If the distribution of differences is approximately normal, the t statistic can be used to make an inference on μ_d.

To construct confidence intervals and test hypothesis for paired data with Minitab, compute the differences between corresponding observations and then use a one sample *t*-test on the sample of differences. You can compare the paired samples graphically by plotting the paired observations on the same graph.

■ **Example 2**   **Comparing Two Population Means: Matched Pairs**

A university wants to compare two methods of teaching Orientation for International Students, a required course for all entering and transfer international students. International students are matched into pairs according to IQ, ethnic background, and other factors that might affect their academic performance. One student from each pair is randomly selected to be taught by method 1; the other student is assigned method 2. After the course, each student's score on a course assessment survey are recorded in the table below. Based on these results, which teaching method would you recommend? Discuss.

Pair	Method 1 Scores	Method 2 Scores
1	78	71
2	63	44
3	72	61
4	89	84
5	91	74
6	49	51
7	68	55
8	76	60
9	85	77
10	55	39

Solution   The data are saved in **Internatl.mtp**. Columns are named Pair, Method1, and Method2. First we graphically compare student performance based on the two teaching methods.

Graph ▸ Plot
  Select Method1 in **Graph 1 Y**
    and Pair in **Graph 1 X**;
  Select Method2 in **Graph 2 Y**
    and Pair in **Graph 2 X**;
  Click **Edit Attributes**, Click **Type**,
    choose Solid circle for **Graph 1**
    and Circle for **Graph 2**;
  Click **Annotation** and **Title**, add a title;
  Click **Frame** and **Multiple Graphs**,
    Select **Overlay graphs on same page**;
  Click **Frame** and **Axis**, Enter Score in **Label 2. OK**

```
MTB > Plot 'Method1'*'Pair' 'Method2'*'Pair';
SUBC>   Symbol;
SUBC>     Type 6 1;
SUBC>     Title "Two Teaching Methods";
SUBC>   Overlay;
SUBC>   Axis 1;
SUBC>   Axis 2;
SUBC>     Label "Score".
```

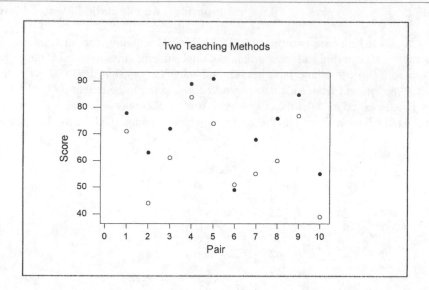

The plot shows that, for most pairs of students, those trained by method 1 denoted by a solid circle, had higher scores. It also shows a lot of variation in assertiveness scores between pairs of students. This variation in scores is accounted for by the matched pairs design; each pair is matched by factors that might affect test scores.

Next we calculate the differences between mean test scores and construct a 95% confidence interval for the difference.

Calc ▸ Calculator
  Enter 'Difference' in **Store result in variable:**
  Enter 'Method1' - 'Method2' in **Expression. OK**

Stats ▸ Basic Statistics ▸ 1-Sample t
  Select Difference in **Variables:**
  Click **Graphs**, choose **Dotplot of data. OK**

MTB > Name C4 = 'Difference'
MTB > Let 'Difference' = 'Method1' - 'Method2'

MTB > OneT 'Difference';
SUBC> GDotplot.

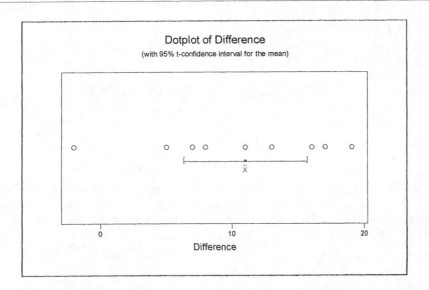

The dot plot shows one negative difference; only one pair resulted in a lower Method 1 test score. The display also illustrates the location of the sample mean difference and a 95% confidence interval relative to the sample differences.

One-Sample T: Difference

```
Variable        N       Mean      StDev     SE Mean         95.0% CI
Difference     10      11.00       6.53        2.07    (    6.33,    15.67)
```

The point estimate of the true mean difference in test scores is 11 points. We are 95% confident that the mean difference in test scores is between 6.3 and 15.7 points; that is, method 1 test scores average from 6.3 to 15.7 points higher than method 2 test scores.

The hypotheses to test whether the method 1 mean score μ_1 exceeds the method 2 mean score μ_2 are

H_0: $\mu_1 - \mu_2 = 0$
H_a: $\mu_1 - \mu_2 > 0$

Stats ▸ Basic Statistics ▸ 1-Sample t
  Select Difference in **Variables;**
  Enter 0 in **Test mean:**
  Click **Options,**
    Choose **greater than** in **Alternative. OK**
	MTB > OneT 'Difference';
	SUBC> Test 0;
	SUBC> Alternative 1.

One-Sample T: Difference

```
Test of mu = 0 vs mu > 0

Variable             N           Mean      StDev    SE Mean
Difference          10          11.00       6.53       2.07


Variable      95.0% Lower Bound            T          P
Difference                 7.21         5.33      0.000
```

Since the observed significance level or *p*-value is 0, we reject the null hypothesis. We have sufficient evidence to conclude the mean difference is greater than 0, or the mean method 1 score exceeds the mean method 2 score. Teaching method 1 results in significantly higher scores than the second teaching method.

8.3   MAKING INFERENCES ABOUT $\pi_1 - \pi_2$

Suppose the proportion of successes in one population is π_1, and π_2 in another population. To make an inference about the difference between these proportions, the point estimate is the difference between corresponding sample proportions $(p_1 - p_2)$, where $p_1 = x_1/n_1$ and $p_2 = x_2/n_2$, and x_1 and x_2 are the number of successes in the two samples of sizes n_1 and n_2. If the sample sizes are large, the sampling distribution of $(p_1 - p_2)$ is approximately normal.

The $(1 - \alpha)100\%$ confidence interval for $(\pi_1 - \pi_2)$ is

$$(p_1 - p_2) \pm z_{\alpha/2} \sqrt{p_1 q_1 / n_1 + p_2 q_2 / n_2} \text{, where } q_1 = 1 - p_1 \text{ and } q_2 = 1 - p_2.$$

The null and alternative hypotheses for a two-tailed test are

$$H_0: \pi_1 - \pi_2 = 0$$
$$H_a: \pi_1 - \pi_2 \neq 0$$

The z test statistic for this test is

$$z = \frac{(p_1 - p_2)}{\sqrt{pq(1/n_1 + 1/n_2)}}$$

where $p = (x_1 + x_2)/(n_1 + n_2)$ and $q = 1 - p$.

MAKING INFERENCES: TWO PROPORTIONS

The following command performs a test of the difference in two proportions and generates a confidence interval, with a default confidence level of 95%. The data can be either unstacked data, where data are entered in separate columns, or stacked data, where the data are entered in one column and code identifying the group in a second column.

Or data can be entered as summarized data. On the command line, enter four integers: the number of trials and the number of successes in the first sample followed by the number of trials and the number of successes in the second sample.

Use POOLED for a pooled estimate of p for the test statistic. Use ALTERNATIVE $= +1$ for H_a: $\pi_1 - \pi_2 > 0$ and ALTERNATIVE $= -1$ for H_a: $\pi_1 - \pi_2 < 0$.

Stat ▸ Basic Statistics ▸ 2 Proportions

PTWO C C *or* K K K K	Use for actual data and for summarized data
CONFIDENCE K	Default if 95%
TEST K	Uses a null hypothesis value of K
ALTERNATIVE K	Specifies a one-tailed test
POOLED	Uses pooled variance
STACKED	Use for stacked data

NOTE

The PTWO command is available with Minitab Release 13 and Student Release 12. If you are using releases without this command, you can use the Minitab Calculator function to evaluate the formulas given above. The Inverse Cumulative Probability command gives the value of $z_{\alpha/2}$ for a $(1 - \alpha)100\%$ confidence interval.

■ **Example 3**   **Comparing Two Population Proportions**

The Women's Institutional Studies group at a Midwestern university wanted to compare the proportions of female faculty members in the various units on campus in Spring, 2000. Of particular interest were the proportions of female faculty in the College of Education and the College of Business. In a random sample of 80 College of Education faculty, there were 36 females, and in a random sample of 70 College of Business faculty, there were 15 females. Based on the two samples, can we conclude that there are differences in the proportion of female faculty in these colleges?

Solution To test whether the proportion of female faculty in the College of Education differs from the proportion of female faculty in the College of Business, the null and alternative hypotheses are

$$H_0: \ \pi_1 - \pi_2 = 0$$
$$H_a: \ \pi_1 - \pi_2 \neq 0$$

We use PTWO to calculate a 90% confidence interval and use $\alpha = .10$ for the hypothesis test.

Stat ▸ Basic Statistics ▸ 2 Proportions   MTB > PTwo 80 36 70 15;
  Click **Summarized data:**   SUBC> Confidence 90.0;
  In **First sample:** enter 80 **Trials:** and 36 **Successes:**   SUBC> Pooled.
  In **Second sample:** enter 70 **Trials:** and 15 **Successes:**
  Click **Options** and enter 90 in **Confidence level:**
  Click **Use pooled estimate of p for test. OK**

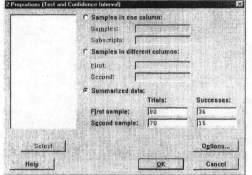 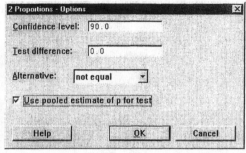

Test and CI for Two Proportions

```
Sample      X       N  Sample p
1          36      80  0.450000
2          15      70  0.214286


Estimate for p(1) - p(2):  0.235714
90% CI for p(1) - p(2):  (0.113740, 0.357689)
Test for p(1) - p(2) = 0 (vs not = 0):  Z = 3.04   P-Value = 0.002
```

The confidence interval is $.11 \leq \pi_1 - \pi_2 \leq .36$. We can be 90% confident that the College of Education has between 11% and 36% more female faculty than the College of Business.

The *p*-value is the probability of obtaining a *z* test statistic as large as 3.04 when $H_0: \ \pi_1 - \pi_2 = 0$ is true. Since the *p*-value is less than α, the samples provide sufficient evidence that the proportion of female education faculty differs from the proportion of female business faculty.

8.4   COMPARING TWO POPULATION VARIANCES

An assumption for using the *t* distribution to compare population means for small independent samples is that both sampled populations have equal variances. A statistical procedure to test for equal variances is available with Minitab. The null and alternative hypotheses for a two-tailed test are

H_0:   The population variances are equal.
H_a: The population variances are not equal.

MAKING INFERENCES: TWO VARIANCES

The following performs the Bartlett's and Levene's tests of the difference in two variances and calculates confidence intervals for the standard deviations, with a default confidence level of 95%. Use Bartlett's test when the data come from normal distributions; and Levene's test when the data come from continuous, but not necessarily normal, distributions.

The data can be either unstacked data, where data are entered in separate columns, or stacked data, where the data are entered in one column and code identifying the group in a second column.

Stat ▸ Basic Statistics ▸ 2 Variances

%VARTEST C C	Test for differences in two variances
UNSTACKED	Use if data are unstacked
CONFIDENCE K	Default if 95%

NOTE

*%VARTEST is available in Minitab Release 13 and Student Release 12. The path for the student release is **Stat ▸ ANOVA ▸ Homogeneity of Variance**. If you are using releases that do not support this macro, you can use the Minitab Calculator function to evaluate formulas for testing the differences in two variances.*

■ **Example 4**   **Comparing Two Population Variances**

Refer to Example 1 of this chapter. Data on home prices for existing single-family homes are compiled by the WEFA Group, an economics consulting firm in Bala Cynwyd, Pa. The data include 1995 home prices, 1995 percentage changes, and projected percentage changes for 1996, for a sample of cities in the eastern and western parts of the United States. Compare the variances of home prices in the eastern and western parts.

Solution   The data are saved in **Cityhomes.mtp**. Columns are named City, HPrice, 1995 Change, 1996 Change and Location. The hypotheses are

H_0:   The population variances of home prices in the east and west are equal.

H_a: The population variances of home prices in the east and west are not equal.

Stat ▸ Basic Statistics ▸ 2 Variances   MTB > %VarTest 'HPrice' 'Location'
   Click **Samples in one column**;
    Select HPrice in **Samples:** and Location in **Subscripts. OK**

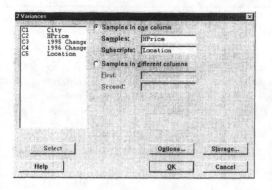

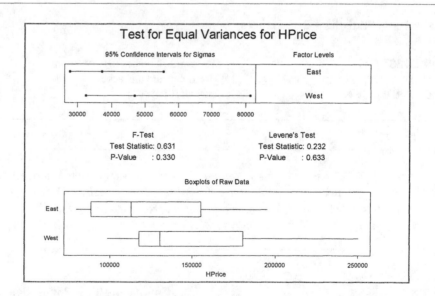

There is overlap in the confidence intervals for the standard deviations. The sample standard deviation of home prices in the west is higher than that of the home prices in the east.

Test for Equal Variances

```
Response      HPrice
Factors       Location
ConfLvl       95.0000

Bonferroni confidence intervals for standard deviations

   Lower     Sigma     Upper    N  Factor Levels

  27773.9   37195.6   55550.3   23  East
  32492.7   46813.9   81355.2   14  West


F-Test (normal distribution)

Test Statistic: 0.631
P-Value        : 0.330


Levene's Test (any continuous distribution)

Test Statistic: 0.232
P-Value        : 0.633
```

The *p*-value is .330 for Bartlett's F-test, which assumes a normal distribution, Since this is greater than an α level as high as .10, we do not have enough evidence to conclude the population variances of home prices in the east and west differ. We reach the same conclusion for Levene's test.

8.5 COMPARING TWO POPULATION MEDIANS

The **Mann-Whitney rank sum** test is a nonparametric counterpart of the *z* or *t* test for the difference between two population means based on independent random samples. The test is used to determine whether one population median is shifted to the right or left of another population median. The test is sometimes referred to as the two-sample **Wilcoxon rank sum** test.

To use the rank sum test, rank all the observations from both samples, and then sum the ranks for each sample. If the two distributions for equal sample sizes are identical, the rank sums should be about the same. If the rank sum of one sample is significantly different then the rank sum of another sample, the data suggest that one population distribution is shifted to the right or left of another. The hypotheses are

H_0: The two population distributions are identical.
H_a: One population distribution median is shifted to the right or to the left of the other population median.

MANN-WHITNEY TWO-SAMPLE RANK SUM TEST

This command performs a two-sample rank test for the differences between two population medians. The output includes the point estimate, confidence interval for the difference between population medians, and the hypothesis test results. The confidence level option specifies the confidence coefficient; the default level is 95%.

Stat ▸ Nonparametrics ▸ Mann-Whitney

MANN-WHITNEY (K%) *data* C ... C   Differences between two medians
    ALTERNATIVE K   Distribution shifted to one direction

■ **Example 5**   **Comparing Two Population Medians**

An educational psychologist claims that the order of questions on an exam affects the student's score on the exam. She believes that students will score better on an exam if the questions are ordered from easiest too hardest. To test the claim, she arranges the same set of questions from easiest to hardest on Exam A, and from hardest to easiest on Exam B. She randomly selects two groups of ten students each to take Exam A and B. The resulting exam scores are given below. Graphically and numerically compare the exam scores; test for normality. Select an appropriate procedure to test the educational psychologist's claim. Use $\alpha = .05$.

Exam A		Exam B	
69	78	72	72
80	82	69	69
86	79	57	61
82	69	72	72
77	77	70	73

Solution   We enter the scores in columns named Exam A and Exam B. First we obtain some numerical statistics and box plots.

Stat ▸ Basic Statistics ▸ Display Descriptive Statistics   MTB > Describe 'Exam A' 'Exam B'
    Select Exam A and Exam B in **Variables**. **OK**

Descriptive Statistics: Exam A, Exam B

Variable	N	Mean	Median	TrMean	StDev	SE Mean
Exam A	10	77.90	78.50	78.00	5.43	1.72
Exam B	10	68.70	71.00	69.63	5.38	1.70

Variable	Minimum	Maximum	Q1	Q3
Exam A	69.00	86.00	75.00	82.00
Exam B	57.00	73.00	67.00	72.00

The two samples have about the same standard deviation; the means differ by about 9 points and the medians by 7.5 points.

Graph ▸ Boxplot
  Select Exam A in **Graph 1 Y** and
   Select Exam B in **Graph 2 Y**,
  Click **Frame**, choose **Multiple Graphs**,
   Choose **Overlay graphs on same page**.
  Click **Annotation**, choose **Title**, add a title;
  Click **Annotation**, choose **Footnote**, add a footnote. **OK**

```
MTB > Boxplot 'Exam A' 'Exam B';
SUBC>  Box;
SUBC>  Title "Exam Scores ";
SUBC>  Footnote "Exam A: Questions   &
CONT >   Easiest to Hardest";
SUBC>  Footnote "Exam B: Questions   &
CONT >   Hardest to Easiest";
SUBC>  Overlay.
```

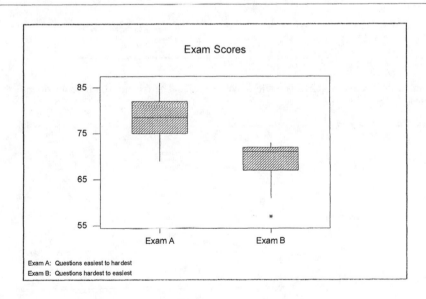

The box plots show a difference in the centers of the data sets. Exam B scores do not appear to be normal, but appear to be skewed toward lower scores.

The null and alternative hypotheses for the normality test for Exam A scores are

H_0: The population of Exam A scores has a normal distribution.

H_a: The population of Exam A scores does not have a normal distribution.

Stat ▸ Basic Statistics ▸ Normality Test   MTB > %NormPlot 'Exam A'
Select Exam A in **Variable. OK**

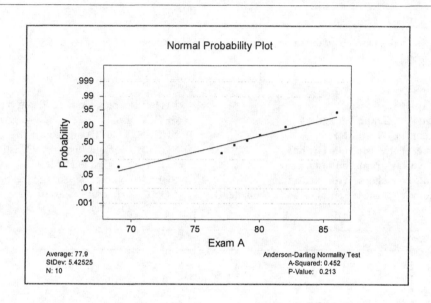

For Exam A, the *p*-value of 0.213 is not less than $\alpha = .05$. There is not significant evidence that the distribution differs from normality.

The null and alternative hypotheses for the normality test for Exam B scores are

H_0: The population of Exam B scores has a normal distribution.

H_a: The population of Exam B scores does not have a normal distribution.

Stat ▸ Basic Statistics ▸ Normality Test
                                          MTB > %NormPlot 'Exam B'
Select Exam B in **Variable. OK**

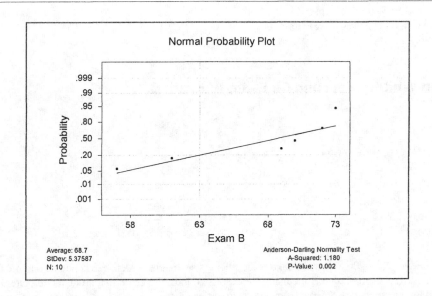

However, for Exam B, the *p*-value of 0.002 is less than $\alpha = .05$. There is significant evidence that the distribution differs from normality. The parametric test procedures for small sample sizes and a normal population are not appropriate for making inferences about the population.

The 2-sample t test is not appropriate, since it assumes each population has a normal distribution. We use the Mann-Whitney test to test if the median for Exam A exceeds the median for Exam B. The hypotheses are

H_0: The medians for Exam A and Exam B are equal.
H_a: The median for Exam A exceeds the median for Exam B.

Stat ▸ Nonparametrics ▸ Mann-Whitney
   Select Exam A in **First sample:**
   Select Exam B in **Second Sample:**
   Click **Alternative**, choose **greater than**. **OK**

MTB > Mann-Whitney 95.0 'Exam A' 'Exam B
SUBC> Alternative 1.

Mann-Whitney Test and CI: Exam A, Exam B

```
Exam A     N =   10     Median =        78.500
Exam B     N =   10     Median =        71.000
Point estimate for ETA1-ETA2 is         8.500
95.5 Percent CI for ETA1-ETA2 is  (4.999,12.998)
W = 141.0


Test of ETA1 = ETA2  vs  ETA1 > ETA2 is significant at 0.0036
The test is significant at 0.0034 (adjusted for ties)
```

Since the *p*-value = .0036 is less than α = .05, there is sufficient evidence to conclude that the Exam A median exceeds the Exam B median. The results support the claim that students do better on an exam if the questions are ordered from easiest to hardest.

The output includes a 95% confidence interval on the difference between the two medians. We are 95% confidence that Exam A median exceeds the Exam B median by between 5 and 13 points.

EXERCISES

1. The price earnings ratio or PE ratio is the price of a share of stock divided by the earnings per share. The PE ratio reflects the price an investor is willing to pay for a dollar of earnings. The following table gives the reported PE ratios as of January 2001 of two random samples of stocks in the financial industry and in the computers and technology industry.

Financial	PE	Technology	PE
BankAmer	10	Micron Tech	14
TCF Fin	20	BroadVision	176
Am Express	27	WebTrends	97
Wells Fargo	23	IBM	21
Chase Manhattan	11	Hewlett-Packard	18
Am Intl Grp	37	Gateway	12
Hartford Fin	17	Celestica	46
Capital One Fin	22	Sun Microsystems	60
Marsh&McLn	36	Texas Instruments	35
US Bancp	14	Foundry Networks	64

a. Graphically and numerically compare the price earnings ratios for the financial industry and the computers and technology industry.
b. Construct a 95% confidence interval for the difference between mean price earnings ratios for the two industries. Interpret. What assumptions are necessary for this analysis?
c. Test whether the mean price earnings ratio of the financial industry is less than that of the computers and technology industry. Use $\alpha = .01$.

2. Many universities have implemented programs to increase the retention rate of students. One reason why students leave a university is the feeling of loneliness. Before and after implementing a program to combat loneliness, students at a large university were given a standardized loneliness survey. The following scores were recorded for a sample of 40 students before, and a sample of 30 students after the program. Higher scores indicate greater loneliness. (File: **LonelinessScores.mtp**)

Loneliness Scores Before

69	39	64	49	37	17	39	54	61	48
32	16	38	63	19	33	49	21	49	47
52	83	58	57	36	24	40	49	42	59
41	40	19	52	36	44	48	30	54	25

Loneliness Scores After

26	61	16	31	63	57	26	53	39	45
52	32	31	5	41	28	23	38	34	40
11	45	24	36	55	52	22	26	2	43

a. Graphically compare the samples of scores for students.
b. Construct a 95% confidence interval for the true difference in the loneliness scores before and after the program. Interpret.
c. Is there sufficient evidence in the samples to conclude that the program was effective in

decreasing the feeling of loneliness? Use $\alpha = .05$.

3.   A class data set containing information on 200 students enrolled in a statistics course is given in the Appendix. Two samples of business and nonbusiness majors were randomly selected from the data set.   The grade point averages of the students are given as follow: (File: **MajorGPAs.mtp**)

Business Major GPAs		Nonbusiness Major GPAs	
3.440	2.650	2.790	3.100
3.941	3.360	3.400	2.890
2.730	3.680	4.000	2.560
3.625	2.760	2.666	3.000
3.330	3.100	3.300	3.900
3.460	3.890	3.750	2.680
2.700	2.500	2.000	2.900
2.690	3.010	3.428	3.650
3.450	3.200	2.750	2.850
3.125	2.800	3.800	2.768

a. Numerically and graphically summarize the grade point averages for the two groups.
b. Construct a 99% confidence interval for the difference between mean grade point averages. Interpret.
c. Is there evidence in the samples that the mean grade point averages differ for business and nonbusiness majors? Use $\alpha = .10$.
d. Test whether the variances in grade point averages differ for business and nonbusiness majors. Use $\alpha = .05$.

4.   The Minnesota Real Estate Research Center compiles information on homes sold in several areas of Minnesota. The following table gives the selling prices of 20 homes randomly selected from all homes sold in St. Cloud and Rochester.   (File: **MNHomes.mtp**)

St. Cloud Homes		Rochester Homes	
$105,000	$124,400	$123,925	$159,900
66,000	110,600	86,000	67,800
98,900	73,500	29,900	116,000
143,000	139,500	73,000	112,330
136,000	74,000	145,500	74,900
66,600	84,500	81,500	164,000
119,875	91,900	84,000	109,000
84,000	89,900	100,750	105,900
72,000	131,900	94,500	155,000
72,500	74,500	149,195	78,000

a. Graphically and numerically compare the samples.
b. Construct a 95% confidence interval for $(\mu_1 - \mu_2)$, the difference in mean selling prices.
c. Construct a 99% confidence interval for $(\mu_1 - \mu_2)$. Compare with the interval of part b.
d. Is there sufficient evidence in the samples that the variances in selling prices differ for St. Cloud and Rochester?

5. Consider the data on heart attack victims given in the Appendix. An ambulance company studied the save rate of heart attack victims to determine what could be done to increase the chance of saving a patient. (File: **Heart.mtp**)

   a. Graphically compare the ambulance response times for metro and non-metro areas.
   b. Is there sufficient evidence that the variances in response times differ for the two locations? Use $\alpha = .05$.
   c. Construct a 95% confidence interval for $(\mu_1 - \mu_2)$, the difference in mean response time for victims in the metro and non-metro areas.

6. The service manager at a quick oil and lube shop was concerned about the length of time it was taking to service automobiles. The old system had one mechanic do everything. He proposed a new system where the mechanic would only change the oil. A second person would lubricate the car while doing a safety check. A random sample of 50 cars using the old system and 50 cars using the new system resulted in the following service times in minutes. (File: **SystemTimes.mtp**)

Old System					New System				
6	10	10	11	11	6	6	7	7	7
11	12	12	12	12	7	8	8	8	8
12	12	13	13	13	8	9	9	9	10
13	13	13	13	13	11	11	11	11	11
13	14	14	14	14	11	11	12	12	12
14	14	14	15	15	12	12	12	12	13
15	15	15	16	16	13	13	14	14	14
16	16	17	17	17	14	14	14	15	15
17	18	19	19	19	15	15	15	15	15
20	20	21	22	28	16	16	19	19	23

   a. Is there sufficient evidence in the samples that the mean service time using the new system is less than the mean service time using the old system? Use $\alpha = .05$.
   b. The service manager also believes that the new system would result in a smaller variance in service time. Is there sufficient evidence in the samples to support this belief? Use $\alpha = .05$.

7. A dentist conducted an experiment to measure the effectiveness of a new type of dental anesthetic. Twenty-five patients receive the standard anesthetic while twenty-five others receive the new anesthetic. Each patient gave a measure of his or her discomfort on a scale from 0 to 100, higher scores indicating greater discomfort. Is there sufficient evidence in the samples that the new anesthetic results in a lower mean discomfort score than the standard anesthetic? Use $\alpha = .05$. Graphically compare the two samples. (File: **Dentist.mtp**)

Standard Scores					New Scores				
23	44	44	50	51	62	82	39	85	75
26	34	53	43	6	50	74	51	57	46
44	26	79	49	30	40	87	72	39	48
32	49	52	33	38	35	30	56	48	56
44	67	33	52	22	52	58	50	64	60

8. A school district is comparing two methods of teaching reading skills to first graders. First graders are matched into pairs according to IQ, ethnic background, and other factors that might affect reading achievement. One student from each pair is randomly selected to be taught by method A; the other student is assigned method B. After the class, students' scores on an achievement test are recorded and provided in the table. (File: **TeachingMethods.mtp**)

Pair	Scores of Students Method A	Method B	Pair	Scores of Students Method A	Method B
1	63	80	11	69	43
2	82	86	12	63	60
3	99	56	13	84	74
4	58	54	14	57	91
5	92	73	15	52	83
6	67	68	16	91	81
7	80	94	17	97	97
8	88	67	18	50	87
9	85	79	19	82	90
10	76	71	20	59	88

a. Graphically compare the two teaching methods.
b. Construct and interpret a 95% confidence interval for the difference between mean test scores. Graphically display the differences.
c. Do the data provide sufficient evidence that the population mean method A test score exceeds the population mean method B test score? Test using $\alpha = .05$.

9. Many people who have been smoking cigarettes for a long time find it very difficult to quit smoking. A group of 30 smokers who have indicated that they want to quit smoking are randomly split into two groups of 15 people each. One group entered a new smoking cessation program and the second group was placed in the current program. One month after the completion of the programs, the following numbers of cigarettes smoked per day were recorded.

New Program			Old Program		
14	12	0	3	0	24
0	0	15	20	1	14
0	0	2	0	8	8
20	5	0	27	0	22
15	3	12	10	19	14

a. Graphically and numerically compare the programs; test for normality.
b. Is there evidence in the samples that the new cessation program is more effective than the old program? Select an appropriate procedure for the test. Use $\alpha = .05$.

10. Example 1 of this chapter analyzes data on home prices for existing single-family homes compiled by the WEFA Group, an economics consulting firm in Bala Cynwyd, Pa. The data include 1995 home prices, 1995 percentage change, and the projected 1996 percentage changes, for a sample of cities in the eastern and western parts of the United States. (File: **Cityhomes.mtp**)

a. Graphically and numerically compare the 1995 and 1996 percentages.
b. Construct and interpret a 95% confidence interval for the difference in mean 1995 and 1996 percentages. Graphically display the differences.
c. Do the data provide sufficient evidence that the mean 1995 and 1996 percentages differ? Test using $\alpha = .05$.

11. A reference librarian is concerned about the length of time that customers have to wait before receiving the information they requested. A new information retrieval system was tried to see if the length of time could be decreased. The librarian randomly selected 30 customers before the new system and 30 after the new system, and recorded the information retrieval time for each customer. The times, in minutes, are shown below. (File: **CustomerWait.mtp**)

Wait Before New System						**Wait After New System**				
13	11	14	12	12		14	12	14	12	6
13	12	13	14	13		9	3	10	15	10
13	17	14	8	13		15	12	10	12	6
13	12	15	11	17		8	5	6	8	2
10	14	15	9	11		9	15	19	11	11
15	13	12	13	16		16	13	16	11	13

a. Is there sufficient evidence in the samples that the mean information retrieval time using the new system is less than the mean time using the old system? Use $\alpha = .05$. Graphically compare the two systems.
b. The reference librarian believed that the new system would not change variance in service times. Is there sufficient evidence that the variances are not the same? Use $\alpha = .05$.

12. During fall quarter 2000 a team of statistics students compared grade point averages of university students who live on campus with students who live off campus. The team was interested in determining whether there are differences in grade point averages distributions for the two student groups. Random samples of grade point averages are given below: (File: **CampusGPA.mtp**)

On-campus GPAs				**Off-campus GPAs**				
2.2	3.4	4.0	3.1	2.8	3.4	2.2	2.9	2.9
2.9	2.9	2.8	2.6	2.6	2.9	3.0	2.8	3.4
3.5	2.2	2.9	3.6	2.9	2.6	3.5	2.5	
3.3	3.8	3.0	2.8	3.7	2.7	2.7	2.7	
3.3	3.2	3.0	2.8	2.9	3.0	2.7	2.9	
3.2	3.0	2.5	2.5	2.5	2.5	3.5	3.2	

a. Graphically and numerically compare the two samples.
b. Construct and interpret a 90% confidence interval on the difference in mean grade point averages for the two groups.
c. Is there sufficient evidence in the two samples that the grade point average means for the two groups differ? Use $\alpha = .10$.

13. A study of married couples where both husband and wife work outside of the home indicated that wives spent more time doing housework. Fifteen married couples were asked what proportion of

the housework each did. The data are given below. (File: **Housework.mtp**)

Couple	Husband	Wife		Couple	Husband	Wife
1	51	64		9	47	62
2	46	57		10	62	61
3	54	65		11	47	65
4	50	69		12	39	57
5	50	59		13	62	57
6	51	63		14	44	55
7	57	57		15	57	60
8	49	65				

a. Estimate the mean difference in the proportion of housework indicated done by husbands and wives using a 95% confidence interval.

b. Is there sufficient evidence in the sample that wives indicated that they do a greater proportion of the housework? Use $\alpha = .10$.

14. Test anxiety is a serious problem for many students. Although the students may understand the course material, taking a traditional exam is very difficult for them. The counseling center at the university developed a program to help students reduce their anxiety so that they could perform better on tests. Twenty students identified as having test anxiety were randomly split into two groups of ten students. One group attended a program developed by the university counseling center to reduce test anxiety. The students in the second group were used as a control group, and were given no special help. After the program completion, both groups were given a standardized anxiety test. Lower scores on the test indicate lower anxiety. The test results are given below.

Program Group Scores		Control Group Scores	
63	64	64	55
59	33	70	62
55	75	72	78
66	66	58	67
62	42	83	70

a. Test for normality of the populations of test scores.

b. Determine whether there is sufficient evidence in the samples that the anxiety reduction program is effective. Use $\alpha = .10$.

15. During the summer of 2000, a nursing home measured the quality of providing medication to the residents. Quality was divided into three categories: excellent - medication received within 15 minutes of scheduled time; acceptable - medication received between 15 and 30 minutes of scheduled time; and poor - medication not received within 30 minutes of scheduled time. A random sample of 200 medication administrations resulted in 128 classified as excellent, 46 as acceptable, and 26 as poor. The nursing home administration instituted a program to improve the quality. After the program was in effect for one month, a second random sample of 200 administering of medications resulted in 166 classified as excellent, 19 as acceptable, and 15 as poor. Was the quality improvement program effective in increasing the proportion of medications classified as excellent? Use $\alpha = .05$.

16. Learning in a course can be split into two types: surface learning and deep learning. Surface learning, similar to memorization, is what one can learn for a test, but is soon forgotten afterwards. Deep learning is what one will retain for a long period of time. Studies have indicated that about 90% of learning in a typical course is surface learning and only 10% is deep learning.

A professor developed a test to measure student understanding of statistical concepts and principles. He administered the test on the first day of his statistics class, and then again one term after his course ended. The difference in the two test scores was a measure of the amount of deep learning about statistics that occurred in his class. The results for a group of 30 students follow. Analyze the data. Write a summary report on deep learning. (File: **Learning.mtp**)

Student	Test Scores Pretest	Final	Posttest	Student	Test Scores Pretest	Final	Posttest
1	33	62	40	16	47	74	50
2	27	81	27	17	26	53	33
3	15	46	20	18	49	91	56
4	44	70	52	19	14	43	18
5	23	52	32	20	15	42	29
6	22	63	18	21	0	62	6
7	21	81	31	22	39	68	42
8	29	80	44	23	23	68	30
9	29	90	32	24	70	100	85
10	53	88	50	25	13	58	19
11	0	58	10	26	25	52	31
12	0	42	7	27	40	91	37
13	37	99	41	28	38	67	41
14	0	54	2	29	6	42	3
15	45	71	52	30	38	99	37

CHAPTER 9

SIMPLE LINEAR REGRESSION

Simple linear regression is a statistical technique used to study the relationship between two variables. An objective of regression analysis is to model the relationship between an independent variable and a response variable. In this chapter, we describe a scatter plot and correlation analysis to hypothesize the form of the model, fit a model to the data, test the usefulness of the model, and use it for estimation and prediction.

NEW COMMANDS

BRIEF   CORRELATION   %FITLINE   REGRESS

9.1 INTRODUCTION TO REGRESSION ANALYSIS

Regression analysis is used to establish the relationship between two variables. The **response variable** y is the **dependent variable** or variable of interest, and the **predictor variable** x is the **independent variable**. For example, heart rate tends to be related to exercise level; interest paid on a checking account may be related to the minimum account balance; and absenteeism in a firm may be related to job satisfaction.

An objective of simple regression analysis is to develop a linear regression model, relating y to x, that can be used to predict values of the response variable. A scatter plot of the data provides information on the type and strength of the relationship between the two variables. The Minitab Plot command, with y on the vertical axis and x on the horizontal axis, gives a scatter plot of the data.

A correlation analysis gives information to hypothesize the regression model. The **Pearson product moment correlation coefficient** r is a numerical measure of the strength of the linear relationship between y and x. If r is positive, there is a direct relationship between y and x; that is, y tends to increase as x increases. If r is negative, there is an inverse relationship and y tends to decrease as x increases.

CORRELATION ANALYSIS

The Pearson product moment correlation coefficient is calculated between the pair of variables listed on the command line. The coefficient can have a value between -1 and 1. A value close to -1 or to +1 implies a strong linear relationship in the sample data; a value close to zero implies no linear relationship.

Stat ▸ Basic Statistics ▸ Correlation

CORRELATION C C   Calculates correlation between two variables

---

If the scatter plot and correlation coefficient suggest a linear relationship between y and x, the simple linear regression model relating y to x is

$$y = \beta_0 + \beta_1 x + \epsilon$$

The two parameters of the model are β_0, the y-intercept, and β_1, the slope of the line. β_0 is the mean value of y when x is 0. β_1 is the change in the mean value of y for a one unit change in x. The random error, ϵ, accounts for the variability in y that is not explained by the independent variable x. This variability could be due to other important independent variables or to some random phenomenon.

The model assumes that the errors are independent; that is, the error associated with any one observation has no effect on the error associated with any other observation. The model also assumes a normal probability distribution of ϵ, with zero mean and constant variance σ^2 for all values of x.

SIMPLE LINEAR REGRESSION

This command determines the simple linear regression equation using the least squares method. Output options include the regression equation; a table of coefficients, standard deviations, and t-ratios; s and R^2; and the analysis of variance table. Use options to store the residuals, standardized residuals and fitted values, and to construct confidence and prediction intervals.

Stat ▸ Regression ▸ Regression

REGRESS C *on* 1 *predictor* C   Determines a regression model
    RESIDUALS C   Stores residuals
    BRIEF K   Controls output
    PREDICT E   Calculates 95% confidence
                                                       and prediction intervals for y

---

CONTROLLING THE REGRESSION OUTPUT

The BRIEF session command entered before the regression command or as a subcommand controls the amount and type of regression output. BRIEF 2 is the default output of the REGRESS command.

BRIEF (K)

The larger the value of K, the more output. The following are the options for K.

K = 0   No regression output; all requested storage is done. Error messages are printed.
K = 1   The regression equation, table of coefficients, s, r^2 and r^2-adjusted, and the basic analysis of variance table.
K = 2   The output of BRIEF 1, plus the sequential analysis of variance table provided there are two or more predictors, and unusual observations.
K = 3   The output of BRIEF 2, plus a table of the data, fitted values and residuals.

PLOTTING THE REGRESSION LINE

This command provides some regression analysis and plots the regression line on a scatter plot of the data. The options store the residuals and fitted values and construct confidence and prediction bands.

Stat ▸ Regression ▸ Fitted Line Plot

%FITLINE C C   Plots the regression line
   CONFIDENCE K   Confidence level of K; default is 95%
   RESIDUALS C   Stores residuals
   FITS C   Stores fitted values
   CI   Displays confidence bands
   PI   Displays prediction bands
   TITLE   Replaces default title

■ **Example 1**   **Simple Linear Regression Problem**

Several college students applied their recently obtained statistical knowledge to their hunt for the best deal on an apartment. One of several determinants of monthly rent was apartment size. The students collected a sample of 20 apartments with the following monthly rental prices and square footage. Conduct a simple linear regression analysis.

Apartment	Rent	Footage	Apartment	Rent	Footage
1	425	825	11	440	825
2	485	950	12	450	830
3	430	800	13	445	925
4	499	950	14	410	750
5	425	825	15	430	850
6	481	900	16	460	980
7	475	900	17	461	850
8	480	958	18	503	950
9	480	829	19	495	980
10	441	800	20	450	830

Solution   The apartment search data are in a file named **Apartment.mtp**. Columns are named Apartment, Rent, and Footage. The following illustrates initial steps in a simple linear regression analysis. We construct a scatter plot, find the correlation coefficient, determine the linear regression equation, discuss the Minitab output, and plot the regression equation on the scatter plot.

Graph ▸ Plot	MTB > Plot 'Rent' * 'Footage';
Select Rent in **Graph 1 Y**	SUBC> Symbol;
and Footage in **Graph 1 X**;	SUBC> Title "Apartment Search".
Click **Annotation**, choose **Title**; add a title. **OK**	

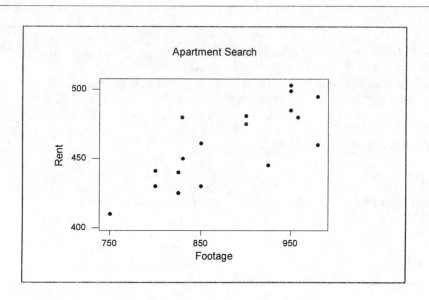

The scatter plot shows a moderate positive linear relationship between monthly rent and square footage. As we would expect, rent increases as the apartment size increases. The slope of the least squares line is positive.

Stat ▸ Basic Statistics ▸ Correlation
  Select Rent and Footage in **Variables**. **OK**

MTB > Correlation 'Rent' 'Footage'

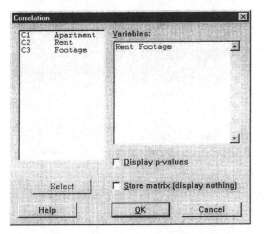

Correlations: Rent, Footage

Pearson correlation of Rent and Footage = 0.786

The coefficient of correlation $r = .786$, confirms the positive linear relationship that we observed in the scatter plot.

Stat ▸ Regression ▸ Regression
  Select Rent in **Response:**
  and Footage in **Predictors:**
Click **Results** and choose the second **Display. OK**

MTB > Regress 'Rent' 1 'Footage';
SUBC>   Constant;
SUBC>   Brief 1.

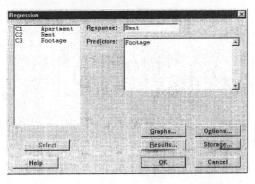

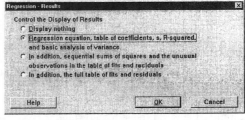

Regression Analysis: Rent versus Footage

```
The regression equation is
Rent = 184 + 0.314 Footage

Predictor          Coef      SE Coef          T          P
Constant         183.70        51.12       3.59      0.002
Footage         0.31364      0.05823       5.39      0.000

S = 17.60        R-Sq = 61.7%      R-Sq(adj) = 59.6%

Analysis of Variance

Source              DF           SS          MS          F          P
Regression           1       8986.6      8986.6      29.01      0.000
Residual Error      18       5575.1       309.7
Total               19      14561.7
```

Least Squares Regression Equation

The first part of the Minitab output gives the regression equation:

```
The regression equation is
Rent = 184 + 0.314 Footage
```

The y-intercept, $\hat{\beta}_0 = 184$, indicates the point at which the line crosses the y axis. In any application, the y-intercept has a practical interpretation only if the range of x values in the sample includes zero. Since the range of apartment square footage is from 750 to 980 square feet, the y-intercept has no practical interpretation in this example.

The slope, $\hat{\beta}_1 = 0.314$, is the estimated change in the mean value of y for every unit increase in x. We estimate monthly rent to increase an average of $0.31 for every 1 square foot increase in apartment size, or an average increase of $31 for every 100 square foot increase in apartment size.

Estimated Standard Error

An estimate of σ is s, the estimated standard error of the regression model. It appears on a line in the regression output before the analysis of variance table.

```
S = 17.60        R-Sq = 61.7%      R-Sq(adj) = 59.6%
```

The estimated standard error is an estimate of the variation of monthly rent from the fitted regression line. If the errors are approximately normal, we can apply the Empirical Rule and estimate that about 68% of all rents will be within $s = \$17.60$ of the fitted line, and about 95% of all rents will be within $2s = \$35.20$ of the fitted regression line.

Coefficient of Determination

The coefficient of determination r^2 is the square of the correlation coefficient, $r = .786$, usually expressed as a percent, $r^2(100)\%$. The coefficient is printed on the same line as s.

```
        S = 17.60        R-Sq = 61.7%        R-Sq(adj) = 59.6%
```

About 62% of the total sum of squared errors of monthly rents about their mean can be explained by using the least squares regression equation. We can reduce the sum of squares of prediction errors by about 62% by using the least squares equation $\hat{y}$, instead of $\bar{y}$, to predict monthly rent. The adjusted r^2 takes into account the degrees of freedom.

Sum of Squared Errors and Mean Squared Error

The sum of squared errors, SSE $= 5575.1$, appears in the analysis of variance table at the intersection of Error and SS. The least squares line minimizes the sum of squared errors.

The mean squared error, $s^2 = 309.7$, is an estimate of the variance σ^2 of the random error. It is in the analysis of variance table at the intersection of Error and MS. It is calculated by dividing the SSE by $(n - 2) = 18$ degrees of freedom.

```
    Analysis of Variance

    Source       DF        SS         MS         F         P
    Regression    1      8986.6     8986.6     29.01     0.000
    Error        18      5575.1      309.7
    Total        19     14561.8
```

Testing the Usefulness of the Model

To test whether the regression model is useful for predicting the amount of rent, we test whether the slope differs from 0. The null and alternative hypotheses are

$$H_0: \beta_1 = 0$$
$$H_a: \beta_1 \neq 0$$

The regression output gives the test statistic $t = 5.39$ and p-value $= 0$ for a two-tailed test in the columns labeled **T** and **P** in the regression coefficients table.

```
    Predictor        Coef        StDev        T         P
    Constant        183.70       51.12       3.59     0.002
    Footage        0.31364      0.05823      5.39     0.000
```

The *p*-value is the probability, assuming the slope is zero, of obtaining a *t*-ratio greater than 5.39 or less than -5.39. Since the *p*-value = 0, we have enough evidence to reject H_0 and conclude that the population slope of the regression model differs from 0 and that the model is useful.

Confidence Interval for the Slope

We can calculate a confidence interval for the slope using the estimates of the slope and standard error of the slope given in the regression coefficients table.

```
Predictor         Coef        StDev           T         P
Constant        183.70        51.12        3.59     0.002
Footage        0.31364      0.05823        5.39     0.000
```

The formula is $\hat{\beta}_1 \pm t_{\alpha/2}(\text{Stdev of } \hat{\beta}_1)$. We find the *t* value for a 95% confidence interval and $(n - 2) =$ 18 degrees of freedom using the *t* distribution There is no Minitab command to calculate the confidence interval, and may be easier with a hand calculator.

Calc ▸ Probability Distributions ▸ t
  Click **Inverse cumulative probability**;
  Enter 18 **Degrees of freedom:**
  Click **Input constant:** enter .975;
  Click **Optional storage:** enter 't'. **OK**

MTB > Name K1 = 't'
MTB > InvCDF .975 't';
SUBC> T 18.

Calc ▸ Calculator
  Enter 'Lower' in **Store result in variable:**
  Enter .31364 - t * .05823 in **Expression**. **OK**

MTB > Name C4 = 'Lower'
MTB > Let 'Lower' = .31364 -'t' * .05823

Calc ▸ Calculator
  Enter 'Upper' in **Store result in variable:**
  Enter .31364 + t * .05823 in **Expression**. **OK**

MTB > Name C5 = 'Upper'
MTB > Let 'Upper' = .31364 + 't' * .05823

Manip ▸ Display Data
  Select Lower and Upper in **Display**. **OK**

MTB > Print 'Lower' 'Upper'

Data Display

```
Row       Lower       Upper

  1     0.191303    0.435977
```

A 95% confidence interval for the slope is $0.19 to $0.44. We are 95% confident that the mean monthly rent increases between $0.19 and $0.44 for every 1 square foot increase in apartment area, or an increase of between $19 and $44 for every 100 square foot increase in apartment area.

Example of a Point Estimate of the Mean Monthly Rent

To illustrate a point estimate, we use the fitted regression equation to find the estimated mean monthly rent for all apartments that have 850 square feet of living area.

Rent = 184 + 0.314 Footage
Rent = 184 + 0.314 (850)
Rent = $451

Fitted Line Plot

The following plots the regression equation on a scatter plot of the data.

Stat ▸ Regression ▸ Fitted Line Plot
  Select Rent in **Response:**
   and Footage in **Predictor:**
  Click **Annotation**, choose **Title**, add a title. **OK**

MTB > %Fitline 'Rent' 'Footage';
SUBC> Confidence 95.0;
SUBC> Title "Apartment Search".

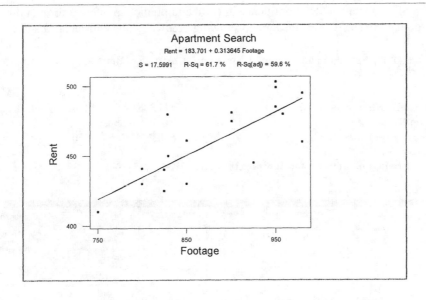

The **Fitted Line Plot** output includes most of the regression output in addition to a plot of the fitted line on a scatter plot. Notice that the fitted line extends from the minimum apartment size of 750 square feet to the maximum size of 980 square feet, emphasizing that all interpretations are limited to the range of x in the sample.

9.2 INTERVAL ESTIMATION AND PREDICTION

If there is a significant linear relationship between two variables and the model assumptions are satisfied, the regression equation can be used for estimation and prediction. You can use it to estimate the mean value of y for a specific value of x using a $(1 - \alpha)100\%$ confidence interval. Or you can use it to predict a particular value of y for a specific value of x using a $(1 - \alpha)100\%$ prediction interval.

The confidence interval is

$$\text{Fit} \pm t_{\alpha/2}(\text{Stdev. Fit})$$

and the prediction interval is

$$\text{Fit} \pm t_{\alpha/2}\sqrt{s^2 + \text{Stdev.Fit}^2}$$

■ Example 2   Confidence and Prediction Intervals

Refer to Example 1. Obtain a 95% confidence interval and prediction interval for monthly rent of an 850 square foot apartment. Construct a graph showing prediction and confidence bands.

Solution The data are saved in a file named **Apartment.mtp**. Columns are named Apartment, Rent and Footage.

Stat ▸ Regression ▸ Regression	MTB > Regress 'Rent' 1 'Footage';
Select Rent in **Response:**	SUBC> Constant;
and Footage in **Predictors:**	SUBC> Predict 850.
Click **Options**;	
Enter 850 in **Prediction intervals for new observations**. **OK**	

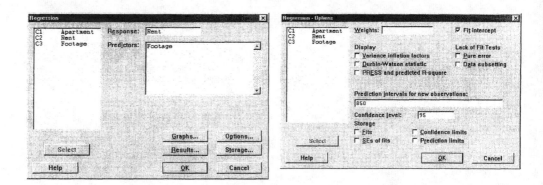

Regression Analysis: Rent versus Footage

```
The regression equation is
Rent = 184 + 0.314 Footage


(Some output omitted)


Predicted Values for New Observations


New Obs     Fit     SE Fit        95.0% CI              95.0% PI
1         450.30      4.20   (  441.47,  459.13) (  412.28,  488.31)


Values of Predictors for New Observations


New Obs    Footage
1              850
```

We are 95% confident that the mean monthly rent for all 850 square foot apartments is from $441 to $459. We are 95% confident that the monthly rent for a particular 850 square foot apartment is from $412 to $488.

The **Fitted Line Plot** provides the prediction and confidence bands.

Stat ▸ Regression ▸ Fitted Line Plot
  Select Rent in **Response:**
   and Footage in **Predictor:**
  Click **Options** and choose **Display confidence bands**
   and **Display prediction bands**;
  Click **Annotation**, choose **Title**; add a title. **OK**

MTB > %Fitline 'Rent' 'Footage';
SUBC>   Confidence 95.0;
SUBC>   Ci;
SUBC>   Pi;
SUBC>   Title "Apartment Search".

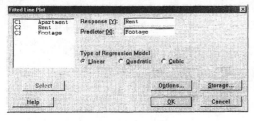

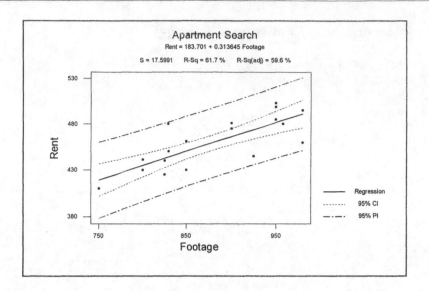

Both confidence and prediction bands are narrowest near the mean square footage. The confidence bands for mean rents are much closer to the fitted regression line than the prediction bands for individual rents: we can estimate mean rent with a greater degree of precision than we can predict an individual apartment rent.

■ **Example 3**   **Simple Linear Regression Problem**

The more digits in a number, the more difficult it is to remember. To illustrate this statement, a psychology professor ran an experiment in three sections of an introductory psychology course. He showed a number to the students for five seconds, waited five seconds, and then had the students write the number down. He than determined the percentage of students who wrote down the number correctly. The data is given in the following table. Conduct a regression analysis to determine the relationship between the percentage of students getting the number correct and the number of digits in the number.

Trial	Digits	%Correct	Section	Trial	Digits	%Correct	Section
1	7	100.0	1	22	10	24.3	2
2	7	97.2	1	23	11	8.1	2
3	8	44.4	1	24	11	21.6	2
4	8	80.6	1	25	12	0.0	2
5	9	52.7	1	26	12	13.5	2
6	9	22.0	1	27	13	8.1	2
7	10	8.3	1	28	13	0.0	2
8	10	25.0	1	29	7	82.8	3
9	11	11.1	1	30	7	85.7	3

10	11	25.0	1	31	8	71.4	3
11	12	0.0	1	32	8	62.8	3
12	12	5.5	1	33	9	40.0	3
13	13	0.0	1	34	9	40.0	3
14	13	0.0	1	35	10	8.6	3
15	7	86.5	2	36	10	20.2	3
16	7	86.5	2	37	11	2.8	3
17	8	56.8	2	38	11	8.6	3
18	8	73.0	2	39	12	0.0	3
19	9	43.2	2	40	12	8.6	3
20	9	32.4	2	41	13	2.8	3
21	10	10.8	2	42	13	0.0	3

Solution The data are saved in a file named **Memory.mtp**; columns are named as in the table above. We begin the analysis with a correlation analysis; the response variable y is the percentage correct and the predictor x is the number of digits in the number.

Stat ▸ Basic Statistics ▸ Correlation   MTB > Correlation 'Digits' '%Correct'
  Select Digits and %Correct in **Variables. OK**

Correlations: Digits, %Correct

Pearson correlation of Digits and %Correct = -0.916

The correlation coefficient, $r = -.916$, indicates a strong inverse linear relationship between the two variables.

The **Fitted Line Plot** provides a graph of the data. It also gives us output for studying the linear relationship between the two variables.

Stat ▸ Regression ▸ Fitted Line Plot   MTB > %Fitline '%Correct' 'Digits';
  Select %Correct in **Response:**   SUBC> Confidence 95.0.
  and Digits in **Predictor. OK**

Regression Analysis: %Correct versus Digits

The regression equation is
%Correct = 179.027 - 14.6387 Digits

S = 13.1454   R-Sq = 83.9 %   R-Sq(adj) = 83.5 %

Analysis of Variance

Source	DF	SS	MS	F	P
Regression	1	36000.9	36000.9	208.337	0.000
Error	40	6912.1	172.8		
Total	41	42913.0			

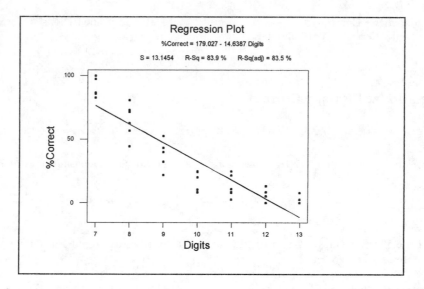

The scatter plot shows a strong inverse relationship between the digits in a number and the percentage of students getting the number correct. However, it appears as though the relationship could be curvilinear. We revisit this example in the next chapter when we study curvilinear relationships.

Least Squares Regression Equation

The regression equation is $\hat{y} = 179 - 14.6x$.

The y-intercept, $\hat{\beta}_0 = 179$, is the estimated percentage of students getting the number correct for a 0-digit number. Since 0 is out of the range of digits in the sample, the y-intercept has no practical interpretation. The slope, $\hat{\beta}_1 = -14.6$, is the estimated decrease in the mean percentage correct for each one digit increase.

Estimated Standard Error

An estimate of σ is $s = 13.15$, the estimated standard error of the regression model. We would expect most actual y values to fall within $2s$ or approximately 26 percentage points of the least squares line.

Coefficient of Determination

The coefficient of determination is $r^2 = 83.9\%$. The linear relationship can explain about 84% of the variation in percentage correct.

Testing the Usefulness of the Model

To test whether the regression model is useful, we test whether the slope differs from 0. The null and alternative hypotheses are

$$H_0: \beta_1 = 0$$
$$H_a: \beta_1 \neq 0$$

The regression output gives the test statistic $t = -14.43$. Since the p-value = 0, there is sufficient evidence to reject H_0 and conclude that the model is useful.

Using the Model

We use the model to estimate the mean percentage correct for a 10-digit number.

Stat ▸ Regression ▸ Regression
  Select %Correct in **Response:**
   and Digits in **Predictors:**
  Click **Options** and enter 10
   in **Prediction intervals for new observations. OK**

MTB > Regress '%Correct' 1 'Digits';
SUBC> Constant;
SUBC> Predict 10.

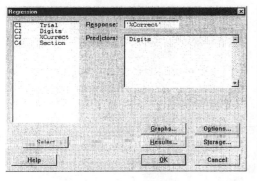

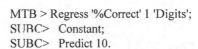

Regression Analysis: %Correct versus Digits

```
The regression equation is
%Correct = 179 - 14.6 Digits

(Some output omitted)

Predicted Values for New Observations

New Obs    Fit    SE Fit        95.0% CI           95.0% PI
1         32.64    2.03    (  28.54,   36.74) (   5.76,   59.52)
Values of Predictors for New Observations

New Obs    Digits
1           10.0
```

A point estimate of the true mean percentage correct for a number with 10 digits is $\hat{y} = 32.6\%$. We are 95% confident that the true mean percentage correct is between 28.5% and 36.7% for 10 digit numbers.

EXERCISES

1. The Minnesota Real Estate Research Center compiled data on the homes sold in St. Cloud, Minnesota during 1998. The selling prices y and living areas in square feet x of 20 homes are given in the following table. (File: **StCloud.mtp**)

Home	Price	Area	Home	Price	Area
1	$ 86,000	870	11	$118,900	2,052
2	86,600	840	12	125,000	1,590
3	92,000	1,032	13	130,600	1,600
4	92,500	1,168	14	139,875	2,044
5	93,500	1,100	15	144,400	1,916
6	94,000	1,430	16	148,000	2,024
7	104,000	1,520	17	156,000	1,840
8	104,500	1,468	18	151,900	1,684
9	109,900	1,160	19	159,500	1,760
10	111,900	1,800	20	163,000	2,260

a. What is the average square footage and selling price of the homes in the sample?
b. Construct a scatter plot and find the correlation coefficient. Interpret.
c. Determine the least squares regression equation. Give a practical interpretation of the parameter estimates and s.
d. Test whether there is a significant linear relationship between selling price and area. Use α = .05.
e. Interpret the coefficient of determination.

2. The Minnesota Real Estate Research Center provided the following table on the selling prices and living areas in square feet of 20 homes randomly selected from the homes sold during 1998 in Rochester, Minnesota. (File: **Rochester.mtp**)

Home	Price	Area	Home	Price	Area
1	$107,800	1,163	11	$ 115,900	1,460
2	93,000	1,280	12	129,000	1,500
3	94,900	1,486	13	132,330	1,576
4	98,000	1,360	14	136,000	1,444
5	101,500	1,440	15	133,925	1,546
6	104,000	1,240	16	175,000	1,933
7	116,000	1,437	17	184,000	2,474
8	109,900	1,272	18	169,900	2,208
9	114,500	1,553	19	165,500	1,936
10	120,750	1,320	20	189,195	2,602

a. Construct and interpret a scatter plot of selling price versus area. Calculate the correlation coefficient. Would a simple linear regression model describe the relationship between the two variables?
b. Use the REGRESS command to find the least squares regression line. Interpret the coefficients and s.

c. Test the usefulness of the hypothesized model. Use $\alpha = .05$.
d. Interpret r^2.
e. If the model is useful, estimate the mean selling price of Rochester homes with living area of 1,500 square feet. Use a 95% confidence interval.

3. An important factor in maintaining employee satisfaction and productivity is adequate compensation for an employee's responsibilities. The personnel manager needs to continually monitor salaries for certain job types, and should compare these salaries with the salaries of the industry. The following table gives job titles, job evaluation points, and comparative starting salaries for 11 jobs in a data processing department. Each job has been assigned points based on responsibilities and requirements. The salaries are the industry benchmark weekly starting salary from the *Occupational Outlook* and the actual starting salary in the department. The objectives of the study are to determine whether any actual salaries are out of line with the industry, and to analyze the relationship between job points and industry benchmark salaries.
    (File: **JobStudy.mtp**)

Job Title	Job Points	Industry Salary	Actual Salary
File Clerk	250	240	220
Data Entry	340	240	250
Receptionist	365	255	300
Wood Processor	390	265	245
General Office Clerk	450	250	255
Computer Operator	490	280	300
Secretary	505	290	330
Accounting Clerk	530	290	280
Statistical Clerk	540	290	300
Programmer	620	330	320
System Analyst I	770	355	400

a. Plot industry salary versus job points and actual salary versus job points on the same graph. Discuss.
b. Find the least squares regression equation that relates industry salary y to job points x. Interpret the regression coefficients.
c. Do the data provide sufficient evidence of a linear relationship between industry salary and job points? Test using $\alpha = .01$.
d. Do any actual salaries in the data processing department seem out of line with industry standards? Explain.

4. As part of a group project in a 1998 statistics course fall semester, students collected data on department, gender, highest degree, years of experience, and salary of college faculty. The data on years of experience and salary follow. Conduct a regression analysis to determine the relationship between the faculty salary y and the years of experience x.
    (File: **FacultySalaries.mtp**)

Faculty	Years	Salary	Faculty	Years	Salary
1	20.3	$65,461	31	10.0	$73,414
2	6.0	67,984	32	15.0	63,057
3	8.3	73,414	33	8.0	70,633
4	14.0	73,414	34	6.0	65,461
5	17.5	73,414	35	12.0	63,057
6	11.5	60,769	36	17.0	65,461
7	29.0	73,414	37	7.0	63,057
8	12.0	73,414	38	*	67,984
9	4.6	73,414	39	11.0	65,461
10	1.5	58,590	40	11.0	63,057
11	9.0	70,633	41	7.0	65,461
12	5.0	58,590	42	9.0	63,057
13	17.0	73,414	43	*	73,414
14	11.5	73,414	44	8.0	67,984
15	6.3	65,461	45	4.0	70,633
16	5.0	73,414	46	17.0	73,414
17	7.0	65,461	47	18.0	73,414
18	12.0	67,984	48	16.0	67,984
19	0.5	73,414	49	*	70,633
20	7.0	73,414	50	0.3	73,414
21	2.7	65,461	51	9.5	73,414
22	12.0	70,633	52	5.3	73,414
23	12.8	58,590	53	6.0	65,461
24	6.0	65,461	54	3.0	60,769
25	5.0	67,984	55	17.8	73,414
26	*	67,984	56	2.9	73,414
27	6.0	65,461	57	10.0	73,414
28	1.0	58,590	58	7.5	60,769
29	14.0	65,461	59	13.0	63,057
30	5.0	60,769			

5. Consider the class data set described in the Appendix. (File: **StudentInfo.mtp**)

    a. Analyze the relationship between the grade point averages reported by the students and their true grade point averages as reported by the university.
    b. Consider only male students. Analyze the relationship between the grade point averages reported by male students and their true grade point averages as reported by the university.
    c. Repeat part b for female students. Compare the results.

6. Consider the student data set described in the Appendix. Analyze the relationship between grade point averages and number of hours worked for all students. What assumptions are necessary for the statistical analysis? (File: **StudentInfo.mtp**)

7. A survey conducted by the UCLA Graduate School of Management on the status of computer development in business schools is reported in the *Sixteenth Annual UCLA Survey of Business School Computer Usage*, November 1999. The survey queries business schools on hardware, software, and resource commitments. The following random sample of 25 schools provides the

sample of 35 schools provides the number of full time equivalent undergraduate students, the number of full time equivalent faculty, the ratio of the computer operating budget to full time equivalent students, the operating budget in thousands of dollars, and the type of institution.

The variable of interest in this exercise is operating budget. Numerically and graphically analyze the data. Conduct a correlation and simple linear regression analysis to explain the variation in operating budget. Prepare a report of the statistical analysis. Include numerical and graphical output. (File: **UCLA.mtp**)

School	UGrad	Faculty	Ratio	Budget	Type
1	1,000	85	70.0	$ 84	Public
2	868	56	114.0	142	Private
3	608	*	120.8	83	Public
4	4,115	285	205.5	1,100	Public
5	400	23	160.0	80	Private
6	937	44	187.4	200	Public
7	3,136	112	167.0	556	Private
8	3,640	260	1,762.1	8,000	Private
9	2,368	105	147.0	434	Private
10	1,540	118	390.2	876	Private
11	4,500	110	19.4	107	Private
12	2,619	149	500.5	1,433	Private
13	550	71	1,191.3	1,700	Public
14	1,250	52	119.1	155	Public
15	715	14	187.5	195	Private
16	296	92	1,041.6	1,282	Private
17	867	39	155.9	147	Public
18	6,000	150	50.4	335	Public
19	248	14	85.0	38	Private
20	630	36	128.3	107	Private
21	3,251	109	38.2	132	Public
22	200	40	107.1	75	Public
23	630	70	59.8	75	Public
24	1,789	80	192.2	463	Public
25	815	40	56.1	65	Private
26	572	25	215.6	130	Public
27	815	40	56.1	65	Private
28	606	65	196.9	190	Public
29	916	42	120.1	125	Public
30	750	23	6.3	5	Private
31	547	69	718.9	873	Private
32	2,200	84	164.1	370	Public
33	5,272	95	110.3	661	Public
34	1,007	128	78.8	210	Private
35	5,000	110	97.3	527	Public

CHAPTER 10

MULTIPLE REGRESSION

In multiple regression, several independent variables are used to describe the variation in a response variable. This chapter illustrates several multiple regression models and residual analysis. We include first-order models, quadratic models, models with qualitative variables. The same Minitab commands of simple linear regression analysis apply in multiple regression analysis.

NEW COMMAND

CORRELATION	INDICATOR	MATRIXPLOT	REGRESS
STEPWISE	%RESPLOTS		

10.1 THE GENERAL LINEAR MODEL

Often, a simple linear regression model containing a single independent variable inadequately describes the variation in a response variable. Predictions of the response variable are too imprecise to be meaningful. In some cases, more than one independent variable may significantly affect the response variable, and a multiple linear regression model may better estimate or predict the value of a response variable. The general form of the model with response variable y and k independent variables $x_1, x_2, ..., x_k$ is

$$y = \beta_0 + \beta_1 x_1 + \beta_2 x_2 + ... + \beta_k x_k + \epsilon$$

where $\beta_0, \beta_1, ..., \beta_k$ are the parameters we wish to estimate and ϵ is the random error term. As before, ϵ accounts for the variability in y that the independent variables in the model do not explain. The model assumes that the errors are independent, and that the probability distribution of ϵ is normal, with zero mean and a constant variance σ^2 for all values of $x_1, x_2, ..., x_k$.

In multiple regression analysis, knowing the type and strength of the relationship between each pair of variables is important. A plot of the response variable versus each independent variable and a correlation analysis provide useful information about the relationships. The Plot command plots one scatter plot at a time, or the Matrix Plot plots all scatter plots. The forms of the correlation and regression commands are about the same as those introduced in Chapter 9.

MATRIX PLOT OF SCATTER PLOTS

A matrix plot is a two-dimensional matrix of separate scatter plots for pairs of variables. There are two options for the matrix plots. In the first option, all pairwise combinations of the variables are displayed. In the second form, called a draftsman plot, only pairwise combinations of the *y*-variable with the independent variables are displayed.

Graph ▸ Matrix Plot
Graph ▸ Draftsman Plot

MATRIXPLOT C ... C	Displays all pairwise combinations
MATRIXPLOT C ... C * C ... C	Displays draftsman plot; list *y*-variable before the asterisk, and *x*-variables after

CORRELATION COEFFICIENTS

The Pearson product moment correlation coefficient is calculated between every pair of columns. The lower triangle of the correlation matrix is printed.

Stat ▸ Basic Statistics ▸ Correlation

CORRELATION C ... C	Displays correlations between all pairs

MULTIPLE REGRESSION

This command determines the multiple linear regression equation using the least squares method. The output includes the regression equation; a table of coefficients, standard deviations, and *t*-ratios; s and R^2; and the analysis of variance table. The optional prediction output includes $\hat{y}$, the standard deviation of $\hat{y}$, and 95% confidence and prediction intervals for specified values of the predictors. You need to enter a value for every predictor. The values may be stored in K columns or as constants.

Stat ▸ Regression ▸ Regression

REGRESS C *on* K *predictors* C ... C	Fits the least squares regression equation
RESIDUALS C	Stores residuals
PREDICT E ... E	Predicts values
BRIEF	Controls output

The BRIEF command described in Chapter 9 entered before REGRESS or as a subcommand changes the amount and type of regression output. BRIEF 2, the default output of the REGRESS command, prints the regression equation, table of coefficients, s, r^2 and r^2-adjusted, sequential analysis of variance table provided there are two or more predictors, and unusual observations.

Consider the following example. Suppose the response is in column C1 and the independent variables are in columns C2, C3, and C4. The Minitab commands for the scatter plots, correlation matrix, and a first-order linear model are

Graph ▸ Matrix Plot   MTB > Matrix C1-C4
  Select C1 C2 C3 and C4 in **Graph Variables**.

Stat ▸ Basic Statistics ▸ Correlation   MTB > Correlation C1-C4
  Select C1 C2 C3 and C4 in **Variables**.

Stat ▸ Regression ▸ Regression   MTB > Regress C1 3 C2-C4
  Select C1 in **Response:**
  Select C2 - C4 in **Predictors**.

We want a high correlation between y and each x. But if the correlation is high between any pair of independent variables, the regression coefficients may be statistically affected. This problem is called **multicollinearity**.

THE FIRST-ORDER LINEAR MODEL

The first-order model is linear in the independent variables. Use the model if the variables independently affect the response variable; that is, if the independent variables do not interact. For example, the first-order regression model for three independent variables is

$$y = \beta_0 + \beta_1 x_1 + \beta_2 x_2 + \beta_3 x_3 + \epsilon$$

The y-intercept β_0 is the value of the mean response when each independent variable is zero. The ith parameter β_i represents the change in the mean value of y for a one unit change in x_i, provided all other variables are held constant.

Analogous to simple linear regression, in which the regression equation is a line, the graph of a first-order regression equation is a hyperplane. For two independent variables, the graph is a three-dimensional plane.

■ **Example 1**   **Multiple Regression Analysis**

When a house needs to be appraised for a mortgage or property taxes, the appraiser typically approaches the problem by selecting four to six comparable homes in the area which have sold recently. Then the price is adjusted up or down to reflect differences between comparable homes and the home in question. However, if homeowners just want to know what their home is worth and don't require an official appraisal, they can obtain information on homes in their area from local realtors or the homes-for-sale section of a paper. Suppose a homeowner in a residential area is interested in predicting the value of her home, and has gathered the following data on homes for sale in her area. The objective is to develop a useful regression model.

House	Price	Bedrooms	SqFtArea	Age
1	$118,000	3	2,300	31
2	137,500	4	2,700	12
3	116,000	3	2,295	31
4	113,900	3	2,052	11
5	123,000	4	1,884	30
6	97,000	3	1,400	25
7	126,000	3	2,288	15
8	112,000	4	2,200	15
9	118,000	4	1,623	30
10	128,000	4	2,716	21
11	118,900	3	1,650	6
12	118,000	3	1,600	30
13	131,130	3	2,398	20
14	140,000	4	2,200	17
15	127,500	3	1,900	24
16	121,900	3	2,113	16
17	146,000	4	2,466	6
18	154,000	4	2,071	6
19	98,000	3	1,724	26
20	176,000	3	2,620	18
21	98,000	2	915	5
22	85,500	3	1,200	27
23	89,900	4	1,671	37
24	93,900	3	1,700	18
25	91,500	3	1,212	16
26	102,000	3	1,952	15
27	115,000	3	1,500	21
28	106,000	2	1,120	7
29	94,700	3	1,820	40
30	109,000	3	2,404	21
31	69,000	2	1,020	14
32	83,500	3	1,128	9
33	82,450	3	1,268	35
34	179,900	4	3,150	17
35	103,000	3	1,162	6
36	101,900	4	1,997	22

Solution   The data are saved in a file named **Appraisal.mtp**; columns are named House, Price, Bedrooms, SqFtArea, and Age.   To develop the model, we construct scatter plots to study the relationship between the response variable and each independent variable, and calculate correlations between all pairs of variables. We consider the first-order linear model

$$y = \beta_0 + \beta_1 x_1 + \beta_2 x_2 + \beta_3 x_3 + \epsilon$$

with y = Price, x_1 = bedrooms, x_2 = area, and x_3 = age.

Graph ▸ Matrix Plot
  Select Price, Bedrooms, SqFtArea, and Age
   in **Graph Variables:**
  Click **Options**, choose **Upper right Matrix Display. OK**

```
MTB > MatrixPlot 'Price' - 'Age';
SUBC>   Symbol;
SUBC>   UR.
```

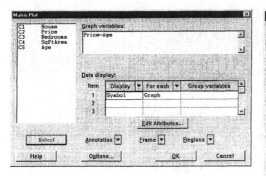

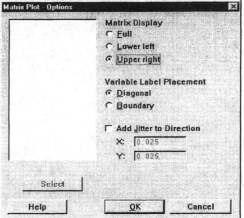

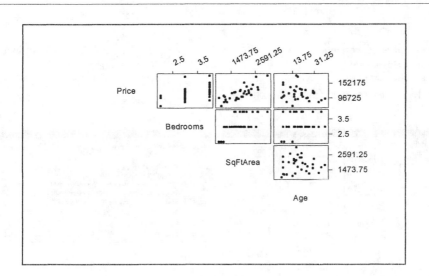

The scatter plots in the first row of the matrix show the relationships between the response variable and the independent variables. The first scatter plot indicates a positive relationship between price and number of bedrooms. The second scatter plot shows a positive relationship between price and area of the home, and the last scatter plot in the first row shows a negative relationship between price and age. The other three scatter plots show the relationship between pairs of independent variables. As we expect, the scatter plot of bedrooms and area shows that the area increases as the number of bedrooms increases.

Stat ▸ Basic Statistics ▸ Correlation   MTB > Correlation 'Price'-'Age'
   Select Price, Bedrooms, SqFtArea, and Age
   in **Variables. OK**

Correlations: Price, Bedrooms, SqFtArea, Age

```
            Price Bedrooms SqFtArea
Bedrooms   0.474
SqFtArea   0.785     0.584
Age       -0.221     0.159    0.038

Cell Contents: Pearson correlation
```

The moderate to high correlations between sale price and number of bedrooms, and sale price and area in square feet, support the evidence found in the scatter plots. The highest correlation is between sale price and area of the home. The moderately high correlation between number of bedrooms and area indicates possible multicollinearity.

Stat ▸ Regression ▸ Regression   MTB > Regress 'Price' 3 'Bedrooms'-'Age';
   Select Price in **Response:**   SUBC>   Constant;
   Select Bedrooms, SqFtArea, and Age in Predictors: SUBC>   Brief 1.
   Click **Results** and choose the second **Display. OK**

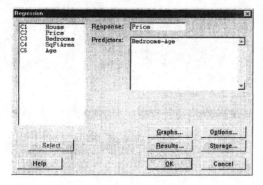
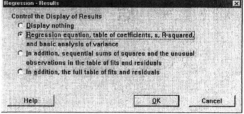

Regression Analysis: Price versus Bedrooms, SqFtArea, Age

```
The regression equation is
Price = 54686 + 3232 Bedrooms + 33.4 SqFtArea - 672 Age

Predictor         Coef      SE Coef           T          P
Constant         54686        13821        3.96      0.000
Bedrooms          3232         5151        0.63      0.535
SqFtArea        33.419        5.474        6.11      0.000
Age             -672.2        258.9       -2.60      0.014


S = 14403        R-Sq = 68.4%      R-Sq(adj) = 65.4%


Analysis of Variance

Source          DF           SS           MS          F        P
Regression       3  14355618414   4785206138      23.07    0.000
Residual Error  32   6637888586    207434018
Total           35  20993507000
```

Least Squares Regression Equation

The first-order linear model

$$y = \beta_0 + \beta_1 x_1 + \beta_2 x_2 + \beta_3 x_3 + \epsilon$$

with x_1 = bedrooms, x_2 = area, and x_3 = age, is fit to the data. The first part of the Minitab output gives the regression equation:

```
The regression equation is
Price = 54686 + 3232 Bedrooms + 33.4 SqFtArea - 672 Age
```

The y-intercept $\hat{\beta}_0$ = \$54,686 is the estimated value of a home with x_1 = 0, x_2 = 0, and x_3 = 0 or no bedrooms, no area, and no age. Since these values are outside the ranges of the sample data, $\hat{\beta}_0$ has no practical interpretation. The slope $\hat{\beta}_1$ = \$3,232 is the estimated change in the mean home value for an increase of one bedroom, holding area and age constant. $\hat{\beta}_2$ and $\hat{\beta}_3$ have similar interpretations.

Estimated Standard Error

An estimate of σ^2, the error variance, is s^2 = 207,434,018, located in the analysis of variance table at the intersection of Error and MS. An estimate of σ, the standard deviation of the random error, is s = \$14,403. We expect this equation to predict the home value to within $2s$, or approximately \$28,806, of its true value.

Coefficient of Determination

The coefficient of determination is $R^2 = 68.4\%$. Approximately 68% of the total variation in home prices is explained by the regression model; 32% is not explained by the regression model.

Testing the Usefulness of the Model

This section describes some hypothesis tests to determine whether the model is useful in predicting sale price. To test whether the overall model is useful, the null and alternative hypotheses are:

H_0: $\beta_1 = \beta_2 = \beta_3 = 0$
H_a: At least one parameter differs from 0

The test statistic $F = 23.07$ and the p-value = 0.000 are given in the analysis of variance table. Since the p-value is 0, we would reject H_0 for any α level. We have strong evidence to conclude the model is useful for predicting the sale price of residential property.

Testing the Usefulness of the Predictors

Next we test the usefulness of the predictors. Although we could test any one of the three predictors, we will test the least useful predictor. The least useful predictor is the one with the highest p-value, which in this example is the number of bedrooms.

To test whether the number of bedrooms, x_1, contributes significant information to predict y, the null and alternative hypotheses are:

H_0: $\beta_1 = 0$
H_a: $\beta_1 \neq 0$

The t-ratio and p-value for the test are given in the regression coefficients table.

Predictor	Coef	StDev	T	P
Bedrooms	3232	5151	0.63	0.535

We do not reject the null hypothesis that $\beta_1 = 0$ because of the high p-value = 0.535. There is not sufficient evidence that the number of bedrooms is a useful predictor.

Our New Model

Since we found that number of bedrooms is not a useful predictor, we remove it from the model. We run the regression analysis again using area and age as predictors

Stat ▸ Regression ▸ Regression
  Select Price in **Response:**
  Select SqFtArea and Age in **Predictors:**
  Click **Results** and choose the second **Display. OK**

MTB > Regress 'Price' 2 'SqFtArea' 'Age';
SUBC>   Constant;
SUBC>   Brief 1.

Regression Analysis: Price versus SqFtArea, Age

```
The regression equation is
Price = 60794 + 35.4 SqFtArea - 645 Age

Predictor          Coef      SE Coef           T          P
Constant          60794         9720        6.25      0.000
SqFtArea         35.432        4.393        8.06      0.000
Age              -644.7        252.8       -2.55      0.016


S = 14270         R-Sq = 68.0%       R-Sq(adj) = 66.1%

Analysis of Variance

Source             DF           SS          MS          F          P
Regression          2  14273985150  7136992575      35.05      0.000
Residual Error     33   6719521850   203621874
Total              35  20993507000
```

The New Model

We fit the first-order linear model to predict the sale price of homes:

$$y = \beta_0 + \beta_1 x_1 + \beta_2 x_2 + \epsilon$$

where x_1 = area and x_2 = age.

To test whether this model is useful for predicting home value, the hypotheses are:

H_0: $\beta_1 = \beta_2 = 0$
H_a: At least one parameter differs from 0

The test statistic $F = 35.05$ and the p-value = 0.000 are given in the analysis of variance table. Since the p-value is 0, we would reject H_0 for any α level. We have strong evidence to conclude the model is useful for predicting the value of residential property.

The p-values of both predictors are less than $\alpha = .05$. We conclude that both area and age of homes are useful predictors.

The Least Squares Regression Equation

```
The regression equation is
Price = 60794 + 35.4 SqFtArea - 645 Age
```

The y-intercept $\hat{\beta}_0 = \$60,794$ is the estimated price of a property with $x_1 = 0$ and $x_2 = 0$, or houses with no area and no age. Since these values are outside the ranges of the sample data, $\hat{\beta}_0$ has no practical interpretation. The slope $\hat{\beta}_1 = \$35.40$ is the estimated change in the mean sale price per one square foot increase in area, for a fixed age. The slope $\hat{\beta}_2 = -\$645$ is the estimated change in the mean price for each additional year in age, for a fixed value of area.

An estimate of σ^2, the error variance, is $s^2 = 203,621,874$, located in the analysis of variance table at the intersection of Error and MS. An estimate of σ, the standard deviation of the random error, is $s = \$14,270$. We expect the model to predict the sale price to within $2s$, or approximately \$28,540, of its true value. This is slightly lower than the first model.

The coefficient of determination is about the same: $R^2 = 68.0\%$. Approximately 68% of the total variation in sale prices is explained by the regression model.

Confidence Interval for a Parameter

A 95% confidence interval for the area parameter, β_1, is defined

$$\hat{\beta}_1 \pm t_{\alpha/2}(\text{Stdev}(\hat{\beta}_1))$$

The coefficient $\hat{\beta}_1$ and its standard deviation are found in the regression coefficients table. The estimates are labeled Coef and Stdev.

Predictor	Coef	StDev	T	P
SqFtArea	35.432	4.393	8.06	0.000
Age	-644.7	252.8	-2.55	0.016

The inverse probability distribution gives the $t_{\alpha/2}$ value for $[n - (k + 1)]$ degrees of freedom. Since $\alpha/2$ is the area in the upper tail, the cumulative area to the left of the t value is $1 - \alpha/2$. For a 95% confidence interval, $1 - \alpha/2 = .975$ and degrees of freedom $(n - 3) = 33$.

Calc ▸ Probability Distributions ▸ t
  Click **Inverse cumulative probability**;
  Enter 33 in **Degrees of freedom:**
  Click **Input constant:** enter .975;
  Click **Optional storage**, enter 't'. **OK**
	MTB > Name K1 = 't'
	MTB > InvCDF .975 't';
	SUBC> T 33.

Calc ▸ Calculator
  Enter 'Lower' in **Store results in variable:**
  Enter 35.432-t*4.393 in **Expression. OK**
	MTB > Name C6 = 'Lower'
	MTB > Let 'Lower' = 35.432 - t * 4.393

Calc ▸ Calculator
  Enter 'Upper' in **Store results in variable:**
  Enter 35.432+t*4.393 in **Expression. OK**
	MTB > Name C7 = 'Upper'
	MTB > Let 'Upper' = 35.432 + t * 4.393

Manip ▸ Display Data **Select** Lower and Upper in **Display. OK**	MTB > Print 'Lower' 'Upper'

Data Display

```
Row      Lower      Upper

  1     26.4944    44.3696
```

We are 95% confidence that the increase in the mean price is $26.49 to $44.37 for a one square foot increase in area, for a fixed age.

■ **Example 2**   **Prediction and Estimation**

Refer to the multiple regression model in Example 1. Suppose a homeowner in the residential area under study has a 15-year-old home with four bedrooms and 2,050 square feet of finished living area. Construct and interpret 95% confidence and prediction intervals.

Solution   Since the model with predictors, area and age, is useful, we construct and interpret 95% confidence and prediction intervals for a home with an area of 2,050 square feet and an age of 15 years.

Stat ▸ Regression ▸ Regression   MTB > Regress 'Price' 2 'SqFtArea' 'Age';
  Select Price in **Response:**   SUBC>   Constant;
  Select SqFtArea and Age in **Predictors:**   SUBC>   Predict 2050 15;
  Click **Options**, enter 2050 and 15   SUBC>   Brief 1.
   in **Prediction intervals for new observations**;
  Click **Results** and choose the second **Display. OK**

Regression Analysis: Price versus SqFtArea, Age

```
The regression equation is
Price = 60794 + 35.4 SqFtArea - 645 Age

(Some output omitted)

Predicted Values for New Observations

New Obs     Fit     SE Fit        95.0% CI             95.0% PI
1         123759     2755   (  118154,  129364)  (  94191,  153327)

Values of Predictors for New Observations

New Obs   SqFtArea        Age
1             2050       15.0
```

A point estimate for the value of the home is $123,759. A 95% confidence interval for the mean value of all homes with 2,050 square feet and 15 years of age is $118,154 to $129,364. A 95% prediction interval for the value of a particular home with 2,050 square feet and 15 years of age is $94,191 to $153,327.

SECOND-ORDER LINEAR MODELS

A second-order polynomial model expresses a curvilinear relationship between a response variable and one or more independent variables. The model with one independent variable includes a second-order term, x^2. If the parameter for x^2 is positive, the graph opens upward. If the parameter for x^2 is negative, the graph opens downward. The form of the model, called a quadratic model, is

$$y = \beta_0 + \beta_1 x + \beta_2 x^2 + \epsilon$$

A complete second-order model with two independent variables is

$$y = \beta_0 + \beta_1 x_1 + \beta_2 x_2 + \beta_3 x_1 x_2 + \beta_4 x_1^2 + \beta_5 x_2^2 + \epsilon$$

where β_0 is the y-intercept, $\beta_1 x_1$ and $\beta_2 x_2$ are the first-order terms, $\beta_3 x_1 x_2$ is the interaction or cross-product term, $\beta_4 x_1^2$ and $\beta_5 x_2^2$ are the quadratic terms. Two variables interact if the effect of changes in one variable on the mean response variable depends on the value of the other independent variable. As before, ϵ accounts for the variability in y that the independent variables in the model do not explain. The multiple regression model assumes that the errors are independent, and that the probability distribution of ϵ is normal, with zero mean and a constant variance σ^2 for any set of values of the independent variables.

The graph of a complete second-order regression equation is generally a complex three-dimensional response surface, such as a paraboloid or a saddle surface. There are many variations to the complete model; a comprehensive graphical and numerical data analysis will help you choose an appropriate model.

■ **Example 3**   **Second-Order Model**

Example 3 of Chapter 9 described the following experiment. The more digits in a number, the more difficult it is to remember. To illustrate this statement, a psychology professor ran an experiment in three sections of an introductory psychology course. He showed a number to the students for five seconds, waited five seconds, and then had the students write the number down. He than determined the percentage of students who wrote down the number correctly. The data is given in the following table. Does a quadratic model provide a better fit than the linear model found in Chapter 9? Discuss.

Trial	Digits	%Correct	Section	Trial	Digits	%Correct	Section
1	7	100.0	1	22	10	24.3	2
2	7	97.2	1	23	11	8.1	2
3	8	44.4	1	24	11	21.6	2
4	8	80.6	1	25	12	0.0	2
5	9	52.7	1	26	12	13.5	2
6	9	22.0	1	27	13	8.1	2
7	10	8.3	1	28	13	0.0	2
8	10	25.0	1	29	7	82.8	3
9	11	11.1	1	30	7	85.7	3
10	11	25.0	1	31	8	71.4	3
11	12	0.0	1	32	8	62.8	3
12	12	5.5	1	33	9	40.0	3
13	13	0.0	1	34	9	40.0	3
14	13	0.0	1	35	10	8.6	3
15	7	86.5	2	36	10	20.2	3
16	7	86.5	2	37	11	2.8	3
17	8	56.8	2	38	11	8.6	3
18	8	73.0	2	39	12	0.0	3
19	9	43.2	2	40	12	8.6	3
20	9	32.4	2	41	13	2.8	3
21	10	10.8	2	42	13	0.0	3

Solution The data are saved in a file named **Memory.mtp**; columns are named as above. The second-order model is

$$y = ß_0 + ß_1 x + ß_2 x^2 + \epsilon$$

where y = Digits and x = %Correct. Minitab has two procedures to fit a second-order model to the data: Fitted Line Plot and Regression. We illustrate both; the testing and interpretation follow both outputs. The Fitted Line Plot command provides some regression output and plots the line on the scatter plot.

Stat ▸ Regression ▸ Fitted Line Plot
  Select %Correct in **Response(Y):**
  Select Digits in **Predictor(X):**
  Choose **Quadratic Regression Model. OK**

MTB > %Fitline '%Correct' 'Digits';
SUBC>   Poly 2;
SUBC>   Confidence 95.0.

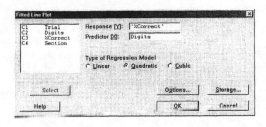

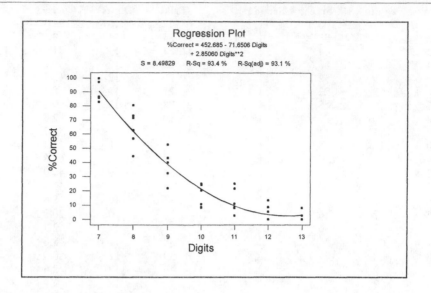

Polynomial Regression Analysis: %Correct versus Digits

```
The regression equation is
%Correct = 452.685 - 71.6506 Digits
 + 2.85060 Digits**2


S = 8.49829       R-Sq = 93.4 %       R-Sq(adj) = 93.1 %

Analysis of Variance

Source            DF          SS          MS          F         P
Regression         2      40096.4     20048.2    277.595    0.000
Error             39       2816.6        72.2
Total             41      42913.0


Source      DF     Seq SS           F        P
Linear       1    36000.9     208.337    0.000
Quadratic    1     4095.5      56.707    0.000
```

This plot shows a curvilinear relationship between the digits in a number and the percentage of students getting the number correct.

The Regression command requires that we create a column of x^2 values, but provides more output than Fitted Line Plot.

Calc ▸ Calculator
  Enter 'DigitsSq' in **Store results in variable:**
  Enter Digits**2 in **Expression. OK**

Stat ▸ Regression ▸ Regression
  Select %Correct in **Response:**
  Select Digits and DigitsSq in **Predictors: OK**

MTB > Name C5 = 'DigitsSq'
MTB > Let 'DigitsSq' = Digits**2

MTB > Regress '%Correct' 2 'Digits' 'DigitsSq';
SUBC> Constant;
SUBC> Brief 2.

Regression Analysis: %Correct versus Digits, DigitsSq

```
The regression equation is
%Correct = 453 - 71.7 Digits + 2.85 DigitsSq

Predictor        Coef     SE Coef         T        P
Constant       452.68       36.95     12.25    0.000
Digits        -71.651        7.599     -9.43    0.000
DigitsSq        2.8506       0.3785     7.53    0.000

S = 8.498       R-Sq = 93.4%     R-Sq(adj) = 93.1%

Analysis of Variance

Source             DF          SS         MS         F        P
Regression          2       40096      20048    277.59    0.000
Residual Error     39        2817         72
Total              41       42913

Source      DF      Seq SS
Digits       1       36001
DigitsSq     1        4095

Unusual Observations
Obs    Digits    %Correct      Fit    SE Fit    Residual    St Resid
  3       8.0       44.40    61.92      1.85      -17.52       -2.11R
  4       8.0       80.60    61.92      1.85       18.68        2.25R
  6       9.0       22.00    38.73      1.85      -16.73       -2.02R

R denotes an observation with a large standardized residual
```

Least Squares Regression Equation

We fit the second-order model is $y = ß_0 + ß_1 x + ß_2 x^2 + \epsilon$, where y = Digits and x = %Correct. The first part of the Minitab output gives the regression equation:

$$\hat{y} = 453 - 71.7\, x + 2.85\, x^2$$

The y-intercept, $\hat{ß}_0 = 453$, doesn't have any practical meaning as $x = 0$ is out of the realistic range of the data. $\hat{ß}_1 = -71.7$ estimates the amount of shift in the quadratic curve along the x axis. $\hat{ß}_2 = 2.85$ is an estimate of the upward curvature.

Estimated Standard Error

An estimate of σ^2, the error variance, is $s^2 = 72$ located in the analysis of variance table at the intersection of Error and MS. An estimate of σ, the standard deviation of the random error, is $s = 8.498$. We expect the model to predict the percentage correct to within $2s$, or approximately 17 percentage points of its true value. This is a substantial improvement over the 26 percentage points we obtained using a linear model in Example 3 of Chapter 9.

Coefficient of Determination

The coefficient of determination is $R^2 = 93.4\%$. Approximately 93% of the total variation in percentages correct is explained by the quadratic regression model. With the linear regression model, the coefficient of determination was approximately 84%.

Testing the Usefulness of the Model

To determine whether the model is useful, we test

H_0: $ß_1 = ß_2 = 0$
H_a: At least $ß_1$ or $ß_2$ differs from 0

The test statistic, $F = 277.59$, and p-value = 0. Thus, there is strong evidence that the model is useful.

The output includes the t test statistics and p-values to test whether the parameters are useful in the model. Since $ß_2$ measures the curvature of the response curve as shown in the graph above, we test its significance.

H_0: $ß_2 = 0$
H_a: $ß_2 \neq 0$

The test statistic is $t = 7.53$ and p-value = 0. There is very strong evidence that the quadratic term is useful in the model.

10.2 MODELS WITH QUALITATIVE INDEPENDENT VARIABLES

A linear regression model can contain one or more qualitative independent variables; qualitative variables are those which are not measured on a numerical scale. Examples include gender, education level, marital status, and severity of disease. **Indicator or dummy variables** with values (0,1) can be used to represent levels of qualitative variables. Each indicator variable x_i is assigned the value 1 for level i, and 0 otherwise.

Suppose the qualitative variable that we want to add to a regression model has k levels. We assign one level as the base level, and use the indicator variables corresponding to the other $(k - 1)$ levels in the regression model.

INDICATOR VARIABLES FOR QUALITATIVE DATA

This command creates indicator or dummy variables with values 1 or 0. Enter the code, usually 1 for the first level, 2 for the second, and so on, in the first column that is specified on the command line. Use the same number of columns to store the indicator variables as the number of levels. The command places a 1 or a 0 in the columns.

Calc ▸ Make Indicator Variables

INDICATOR C *put values in* C ... C

For example, consider the class data set given in the Appendix of this guide. Suppose a random sample of 10 students have the following type of car: No car, foreign car, or US car.

Student	Car	Student	Car
1	NoCar	6	USCar
2	Foreign	7	No Car
3	Foreign	8	USCar
4	USCar	9	No Car
5	USCar	10	Foreign

Since the type of car has three levels, we need three indicator variables for the indicator command.

Calc ▸ Make Indicator Variables   MTB > Indicator 'CarType' C3-C5
  Select CarType in **Indicator variables for:**
  Enter C3-C5 in **Store results in**. **OK**

Manip ▸ Display Data   MTB > Print C1-C5
  Select C1-C5 in **Display**. **OK**

Data Display

Row	Car	CarType	C3	C4	C5
1	1	NoCar	0	1	0
2	2	Foreign	1	0	0
3	3	Foreign	1	0	0
4	4	USCar	0	0	1
5	5	USCar	0	0	1
6	6	USCar	0	0	1
7	7	NoCar	0	1	0
8	8	USCar	0	0	1
9	9	NoCar	0	1	0
10	10	Foreign	1	0	0

Suppose CarType is the qualitative variable that we want to add to a regression model. We assign one level as the base level, for example, Foreign, and use indicator variables for NoCar and USCar in the regression model.

■ Example 4   **Model with A Qualitative Variable**

Refer to Example 3 of this chapter. A psychology professor ran an experiment in three sections of an introductory psychology course to show that the more digits in a number, the more difficult it is to remember. Since sections meet at different times of the day, percentage correct may depend on the section in which the experiment takes place. Analyze a regression model which includes the section.

Solution   The data are saved in a file named **Memory.mtp**; columns are named Trial, Digits, %Correct, and Section. The column DigitsSq has been added to the data. Since we found in the last example that the quadratic model was a better fit to the data, we add two indicators, x_2 and x_3, for the qualitative variable Section to the quadratic model

$$y = ß_0 + ß_1 x_1 + ß_2 x_1^2 + ß_3 x_2 + ß_4 x_3 + \epsilon$$

where $x_2 = 1$ if the students were in section 1 and 0 if not, and $x_3 = 1$ if the students were in section 2 and 0 if not. Section 3 is the base level.

Calc ▸ Make Indicator Variables
  Select Section in **Indicator variables for:**
  Enter 'Sec1' 'Sec2' 'Sec3' in **Store results in. OK**

Stat ▸ Regression ▸ Regression
  Select %Correct in **Response:**
  Select Digits, DigitsSq, Sec1, Sec2 in **Predictors:**
  Click **Results** and choose the second **Display. OK**

MTB > Name C6 'Sec1' C7 'Sec2' C8 'Sec3'
MTB > Indicator 'Section' 'Sec1' 'Sec2' 'Sec3'

MTB > Regress '%Correct' 4 'Digits' &
CONT> 'DigitsSq' 'Sec1' 'Sec2';
SUBC> Constant;
SUBC> Brief 1.

Regression Analysis: %Correct versus Digits, DigitsSq, Sec1, Sec2

```
The regression equation is
%Correct = 451 - 71.7 Digits + 2.85 DigitsSq + 2.68 Sec1 + 2.18 Sec2

Predictor          Coef      SE Coef          T          P
Constant         451.07        37.60      12.00      0.000
Digits          -71.651         7.723      -9.28      0.000
DigitsSq          2.8506        0.3847       7.41      0.000
Sec1              2.679         3.264       0.82      0.417
Sec2              2.179         3.264       0.67      0.509

S = 8.637        R-Sq = 93.6%      R-Sq(adj) = 92.9%

Analysis of Variance

Source             DF           SS          MS          F          P
Regression          4        40153       10038     134.58      0.000
Residual Error     37         2760          75
Total              41        42913
```

Testing the Usefulness of the Model

The regression analysis indicates that the regression model is useful for the prediction of y. The test statistic is $F = 134.58$ and the p-value $= 0.000$. The coefficient of determination, $R^2 = 93.6\%$, indicates that nearly all of the variation in y is explained by the regression model.

However the p-values for x_2 and x_3 are high, which leads one to wonder whether section is significant in the model. The hypothesis test to determine whether the indicator variables simultaneously add information to the prediction of percentage correct is described in the next section.

10.3 TESTING PORTIONS OF A MODEL

Oftentimes, we want to test whether several regression coefficients simultaneously equal zero. That is, we want to test whether a reduced model is a better model than a complete model. The F test statistic is used to test the null hypothesis that a particular set of $(k - g)$ parameters simultaneously equals 0. To do the test, the complete model with k predictors and the reduced model with g predictors are fit to the data. The difference in the sums of squares for error is used to test if the particular set of parameters contributes significant information to predict y. The form of the hypothesis test is

H_0: The set of $(k - g)$ parameters simultaneously equal 0
H_a: At least one of the parameters in the set is not 0

The test statistic is

$$F = \frac{(\text{SSE}_R - \text{SSE}_C)/(k - g)}{\text{SSE}_C / [n - (k + 1)]}$$

where SSE_R and SSE_C are the sums of squares for error for the reduced and complete models respectively. When H_0 is true, and the assumptions of the regression model are satisfied, this test statistic has an F distribution with $(k - g)$ and $[n - (k + 1)]$ degrees of freedom.

■ **Example 5**   **Testing Portions of a Model**

In the last example, the qualitative variable section was added to the quadratic model to model the percentage correct in a memory experiment. Test whether the section in which the experiment is held is significant.

Solution   In the last example, the complete model $y = ß_0 + ß_1 x_1 + ß_2 x_1^2 + ß_3 x_2 + ß_4 x_3 + \epsilon$ was fit to the data, and in Example 3, the reduced model $y = ß_0 + ß_1 x + ß_2 x^2 + \epsilon$ was fit to the data. The following provides the regression equation and analysis of variance for each model.

Regression Analysis: %Correct versus Digits, DigitsSq

```
The regression equation is
%Correct = 453 - 71.7 Digits + 2.85 DigitsSq
```

Analysis of Variance

Source	DF	SS	MS	F	P
Regression	2	40096	20048	277.59	0.000
Residual Error	39	2817	72		
Total	41	42913			

Regression Analysis: %Correct versus Digits, DigitsSq, Sec1, Sec2

```
The regression equation is
%Correct = 451 - 71.7 Digits + 2.85 DigitsSq + 2.68 Sec1 + 2.18 Sec2
```

Analysis of Variance

Source	DF	SS	MS	F	P
Regression	4	40153	10038	134.58	0.000
Residual Error	37	2760	75		
Total	41	42913			

The test to determine whether the qualitative terms are useful is

H_0: $\beta_3 = \beta_4 = 0$
H_a: At least one of β_3 and β_4 differs from 0

The sums of squares error, $SSE_R = 2,817$ and $SSE_C = 2,760$, are found in the analysis of variance tables for the reduced model and complete model. Since $k = 4$, $n = 42$, and $g = 2$, the degrees of freedom are 2 and 37.

Calc ▶ Calculator   MTB > Let K1= ((2817-2760)/2)/(2760/37)
  Enter K1 in **Store results in variable:**
  Enter ((2817-2760)/2)/(2760/37) in **Expression. OK**

Manip ▶ Display Data   MTB > Print K1
  Select K1 in **Display. OK**

Data Display

```
K1
   0.382065
```

There does not appear to be a significant difference in the sums of squares for error in the complete model over the reduced model to warrant the inclusion of the qualitative variable.

We use CDF to obtain the *p*-value of the test. The *p*-value is defined as $P(F > .382) = 1 - P(F \leq .382)$, assuming the null hypothesis is true.

Calc ▶ Probability Distributions ▶ F   MTB > CDF K1;
  Click **Cumulative probability**;   SUBC> F 2 37.
  Enter 2 in **Numerator degrees of freedom:**
  and 37 in **Denominator degrees of freedom:**
  Enter K1 in **Input constant. OK**

Cumulative Distribution Function

```
F distribution with 2 DF in numerator and 37 DF in denominator

        x      P( X <= x )
   0.3821         0.3149
```

The *p*-value is 1 - .315 = .685. There is not enough evidence to reject the null hypothesis and conclude that at least one qualitative term is useful in the model. The percentage correct is not significantly affected by the section in which the experiment is held.

10.4 RESIDUAL ANALYSIS

Some uses of **residual analysis** are to determine whether the regression model is misspecified, whether there are unusual observations or outliers, and whether any assumptions are violated. The model assumes that the errors are independent, and that the probability distribution of ϵ is normal, with zero mean and a constant variance σ^2 for all values of $x_1, x_2, ..., x_k$.

The **residual** is the difference between the observed and fitted value of the response variable. A plot of the residuals versus the fitted values or an independent variable may indicate a nonrandom pattern in the residuals, or may indicate outliers or unusual observations. A normal probability plot and histogram give information on the normality of the random errors.

Minitab labels unusual observations on some regression printouts. If you use BRIEF 3, Minitab prints a table of residuals for all values of the independent variables. If you use the default BRIEF 2, Minitab prints the residuals for the unusual observations only. An observation is marked X if a value of an independent variable is unusual, and marked R if the value of the response variable is unusual. Since almost all values of y should lie within 2σ of the fitted values $\hat{y}$, a standardized residual greater than 2 or less than -2 suggests an outlier.

RESIDUAL PLOTS FOR REGRESSION MODELS

This command provides a normal plot of the residuals, an I Chart, a histogram of the residuals, and a plot of residuals versus the fitted values.

Stat ▸ Regression ▸ Residual Plots

%RESPLOTS *residuals* C, *fitted values* C   Constructs residual plots
    TITLE   Adds a title to the plots

NOTE

The output of the %RESPLOT includes some tests and an I Chart. Details for the tests and I Chart are given in Chapter 12, Introduction to Quality and Process Control.

■ **Example 6**   **Residual Analysis**

In Example 3 of Chapter 9 and in Example 3 of this chapter, we used a first-order and a second-order regression model to predict the percentage of students correctly recalling a number. Analyze the residual plots for both models.

Solution The data are saved in a file named **Memory.mtp**; columns are named Trial, Digits, %Correct, and Section. The default column names to store residuals and fitted values are RESI1 and FITS1 for the first model, and RESI2 and FITS2 for the second model.

Stat ▸ Regression ▸ Regression
  Select %Correct in **Response(Y):**
    and Digits in **Predictor(X):**
  Click **Storage,**
    choose **Residuals** and **Fits;**
  Click **Results** and choose the second **Display. OK**

```
MTB > Name C6 = 'RESI1' C7 = 'FITS1'
MTB > Regress '%Correct' 1 'Digits';
SUBC>   Resid 'RESI1';
SUBC>   Fits 'FITS1';
SUBC>   Brief 1.
```

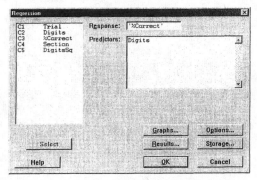

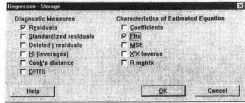

Regression Analysis: %Correct versus Digits

```
The regression equation is
%Correct = 179 - 14.6 Digits

Predictor        Coef      SE Coef           T          P
Constant       179.03        10.34       17.31      0.000
Digits        -14.639         1.014      -14.43      0.000

S = 13.15        R-Sq = 83.9%       R-Sq(adj) = 83.5%

Analysis of Variance

Source          DF           SS          MS           F          P
Regression       1        36001       36001      208.34      0.000
Residual Error  40         6912         173
Total           41        42913
```

Stat ▸ Regression ▸ Residual Plots
  Select RESI1 in **Residuals:**
  Select FITS1 in **Fits:**
  Enter a **Title. OK**

```
MTB > %Resplots 'RESI1' 'FITS1';
SUBC>   Title "Simple Linear Model".
```

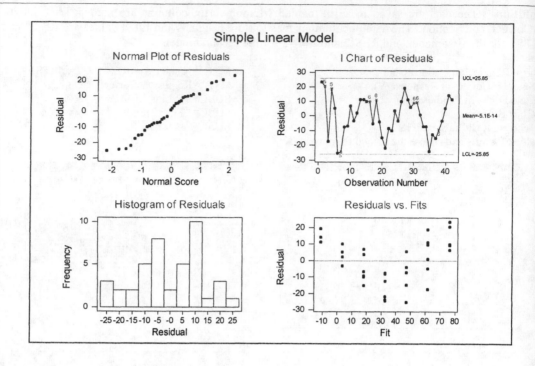

Residual Plots: RESI1 vs FITS1

```
TEST 5. 2 out of 3 points more than 2 sigmas from center line
        (on one side of CL).
Test Failed at points: 2 4 7

TEST 6. 4 out of 5 points more than 1 sigma from center line
        (on one side of CL).
Test Failed at points: 16 18 30 31 38
```

A normal distribution of residuals would plot as a straight line on the normal plot, and as a mound-shaped histogram. Both plots indicate a nonnormal distribution. The I Chart and Residuals vs. Fits plot reveal a nonrandom pattern in the residuals. The curvilinear pattern of the residuals suggests that the model is misspecified; a quadratic model may be a better model. The failed tests given with the output indicate that the errors may not be random; there are some unusual residuals.

Stat ▸ Regression ▸ Regression
  Select %Correct in **Response(Y):**
    and Digits DigitsSq in **Predictor(X):**
  Click **Storage,**
    choose **Residuals** and **Fits;**
  Click **Results** and choose the second **Display. OK**

MTB > Name C8 = 'RESI2' C9 = 'FITS2'
MTB > Regress '%Correct' 2 'Digits' 'DigitsSq';
SUBC>   Resid 'RESI2';
SUBC>   Fits 'FITS2';
SUBC>   Brief 1.

Regression Analysis: %Correct versus Digits, DigitsSq

```
The regression equation is
%Correct = 453 - 71.7 Digits + 2.85 DigitsSq

Predictor        Coef      SE Coef           T          P
Constant       452.68        36.95       12.25      0.000
Digits        -71.651         7.599       -9.43      0.000
DigitsSq       2.8506        0.3785        7.53      0.000


S = 8.498       R-Sq = 93.4%       R-Sq(adj) = 93.1%

Analysis of Variance

Source            DF           SS          MS         F          P
Regression         2        40096       20048    277.59      0.000
Residual Error    39         2817          72
Total             41        42913
```

Stat ▸ Regression ▸ Residual Plots
Select RESI2 in **Residuals:**
Select FITS2 in **Fits:**
Enter a **Title. OK**

MTB > %Resplots 'RESI2' 'FITS2';
SUBC>   Title "Quadratic Model".

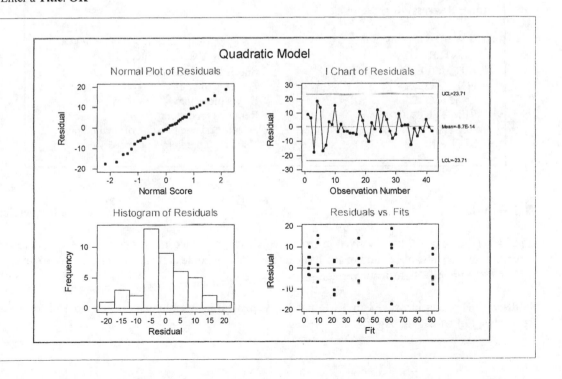

The normal probability plot and histogram indicate approximate normal distribution of residuals; the I Chart and Residuals vs. Fits plot show somewhat random residuals. The curvilinear pattern of the straight-line residual plot has disappeared with the addition of the squared term. The quadratic model provides a better fit than the simple linear model.

10.5 STEPWISE REGRESSION

Stepwise regression is a screening process that selects a useful set of predictors for a response variable y. To use stepwise, identify the set of all possible predictors that you want to include in the regression analysis. This set may include interaction and higher order terms. An F test determines which predictors in this set are useful.

STEPWISE REGRESSION

Stepwise regression identifies a useful subset of predictors from up to 100 predictors listed on the command line. An α test determines if a predictor is to be entered or removed from the equation. The default α value is 0.15. For each step, Minitab prints the constant term, the coefficient and t-ratio for each predictor in the model, s, R^2, and R^2-Adjusted.

Stat ▸ Regression ▸ Stepwise

STEPWISE C *predictors* C ... C	Uses stepwise regression to build model
AENTER K	Specifies α value to enter
AREMOVE K	Specifies α value to remove
FORCE C...C	Forces predictors
ENTER C...C	Enters predictors
REMOVE C...C	Removes predictors
BEST K	Selects best combination of predictors
STEPS K	Number of predictors per page

■ **Example 7**   **Stepwise Regression**

Consider the data on 36 homes given in Example 1. A homeowner in a residential area is interested in predicting the value of her home, and has gathered data on homes for sale in her area. Use stepwise regression to identify significant variables.

Solution   The data are saved in a file named **Appraisal.mtp**; columns are named House, Price, Bedrooms, SqFtArea, and Age.

Stat ▸ **Regression** ▸ **Stepwise**
  Select Price in **Response:**
  Select Bedrooms, SqFtArea, Age in **Predictors. OK**

MTB > Stepwise 'Price' 'Bedrooms'-'Age';
SUBC>   AEnter 0.15;
SUBC>   ARemove 0.15;
SUBC>   Constant.

Stepwise Regression: Price versus Bedrooms, SqFtArea, Age

```
     Alpha-to-Enter: 0.15  Alpha-to-Remove: 0.15

     Response is  Price   on  3 predictors, with N =    36


          Step          1          2
     Constant        49046      60794

     SqFtArea         35.0       35.4
     T-Value          7.40       8.06
     P-Value         0.000      0.000

     Age                        -645
     T-Value                   -2.55
     P-Value                   0.016

     S               15381      14270
     R-Sq            61.68      67.99
     R-Sq(adj)       60.56      66.05
     C-p               6.8        2.4
       More? (Yes, No, Subcommand, or Help)
```

At Step 1, SqFtArea was selected as the most useful predictor. The model at Step 1 is

```
Price = 49,046 + 35.0 SqFtArea
```

with an $R^2 = 61.7\%$ and s = 15,381.

At Step 2, Age was added as a useful predictor. The model at Step 2 is

```
Price = 60,794 + 35.4 SqFtArea + -645 Age
```

with an $R^2 = 68.0\%$ and s = 14,270.

Stepwise regression has selected the variables SqFtArea and Age, the same variables which we had selected in the regression analysis process of Example 1.

EXERCISES

1. The accountant at Fandels Department store wants to study the relationship between the amount of purchases y and customer income x. A random sample of 15 customers provided the following data on income and total purchases made at Fandels during 1999.   (File: **Fandels.mtp**)

Customer	Purchases	Income
1	$ 740	$ 34,000
2	1,360	71,500
3	1,280	46,000
4	1,640	73,000
5	1,100	42,500
6	1,480	110,500
7	680	31,500
8	1,000	37,000
9	1,440	97,500
10	1,520	85,000
11	1,560	72,000
12	2,080	178,000
13	1,920	157,000
14	1,200	51,000
15	1,140	18,000

a. Analyze the relationship between the amount of purchases and income. What model is appropriate?
b. Fit the model to the data. Test whether the overall model is useful. Test whether each predictor is useful. Use $\alpha = .05$.
c. Find and interpret a 95% prediction interval for a customer with an income of $30,000.

2. Consider the class data set described in the Appendix. Use a quadratic model to analyze the relationship between the grade point averages and the number of hours worked. Conduct a complete analysis. (File: **StudentInfo.mtp**)

3. The following data compiled by the Minnesota Real Estate Research Center gives the area in square feet x_1, the age x_2, and price y of a random sample of 20 homes that were sold during 1999 in the St. Cloud area. Any home less than one year old is given an age of one.
(File: **20Homes.mtp**)

Home	Area	Age	Price
1	770	15	$69,000
2	740	40	69,900
3	832	40	78,000
4	768	16	78,750
5	700	*	80,250
6	1,030	27	81,000
7	1,120	24	96,000
8	1,068	11	96,750
9	760	4	104,850

10	1,400	26	107,850
11	1,652	13	118,350
12	1,190	3	127,500
13	1,200	11	135,900
14	1,444	2	149,813
15	1,516	1	156,600
16	2,024	1	162,000
17	1,840	1	174,000
18	1,684	1	167,850
19	1,760	1	179,250
20	1,870	1	184,500

a. Graphically analyze the data to determine whether the two independent variables interact in their effect on the price of homes.
b. Fit the interaction model to the data. Test whether the model is useful for predicting the price of a home. Use $\alpha = .05$. Interpret R^2.
c. Is there significant evidence that the interaction term contributes to the prediction of the price of a home?
d. If the model is useful, find the 95% prediction interval for a 1500 square foot home that is 10 years old.

4. The accountant at Fandels Department Store wants to determine the relationship between customers purchases y, and the two independent variables, yearly income and type of residence. A sample of 15 customers provided the following data. (File: **Fandels.mtp**)

Customer	Purchases	Income	Residence
1	$ 740	$ 34,000	Rent home
2	1,360	71,500	Own Home
3	1,280	46,000	Own Home
4	1,640	73,000	Own Home
5	1,100	42,500	Apartment
6	1,480	110,500	Apartment
7	680	31,500	Apartment
8	1,000	37,000	Own Home
9	1,440	97,500	Apartment
10	1,520	85,000	Apartment
11	1,560	72,000	Own Home
12	2,080	178,000	Rent home
13	1,920	157,000	Rent home
14	1,200	51,000	Own Home
15	1,140	18,000	Apartment

a. Create indicator variables for the type of residence.
b. Fit a first-order model to the data.
c. Test whether the overall model is useful. Use $\alpha = .05$.
d. Test whether the type of residence is useful in the model. Use $\alpha = .05$.
e. Find and interpret a 95% prediction interval for a homeowner with $30,000 annual income.

5.   An investor is interested in the relationship between the average annual investment yield for three types of mutual funds, and the size of the funds, the fees charged, and the annual expenses. The table provides the data for a random sample of 43 mutual funds. The three types of funds are stock (1), stock and bond (2), and foreign (3). Yield is the average annual percent return on investment over the past ten years. Assets gives the size of the funds in millions of dollars. The sales fee is the maximum percentage sales charge on money invested in a mutual fund. Annual expense is the annual percentage charge for operating the fund. (File: **MutualFunds.mtp**)

Fund	Type	Yield	Assets	Fee	Expenses
1	1	14.8	$ 738	0.00	0.80
2	1	16.2	149	4.50	1.00
3	1	14.5	546	0.00	1.31
4	1	14.7	72	4.00	1.10
5	1	8.5	161	0.00	1.02
6	1	14.8	991	0.00	0.67
7	1	12.0	833	0.00	0.47
8	1	5.0	19	8.50	1.30
9	1	15.3	464	5.75	0.71
10	1	12.5	32	15.00	0.68
11	1	6.8	184	0.00	1.35
12	1	20.1	534	0.00	0.92
13	1	12.2	233	7.25	0.89
14	1	7.0	1019	8.50	0.85
15	1	16.2	529	1.00	1.01
16	1	11.0	644	8.50	0.68
17	1	8.4	275	0.00	1.31
18	1	11.3	79	5.75	0.82
19	1	16.3	186	0.00	1.14
20	1	1.9	161	0.00	0.87
21	2	16.2	143	5.50	1.42
22	2	12.0	6	3.00	1.23
23	2	4.4	46	0.00	0.73
24	2	12.6	164	8.00	0.80
25	2	14.3	266	7.25	0.91
26	2	5.7	1826	0.00	0.45
27	2	9.7	139	0.00	0.89
28	2	13.1	873	8.50	0.92
29	2	3.7	1052	4.00	0.59
30	2	12.9	72	4.00	1.12
31	3	11.5	31	5.50	1.93
32	3	0.7	528	0.00	1.40
33	3	4.7	280	4.00	0.82
34	3	17.0	89	4.75	2.20
35	3	0.5	303	0.00	1.01
36	3	12.4	114	4.00	2.19
37	3	12.5	62	0.00	2.31
38	3	3.8	288	6.50	1.02
39	3	16.0	100	5.75	0.69
40	3	14.7	455	8.50	1.89
41	3	7.3	466	8.50	1.61
42	3	16.0	564	0.00	1.22
43	3	3.5	727	8.50	0.83

a. Construct scatter plots of the response variable versus each independent variable. Find the correlation matrix. Summarize the relationships between the variables.

b. Fit the regression model

$$y = ß_0 + ß_1x_1 + ß_2x_2 + ß_3x_3 + ß_4x_4 + ß_5x_5 + \epsilon$$

where y = Average annual yield, x_1 = Assets, x_2 = Sales fee, x_3 = Annual expenses, x_4 = 1 if stock fund, 0 otherwise, and x_5 = 1 if stock and bond fund, 0 otherwise.

c. Interpret s and R^2.

d. Test whether the model is useful for predicting fund yield. Use $\alpha = .05$.

e. Use STEPWISE to select a subset of useful predictors.

f. Write a short summary of the implications of this data analysis.

6. Consider the class data set given in the Appendix of this guide. Model the relationship between grade point average y and the following independent variables: Age x_1, numbers of hours worked x_2, and distance in miles from school x_3. (File: **Classdata.mtp**)

a. Construct scatter plots to study the relationship between grade point average and each independent variable. Calculate and interpret the correlations between all pairs of variables.

b. Fit the first-order linear model to the data. Interpret the least squares estimates of the parameters.

c. Interpret the estimate of σ. Interpret R^2.

d. Test whether the number of hours worked x_2 contributes significantly to the prediction of grade point average. Use $\alpha = .05$.

e. Construct and interpret a 95% confidence interval for $ß_2$.

f. Test whether the model is useful for predicting grade point average.

g. If the model is useful, construct and interpret 95% confidence and prediction intervals for a 25 year old student who works 20 hours a week and lives 10 miles from class.

h. Perform a residual analysis. Discuss.

7. A survey conducted by the UCLA Graduate School of Management on the status of computer development in business schools is reported in the *Sixteenth Annual UCLA Survey of Business School Computer Usage*, November 1999. The survey queries business schools on hardware, software, and resource commitments. The following random sample of 35 schools provides the number of full time equivalent undergraduate students, the number of full time equivalent faculty, the ratio of the computer operating budget to full time equivalent students, the operating budget in thousands of dollars, and the type of institution. Conduct a regression analysis of the data to model the relationship between operating budget and the other variables. Write a report summarizing the analysis. (File: **UCLA.mtp**)

School	UGrad	Faculty	Ratio	Budget	Type
1	1,000	85	70.0	$ 84	Public
2	868	56	114.0	142	Private
3	608	*	120.8	83	Public
4	4,115	285	205.5	1,100	Public
5	400	23	160.0	80	Private
6	937	44	187.4	200	Public
7	3,136	112	167.0	556	Private
8	3,640	260	1,762.1	8,000	Private
9	2,368	105	147.0	434	Private
10	1,540	118	390.2	876	Private
11	4,500	110	19.4	107	Private
12	2,619	149	500.5	1,433	Private
13	550	71	1,191.3	1,700	Public
14	1,250	52	119.1	155	Public
15	715	14	187.5	195	Private
16	296	92	1,041.6	1,282	Private
17	867	39	155.9	147	Public
18	6,000	150	50.4	335	Public
19	248	14	85.0	38	Private
20	630	36	128.3	107	Private
21	3,251	109	38.2	132	Public
22	200	40	107.1	75	Public
23	630	70	59.8	75	Public
24	1,789	80	192.2	463	Public
25	815	40	56.1	65	Private
26	572	25	215.6	130	Public
27	815	40	56.1	65	Private
28	606	65	196.9	190	Public
29	916	42	120.1	125	Public
30	750	23	6.3	5	Private
31	547	69	718.9	873	Private
32	2,200	84	164.1	370	Public
33	5,272	95	110.3	661	Public
34	1,007	128	78.8	210	Private
35	5,000	110	97.3	527	Public

8. Time series analysis uses a linear regression model to predict future values. Quarterly or monthly data are included in a regression model with indicator variables. In Chapter 14, Exercise 4 gives quarterly enrollment at St. Cloud State University for Fall 1985 through Summer 1998. Fit a multiple regression model to the data. Predict the enrollment for the 1998-99 academic year. Summarize your results. (File: **SCSUEnroll.mtp**)

9. Repeat the analysis described in Exercise 8 for male enrollment. Summarize your results. (File: **SCSUEnroll.mtp**)

10. Repeat the analysis described in Exercise 8 for female enrollment. How does this model compare with the model to estimate male enrollment? Summarize your results. (File: **SCSUEnroll.mtp**)

CHAPTER 11

ANALYSIS OF VARIANCE

In an earlier chapter we presented methods for making inferences about the difference between two population means. This chapter presents methods to compare more than two population means. The appropriate method to use depends on the design of the experiment. We describe several experimental designs, and show how to use Minitab to graphically display the data and do the analysis of variance. The last sections describe multiple comparison of the means and residual analysis.

NEW COMMANDS

ANOVA   AOVONEWAY   %INTERACT   KRUSKAL-WALLIS
ONEWAY   TWOWAY

11.1 THE COMPLETELY RANDOMIZED DESIGN

The **completely randomized design** is one in which independent samples are randomly selected from each treatment population. This design is perhaps the simplest experimental design for comparing more than two population means. For example, a health researcher, interested in studying the diastolic blood pressure among different populations, measures blood pressure for a random sample chosen from each population, or a financial analyst, interested in the annual rate of investment return in stock, bond, and foreign mutual funds, independently selects a random sample from each type of fund.

An objective of a completely randomized design is to compare treatment means. The variable of interest is the dependent or response variable, and the independent variables are called factors. A treatment is a factor level in an experiment with one factor, or a combination of factor levels if two or more factors are studied simultaneously. Different treatments are applied to objects called experimental units.

The analysis of variance is used to determine whether a factor affects the response variable. If the factor is significant, the mean response differs for the various treatments. Minitab will do an analysis of variance for single factor balanced and unbalanced completely randomized designs. A balanced design has an equal number of observations per treatment and an unbalanced design has an unequal number. We recommend the use of descriptive statistics and graphical analysis to summarize data and to verify assumptions.

ONE FACTOR ANALYSIS OF VARIANCE

These commands provide the analysis of variance table; the number of observations, mean, standard deviation, and 95% confidence interval for each treatment mean; and the pooled standard deviation. Graphical display options include dot plots and box plots of the samples.

Stat ▸ ANOVA ▸ One-way (Unstacked)

AOVONEWAY C ... C	Use for unstacked data
GDOTPLOT	Displays dot plots
GBOXPLOT	Displays box plots

The following command for stacked data is a more versatile command in that it also provides optional storage of residuals and fits, residual plot options and multiple comparison options including the Tukey, Fisher, Dunnett, and MCB methods. Enter the observations in one column, and codes identifying the treatments in a second column. The codes can be either alpha or numeric, for example, 1, 2, ...

Stat ▸ ANOVA ▸ One-way

ONEWAY C C (*residuals in* C (*fits in* C))	Use for stacked data
GDOTPLOT	Displays dot plots
GBOXPLOT	Displays box plots
TUKEY (K)	Family error rate K; default .05
FISHER (K)	Individual error rate K; default .05

■ **Example 1**   **Analysis of Variance: Unstacked Data**

The price earnings or PE ratio is the price of a share of stock divided by the earnings per share. The ratio reflects the price an investor is willing to invest for a dollar of earnings. To test whether the mean PE ratios differ for the financial, medical, technology, and consumer industries, the following random samples were selected from the Standard and Poor's Stock Guide in December 2000. Graphically compare the PE ratios in the four industries. Test whether there is a difference in group means using $\alpha = .05$. Interpret the *p*-value. Interpret the 95% confidence intervals given on the printout.

Financial	Medical	Technology	Consumer
24	23	64	15
20	19	29	14
13	34	142	23
31	20	60	38
40	19	97	53
11	28	35	24
14		46	31

Solution The data are saved in a file named **PERatios.mtp**. PE ratios are unstacked in four columns named Financial, Medical, Technology, and Consumer.

Stat ▸ ANOVA ▸ One-way (Unstacked)
  Select 'Financial' - 'Consumer'
  in **Responses [in separate columns]:**
  Click **Graphs**, choose **Boxplots of data**. **OK**

MTB > AOVOneway 'Financial'-'Consumer';
SUBC> GBoxplot.

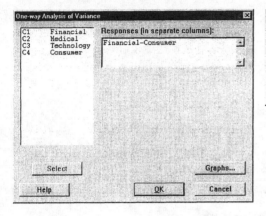

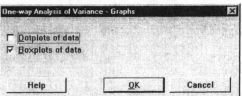

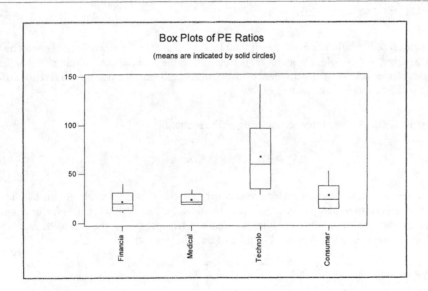

The box plots indicate that the technology industry has higher and more variable PE ratios than the other industries. There is a lot of overlap between the observations for the other industries. Medical has lower variability than the other industries.

One-way ANOVA: Financial, Medical, Technology, Consumer

```
Analysis of Variance
Source      DF          SS         MS       F        P
Factor       3        9681       3227     6.46    0.002
Error       23       11491        500
Total       26       21172
```

```
                                    Individual 95% CIs For Mean
                                    Based on Pooled StDev
Level        N       Mean     StDev  ---------+---------+---------+-----
Financial    7      21.86     10.64     (------*------)
Medical      6      23.83      6.05     (-------*------)
Technology   7      67.57     39.77                        (------*------)
Consumer     7      28.29     13.78        (------*------)
                                    ---------+---------+---------+-----
Pooled StDev =      22.35                   25        50        75
```

To test whether the mean PE ratios for the industries differ, the null and alternative hypotheses are

H_0: $\mu_1 = \mu_2 = \mu_3 = \mu_4$
H_a: At least two means differ.

The test statistic, $F = 6.46$ has a p-value of 0.002. The p-value is the probability of obtaining a test statistic as large as $F = 6.46$, assuming H_0 is true. Since the p-value is less than $\alpha = .05$, the null hypothesis is rejected. We have sufficient evidence to conclude that the true mean PE ratios differ for at least two of the four industries.

The formula for the 95% confidence intervals on the printout is

$$\bar{x} \pm t_{.025} \text{ (Pooled Stdev)}/\sqrt{n}$$

The confidence intervals indicate which means may differ. If two intervals do not overlap, it is possible that the corresponding mean ratios differ significantly. The confidence interval for technology does not overlap with any other confidence interval. It appears that the mean PE ratio for the technology industry exceeds the mean PE ratios of the other industries.

■ **Example 2**   **Analysis of Variance: Stacked Data**

The price earnings or PE ratios for four industries are given in Example 1. Repeat the analysis of variance using stacked data. This means that the PE ratios for each industry are placed in one columns and a code identifying the industry in another. Compare this printout with that of Example 1.

Solution   The data are saved in a file named **PERatios.mtp**; data are unstacked in four columns named Financial, Medical, Technology, and Consumer. For this example, we stack the data.

Manip ▸ Stack ▸ Stack Columns
  Stack the following columns:
    Select Financial - Consumer;
  Click **Column of current worksheet:** enter 'Ratio',
    Enter 'Industry' in **Store subscripts in:**
  Click **Use variable names in subscript column OK**

MTB > Name C5 = 'Ratio' C6 = 'Industry'
MTB > Stack 'Financial'-'Consumer' 'Ratio';
SUBC>   Subscripts 'Industry';
SUBC>   UseNames.

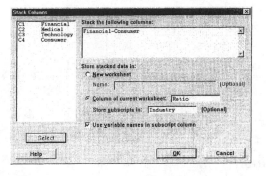

Stat ▸ ANOVA ▸ One-way
  Select Ratio in **Response:** and Industry in **Factor:**
  Click **Graphs**, choose **Boxplots of data**. **OK**

MTB > Oneway 'Ratio' 'Industry';
SUBC>   GBoxplot.

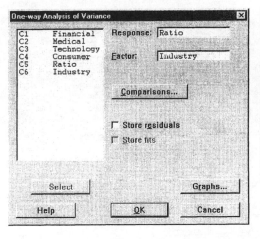

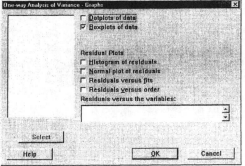

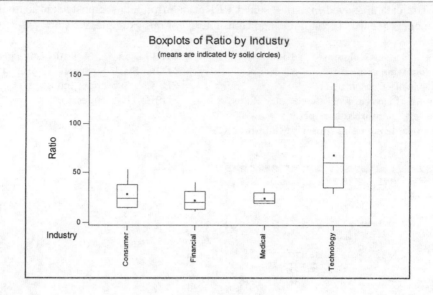

Boxplots of Ratio by Industry
(means are indicated by solid circles)

One-way ANOVA: Ratio versus Industry

```
Analysis of Variance for Ratio
Source      DF        SS         MS        F        P
Industry     3      9681       3227     6.46    0.002
Error       23     11491        500
Total       26     21172
```

```
                                 Individual 95% CIs For Mean
                                 Based on Pooled StDev
Level        N    Mean    StDev  ---------+---------+---------+-----
Consumer     7   28.29    13.78     (------*------)
Financial    7   21.86    10.64  (------*------)
Medical      6   23.83     6.05  (-------*------)
Technology   7   67.57    39.77                        (------*------)
                                 ---------+---------+---------+-----
Pooled StDev =     22.35                   25        50        75
```

For stacked data, the box plot and analysis of variance output differ only in some labeling and ordering of industries in the graph and summary table.

■ **Example 3**   **Completely Randomized Design**

A research laboratory was developing new treatments for the relief of hay fever. The interest in this phase of development was in the length of time it took for hay fever patients to react to three different experimental treatments. Twenty patients were randomly assigned to each treatment. The following table gives reaction times in minutes. Graphically compare the reaction times of the three treatments. Test whether the mean reaction times differ. Use $\alpha = .05$. Interpret the *p*-value and the confidence intervals on the printout.

Treatment 1		Treatment 2		Treatment 3	
20	16	20	12	22	21
25	20	21	24	29	24
25	26	35	20	19	21
31	22	18	33	21	31
18	19	14	14	19	15
17	35	24	25	17	20
17	21	20	20	31	14
33	34	22	24	12	16
17	30	19	24	27	12
20	22	21	21	21	10

Solution   The data are saved in a file named **Treatment.mtp**; reaction times and the codes for treatments are stacked in columns named Time and Treatment.

Stat ▸ ANOVA ▸ One-way   MTB > Oneway 'Time' 'Treatment';
  Select Time in **Response:** and Treatment in **Factor:**   SUBC> GBoxplot.
  Click **Graphs**; choose **Boxplots of data. OK**

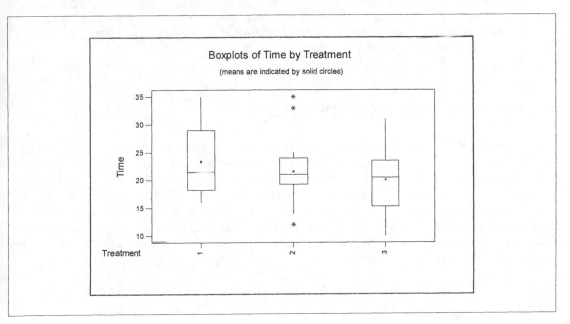

One-way ANOVA: Time versus Treatment

```
Analysis of Variance for Time
Source        DF        SS        MS        F        P
Treatment      2      109.4      54.7      1.55    0.222
Error         57     2017.6      35.4
Total         59     2127.0
                                 Individual 95% CIs For Mean
                                 Based on Pooled StDev
Level    N     Mean      StDev    -+---------+---------+---------+-----
1       20    23.400     6.168                   (----------*---------)
2       20    21.550     5.539             (---------*----------)
3       20    20.100     6.121     (---------*----------)
                                 -+---------+---------+---------+-----
Pooled StDev =    5.949         17.5      20.0      22.5      25.0
```

The box plots show that the sample mean and median times differ slightly, but there is much overlap in the times for the three treatments.

To test whether the mean times differ significantly, the null and alternative hypotheses are

H_0: $\mu_1 = \mu_2 = \mu_3$
H_a: At least two of the mean times differ.

The p-value is the probability, assuming the mean times are equal, of observing a test statistic value as large as $F = 1.55$. The p-value of 0.222 is not less than $\alpha = .05$. There is not sufficient evidence of a difference among the mean times for the three treatments. The overlap in the confidence intervals also indicates there is no difference in means.

11.2 RANDOMIZED BLOCK DESIGNS

In a **randomized block design**, the experimental units are grouped into blocks, and treatments are randomly assigned within the blocks. The objective of a blocked experiment is to increase the precision of the experimental results by reducing the sampling variability. The variable selected for blocking should be one which accounts for some variability among the responses; that is, one which is correlated with the response or in some way affects the response. A **blocking variable** can be one associated with the experiment itself, such as the subject, time, or the measuring instrument. Or a blocking variable can be a characteristic of the experimental unit, such as the age and education of an individual, or the population size of a geographical area.

ANALYSIS OF VARIANCE FOR TWO FACTORS

This command constructs the analysis of variance table. The response data are stacked in the first column and codes for the factor levels in the other columns. The factor levels are usually coded 1, 2, and so on. Options include storing residuals and fits, residual plots, confidence intervals for the factor level means, and additive model.

Stat ▸ ANOVA ▸ Two-way

TWOWAY *data* C *factors* C C (*resids* C (*fits* C))	Does analysis of variance
MEANS FOR C (AND C)	Displays means
ADDITIVE	Use for additive model

The next ANOVA command described below does an analysis of variance for single factor balanced and unbalanced designs, and for more complex balanced designs. Factors may be fixed or random. A factor is considered fixed if the conclusions pertain only to those factor levels included in the study. A factor is random if the levels are sampled from a population, and interest is in the population. The single factor F test statistic does not depend on whether the factor is fixed or random; the multifactor F test statistic does.

ANALYSIS OF VARIANCE FOR TWO OR MORE FACTORS

This command does an analysis of variance for balanced multifactor designs. All the observations are stacked in the first column, and codes identifying the factor levels are in separate columns. Usually the levels are coded 1, 2, and so on. Use an asterisk * to denote an interaction term.

The output includes a factor table and an analysis of variance table. The factor table lists the factors and codes for each factor. The analysis of variance table includes the F test statistics and *p*-values. Options include storing residuals and fits, residual plots, factor level means, and fitting random effects models.

Stat ▸ ANOVA ▸ Balanced ANOVA

ANOVA C = C ... C	Does analysis of variance
MEANS C...C	Displays means
RANDOM C...C	Indicates random factors
RESIDUALS C...C	Stores residuals
FITS C...C	Stores fitted values

■ Example 4   Randomized Block Design

The University Chronicle conducted a survey of prices at four local grocery stores. The objective was to compare the stores in terms of grocery prices. They recorded the following prices of eight items often purchased by university students at each store. Graphically analyze the data. Is grocery item a good blocking variable? Do some stores have consistently higher or lower prices? Test using $\alpha = .05$.

Product	Grocery Store			
	1	2	3	4
Ground Beef	2.18	2.09	2.16	1.99
Mac & Cheese	0.89	0.96	0.87	1.09
Heinz Ketchup	1.39	1.59	1.39	2.25
Gallon Milk	2.73	2.73	2.88	2.73
Fruit Loops	2.73	2.73	2.73	3.19
Campbell's Soup	0.79	0.83	0.79	0.95
Northern Tissue	1.39	1.59	1.39	1.89
Ragu Sauce	2.26	2.40	2.26	2.65

Solution   The data are saved in a file named **Store.mtp**. Since we need stacked data to analyze a randomized block design, prices are entered in C1 named Price, a code (1 to 4) for store in C2 named Store, and a code (1 to 8) for product in C3 named Product. First we plot the product prices versus product using different symbols for each store.

Graph ▸ Plot   MTB > Plot 'Price'*'Product';
  Select Price in **Graph 1 Y** and Product in **Graph 1 X**;   SUBC>   Symbol 'Store';
  Click **For each**, choose **Group**;   SUBC>   Title "Grocery Store Prices".
  Select Store in **Group variables**;
  Click **Annotation**, choose **Title**, add a title. **OK**

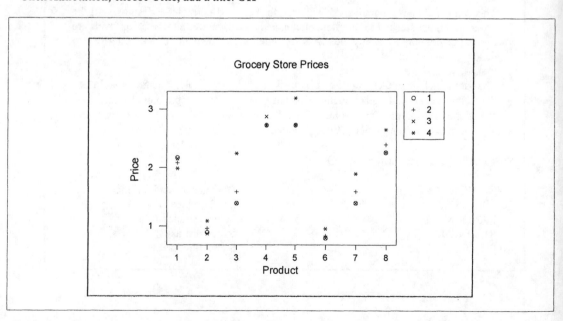

The plot shows that product may be a good blocking variable since there is much price variability from one product to the next. Grocery store 4 has the highest prices for many products.

To test whether grocery product is a significant blocking variable and whether the mean prices differ significantly for the four grocery stores, we obtain the analysis of variance table.

Stat ▸ ANOVA ▸ Balanced ANOVA   MTB > ANOVA 'Price' = Store Product
  Select Price in **Responses:**
  Select Store and Product in **Model. OK**

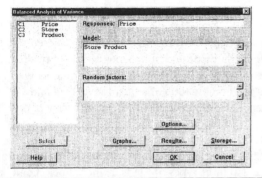

ANOVA: Price versus Store, Product

```
Factor      Type Levels Values
Store       fixed    4    1    2    3    4
Product     fixed    8    1    2    3    4    5    6    7
                          8
```

Analysis of Variance for Price

Source	DF	SS	MS	F	P
Store	3	0.4581	0.1527	5.79	0.005
Product	7	16.4921	2.3560	89.28	0.000
Error	21	0.5542	0.0264		
Total	31	17.5043			

The hypothesis test for block effects is

  H_0: The product price means are equal.
  H_a: At least two product price means differ.

From the ANOVA printout, the test statistic is $F = 89.28$ and the p-value of 0 is less than $\alpha = .05$. We have enough evidence to conclude mean prices differ for at least two products. Grocery product is a useful blocking variable.

To test whether the mean prices differ significantly for the four grocery stores, we test

H_0: $\mu_1 = \mu_2 = \mu_3 = \mu_4$
H_a: At least two grocery store price means differ.

The test statistic is $F = 5.79$, and the p-value = 0.005 is less than $\alpha = .05$. We have enough evidence to conclude that the mean prices differ for at least two grocery stores.

11.3 FACTORIAL DESIGNS

Often, more than one factor affects a response variable. For example, the price of a product and the type of advertising campaign affects the sales of a product. Work environment and perceived job security affect job satisfaction. A **factorial experiment** studies the simultaneous effects of two or more factors on a response variable. In this section, we describe complete factorial experiments with two factors, referred to as factors A and B. A treatment is a combination of a factor level of A and a factor level of B. If factor A has a levels, and factor B has b levels, a complete factorial experiment consists of all ab possible treatments.

For example, the type of fund and the fee structure may affect the rate of return on investment of a mutual fund. Suppose a financial analyst is interested in three types of funds, namely stock, bond, and foreign, and two types of fee structures, load and no load. A load refers to the sales commissions and other distribution expenses. Since the type of fund has three levels and fee structure has two levels, there are six treatments. These are load stock fund, no load stock fund, load bond fund, no load bond fund, load foreign fund, and no load foreign fund. The response variable is the rate of return over a fixed period of time.

If the treatments are randomly assigned to experimental units, the design is a completely randomized design. The analysis of variance for a two factor experiment is an extension of the analysis of variance for a single factor experiment. The analysis evaluates the effects of factor A and B, called main effects, and the joint effects of the two factors, called **interactions**. Two factors interact if the effect of one factor on the response depends on the level of the other factor. Use Two-way or Balanced ANOVA to construct the analysis of variance table for a factorial design.

INTERACTION PLOT

This command constructs a single interaction plot if two factors are entered, or a matrix of interaction plots if more than two factors are entered.

Stat ▸ ANOVA ▸ Interactions Plot

%INTERACT C ... C	Constructs an interaction plot
RESPONSES C	Contains response data
TITLE	Adds a title to the plot

NOTE

The Cross Tabulation command (TABLE session command) introduced in Chapter 4 organizes the data in cells according to factor levels, and gives treatment means, factor level means, and the overall mean.

■ **Example 5**   **Factorial Design**

A mail order company recently purchased an integrated computer software package. Suppose the company wants to study the effects of employees' computer experience and the type of training method on task times. The company identified fifteen employees with considerable experience (coded 1) and fifteen with almost no experience (coded 2). They randomly assigned each of three types of training method to five employees in each experience category. After completing the training, they gave the employees the same computer task. The times to complete the task were recorded as follow.

Considerable Experience			Little/No Experience		
Employee	Time	Training	Employee	Time	Training
1	19	2	16	18	2
2	27	1	17	27	1
3	18	1	18	20	1
4	12	2	19	22	3
5	26	3	20	26	3
6	20	3	21	30	3
7	17	2	22	23	3
8	25	1	23	21	2
9	23	1	24	23	2
10	27	3	25	30	2
11	8	2	26	24	1
12	23	2	27	24	2
13	22	3	28	28	1
14	17	1	29	35	3
15	30	3	30	22	1

Solution   The two factors of interest are training and experience. Since there are three training methods and two experience levels, the experiment is a 3x2 factorial experiment consisting of six treatment combinations. Columns in **Experience.mtp** are named TaskTime, Method, and Experience.

We use the Cross Tabulation command to print a table of data and means. The Interactions Plot plots the treatment means and checks for interaction between computer experience and training method.

Stat ▸ Tables ▸ Cross Tabulation
  Select Method and Experience
  in **Classification variables:**
  Click **Summaries** and
  select TaskTime in **Associated variables:**
  Under **Display**, choose **Means** and **Data. OK**

MTB > Table 'Method' 'Experience',
SUBC>   Means 'TaskTime';
SUBC>   Data 'TaskTime'.

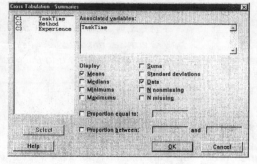

Tabulated Statistics: Method, Experience

```
Rows: Method      Columns: Experience

              1          2        All

   1      22.000     24.200    23.100
          27.000     27.000      --
          18.000     20.000
          25.000     24.000
          23.000     28.000
          17.000     22.000


   2      15.800     23.200    19.500
          19.000     18.000      --
          12.000     21.000
          17.000     23.000
           8.000     30.000
          23.000     24.000


   3      25.000     27.200    26.100
          26.000     22.000      --
          20.000     26.000
          27.000     30.000
          22.000     23.000
          30.000     35.000
  All     20.933     24.867    22.900
            --         --         --


   Cell Contents --
          TaskTime: Mean
                    Data
```

The table gives the data and means of the treatment combinations, the means for levels of computer experience and training methods, and the overall mean. The sample of employees with considerable experience (coded 1) have a lower mean time than the almost no experience group for each training method. The second training method has a lower mean task time and the third method a higher mean task time than the overall average of 22.9 minutes.

Stat ▸ ANOVA ▸ Interactions Plot
   Select TaskTime in **Responses:**
   Select Method and Experience in **Factors: OK**

MTB > %Interact 'Method' 'Experience';
SUBC>   Response 'TaskTime'.

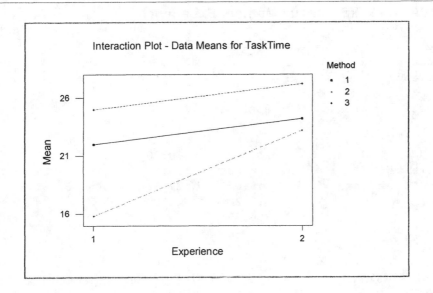

Employees with considerable experience (coded 1) take less time than the employees with almost no experience for each training method. The second method has a lower mean task times at both experience levels. The lines on the display should be approximately parallel when there is no interaction between method and experience. The method three line is not parallel to the other two lines, indicating possible interaction.

Balanced ANOVA and Two-way give the analysis of variance table for factorial experiments. We use
$\alpha = .05$ for each F test to analyze this factorial experiment.

Stat ► ANOVA ► Balanced ANOVA   MTB > ANOVA 'TaskTime' = Method|Experience
  Select TaskTime in **Responses:**
  Select Method | Experience in **Model. OK**

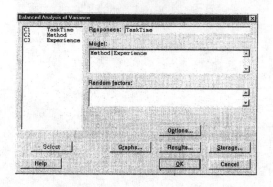

ANOVA: TaskTime versus Method, Experience

Factor	Type	Levels	Values		
Method	fixed	3	1	2	3
Experience	fixed	2	1	2	

Analysis of Variance for TaskTime

Source	DF	SS	MS	F	P
Method	2	218.40	109.20	5.07	0.015
Experience	1	116.03	116.03	5.38	0.029
Method*Experience	2	45.07	22.53	1.05	0.367
Error	24	517.20	21.55		
Total	29	896.70			

Stat ► ANOVA ► Two-way   MTB> Twoway 'TaskTime' 'Method' 'Experience';
  Select TaskTime in **Response:**   SUBC>   Means 'Method' 'Experience'.
  Select Method in **Row factor:**
   and click **Display means**;
  Select Experience in **Column factor:**
   and click **Display means. OK**

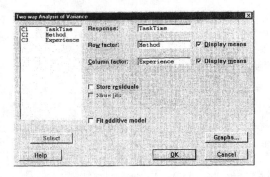

Two-way ANOVA: TaskTime versus Method, Experience

```
Analysis of Variance for TaskTime
Source        DF        SS        MS        F         P
Method         2     218.4     109.2      5.07     0.015
Experience     1     116.0     116.0      5.38     0.029
Interaction    2      45.1      22.5      1.05     0.367
Error         24     517.2      21.6
Total         29     896.7

                      Individual 95% CI
Method     Mean    ---+---------+---------+---------+--------
1          23.1                 (--------*--------)
2          19.5    (--------*-------)
3          26.1                        (--------*-------)
                   ---+---------+---------+---------+--------
                   17.5      21.0      24.5      28.0

                      Individual 95% CI
Experience Mean    -------+---------+---------+---------+----
1          20.9     (---------*---------)
2          24.9                   (--------*---------)
                   -------+---------+---------+---------+----
                       20.0      22.5      25.0      27.5
```

Summary of Analysis of Variance Output

The **Balanced ANOVA** command provides a factor table and analysis of variance table for factorial experiments. The **Two-way** output includes the analysis of variance table and confidence intervals for the factors. Both commands provide the *F* test statistics and *p*-values for all exact *F* tests.

The tests for differences in the mean times of methods and experience are relevant only if the factors do not interact. To test whether the interactions are significant, the null and alternative hypotheses are

H_0: There is no interaction between methods and experience.
H_a: Methods and experience interact.

The test statistic, $F = 1.05$, has a p-value of 0.367. Since the p-value is greater than $\alpha = .05$, there is not significant interaction between methods and experience. The tests to determine whether there are differences in the means for methods and experience are relevant.

Since there is no significant interaction, we test for differences between factor level means. The null and alternative hypotheses for significant training method effects are

H_0: The three methods have equal mean task times.
H_a: At least two of the means differ.

The test statistic, $F = 5.07$, has a p-value of 0.015. Since the p-value is less than $\alpha = .05$, there is significant evidence that at least two of the mean task times differ. The confidence intervals for Methods 2 and 3 do not overlap, indicating that method 2 is superior to method 3 in time to complete a task.

The null and alternative hypotheses for significant computer experience effects are

H_0: The two computer experience levels have equal mean task times.
H_a: The two means differ.

The test statistic, $F = 5.38$, has a p-value of 0.029. Since the p-value is less than $\alpha = .05$, there is significant evidence that the two means differ. Employees with considerable computer experience take less time, on average, than employees with almost no experience.

11.4   MULTIPLE COMPARISONS OF MEANS

If the conclusion of the F test is that there is a significant difference in treatment means, we want to know which pairs of treatment means differ. There are several procedures for multiple comparisons, some of which can be done with **Stat ▸ ANOVA ▸ One-way** with stacked data. Two procedures we illustrate are Tukey and Fisher. *Tukey* requires a family error rate α. *Fisher* requires an individual error rate α/c, where c equals the number of pairs of means. The Tukey and Fisher results are comparable for corresponding family and individual rates. Other procedures for multiple comparisons with One-way include Dunnett and MCB. Refer to the HELP facility for specific information on these procedures.

■ Example 6   **Multiple Comparisons**

In Example 1 of this chapter, we found a difference in the mean PE ratios for four industries. Use the Tukey and Fisher multiple comparison procedures to determine which pairs of means differ.

Financial	Medical	Technology	Consumer
24	23	64	15
20	19	29	14
13	34	142	23
31	20	60	38
40	19	97	53
11	28	35	24
14		46	31

Solution The data are entered in a file named **PERatios.mtp** as unstacked data. PE ratios are put in one column, and names for the four industries are put in a second column. We use a family error rate $\alpha = .10$ for Tukey, and an individual error rate $\alpha = .05$ for Fisher.

Manip ▸ Stack ▸ Stack Columns
  Stack the following columns:
    Select Financial - Consumer;
  Click **Column of current worksheet:** enter 'Ratio',
  Enter 'Industry' in **Store subscripts in:**
  Click **Use variable names in subscript column OK**

```
MTB > Name C5 = 'Ratio' C6 = 'Industry'
MTB > Stack 'Financial'-'Consumer' 'Ratio';
SUBC>   Subscripts 'Industry';
SUBC>   UseNames.
```

Stat ▸ ANOVA ▸ One-way
  Select Ratio in **Response:** and Industry in **Factor:**
  Click **Comparisons,**
    Choose **Tukey's**, enter 10;
    Choose **Fisher's**, enter 5. **OK**

```
MTB > Oneway 'Ratio' 'Industry';
SUBC>   Tukey 10;
SUBC>   Fisher 5.
```

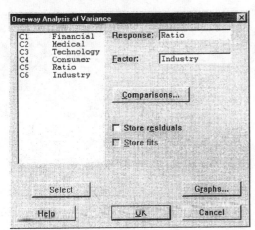

One-way ANOVA: Ratio versus Industry

```
Analysis of Variance for Ratio
Source      DF         SS        MS        F        P
Industry     3       9681      3227     6.46    0.002
Error       23      11491       500
Total       26      21172
                                Individual 95% CIs For Mean
                                Based on Pooled StDev
Level       N      Mean     StDev  ---------+---------+---------+-----
Consumer    7     28.29     13.78     (------*------)
Financial   7     21.86     10.64   (------*------)
Medical     6     23.83      6.05   (-------*------)
Technology  7     67.57     39.77                    (------*------)
                                   ---------+---------+---------+-----
Pooled StDev =   22.35                    25        50        75
```

Tukey's pairwise comparisons

    Family error rate = 0.100
Individual error rate = 0.0235

Critical value = 3.43

Intervals for (column level mean) - (row level mean)

```
               Consumer    Financial    Medical

Financial       -22.55
                 35.41

Medical         -25.71       -32.14
                 34.61        28.18

Technology      -68.26       -74.69      -73.90
                -10.31       -16.74      -13.58
```

Fisher's pairwise comparisons

    Family error rate = 0.193
Individual error rate = 0.0500

Critical value = 2.069

```
Intervals for (column level mean) - (row level mean)

            Consumer    Financial    Medical

Financial    -18.29
              31.15

Medical      -21.28       -27.70
              30.18        23.75

Technology   -64.01       -70.43      -69.47
             -14.57       -20.99      -18.01
```

The columns and rows in the TUKEY and FISHER confidence interval tables are labeled by industry. For example, the TUKEY interval for the difference between the mean PE ratios for Technology (μ_3) and Consumer (μ_4) is $-68.26 \le \mu_3 - \mu_4 \le -10.31$; the Fisher interval is $-64.01 \le \mu_3 - \mu_4 \le -14.57$. intervals do not contain 0, indicating a difference. Other intervals that do not contain 0 are the intervals for the difference between means for Technology and Financial, and Technology and Medical. We conclude that there are significant differences between Technology and the other three industries in mean PE ratios.

There are no subcommands with Two-way and ANOVA for multiple comparison procedures. You can, however, sort the means and compare differences between means with the half-width for the **Bonferroni multiple comparison** procedure. To obtain a family error rate of at most α for g pairwise comparisons, the confidence coefficient for each pair is $(1 - \alpha/g)$. The procedure determines the Bonferroni critical difference:

$$B_{ij} = t_{\alpha/2g}\, s\, \sqrt{1/n_i + 1/n_j}$$

where $s = \sqrt{\text{MSE}}$ and $g = k(k - 1)/2$ pairwise comparisons. All pairs that differ by more than B_{ij} are significantly different.

The next example illustrates these calculations. The inverse probability distribution gives the critical value of t, where the degrees of freedom are the error degrees of freedom given in the analysis of variance table.

■ **Example 7**   **Bonferroni Confidence Intervals**

Refer to Example 4 of this chapter. The University Chronicle conducted a survey of prices at four local grocery stores. The analysis of variance procedure showed that there was a difference in the four stores in terms of grocery prices. Use the Bonferroni multiple comparison procedure to determine which pairs of mean prices for stores differ. Use $\alpha = .05$.

	Grocery Store			
Product	**1**	**2**	**3**	**4**
Ground Beef	2.18	2.09	2.16	1.99
Mac & Cheese	0.89	0.96	0.87	1.09
Heinz Ketchup	1.39	1.59	1.39	2.25
Gallon Milk	2.73	2.73	2.88	2.73
Fruit Loops	2.73	2.73	2.73	3.19
Campbell's Soup	0.79	0.83	0.79	0.95
Northern Tissue	1.39	1.59	1.39	1.89
Ragu Sauce	2.26	2.40	2.26	2.65

Solution All pairs of treatment means that differ by more than the Bonferroni critical difference are significantly different. For four treatment means, there are $4(3)/2 = 6$ pairwise comparisons. We order the treatment means to determine critical differences. Data are saved in **Store.mtp**.

Stat ▸ ANOVA ▸ Balanced ANOVA
  Select Price in **Responses:**
  Select Store and Product in **Model:**
  Click **Results** and **Select** Store in
  Display means according to the terms. OK

MTB > ANOVA 'Price' = Store Product;
SUBC>   Means Store.

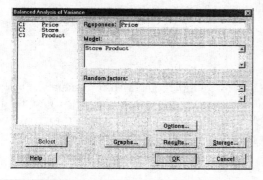
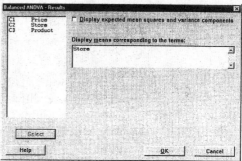

ANOVA: Price versus Store, Product

```
Factor      Type Levels Values
Store       fixed    4    1    2    3    4
Product     fixed    8    1    2    3    4    5    6    7
                          8


Analysis of Variance for Price

Source      DF        SS        MS        F       P
Store        3    0.4581    0.1527     5.79   0.005
Product      7   16.4921    2.3560    89.28   0.000
Error       21    0.5542    0.0264
Total       31   17.5043
```

```
Means

Store    N     Price
1        8     1.7950
2        8     1.8650
3        8     1.8088
4        8     2.0925
```

Calc ▸ Calculator
  Enter K1 in **Store results in variable:**
  Enter 1 - (.05/(2*6)) in **Expression. OK**

MTB > Let K1 = 1 - (.05/(2*6))

Calc ▸ Probability Distributions ▸ t
  Click **Inverse cumulative probability**;
  Enter 21 in **Degrees of Freedom:**
  Enter K1 in **Input constant. OK**

MTB > InvCDF K1;
SUBC> T 21.

Inverse Cumulative Distribution Function

```
Student's t distribution with 21 DF

P( X <= x )          x
   0.9958        2.9121
```

Calc ▸ Calculator
  Enter K2 in **Store results in variable:**
  Enter 2.9121*SQRT(.0264*(1/8+1/8))
    in **Expression. OK**

MTB > Let K2=2.9121*SQRT(.0264*(1/8+1/8))

Manip ▸ Display Data
  Select K2 in **Display. OK**

MTB > Print K2

Data Display

```
K2      0.236579
```

All pairs of treatment means that differ by more than the Bonferroni critical difference B_{ij} = .237 differ significantly. Listing the means in order makes it easier to find differences. From the ANOVA output, we order from highest to lowest.

Store	Price
4	2.0925
2	1.8650
3	1.8088
1	1.7950

The highest mean price of $2.09 differs by more than $0.24 from the two lowest means. Store 4 has significantly higher mean prices than stores 1 and 3.

11.5 CHECKING MODEL ASSUMPTIONS

The assumptions underlying the analysis of variance for each experimental design are similar to those required for a regression analysis. For example, assumptions for a completely randomized design are that the data for the treatments must have normal probability distributions with equal variances. The assumptions can be checked with %RESPLOTS which was described in Chapter 10.

■ **Example 8**   **Analysis of Variance Assumptions**

In Example 1, we found a difference in the mean price earnings or PE ratio for four industries. Obtain and interpret residual plots for the analysis of variance.

Solution   The data are saved in a file named **PERatios.mtp**; data are unstacked in four columns named Financial, Medical, Technology, and Consumer. For this example, we stack the data.

Manip ▸ Stack ▸ Stack Columns
  Stack the following columns:
    Select Financial - Consumer;
  Click **Column of current worksheet:** enter 'Ratio',
    Enter 'Industry' in **Store subscripts in:**
  Click **Use variable names in subscript column OK**

MTB > Name C5 = 'Ratio' C6 = 'Industry'
MTB > Stack 'Financial'-'Consumer' 'Ratio';
SUBC>   Subscripts 'Industry';
SUBC>   UseNames.

Stat ▸ ANOVA ▸ One-way
  Select Ratio in **Response:** and Industry in **Factor:**
  Click **Store Resids**; click **Store Fits. OK**

MTB > Name C7 = 'RESI1' C8 = 'FITS1'
MTB > Oneway 'Ratio' 'Industry' 'RESI1' 'FITS1'

One-way ANOVA: Ratio versus Industry

```
Analysis of Variance for Ratio
Source      DF        SS       MS       F        P
Industry     3      9681     3227    6.46    0.002
Error       23     11491      500
Total       26     21172
```

Manip ▸ Display Data
  Select Ratio - FITS1 in **Display. OK**

MTB > Print 'Ratio'-'FITS1'

Data Display

Row	Ratio	Industry	RESI1	FITS1
1	24	Financial	2.1429	21.8571
2	20	Financial	-1.8571	21.8571
3	13	Financial	-8.8571	21.8571
4	31	Financial	9.1429	21.8571
5	40	Financial	18.1429	21.8571
6	11	Financial	-10.8571	21.8571
7	14	Financial	-7.8571	21.8571
8	23	Medical	-0.8333	23.8333
9	19	Medical	-4.8333	23.8333
10	34	Medical	10.1667	23.8333
11	20	Medical	-3.8333	23.8333
12	19	Medical	-4.8333	23.8333
13	28	Medical	4.1667	23.8333
14	64	Technology	-3.5714	67.5714
15	29	Technology	-38.5714	67.5714
16	142	Technology	74.4286	67.5714
17	60	Technology	-7.5714	67.5714
18	97	Technology	29.4286	67.5714
19	35	Technology	-32.5714	67.5714
20	46	Technology	-21.5714	67.5714
21	15	Consumer	-13.2857	28.2857
22	14	Consumer	-14.2857	28.2857
23	23	Consumer	-5.2857	28.2857
24	38	Consumer	9.7143	28.2857
25	53	Consumer	24.7143	28.2857
26	24	Consumer	-4.2857	28.2857
27	31	Consumer	2.7143	28.2857

The fitted values are the industry means of the PE ratios, and the residuals are the differences between the actual data and the means.

Stat ▸ Regression ▸ Residual Plots
  Select RESI1 in **Residuals:** and FITS1 in **Fits:**
  Add **Title. OK**

MTB > %Resplots 'RESI1' 'FITS1';
SUBC>   Title "Residual Plots".

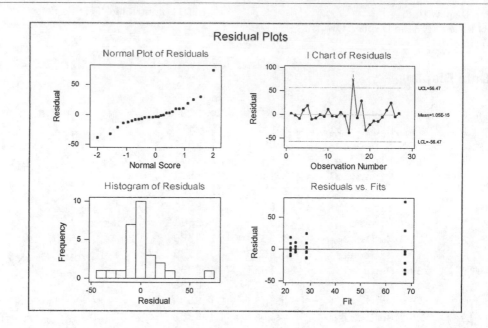

To meet the normality assumption, points should fall close to a straight line on the normal plot. The normality assumption may not be appropriate. The residuals versus the fits plot indicates that there are some differences in variances for the four groups. If the ANOVA assumptions are not satisfied, a nonparametric procedure such as that described in the next section can be used to compare the locations of more than two populations.

11.6   NONPARAMETRIC TEST FOR A COMPLETELY RANDOMIZED DESIGN

The analysis of variance F test assumes that independent random samples are selected from normally distributed populations with equal variances. If these assumptions are not satisfied, the nonparametric **Kruskal-Wallis H test** can be used to compare the locations of more than two populations.

The Kruskal-Wallis test assumes that independent random samples are selected from continuous distributions. All the observations from k samples are ranked, and rank sums are calculated for each sample. The H test statistic is calculated using the rank sum for each sample. The hypotheses are

H_0: The k probability distributions have the same median.
H_a: At least two of the k distributions have different medians.

Under the null hypothesis, the H statistic has an approximate chi-square distribution, with $(k-1)$ degrees of freedom. The rejection region is located in the upper tail of the chi-square distribution.

KRUSKAL-WALLIS H TEST

This command performs a test of differences in k population medians.   The factor column may be numeric or text.

In addition to the H test statistic and p-value, the output includes a table of the number of observations, median, average rank, and z value of each sample. The z value measures the difference between the mean rank for each sample and the mean rank for all observations.

Stat ▸ Nonparametrics ▸ Kruskal-Wallis

KRUSKAL-WALLIS *data* C, *factor levels* C   Tests differences in medians

■ **Example 9**   **Kruskal-Wallis H Test**

Not only is the type of medication important for the control of migraine headaches, but also how the medication is administrated. Suppose that three methods of administering Isomet are studied. Twenty-four people who suffer from migraines were randomly split into three groups of eight, and one method was used on each group. After three hours the people rated their pain on a scale of 0 to 10. The higher the number, the greater the pain. Is there sufficient evidence that the method of administering Isomet has an effect on the relief of migraine headaches? Use $\alpha = .10$.

Method 1	Method 2	Method 3
5	5	9
2	2	3
2	5	9
5	8	2
6	2	7
2	4	4
2	6	9
5	6	4

Solution   The data are saved in a file named **Pain.mtp.** Pain scores are stacked in a column named Score; corresponding methods are stacked in Method. We compare the methods graphically using box plots.

Graph ▸ Boxplot
  Select Score in **Graph 1 Y**
   and Method in **Graph 1 X**;
  Click **Annotation**, choose **Title**, add a title, **OK**

MTB > Boxplot 'Score' * 'Method';
SUBC> Box;
SUBC> Symbol;
SUBC>   Outlier;
SUBC> Title "Isomet for Pain".

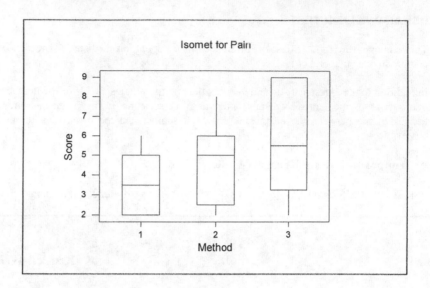

Isomet for Pain

The display indicates that Method 1 has the lowest median score, and has the least variation in scores.

The hypothesis test to test whether the methods have the same median is

H_0: The three probability distributions have the same median.
H_a: At least two distributions have different medians.

Stat ▸ Nonparametrics ▸ Kruskal-Wallis   MTB > Kruskal-Wallis 'Score' 'Method'
  Select Score in **Response:**
  Select Method in **Factor. OK**

Kruskal-Wallis Test: Score versus Method

Kruskal-Wallis Test on Score

Method	N	Median	Ave Rank	Z
1	8	3.500	9.5	-1.47
2	8	5.000	12.9	0.18
3	8	5.500	15.1	1.29
Overall	24		12.5	

H = 2.57 DF = 2 P = 0.277
H = 2.67 DF = 2 P = 0.264 (adjusted for ties)

The p-value is the probability, assuming the null hypothesis is true, of obtaining an $H > 2.57$. Since the p-value $= 0.277$ is not less than $\alpha = .10$, there is not sufficient evidence in the samples to conclude that at least two of the distributions differ. The z-values reflect the relative differences between the mean scores for the methods.

EXERCISES

1. Several school districts are considering delaying the start of a school day by two hours. Studie have indicated that many students are not ready to start classes at 8:00 in the morning. A researcher developed a 15 point test that measured student learning ability. Higher scores indicate greater learning ability. Forty-eight students were randomly assigned to four groups of twelve students each. One group took the test at 7:00 am, a second group at 8:00 am, a third group a 9:00 am, and a last group at 10:00 am. The scores are shown below. (File: **SchoolTime.mtp**)

7 am	8 am	9 am	10 am
3	7	9	12
7	8	13	8
2	11	10	8
8	10	10	10
3	10	12	9
8	7	9	12
5	4	12	9
2	8	10	8
3	7	11	13
9	7	13	10
6	9	6	11
5	9	6	12

a. Graphically summarize the data.
b. Is there significant evidence that school start time has an effect on student learning ability? Use $\alpha = .05$.
c. Interpret the 95% confidence intervals given on the printout.
d. If there is a difference in means, determine which means differ significantly. Use a family error rate of $\alpha = .10$.

2. A large mail order company recently purchased a new integrated computer software package, and is considering three different training methods for its employees. Fifteen employees with comparable computer experience were selected, and five were randomly assigned to each training method. After completing the training, each employee was given an identical computer task. The times to complete the task were recorded as follow.

Method 1	Method 2	Method 3
26	19	30
14	29	38
26	31	30
21	11	19
33	13	35

a. Construct and interpret dot plots of the times to complete the task for the three methods.
b. Test whether there are significant differences between the mean task times for the three training methods. Use $\alpha = .05$.
c. If there is a difference in mean task times, determine which means differ. Use a family error rate of $\alpha = .10$.

. A mutual fund is a financial instrument that pools the investments of many people, and invests in stocks and bonds. Many types of mutual funds are available. These include stocks, bonds, small company stocks, and gold stocks. A sound mutual fund performs well in both strong and weak markets. Because of business cycles, the ten year performance record of a fund provides a good indication of the performance of a fund. Suppose an investor wants to compare the rates of return for the stock, stock and bond, and foreign funds. Random samples of the three types of funds were selected, and the following average annual returns for a period of ten years were reported in Forbes. (File: **Funds.mtp**)

Stock		Stock and Bond	Foreign	
14.8	16.8	16.2	11.5	23.8
16.2	20.1	12.0	0.7	16.0
14.5	12.2	14.4	4.7	14.7
14.7	17.0	12.6	17.0	17.3
8.5	16.2	14.3	20.5	16.0
14.8	11.0	15.7	12.4	3.5
12.0	8.4	9.7	12.5	
5.0	11.3	13.1		
15.3	16.3	13.7		
12.5				

a. Construct and interpret dot plots of the annual rates of return for the three funds.
b. Obtain the analysis of variance table. Is there significant evidence that the mean annual rates differ for the three funds? Use $\alpha = .05$. Interpret the p-value.
c. Interpret the 95% confidence intervals given on the printout.
d. If there is a difference in mean annual rates, determine which means differ significantly. Use a family error rate of $\alpha = .10$.

4. Suppose thirty people over 65 are randomly assigned to one of three treatments. In treatment group one, ten people are taught a series of strategies to improve their memory. In treatment group two, ten people are given a placebo pill and told that it will improve their memory. Group three is a control group that does not receive the strategies to improve memory or a placebo pill. At the end of the experiment the scores on a memory test are recorded as follow.
(File: **MemoryTest.mtp**)

Memory Strategies	Placebo Pill	Control Group
80	79	78
83	82	69
79	89	69
71	78	74
72	86	61
76	81	73
79	89	80
69	85	74
85	69	61
92	74	70

a. Graphically compare the three groups.
a. Is there sufficient evidence in the samples that there is a difference in average scores? Us $\alpha = .05$.
c. Interpret the 95% confidence intervals given on the printout.
d. If there is a difference in means, determine which means differ significantly. Use a famil error rate of $\alpha = .10$.

5. A foods company recently produced a new snack food and wants to determine whether sales are affected by age and type of television advertising. Three age groups and two types of television advertising to promote the product have been identified for the study. One type included the endorsement of a professional football player; the other type emphasized the nutritional value o: the snack food. Twenty consumers from each age group were randomly selected for the study and each type of TV ad was randomly assigned to ten consumers in each group. After viewing the ad, each person was asked to complete a questionnaire concerning interest in the product. The composite scores, based on a 100-point scale, are given in the following table. A higher score indicates more interest in the product. (File: **TVAds.mtp**)

	Endorsement Ad			Nutritional Ad	
Age 1	**Age 2**	**Age 3**	**Age 1**	**Age 2**	**Age 3**
26	13	16	29	14	29
24	15	16	20	15	34
11	24	8	21	9	26
21	23	18	10	25	26
28	16	32	14	28	48
32	7	22	2	11	26
35	41	28	8	12	20
21	26	14	3	19	10
37	24	7	20	37	14
36	23	15	19	24	31

a. Calculate the treatment means, factor level means, and overall mean.
b. Obtain the analysis of variance table. Test for factor interactions. If there is not significant interaction, test for differences in factor level means. Use $\alpha = .10$.
c. Numerically compare relevant means. Use a family error rate of $\alpha = .10$.

6. An investor is interested in studying the effects of the type of mutual fund and fee structure on fund performance. The fund types of interest are stock, bond, and foreign. Fee structures of mutual funds are of two types: load or no load. Load refers to the sales commissions and other distribution expenses charged to the investor. The load is usually between 4% and 8% of the invested amount. No load refers to no fees at the time of purchase. For the study, random samples of five funds of each type, load and no load, were observed from 1980 to 1989. The average annual yields are given in the table.

	Stock	Stock/Bond	Foreign
Load Funds	16.2	16.2	11.5
	14.7	12.0	17.0
	5.0	12.6	12.4
	15.3	14.3	23.8
	12.5	13.1	16.0
No Load Funds	14.8	14.4	0.7
	14.5	15.7	20.5
	8.5	9.7	12.5
	14.8	16.4	16.0
	12.0	15.1	14.2

a. Obtain a table of the data and the means. Summarize.
b. Graphically compare treatment means. Interpret.
c. Construct the analysis of variance tables using TWOWAY and ANOVA. Compare the output.
d. Test whether there is evidence of significant interaction between the two factors. If there is not evidence, test whether there are significant main effects. Use $\alpha = .10$.
e. Compare the relevant pairs of treatment means. Use $\alpha = .10$.

7. An elementary school researcher claims that students who are awarded for reading, and also are read aloud to, perform better in school. To test the claim, she randomly assigns 20 students to four reading groups of five students each. In group one the students are not awarded to read and do not read aloud within their group. Group two is awarded but do not read aloud. Group three are not award and read aloud. Group four are awarded and read aloud within their group. After two months, the following performance scores are observed. (File: **Reading.mtp**)

Student	Score	Award	Aloud
1	30	no	no
2	37	no	no
3	30	no	no
4	19	no	no
5	26	no	no
6	30	yes	no
7	44	yes	no
8	35	yes	no
9	26	yes	no
10	38	yes	no
11	42	no	yes
12	55	no	yes
13	58	no	yes
14	53	no	yes
15	54	no	yes
16	40	yes	yes
17	48	yes	yes
18	32	yes	yes
19	36	yes	yes
20	41	yes	yes

a. Construct a table of the data grouped by Award and Aloud, and a table of treatment means factor level means, and the overall mean. Summarize.
b. Obtain the analysis of variance tables using TWOWAY and ANOVA. Compare the outputs
c. Test whether there is evidence of significant interaction between the two factors. If there i not evidence, test whether there are significant factor effects. Use $\alpha = .05$.
d. If there are significant effects, determine which means for the reading groups differ. Use family error rate of $\alpha = .10$.

CHAPTER 12

INTRODUCTION TO PROCESS AND QUALITY CONTROL

This chapter considers some statistical control procedures for measuring and regulating product and service characteristics. A control chart continuously monitors a quantitative or qualitative characteristic of a process. We illustrate statistical control charts for individual observations, process means, variation, and proportions and number of defectives per item.

NEW COMMANDS

CCHART	ICHART	PCHART	RCHART
SCHART	XBARCHART		

12.1 GENERAL CHARACTERISTICS OF CONTROL CHARTS

Control charts are plots of sample observations or statistics obtained periodically from a continuing process. Examples of sample statistics include the mean and variation of a process and the fraction of defective items produced by a process.

To construct a control chart, samples of the process output are taken at periodic points, and then statistics are calculated and plotted over time. The center line of the control chart is the process mean. The upper and lower control limits (UCL and LCL) are generally the process mean plus or minus three standard deviations. If unknown, the mean and standard deviation are estimated from the sample data.

Changes in the values of the sample statistics over time provide useful information about the underlying process. The process may be out of control if a sample statistic falls outside the control limits, or if there are patterns in the data suggesting a nonrandom process. Control charts indicate whether corrective action should be taken to change the process.

MINITAB OPTIONS AND SUBCOMMANDS

This section describes some options that are common to most Minitab control charts. These charts include the I chart, $\bar{x}$-chart, S-chart, R-chart, C-chart, and P-chart presented in this chapter.

GRAPHICAL OPTIONS FOR CONTROL CHARTS

The following are some options available for constructing Minitab control charts. Several options are available for estimating σ; the upper and lower control limits are usually at $\mu \pm 3\sigma$, but can be set at any level.

SLIMITS K ... K	Changes σ upper and lower control limits
HLINES E ... E	Adds horizontal lines at specified values
ESTIMATE K ... K	Specifies the samples used for charts
XSTART K (END K)	Specifies the portion of the chart to be printed
YSTART K (END K)	Controls the y-axis scaling
YINCREMENT = K	Controls the y-axis scaling
XLABEL	Adds label for x-axis
YLABEL	Adds label for y-axis
TITLE	Adds a title on control chart
FOOTNOTE	Adds footnote(s)

STATISTICAL TESTS

Minitab has eight statistical tests to monitor a process. Some or all of the tests are available with control charts.

TESTS FOR CONTROL CHART

The following are eight possible tests for detecting specific patterns of variation. The numerical value given in each test is the default; this can be changed within a range.

1. One point beyond 3σ of the center line
2. Nine consecutive points on one side of the center line
3. Six consecutive increasing or decreasing points
4. Fourteen consecutive points, alternating up and down
5. Two out of three consecutive points beyond 2σ on one side of the center line
6. Four out of five consecutive points beyond one σ on one side of the center line
7. Fifteen consecutive points within one σ of the center line
8. Eight consecutive points beyond one σ of the center line

12.2 CHART FOR INDIVIDUAL OBSERVATIONS: I CHART

The I Chart monitors a product's quantitative characteristic, such as weight, length, or diameter. This chart plots individual measurements taken at periodic points of time.

CONTROL CHART FOR INDIVIDUAL OBSERVATIONS

This is a control chart for individual observations. The center line of the chart is the process mean μ. The upper and lower control limits are given by

$$UCL = \mu + 3\sigma \qquad LCL = \mu - 3\sigma$$

where σ is the population standard deviation. If unknown, μ and σ are estimated from the data. A measurement could fall beyond these control limits if a rare event occurs or if the process goes out of control.

Stat ▸ Control Charts ▸ Individuals

ICHART C	Constructs a control chart for individual observations
MU = K	Specifies the mean
SIGMA = K	Specifies the standard deviation
RSPAN = K	Specifics the number of observations to estimate σ
TEST K ... K	Specifies one or more of the eight tests

◀ **Example 1**   **Individual Control Chart**

A large grocery store has a machine to weigh and package ground meat. An adjustment on the machine allows the operator to fill packages at different weights. Suppose the operator adjusts the machine to fill one pound packages. To monitor the fill process, the operator randomly selects a package every five minutes and measures its weight. The weights of 20 packages are given in the following table. Construct a control chart. Determine whether the process is in control.

Package	Weight	Package	Weight
1	1.00	11	1.01
2	0.99	12	0.99
3	0.98	13	0.98
4	1.01	14	0.99
5	1.01	15	0.87
6	0.99	16	1.01
7	1.06	17	0.99
8	0.99	18	0.99
9	0.99	19	0.97
10	1.03	20	0.99

Solution   The data are saved in a file named **Weight-1.mtp**; weights are in a column named Weight.

Stat ▸ **Control Charts ▸ Individuals**
  Select Weight in **Variable:**
  Click **Tests**, check **Perform all eight tests. OK**

MTB > Ichart 'Weight';
SUBC> Slimits;
SUBC> Symbol;
SUBC> Connect;
SUBC> Test 1 2 3 4 5 6 7 8.

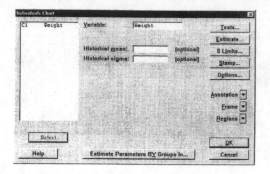

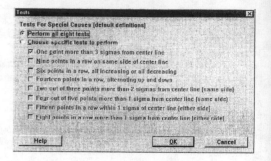

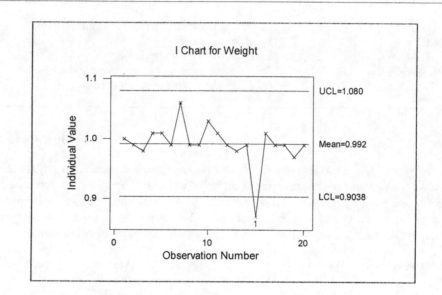

```
TEST  One point more than 3.00 sigmas from center line.
Test Failed at points: 15
```

The chart shows that the weight of package 15 falls below three standard deviations of the mean. The process is not in control. This control chart should not be used to monitor future process output.

12.3 CONTROL CHART FOR MEANS: $\bar{x}$-CHART

The $\bar{x}$-chart monitors a quantitative characteristic of a process, such as weight, length, or diameter. This chart shows the means of random samples taken at periodic points in time. The center line of an $\bar{x}$-chart is the process mean μ. The upper and lower control limits are given by

$$UCL = \mu + 3\sigma/\sqrt{n} \qquad LCL = \mu - 3\sigma/\sqrt{n}$$

where σ is the population standard deviation and n is the sample size. If unknown, μ and σ are estimated from the data. A sample mean could fall beyond these control limits if a rare event occurs or if the process goes out of control. The process variation is assumed to be stable.

CONTROL CHART TO MONITOR A PROCESS MEAN

This command plots the sample means. If the subgroups are in columns, enter a data column followed by a constant or column which specifies the sample sizes. If the subgroups are in rows, omit the arguments on the command line and use the RSUB subcommand. If unknown, μ and σ are estimated from the data.

Stat ▸ Control Charts ▸ Xbar

XBARCHART (C *sample size* E)	Constructs a control chart for the means
RSUB C ... C	Use if subgroups are in rows
MU = K	Specifies the mean
SIGMA = K	Specifies the standard deviation
TEST K ... K	Tests for detecting patterns of variation

◼ **Example 2**   **Control Chart: Process Mean**

Refer to Example 1. A large grocery store has a machine to weigh and package ground meat. An adjustment on the machine allows the operator to fill packages at different weights. Suppose the operator adjusts the machine to fill one pound packages. To monitor the fill process, the operator randomly selects a sample of five packages every 15 minutes. The weights of 20 samples are given in the table below. Construct and interpret an $\bar{x}$-chart using the data to estimate μ and σ. Include all tests for special causes of variation.

Sample	Weights of Packages				
1	1.01	1.03	1.00	1.06	1.02
2	1.05	1.05	1.05	1.04	1.08
3	1.09	1.03	0.97	1.04	0.96
4	1.01	1.07	1.07	1.07	1.11
5	1.03	0.99	0.92	1.00	1.04
6	1.07	1.03	1.00	1.04	0.99
7	0.99	1.00	1.09	0.97	1.03
8	0.87	1.00	1.03	1.05	1.07
9	0.99	0.93	1.01	0.95	0.96
10	1.02	1.02	1.00	1.02	0.93
11	0.94	1.09	1.06	1.05	1.01
12	0.98	0.98	1.05	1.00	1.07
13	1.05	1.00	1.03	1.14	1.09
14	0.95	0.97	1.06	1.00	1.08

15	1.06	0.99	1.00	0.98	1.01
16	1.06	1.03	1.03	1.01	1.09
17	1.09	1.09	1.17	1.05	0.89
18	1.02	1.01	1.04	0.98	1.08
19	1.10	0.99	1.05	0.96	1.10
20	1.08	0.91	0.94	0.97	0.98

Solution   The data are saved in a file named **Weight-5.mtp**; weights are in columns C1 to C5. Eac row of the Minitab worksheet gives the five observations in a sample.

Stat ▸ Control Charts ▸ Xbar
  Click **Subgroups across rows of:**
  Select C1-C5;
  Click **Tests**, check **Perform all eight tests**;
  Click **Annotation**, choose **Title**, add a title. **OK**

MTB > Xbarchart;
SUBC>   Rsub C1-C5;
SUBC>   Title"Package Weight Control Chart
SUBC>   Slimits;
SUBC>   Symbol;
SUBC>   Connect;
SUBC>   Test 1 2 3 4 5 6 7 8.

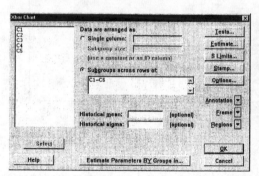

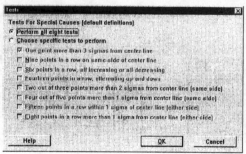

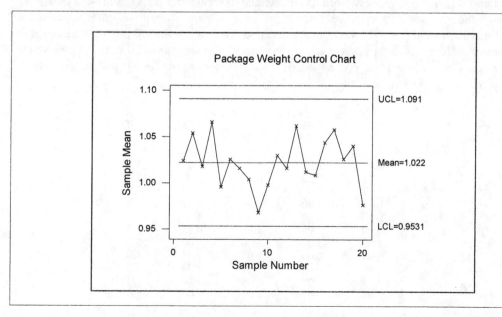

Package Weight Control Chart

No special causes of variation are indicated in the $\bar{x}$-chart. The fill process is not out of control. The control limits can be used to monitor future process output.

12.4 CONTROL CHARTS FOR PROCESS VARIATION

Control charts for process variation typically precede an $\bar{x}$-chart. The *S*-chart monitors variation, as measured by standard deviations. The production process variation is in control if all sample standard deviations fall within the control limits and no special causes of variation are detected.

CONTROL CHART FOR PROCESS STANDARD DEVIATION

This command prints a control chart of sample standard deviations. If the subgroups are in columns, enter a data column followed by a constant or column which specifies the sample sizes. If the subgroups are in rows, omit the arguments on the command line and use the RSUB subcommand.

The default estimate of sigma is the average of the subgroup standard deviations. You can enter a historical value with SIGMA.

Stat ▸ Control Charts ▸ S

SCHART (C *samples size* E)	Constructs a standard deviation control chart
RSUB C ... C	Use if subgroups are in rows
SIGMA = K	Specifies the standard deviation
TEST K ... K	First four tests are available

The *R*-chart monitors process variation, as measured by sample ranges. The range is the difference between the maximum and minimum value of each sample. The production process variation is in control if all sample ranges fall within the control limits and no special causes of variation are detected. The center line of the *R*-chart is located at μ_R, the mean of the ranges, and the upper and lower control limits are located at $\mu_R \pm 3\sigma_R$. If unknown, μ_R and σ_R are estimated from the sample data.

CONTROL CHART FOR PROCESS RANGES

This command prints a control chart of sample ranges. If the subgroups are in columns, enter a data column followed by a constant or column which specifies the sample sizes. If the subgroups are in rows, omit the arguments on the main command line and use the RSUB subcommand.

Stat ▸ Control Charts ▸ R

RCHART (C *samples size* E)	Constructs a control chart of ranges
RSUB C ... C	Use if subgroups are in rows
SIGMA = K	Specifies the standard deviation
TEST K ... K	First four tests are available

■ **Example 3**   **Control Charts for Process Variation**

Consider the fill process described in the previous example. A large grocery store has a machine to weigh and package ground meat. An operator selects a random sample of five packages every 15 minutes. Construct and interpret an *S*-chart and an *R*-chart.

Solution   The data are saved in a file named **Weight-5.mtp**. Sample observations are in rows of columns C1 to C5.

Stat ▸ Control Charts ▸ S	MTB > Schart;
Click **Subgroups across rows of:**	SUBC> Rsub C1-C5;
Select C1-C5;	SUBC> Title "Package Weight Standard Deviations";
Click **Tests**, check **Perform all four tests**;	SUBC> Rbar;
Click **Annotation**, choose **Title**, add a title. **OK**	SUBC> Symbol;
	SUBC> Connect;
	SUBC> Test 1 2 3 4.

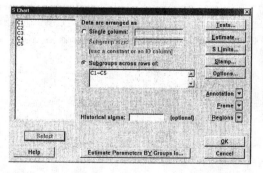

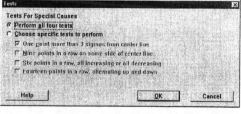

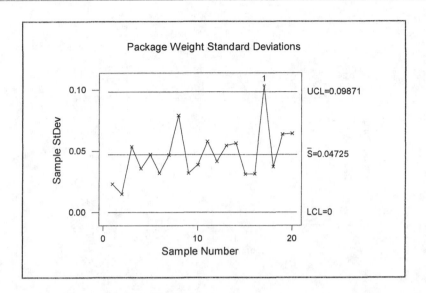

TEST 1. One point more than 3.00 sigmas from center line.
Test Failed at points: 17

The S-chart indicates that the process variation is out of control. One test fails at sample number 17 because of an unusually large standard deviation.

Stat ▸ Control Charts ▸ R
  Click **Subgroups across rows of:**
   Select C1-C5;
  Click **Tests**, check **Perform all four tests**;
  Click **Annotation**, choose **Title**, add a title. **OK**

MTB > Rchart;
SUBC> Rsub C1-C5;
SUBC> Title "Package Weight Ranges";
SUBC> Rbar;
SUBC> Symbol;
SUBC> Connect;
SUBC> Test 1 2 3 4.

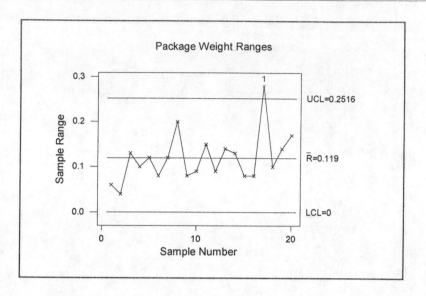

Package Weight Ranges

TEST 1. One point more than 3.00 sigmas from center line.
Test Failed at points: 17

The *R*-chart also indicates that the process variation is out of control. This test failed at the same sample as the *S*-chart did. The machine operator should determine a cause for the unusually large sample range.

NOTE

*An Xbar Chart and Standard Deviation Chart or Range Chart can be constructed at the same time by using the Xbar/S or Xbar/R commands. Use **Stat ▸ Control Charts ▸ Xbar-S** or **Stat ▸ Control Charts ▸ Xbar-R**.*

12.5   CONTROL CHART FOR A PROCESS PROPORTION: P-CHART

The *P*-chart monitors a qualitative characteristic of a process, such as the proportion of nonconforming or defective items. It indicates the proportion of nonconformities observed in samples collected over time.

The center line is *p*, the process proportion of nonconformities. The upper and lower control limits are

$$UCL = p + 3\sqrt{p(1-p)/n} \qquad LCL = p - 3\sqrt{p(1-p)/n}$$

where n is the sample size. Since $0 \le p \le 1$, UCL is set at 1 if the value of UCL is greater than 1, and LCL is set at 0 if the value of LCL is less than 0. If unknown, p is the proportion of nonconformities in the sample data.

CONTROL CHART FOR PROPORTIONS

This command prints a *P*-chart of the proportion of nonconformities. The input column contains the number of nonconformities in the samples. A constant or column specifies the sample size. If E is a constant, all samples are of size E. If E is a column, the numbers in the column determine the sample sizes.

Stat ▸ Control Charts ▸ P

PCHART *nonconformities* C *sample size* E	Plots the proportion of defectives
P = K	Specifies the binomial *p*
TEST K ... K	First four tests are available

■ **Example 4**   **P-Chart: Process Proportion**

The Federal Aviation Administration continually monitors the performance of United States airlines. Of particular interest is the proportion of flights that are not on time. Historically, about 30% of flights do not arrive within 15 minutes of their scheduled time, and are classified as delays. Suppose that a major airline with a 30% delay rate launched a program to decrease its flight delays. To monitor the success of the program, the airline randomly selected 25 flights per day for 28 days and recorded the following delays. Construct and interpret a *P*-chart of the proportion of delayed flights.

Day	1	2	3	4	5	6	7	8	9	10	11	12	13	14
Delays	12	6	8	6	13	8	10	6	9	7	3	5	11	7

Day	15	16	17	18	19	20	21	22	23	24	25	26	27	28
Delays	3	4	7	7	9	6	5	7	2	7	3	2	4	5

Solution The data are saved in a file named **Airline.mtp**; delays are in a column named Delays. The sample size, $n = 25$, for each day and the historical proportion, $p = .3$, are specified in the dialog box.

Stat ▸ Control Charts ▸ P	MTB > PChart 'Delays' 25;
Select Delays in **Variable:**	SUBC> P .3;
Enter 25 in **Subgroup size:**	SUBC> Title "Daily Flight Delays";
And 0.3 in **Historical p:**	SUBC> Slimits;
Click **Tests**, check **Perform all four tests**;	SUBC> Symbol;
Click **Annotation**, choose **Title**, add a title. **OK**	SUBC> Connect.
	SUBC> Test 1 2 3 4.

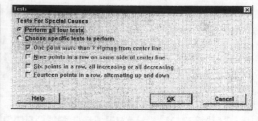

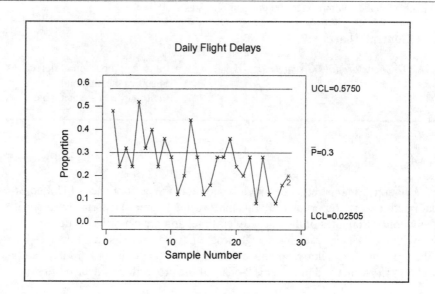

Daily Flight Delays

TEST 2. 9 points in a row on same side of center line.
Test Failed at points: 28

The *P*-chart shows that the airline's program has resulted in a decreasing trend in delayed flights over time. However, it was not until the last day that the failure of test 2 indicated a decrease in the proportion of delayed flights from the historical rate of 30%.

12.6   CONTROL CHART FOR NUMBER OF DEFECTS: C-CHART

A *C*-chart monitors the number of defects per item. The number of defectives *c* contained in each item is assumed to have a Poisson probability distribution, with mean μ. The center line is located at the average number of defectives per item, and the upper and lower control limits are located 3σ above and below the center line.

CONTROL CHART FOR NUMBER OF DEFECTS

This command gives a control chart for the number of nonconformities in each sample. The samples are assumed to come from a Poisson distribution with mean μ.

Stat ▸ Control Charts ▸ C

CCHART *nonconformities in* C	Constructs a control chart for defects
MU = K	Specifies a value for μ
TEST K ... K	First four tests are available

■ **Example 5**   **C-Chart: Nonconformities**

Each hour, an automobile manufacturer selects the next car off a product line, and counts the number of paint defects on the surface of the car. The results for a 20-hour period are given below. Construct a control chart to monitor the quality of the paint surface.

Hour	1	2	3	4	5	6	7	8	9	10
Defects	11	14	10	8	3	9	10	2	5	6

Hour	11	12	13	14	15	16	17	18	19	20
Defects	12	3	4	5	6	8	11	8	7	9

Solution   The data are saved in a file named **Auto.mtp**; defects are in a column named Defects. A *C*-chart monitors the number of defects per car.

Stat ▸ Control Charts ▸ C	MTB > CChart 'Defects';
Select Defects in **Variable:**	SUBC> Title "Automobile Paint Defects";
Click **Tests**, check all four tests;	SUBC> Slimits;
Click **Annotation**, choose **Title**, add a title. **OK**	SUBC> Symbol;
	SUBC> Tests 1 2 3 4.

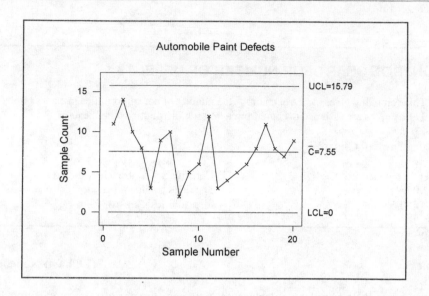

All 20 observations are within the control limits. The statistical tests to monitor the paint surface quality did not detect any unusual patterns of variation. The process appears to be in control.

EXERCISES

1. A quality control engineer at a cola bottling manufacturing company randomly samples one finished bottle from the production process each day for 20 days and records the weight in ounces of each bottle. The data are given below. Construct an individual control chart, including the eight tests. Does the process appear to be in control? (File: **Cola.mtp**)

Day	Weight	Day	Weight
1	5.6	11	6.2
2	5.7	12	5.9
3	6.1	13	5.2
4	6.3	14	6.0
5	5.2	15	6.3
6	6.0	16	5.8
7	5.8	17	6.1
8	5.8	18	6.2
9	6.4	19	5.3
10	6.0	20	6.0

2. A machine that packages a dry breakfast cereal is set to fill a 300 cubic inch box with 20 ounces of cereal. The manufacturer is interested in monitoring both the weight and volume of the packaging process. The accompanying table shows the data for 20 samples of three boxes each. (File: **Cereal.mtp**)

	Weights			Volumes		
Sample	Box 1	Box 2	Box 3	Box 1	Box 2	Box 3
1	20.0	19.9	19.9	284	280	275
2	20.1	19.9	20.0	279	279	282
3	20.0	19.8	19.9	281	279	277
4	19.9	19.9	19.9	280	279	276
5	20.1	20.4	20.0	285	287	276
6	20.3	20.2	20.0	285	284	284
7	20.1	20.7	19.9	282	294	278
8	20.0	19.9	20.2	278	279	286
9	20.2	20.4	20.0	281	287	280
10	20.2	20.2	20.3	280	283	286
11	20.0	19.8	19.8	278	277	275
12	20.0	20.0	20.1	283	276	281
13	20.0	19.5	20.0	275	272	284
14	19.9	20.1	19.9	279	283	274
15	19.9	20.1	20.1	275	281	282
16	19.8	19.9	20.1	281	277	280
17	20.1	20.1	20.3	283	287	283
18	19.9	20.1	20.1	276	283	280
19	20.0	20.2	20.2	277	277	281
20	20.2	20.1	20.1	282	279	282

a. Construct and interpret S-charts and R-charts for the weight and volume of cereal in the packages.

342   *Chapter 12*

b. An $\bar{x}$-chart should only be constructed if the variation of a process is in control. Is it appropriate to construct $\bar{x}$-charts for the weight and volume of cereal in the packages? If so, construct the charts. Include the eight tests for patterns of variation in the packaging process.
c. Plot weight versus volume. Calculate the coefficient of correlation. Does there seem to be a relationship between the two variables?

3. The following data was collected to monitor the amount of diet cola put into 16-ounce bottles. Four consecutive bottles of the automated process were sampled each hour for 24 hours. (File: **DietCola.mtp**)

Hour	Cola Measurements			
1	16.01	16.03	15.98	16.00
2	16.03	16.02	15.97	15.99
3	15.98	16.00	16.03	16.04
4	16.00	16.03	16.02	15.98
5	15.97	15.99	16.03	16.01
6	16.01	16.03	16.04	15.97
7	16.04	16.05	15.97	15.96
8	16.02	16.05	16.03	15.97
9	15.97	15.99	16.02	16.03
10	16.00	16.01	15.95	16.04
11	15.95	16.04	16.07	15.93
12	15.98	16.07	15.94	16.08
13	15.96	16.00	16.01	16.00
14	15.98	16.01	16.02	15.99
15	15.99	16.03	16.00	15.98
16	16.02	16.02	16.01	15.97
17	16.01	16.05	15.99	15.99
18	15.98	16.03	16.04	15.98
19	15.97	15.96	15.99	15.99
20	16.03	16.01	16.04	15.96
21	15.99	16.03	15.97	16.05
22	15.98	15.95	16.07	16.01
23	15.99	16.06	15.95	16.03
24	16.00	16.01	16.08	15.94

a. Construct and interpret an S-chart, R-chart, and $\bar{x}$-chart using the desired process parameters $\mu = 16$ ounces and $\sigma = .05$.
b. Construct and interpret an S-chart, R-chart, and $\bar{x}$-chart using the data to estimate μ and σ. Compare these charts with those in part b.

4. An electronics company manufactures computer monitors. Fifty monitors are randomly selected on each of 21 days, and the following number of defective monitors observed. Construct and interpret a P-chart for the production process.

Day	1	2	3	4	5	6	7	8	9	10	11
Defectives	3	7	4	2	1	4	4	6	1	5	7

Day	12	13	14	15	16	17	18	19	20	21
Defectives	15	7	4	3	3	8	7	2	5	4

5. A manufacturer of rubber strips for sealing windows wants to monitor the production process. A random sample of 100 strips is tested at the end of each sixteen-hour period. The accompanying table gives the number of defective strips in each sample. Construct and interpret a *P*-chart for the production process.

Hour	1	2	3	4	5	6	7	8	9	10	11	12	13	14	15	16
Defectives	2	6	1	4	4	8	3	3	3	5	3	2	3	2	1	3

6. Printing errors are found in many books. The following table gives the total number of errors per ten randomly selected pages for the 25 books most recently published by an book publisher. Construct and interpret a *C*-chart for the number of errors per ten pages of a book. Can the control limits be used for future data? Explain.

Book	1	2	3	4	5	6	7	8	9	10	11	12	13
Errors	7	6	6	7	4	7	8	12	9	9	8	5	5

Book	14	15	16	17	18	19	20	21	22	23	24	25
Errors	9	8	15	6	4	13	7	8	15	6	6	10

7. Refer to Exercise 6. The number of printing errors for each of the next 25 books is given in the table below. Add these numbers of errors to the *C*-chart produced in Exercise 6 above. Use the data from the first 25 books to determine the control chart limits. Is the process still in control?

Book	26	27	28	29	30	31	32	33	34	35	36	37	38
Errors	7	13	4	5	9	3	4	6	7	14	18	11	11

Book	39	40	41	42	43	44	45	46	47	48	49	50
Errors	11	8	10	8	7	16	13	12	9	11	11	8

8. A manufacturer of hard disk drives continually monitors the disk drives for flaws on the storage surface. Flaws reduce the storage space on the disks. One disk drive is randomly selected each hour and the number of flaws determined. The accompanying table gives the results for 50 samples. (File: **DiskDrives.mtp**)

Construct and interpret a *C*-chart for the number of flaws per disk drive.

Sample	1	2	3	4	5	6	7	8	9	10	11	12	13	14	15
Flaws	8	11	7	11	10	10	8	9	6	14	11	8	11	9	18

Sample	16	17	18	19	20	21	22	23	24	25	26	27	28	29	30
Flaws	13	7	14	8	9	17	11	12	12	16	10	20	13	12	22

Sample	31	32	33	34	35	36	37	38	39	30	41	42	43	44	45
Flaws	14	8	12	6	11	6	10	9	8	10	13	11	9	14	15

Sample	46	47	48	49	50
Flaws	11	12	11	6	13

CHAPTER 13

TIME SERIES AND INDEX NUMBERS

Time series are numerical data collected sequentially over time. In this chapter, we use Minitab to graph time series and to calculate simple, composite, and weighted composite index numbers. We also illustrate moving average and exponential smoothing methods for characterizing the components of a time series.

NEW COMMANDS

MTSPLOT   TSPLOT   %MA   %SES

13.1 GRAPHICAL DESCRIPTION OF TIME SERIES

Time series are observations calculated, measured, or observed at equally spaced points in time. A graph of the sequence of observations versus time gives a useful description of the time series. Minitab plots a single or several time series on the same axes.

PLOTTING TIME SERIES

A time series plot has time on the *x*-axis and the variable of interest on the *y*-axis. By default, Minitab displays symbols for each point and joins the points with a line. Options include changing the display method, time scale, and start point.

Graph ▸ Time Series Plot
Stat ▸ Time Series ▸ Time Series Plot

TSPLOT C	Plots a single time series
MTSPLOT C...C	Character plot for multiple time series
START K	Time of first observation

■ Example 1

The numbers of transactions per month at a bank's ATM machine located on the St. Cloud State University campus are given in the following table. Graph and describe the series.

Month	Usage	Month	Usage
January	984	July	279
February	1,706	August	241
March	743	September	996
April	1,420	October	1,452
May	1,310	November	1,588
June	341	December	1,316

Solution   We enter the data in Month and Usage and save the file in **ATM-Univ.mtp**.

Graph ▸ Time Series Plot
  Enter Usage in **Graph 1 Y**;
  Click **Calendar**, choose **Month**;
  Click **Annotation**, choose **Title**, add a title. **OK**

MTB > TSPlot 'Usage';
SUBC>   Month;
SUBC>   Connect;
SUBC>   Title "Campus ATM Transactions".

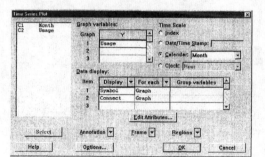

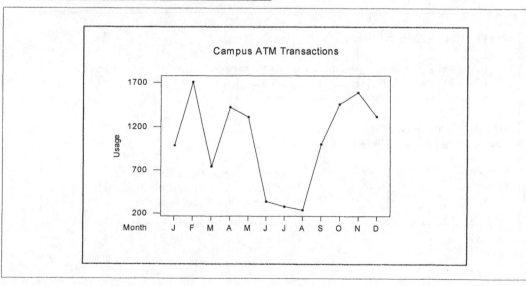

The plot shows the fluctuations in the number of transactions over time. It's not surprising to see the lower usage in the summer when fewer students are on campus.

13.2 INDEX NUMBERS

Index numbers are often used to describe time series data. In this section, we describe simple, simple composite, and weighted composite index numbers.

SIMPLE INDEX NUMBERS

A simple index number is a measure of change over time in a single time series variable, relative to a base period. The **simple index** I_t for a time series variable at each time t, expressed as a percentage, is given as

$$I_t = (y_t/y_0)100$$

where y_t is the value of the variable at time t and y_0 is the value at the base period. The index number is always 100% for the base period.

■ **Example 2**   **Simple Index Numbers**

In Example 1 we plotted the numbers of transactions per month at a bank's ATM machine located on the St. Cloud State University campus. Calculate the simple index values using January as the base period. Graph the simple index time series. Interpret the index values for May and June.

Solution   The transactions data are in columns named Month and Usage saved in the file named **ATM-Univ.mtp**. The first row indicated by Usage(1) contains the January base period number. To obtain the simple index values, we need to divide each monthly usage by the base period usage. The formula is

$$I_t = (\text{Usage}/\text{Usage}(1))100.$$

Calc ▸ Calculator   MTB > Name C3 = 'Index'
  Enter 'Index' in **Store results in variable:**   MTB > Let 'Index' = Usage / Usage(1) * 100
  Enter Usage / Usage(1) * 100 in **Expression. OK**

Manip ▸ Display Data
  Select Month - Index in **Display**. **OK**

MTB > Print 'Month'- 'Index'

Data Display

Row	Month	Usage	Index
1	January	984	100.000
2	February	1706	173.374
3	March	743	75.508
4	April	1420	144.309
5	May	1310	133.130
6	June	341	34.654
7	July	279	28.354
8	August	241	24.492
9	September	996	101.220
10	October	1452	147.561
11	November	1588	161.382
12	December	1316	133.740

The number of transactions in May was 133% of the number of transactions in the base month of January. In other words, the usage was 33% higher in May than in January. The usage in June was only 35% of the usage in January, or the usage was 65% lower in June than in January. The large difference between May and June is because classes are not in session in June.

Graph ▸ Time Series Plot
  Select Index in **Graph 1 Y**;
  Click **Calendar**, choose **Month**;
  Click **Annotation**, choose **Title**, add a title. **OK**

MTB > TSPlot 'Index';
SUBC> Month;
SUBC> TDisplay 11;
SUBC> Symbol;
SUBC> Connect;
SUBC> Title "Campus ATM Transactions";
SUBC> Title "Simple Index Series".

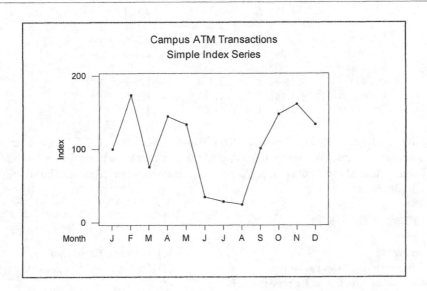

The simple index time series plot shows the low usage in the summer months; there is also a dip in March when the usage was about 75% of that in January.

COMPOSITE INDEX NUMBERS

A **simple composite index** is a simple index for a time series consisting of several time series variables. It is the change over time in the sum of the values of several variables, relative to a base period. To calculate this index, add the values for each time period. Then use the totals for the time periods in the same formula that is used for a simple index.

■ **Example 3**   **Simple Composite Index Numbers**

Consider the ATM usage data given in Example 1. The numbers of transactions per month at a bank's ATM machine located on the St. Cloud State University campus are given. In addition to the ATM machine on campus the bank has an ATM machine at a shopping mall and at a gas station. Calculate a table of the composite index series using January as the base period. Graph the composite index time series. Interpret the index values for May and June.

Month	Campus	Mall	Station
January	984	2,410	1,536
February	1,706	2,696	1,920
March	743	2,175	1,630
April	1,420	2,234	1,673

May	1,310	2,370	2,114
June	341	2,280	2,121
July	279	2,325	2,326
August	241	2,744	2,676
September	996	2,618	2,347
October	1,452	2,284	1,842
November	1,588	2,398	1,968
December	1,316	3,705	1,796

Solution   The data are saved in a file named **ATM.mtp** in columns C1-C4 named as in the table above. To compute a simple composite index, we add the three transactions for each month and enter the sum in Total. The first row, Total(1), contains the January base period total. The simple composite index for each month is

$$I_t = (\text{Total}/\text{Total}(1))100$$

Calc ▸ Calculator
   Enter 'Total' in **Store results in variable:**
   Enter Campus + Mall + Station in **Expression. OK**

MTB > Name C5 = 'Total'
MTB > Let 'Total'=Campus+Mall+Station

Calc ▸ Calculator
   Enter 'Index' in **Store results in variable:**
   Enter Total / Total(1) * 100 in **Expression. OK**

MTB > Name C6 = 'Index'
MTB > Let 'Index' = Total / Total(1) * 100

Manip ▸ Display Data
   Select Month - Index in **Display. OK**

MTB > Print 'Month'-'Index'

Data Display

Row	Month	Campus	Mall	Station	Total	Index
1	January	984	2410	1536	4930	100.000
2	February	1706	2696	1920	6322	128.235
3	March	743	2175	1630	4548	92.252
4	April	1420	2234	1673	5327	108.053
5	May	1310	2370	2114	5794	117.525
6	June	341	2280	2121	4742	96.187
7	July	279	2325	2326	4930	100.000
8	August	241	2744	2676	5661	114.828
9	September	996	2618	2347	5961	120.913
10	October	1452	2284	1842	5578	113.144
11	November	1588	2398	1968	5954	120.771
12	December	1316	3705	1796	6817	138.276

The simple composite index is interpreted about the same as the simple index. The number of transactions in May was about 118% of the number of transactions in the base month of January. In other words, the usage in May was 18% higher than in January. The usage in June was 96% of the usage in January; or the usage in June was 4% lower than in January.

Graph ► Time Series Plot	MTB > TSPlot 'Index';
Select Index in **Graph 1 Y**;	SUBC> Month;
Click **Calendar**, choose **Month**;	SUBC> TDisplay 11;
Click **Annotation**, choose **Title**, add a title. **OK**	SUBC> Symbol;
	SUBC> Connect;
	SUBC> Title "ATM Transactions";
	SUBC> Title "Simple Composite Index Series".

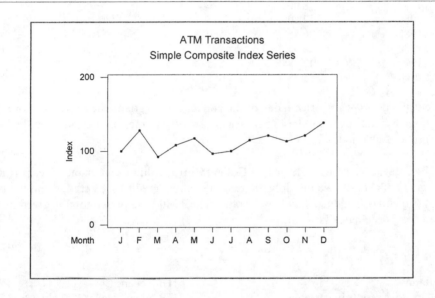

Using three ATM locations has removed a lot of the ups and downs of the simple index calculated in Example 2. There is not the dip in the summer composite index values because the other two ATM machine usages are not affected by fewer students on campus in the summer. The December index is high reflecting the large number of holiday shoppers.

WEIGHTED COMPOSITE INDEX

A simple composite index is easy to compute and interpret; however, the time series variables with large values tend to dominate the index. In these cases, a **weighted composite index**, which uses a weighted sum of the time series variables, is a more meaningful index. The weight reflects the relative importance of each variable. The Consumer Price Index is an example of a weighted composite index.

There are several types of indexes that use different weighting factors. The most popular price indexes use the base period quantity or the quantity associated with each time period. To calculate a weighted composite price index, multiply the price for each time period by some measure of quantity.

■ **Example 4**   **Weighted Composite Index Numbers**

The cost to attend college has risen rapidly in the past years. The following table provides the cost per credit, and room and board costs per quarter to attend a Midwestern university for selected years.

Year	Tuition	Room&Board
1970	$ 6.75	$ 275
1975	8.00	326
1980	12.50	415
1985	26.85	560
1990	32.05	705
1995	42.35	845
2000	55.45	1,055

Calculate a weighted composite price index of the annual cost to attend the university for a full-time student carrying 16 credits per quarter (48 per year). Use 1980 as the base period. Plot the index time series. Interpret the 2000 index value.

Solution   The data are saved in a file named **College$.mtp**; columns are named Year, Tuition, and RmBrd. To get annual costs, we multiply the tuition cost per credit by 48 credits and the room and board cost by 3 quarters, and then sum to get Total. The 1980 base period total is given in Total(3). The weighted composite index is

$$I_t = (Total/Total(3))100$$

Calc ▸ Calculator
   Enter 'Total' in **Store results in variable:**
   Enter 48*Tuition + 3*RmBrd in **Expression. OK**

MTB > Name C4 = 'Total'
MTB > Let 'Total' = 48*Tuition+ 3* RmBrd

Calc ▸ Calculator
   Enter 'Index' in **Store results in variable:**
   Enter Total / Total(3) * 100 in **Expression. OK**

MTB > Name C5 = 'Index'
MTB > Let 'Index' = Total / Total(3) * 100

Manip ▸ Display Data
   Select Year - Index in **Display. OK**

MTB > Print 'Year'-'Index'

Data Display

Row	Year	Tuition	RmBrd	Total	Index
1	1970	6.75	275	1149.0	62.276
2	1975	8.00	326	1362.0	73.821
3	1980	12.50	415	1845.0	100.000
4	1985	26.85	560	2968.8	160.911
5	1990	32.05	705	3653.4	198.016
6	1995	42.35	845	4567.8	247.577
7	2000	55.45	1055	5826.6	315.805

The annual cost in 2000 is about 315% of the cost in 1980. The cost to attend college has increased over 200% between 1980 and 2000.

Graph ▸ Time Series Plot
Select Index in **Graph 1 Y**;
Click **Options**; Enter 1970:2000/5;
 in **Assignment of time to data**;
Click **Annotation**, choose **Title**, add a title;
Click **Frame**, choose **Axis**, add a label. OK

MTB > TSPlot 'Index';
SUBC> Index 1970:2000/5;
SUBC> TDisplay 11;
SUBC> Symbol;
SUBC> Connect;
SUBC> Title "Annual College Cost";
SUBC> Title "Weighted Composite Index Series";
SUBC> Axis 11;
SUBC>   Label "Year";
SUBC> Axis 2.

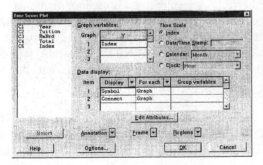

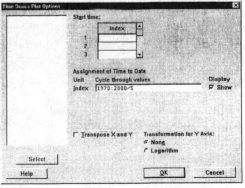

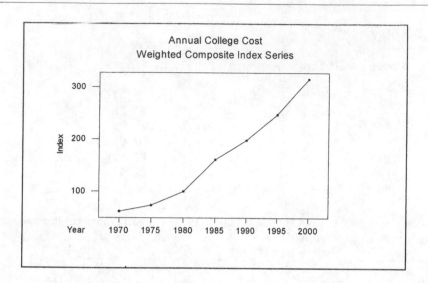

The year 1980 is the base period with an index value of 100. The graph shows the rapid increase in annual college costs since 1970.

13.3   SMOOTHING METHODS

Time series can generally be separated into one or more of the following components: secular trend, cyclical fluctuation, seasonal variation, and residual effect. A secular trend is the long-term increase or decrease in a time series. Cyclical fluctuation is attributed to changes in business and economic conditions. Seasonal variations are monthly, quarterly, or other periodic changes that occur within a year. The residual effects are fluctuations that cannot be attributed to trend, cyclical, or seasonal components. Modeling time series and forecasting future values depend on the components that are present in the series.

Smoothing methods are descriptive methods for identifying and characterizing the components of a time series. These methods generally attempt to describe the secular trend in a series by removing fluctuations caused by other time series components. This section illustrates the moving average and exponential smoothing methods.

MOVING AVERAGE METHOD

The **moving average** method is a simple smoothing method that removes some fluctuations from a time series. A N-point moving average is formed by averaging the time series values over successive time periods of length N. The graph of a moving average gives a smooth curve which describes the general trend.

The formula to calculate a N-point moving average M_t for time t is given as $M_t = S_t/N$, where S_t is the sum of the time series values over N adjacent time periods. The first step in calculating a moving average is to average the first N time series values. This average is the moving average for the midpoint of the first N time periods. To calculate successive moving averages, delete the first time series value from the current sum S_t, add the next time series value, and divide the new sum by N.

MOVING AVERAGE SMOOTHING

This command calculates a moving average by averaging consecutive time series values. It generates a time series plot of the actual data and smoothed or predicted values.

Stat ▸ Time Series ▸ Moving Average

%MA *data* C *length* K	Calculates and plots moving averages
CENTER	Centers the moving averages
FORECASTS K	Generates K forecasts
ORIGIN K	Generates forecasts from time K
SMPLOT	Plots smoothed vs. actual
TABLE	Displays data and calculated values
TITLE	Adds a title

■ **Example 5**   **Moving Average Method**

The following table gives the numbers of computers (in thousands) sold by an electronics retailer from 1988 to 1999. Calculate a 3-point moving average for the time series. Plot the time series and the moving average on the same plot.

Year	Number	Year	Number
1988	64	1994	56
1989	61	1995	55
1990	57	1996	68
1991	60	1997	68
1992	53	1998	57
1993	70	1999	68

Solution We enter the data in columns named Year and Number and save in **ComputerSales.mtp**.

Stat ▸ Time Series ▸ Moving Average
  Select Number in **Variable:**
    Enter 3 in **MA length:** add a **Title:**
  Click **Center the moving averages;**
  Click **Results,** choose **Plot smoothed vs. actual;**
  Click **Storage,** choose **Moving averages. OK**

MTB > Name C3 = 'AVER1'
MTB > %MA 'Number' 3;
SUBC> Center;
SUBC> Averages 'AVER1';
SUBC> Smplot;
SUBC> Title "Computer Sales Time Series".

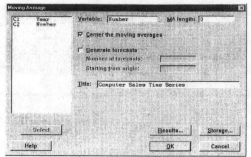

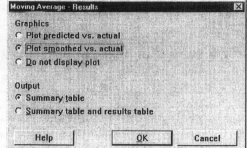

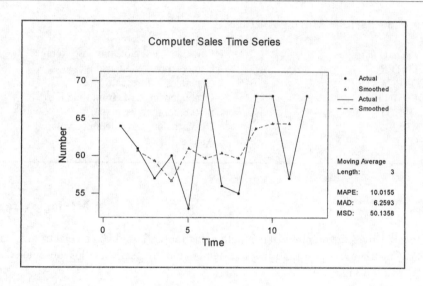

Moving average

```
Data        Number
Length      12.0000
NMissing    0

Moving Average
Length: 3

Accuracy Measures
MAPE: 10.0155
MAD:   6.2593
MSD:  50.1358
```

The time series graph shows that the moving average has removed some fluctuation in the original time series. We will use the accuracy measures in the next chapter.

Manip ▸ Display Data
Select Year - AVER1 in **Display. OK**

MTB > Print 'Year'-'AVER1'

Data Display

Row	Year	Number	AVER1
1	1988	64	*
2	1989	61	60.6667
3	1990	57	59.3333
4	1991	60	56.6667
5	1992	53	61.0000
6	1993	70	59.6667
7	1994	56	60.3333
8	1995	55	59.6667
9	1996	68	63.6667
10	1997	68	64.3333
11	1998	57	64.3333
12	1999	68	*

Because of the averaging of three data points, there is no moving average for the first and last years.

EXPONENTIAL SMOOTHING

Exponential smoothing is a smoothing method for removing random effects from a time series. This method differs from moving average in that a smoothed value can be calculated for every time period t, and greater weight can be given to more recent values. An exponentially smoothed value E_t is a weighted average of the current time series value y_t and the previous smoothed value E_{t-1}. The first smoothed value is the average of the first few time series values. Each succeeding smoothed value is a function of

$$E_t = wy_t + (1-w)E_{t-1}$$

where w is a smoothing constant between 0 and 1. Generally the smaller the value of w, the smoother the resulting series. However, if you want to give the most recent time series more weight than previous values, choose a larger value for w.

EXPONENTIAL SMOOTHING

This command calculates an exponentially smoothed series. It generates a time series plot of the actual data and smoothed or predicted values. The default for the first smoothed value is the average of the first six time series values.

Stat ▸ Time Series ▸ Single Exp Smoothing

%SES *data* C	Calculates an exponentially smoothed series
WEIGHT K	Weight to smooth the data
SMOOTHED	Stores the smoothed values
FORECASTS K	Generates K forecasts
ORIGIN K	Generates forecasts from time K
SMPLOT	Plots smoothed vs. actual
TABLE	Displays data and calculated values
TITLE	Adds a title

■ **Example 6**   **Exponential Smoothing Method**

Refer to Example 5 of this chapter which gives the numbers of computers (in thousands) sold by an electronics retailer from 1988 to 1999 Use $w = .3$ to calculate an exponentially smoothed series. Plot both series on the same graph.

Solution   The data are saved in a file named **ComputerSales.mtp**.

Stat ▸ Time Series ▸ Single Exp Smoothing
  Select Number in **Variable:**
  Click **Use:** enter 0.3;
  Click **Options**; choose **Plot smoothed vs. actual**;
  Click **Storage**; choose **Smoothed data**;
  Add a **Title. OK**

MTB > Name C3 = 'SMOO1'
MTB > %SES 'Number';
SUBC>   Weight .3;
SUBC>   Smoothed 'SMOO1';
SUBC>   Smplot;
SUBC>   Initial 6;
SUBC>   Title "Computer Sales Time Series".

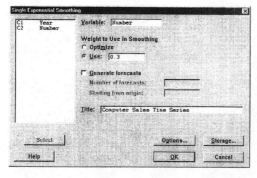
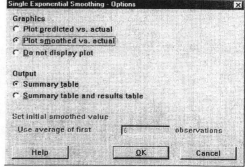

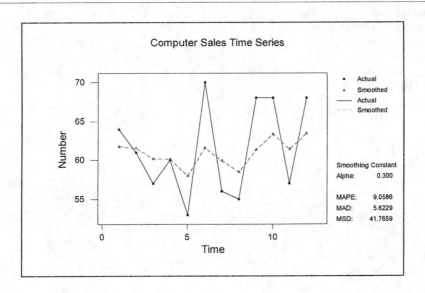

Single Exponential Smoothing

```
Data          Number
Length        12.0000
NMissing      0

Smoothing Constant
Alpha: 0.3

Accuracy Measures
MAPE:   9.0586
MAD:    5.6229
MSD:   41.7659
```

The graph shows that exponential smoothing has removed some fluctuations in the original time series values. Note that exponential smoothing with a $w = .3$ reacts slowly to the number of computers sold.

Manip ▸ Display Data
  Select Year - SMOO1 in **Display. OK**

MTB > Print 'Year'-'SMOO1'

Data Display

Row	Year	Number	SMOO1
1	1988	64	61.7833
2	1989	61	61.5483
3	1990	57	60.1838
4	1991	60	60.1287
5	1992	53	57.9901
6	1993	70	61.5931
7	1994	56	59.9151
8	1995	55	58.4406
9	1996	68	61.3084
10	1997	68	63.3159
11	1998	57	61.4211
12	1999	68	63.3948

The first smoothed value for 1988 is the average of the first six computers sold. A small value such as $w = .3$ tends to give a smooth time series. A larger value of w will give more weight to recent data, and follow more closely the actual series.

EXERCISES

1. The Consumer Price Index (CPI) is a weighted composite index of the prices of a "market basket" of goods and services purchased by the typical consumer. The index, designed to compare relative price changes over time, is used as a measure of inflation. The three-year period 1982-84 is used as the base, and price indices for other periods are percentage changes from the base. Plot the Consumer Price Index for the years 1950 to 1999. Describe the time series. Interpret the 1999 Consumer Price Index. (File: **CPI.mtp**)

Year	CPI	Year	CPI	Year	CPI
1950	24.1	1967	33.4	1984	103.4
1951	26.0	1968	34.8	1985	107.6
1952	26.5	1969	36.7	1986	109.6
1953	26.7	1970	38.8	1987	113.6
1954	26.9	1971	40.5	1988	118.3
1955	26.8	1972	41.8	1989	124.0
1956	27.2	1973	44.4	1990	130.7
1957	28.1	1974	49.3	1991	136.2
1958	28.9	1975	53.8	1992	140.3
1959	29.1	1976	56.9	1993	144.5
1960	29.6	1977	60.6	1994	148.2
1961	29.9	1978	65.2	1995	152.4
1962	30.2	1979	72.6	1996	156.9
1963	30.6	1980	82.4	1997	160.5
1964	31.0	1981	90.9	1998	163.0
1965	31.5	1982	96.5	1999	166.6
1966	32.4	1983	99.6	2000	172.3*

* Estimate based on first nine months

2. A reciprocal of the CPI gives a measure of the purchasing power of the dollar relative to the base period. Calculate the purchasing power series for the years 1950 to 1999 by first dividing CPI by 100 and then taking the reciprocal. Plot the purchasing power of the dollar for the years 1950 to 1999. Describe the time series. Interpret the 1999 purchasing power.

3. Real income is actual or current income multiplied by the purchasing power to adjust for inflation. During periods of high inflation, increases in actual income are distorted by the impact of inflation. For example, in 1979, actual wages were growing at an annual rate of 10 percent a year, but that was not enough to offset a 15% rate of inflation. Real wages actually declined by 5 percent. Consider the income of an anesthesiologist over the years 1973 to 1999. (File: **RealIncome.mtp**)

Year	Income	Year	Income	Year	Income
1973	$15,763	1982	$34,578	1991	$52,977
1974	16,351	1983	39,930	1992	55,626
1975	18,362	1984	40,329	1993	57,250
1976	19,325	1985	41,942	1994	58,414
1977	20,501	1986	43,744	1995	60,166
1978	21,806	1987	45,713	1996	62,573
1979	23,437	1988	47,598	1997	65,701
1980	25,508	1989	49,978	1998	68,330
1981	29,487	1990	52,452	1999	71,746

a. Use the purchasing power index calculated in Exercise 2 to determine the real income of an anesthesiologist.
b. Plot the real income on a time series plot. Describe the trend.
c. Graphically compare the actual income and real income. Discuss.

4. Consider the following data given in the *Statistical Abstract of the United States* on the average price of electricity sold for residential, commercial, and industrial usage during the years 1980 to 1997. The prices in cents per kilowatt hour are in current dollars. (File: **Electricity.mtp**)

Year	Residential	Commercial	Industrial
1980	5.4	5.5	3.7
1981	6.2	6.3	4.3
1982	6.9	6.9	5.0
1983	7.2	7.0	5.0
1984	7.2	7.1	4.8
1985	7.4	7.3	5.0
1986	7.4	7.2	4.9
1987	7.4	7.1	4.8
1988	7.5	7.0	4.7
1989	7.6	7.2	4.7
1990	7.8	7.3	4.7
1991	8.0	7.5	4.8
1992	8.2	7.7	4.8
1993	8.3	7.7	4.8
1994	8.4	7.7	4.8
1995	8.4	7.7	4.7
1996	8.4	7.6	4.6
1997	8.5	7.6	4.6

a. Calculate numerical descriptive measures for each of the three price series. Summarize.
b. A price index measures the change in the price of a commodity over time, in terms of a base period. Calculate price indices for each type of electricity usage, using 1990 as the base period. Print a table of the price indices.
c. Plot the price indices on one graph. Compare the price indices.

5. The following table gives the average annual price of gold and silver for the years 1971 to 1999.

Both are measured in dollars per ounce. (Files: **Gold.mtp** and **Silver.mtp**)

Year	Gold	Year	Silver
1971	$ 41.25	1971	$ 1.55
1972	58.61	1972	1.69
1973	97.81	1973	2.56
1974	159.70	1974	4.71
1975	161.40	1975	4.42
1976	124.80	1976	4.35
1977	148.30	1977	4.62
1978	193.50	1978	5.40
1979	307.80	1979	11.09
1980	606.01	1980	20.60
1981	450.63	1981	10.50
1982	374.18	1982	7.95
1983	449.03	1983	11.44
1984	360.29	1984	8.14
1985	317.30	1985	6.14
1986	367.87	1986	5.47
1987	408.91	1987	7.01
1988	436.93	1988	6.53
1989	381.28	1989	5.50
1990	384.07	1990	4.82
1991	362.04	1991	4.04
1992	344.50	1992	3.94
1993	359.82	1993	4.30
1994	384.15	1994	5.29
1995	384.05	1995	5.19
1996	387.87	1996	5.20
1997	331.29	1997	4.90
1998	294.09	1998	5.54
1999	284.10	1999	5.22

a. Plot the annual gold price series. Describe the time series.
b. Plot the annual silver price series. Describe the time series.
c   Calculate the simple index numbers using 1990 as the base for both the gold and the silver time series. Interpret the 1999 index numbers.
d. Plot both index time series on the same graph. Compare the series.

6. Calculate 3-point moving averages for the gold and silver simple indexes calculated in Example 5. Plot the moving averages for both index series on the same graph. Use the moving averages to compare the trend of the two series.

7. Use $w = .3$ to calculate the exponentially smoothed series for the gold and silver simple indexes calculated in Example 5. Plot the exponentially smoothed index series on the same graph. Compare the trend of the two series.

8. The following table gives the 1970 to 1999 average annual baseball player salary in thousands of

dollars. (File: **Baseball.mtp**)

Year	Salary	Year	Salary
1970	$ 29.30	1985	$ 371.57
1971	31.54	1986	412.52
1972	34.09	1987	412.45
1973	36.57	1988	438.73
1974	40.84	1989	497.25
1975	44.68	1990	597.54
1976	51.50	1991	851.49
1977	76.07	1992	1,028.67
1978	99.88	1993	1,089.51
1979	113.56	1994	1,183.42
1980	143.76	1995	955.92
1981	185.65	1996	1,010.12
1982	241.50	1997	1,219.83
1983	289.19	1998	1,445.86
1984	329.41	1999	1,720.05

a. Plot the baseball salary time series. Describe the time series.
b. Calculate a 5-point moving average. Plot the actual series and the moving average on the same graph. Describe the series.

9. Consider the baseball salary time series given in Exercise 8. (File: **Baseball.mtp**)

a. Use $w = .3$ to calculate the exponentially smoothed series.
b. Use $w = .7$ to calculate the exponentially smoothed series. Compare with the exponentially smoothed series of part a.
c. Plot both exponentially smoothed series from parts a and b on the same graph. Which do you think will give better forecasts for the next year's salary? Explain.

10. Information on air travel and the number of flights resulting in accidents and fatalities in the United States beginning in 1938 is given in the Appendix. (File: **AirFatal.mtp**)

a. Display the number of passengers carried on a time series plot. Describe the trend.
b. Is air travel becoming safer? Create a time series plot of the number of aircraft accidents. Describe the trend in the number of accidents.
c. An increase in the number of accidents over time does not necessarily mean that air travel is becoming less safe, but could be due to an increase in the number of flights. Calculate a ratio of the number of accidents per million departures. Display the ratio on a time series plot. Describe the trend.

11. The Dow Jones Industrial Average, a measure of the share prices of 30 blue chip industrial corporations, is a widely used indicator of stock market activity. The data file gives the closing average for each year and the percentage change from the prior year, since inception in 1896. The following table shows data since 1970. (File: **DJIA.mtp**)

Year	DJIA	% Change	Year	DJIA	% Change
2000	10,786.85	-6.18	1984	1,211.57	-3.74
1999	11,497.12	25.22	1983	1,258.64	20.27
1998	9,181.43	16.10	1982	1,046.54	19.60
1997	7,908.25	22.64	1981	875.00	-9.23
1996	6,448.27	26.01	1980	963.99	14.93
1995	5,117.12	33.45	1979	838.74	4.19
1994	3,834.44	2.14	1978	805.01	-3.15
1993	3,754.09	13.72	1977	831.17	-17.27
1992	3,301.11	4.17	1976	1,004.65	17.86
1991	3,168.83	20.32	1975	852.41	38.32
1990	2,633.66	-4.34	1974	616.24	-27.57
1989	2,753.20	26.96	1973	850.86	-16.58
1988	2,168.57	11.85	1972	1,020.02	14.58
1987	1,938.83	2.26	1971	890.20	6.11
1986	1,895.95	22.58	1970	838.92	4.82
1985	1,546.67	27.66			

a. Plot the Dow Jones Industrial Average closing series since 1896. Discuss characteristics of the series. Calculate the percentage change since 1970.

b. Calculate a 5-point moving average for the years since 1970. Plot the time series and the moving average on the same plot.

c. Calculate the exponentially smoothed series for the years since 1970, using $w = .3$. Plot the time series and the smoothed series on the same plot.

d. Suppose you are asked to estimate the Dow Jones Industrial Average closing for 2001. What would your estimate be? Use the plots. Explain your estimate.

CHAPTER 14

TIME SERIES MODELS AND FORECASTING

In the last chapter you learned about index numbers, and how to smooth a time series. This chapter presents statistical models for forecasting future time series values. These include moving average, exponential smoothing, linear and seasonal regression models, and Winters' forecasting method. The final section covers autocorrelation.

NEW COMMANDS

%ACF	ARIMA	%DECOMP	%DES
%TREND	%WINTMULT		

14.1 FORECASTING MODELS AND ACCURACY MEASURES

Minitab uses several models for forecasting time series. Model selection depends on the components and sources of variation in a time series. The components include secular trend, seasonal variation, cyclical variation, and residual effect. The following table lists time series characteristics, forecasting range, and the type of the models that might be useful in forecasting future values.

Time Series Characteristics	Forecasting Range	Models
No trend or seasonality	Short	Moving Average Single Exponential Smoothing
Trend but no seasonality	Long	Trend Analysis
Trend but no seasonality	Short	Double Exponential Smoothing
Trend and seasonality	Long	Decomposition
Seasonality with and without trend	Short to Medium	Winters' Method

Each method displays three measures to help determine the accuracy of the fitted values. The **Mean**

Absolute Percentage Error (MAPE) expresses accuracy as a percentage. The **Mean Absolute Deviation** (MAD) expresses accuracy as the average absolute error. The **Mean Squared Deviation** (MSD) expresses accuracy as the mean squared error.

Suppose y_t is the actual value and n is the number of forecasts. The formulas to calculate the error measures are as follow:

$$\text{MAPE} = \{[\textstyle\sum (y_t - \text{forecast})/y_t]/n\}\,100$$

$$\text{MAD} = \{[\textstyle\sum |y_t - \text{forecast}|]/n\}\,100$$

$$\text{MSD} = \{[\textstyle\sum (y_t - \text{forecast})^2]/n\}\,100$$

14.2 FORECASTING USING SMOOTHING METHODS

This section considers useful forecasting models if there is no trend in the time series. We illustrate moving average and single exponential smoothing. Both of these are useful for short term forecasting.

MOVING AVERAGE FORECASTING

The last chapter illustrated the moving average method, a simple smoothing technique that removes the rapid fluctuations in a time series. An **N-point moving average** is formed by averaging the time series values over N successive time periods. The graph of a moving average gives a smooth curve which describes the general pattern.

The formula to calculate a N-point moving average M_t for time t is given as $M_t = S_t/N$, where S_t is the sum of the time series values over N adjacent time periods. If the time series, consisting of N equally spaced values, has minimal trend and seasonal components, moving average should provide reliable forecasts of future time series values. To forecast using a N-point moving average, the graph of the moving average M_t is extended horizontally to a future time period t. The forecast F_t is equal to the last moving average, $F_t = M_n$.

■ **Example 1**   **Moving Average Forecasts**

The following table gives the numbers of computers (in thousands) sold by an electronics retailer from 1988 to 1999. Use a 3-point moving average to forecast sales for the next three years.

Year	Number	Year	Number
1988	64	1994	56
1989	61	1995	55
1990	57	1996	68
1991	60	1997	68
1992	53	1998	57
1993	70	1999	68

olution   The data are saved in columns named Year and Number in a file named **ComputerSales.mtp.**

tat ▸ Time Series ▸ Moving Average
Select Number in **Variable:**
  Enter 3 in **MA length:**
Click Generate forecasts;
  Enter 3 in **Number of forecasts:**
Click Results; choose **Plot predicted vs. actual;**
Add a **Title. OK**

MTB > %MA 'Number' 3;
SUBC>   Forecasts 3;
SUBC>   Title "Computer Sales Time Series".

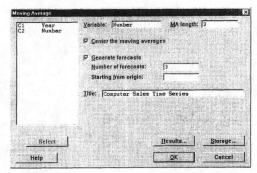

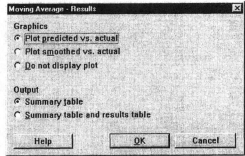

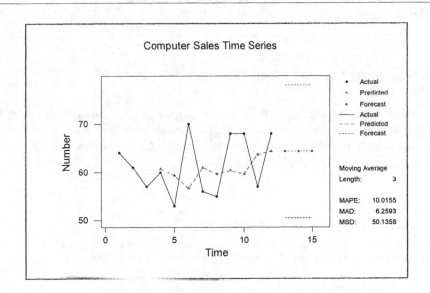

The moving average forecasting method may be appropriate since the plot shows little secular trend. The forecast, upper, and lower limits are plotted on the graph.

Moving average

```
Data          Number
Length        12.0000
NMissing      0

Moving Average
Length: 3

Accuracy Measures
MAPE: 10.0155
MAD:   6.2593
MSD:  50.1358
```

Row	Period	Forecast	Lower	Upper
1	13	64.3333	50.4552	78.2114
2	14	64.3333	50.4552	78.2114
3	15	64.3333	50.4552	78.2114

The number of computer sales are in thousands. The sales forecast for each of the next three years is about 64,000 computers. The lower and upper sales limits are about 50,000 and 78,000.

EXPONENTIAL SMOOTHING FORECASTING

Exponential smoothing was defined in the previous chapter as a smoothing method for removing random effects from a time series. An exponentially smoothed value E_t is a weighted average of the current time series value y_t and the previous smoothed value E_{t-1}. The first smoothed value is the average of the first few time series values. Each succeeding smoothed value is defined by

$$E_t = wy_t + (1-w)E_{t-1}$$

where w is a smoothing constant between 0 and 1. If the time series, consisting of N equally spaced values, has minimal trend and seasonal components, exponential smoothing should provide reliable forecasts of future time series values. The exponentially smoothed forecast for F_t, with $t = N + 1$, $N + 2$, ..., is

$$F_t = wy_n + (1 - w)E_{n-1}$$

Example 2   **Exponential Smoothing Forecasts**

Consider the data on number of computers (in thousands) sold by an electronics retailer from 1988 to 1999 given in Example 1. Use exponential smoothing with a weight $w = .3$ to forecast computer sales for the next three years.

Solution The data are saved in a file named **ComputerSales.mtp.**

Stat ▸ Time Series ▸ Single Exp Smoothing	MTB > %SES 'Number';
Select Number in **Variable:**	SUBC> Weight .3;
Click **Use:** enter 0.3;	SUBC> Forecasts 3;
Click **Options**; choose **Plot predicted vs. actual**;	SUBC> Initial 6;
Click **Generate forecasts**	SUBC> Title "Computer Sales Time Series".
Enter 3 in **Number of forecasts:**	
Add a **Title. OK**	

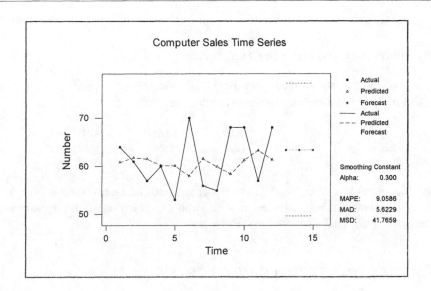

The single exponential smoothing forecasts do not consider the secular or seasonal trend. The forecast, upper, and lower limits are shown on the graph.

Single Exponential Smoothing

```
Data        Number
Length      12.0000
NMissing    0
```

```
    Smoothing Constant
    Alpha: 0.3

    Accuracy Measures
    MAPE:   9.0586
    MAD:    5.6229
    MSD:    41.7659


    Row   Period  Forecast    Lower      Upper

     1      13    63.3948    49.6187    77.1709
     2      14    63.3948    49.6187    77.1709
     3      15    63.3948    49.6187    77.1709
```

The number of computer sales are in thousands. The sales forecast for each of the next three years is about 63,000. The lower and upper sales limits are about 50,000 and 77,000 computers.

Accuracy Summary for Computer Sales Time Series

We have illustrated the moving average and exponential smoothing forecasts. To find which model is the better fit for the time series, we compare accuracy measures.

	MAPE	MAD	MSD
Moving Average	10.02	6.26	50.14
Single Exponential Smoothing	9.06	5.62	41.77

Because the exponential smoothing model has smaller accuracy measures, it provides a better fit for this time series. However, this conclusion may be valid only for the 3-point moving average and smoothing constant $w = .3$ that were used in the forecasts.

14.3 FORECASTING MODELS WITH TREND

This section considers some useful forecasting models if there is trend in the time series. We illustrate linear regression and double exponential smoothing.

If there is a linear trend in the series, the simple linear regression model with time t as the independent variable, is

$$y_t = \beta_0 + \beta_1 t + \epsilon$$

Minitab's trend analysis fits a trend line and generates a plot of the actual data and fitted values.

TREND ANALYSIS

Trend analysis fits a trend line to a time series or detrends a time series. It uses one of four models; the default model is linear trend.

Stat ▸ Time Series ▸ Trend Analysis

%TREND *data* C	Fits a trend line to a time series
QUADRATIC	Quadratic trend model
GROWTH	Exponential growth trend model
SCURVE	Logistic trend model
FORECASTS K	Generates forecasts
RESIDUALS C	Stores the residuals
FITS C	Stores the fitted values
FSTORE C	Stores the forecasts
TITLE	Adds a title

■ **Example 3**   **Linear Trend Model**

The number of students majoring in education is increasing at many universities. Consider the following enrollment data showing the number of education majors at one university. Fit a linear trend model to the data. Forecast the number of majors in 2000 and 2001.

Year	Majors	Year	Majors
1988	188	1994	252
1989	192	1995	260
1990	198	1996	266
1991	210	1997	281
1992	225	1998	289
1993	240	1999	307

Solution The data are saved in a file named **Majors.mtp**.

Stat ▸ Time Series ▸ Trend Analysis
  Select Majors in **Variable:**
  Click **Generate forecasts**;
    Enter 2 in **Number of forecasts:**
  Add a **Title. OK**

MTB > %Trend 'Majors';
SUBC>   Forecasts 2;
SUBC>   Title "Education Majors".

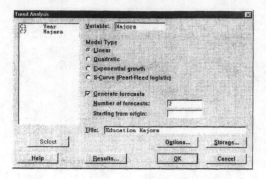

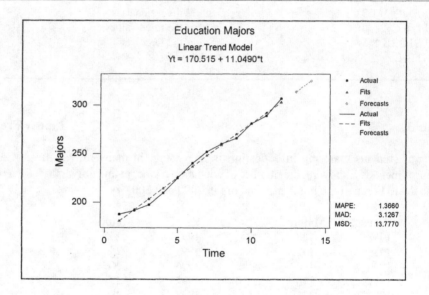

The time series plot shows a fairly strong linear trend in the number of education majors. The slope $\hat{\beta}_1 = 11.049$ indicates that the number of majors increases at an average rate of 11 per year.

Trend Analysis

```
Data        Majors
Length      12.0000
NMissing    0
```

```
Fitted Trend Equation
```

```
Yt = 170.515 + 11.0490*t
```

```
Accuracy Measures

MAPE:        1.36600
MAD:         3.12665
MSD:         13.7770


 Row   Period   Forecast

   1       13    314.152
   2       14    325.200
```

The forecasts for education majors are 314 in 2000 and 325 in 2001.

DOUBLE EXPONENTIAL SMOOTHING FOR TREND ANALYSIS

Use **double exponential smoothing** to smooth out the residual effect and to forecast data that exhibit a trend. By default, Minitab computes optimal values based on the data.

Stat ▸ Time Series ▸ Double Exp Smoothing

%DES *data* C	Uses double exponential smoothing
WEIGHTS K, K	Uses weights for smoothing and trend
FORECASTS K	Generate forecasts
SMOOTHED C	Stores the smoothed data
TREND C	Stores the trend component values
FITS C	Stores the fits
RESIDUALS C	Stores the residuals
FSTORE C	Stores the forecasts
UPPER C	Stores the upper prediction limits
LOWER C	Stores the lower prediction limits
SMPLOT	Plots smoothed vs. actual
NOPLOT	Does not draw the default plot
TABLE	Includes the table in the output
TITLE	Adds a title

◀ **Example 4**   **Double Exponential Smoothing Model**

Consider the enrollment data showing the number of education majors at a university given in Example 3. Fit a double exponential smoothing model to the data. Forecast the number of majors for 2000 and 2001.

Solution The years and numbers of majors are saved in a file named **Majors.mtp**.

Stat ▸ Time Series ▸ Double Exp Smoothing
  Select Majors in **Variable:**
  Click **Use:** enter .3 **for level** and .5 **for trend**;
  Click **Generate forecasts**
   Enter 2 in **Number of forecasts:**
  Add a **Title. OK**

MTB > %DES 'Majors';
SUBC>   Weight .3 .5;
SUBC>   Forecasts 2;
SUBC>   Title "Education Majors".

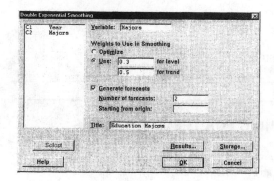

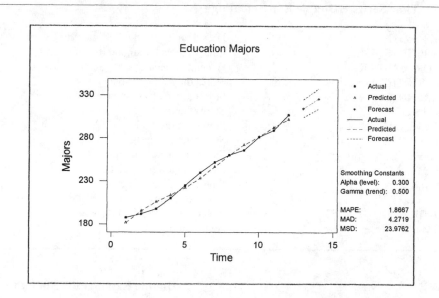

This time series plot also shows the strong linear trend in the data. The double exponential smoothing forecasts take into account the secular trend in the time series.

Double Exponential Smoothing

```
Data        Majors
Length      12.0000
NMissing    0

Smoothing Constants
Alpha (level): 0.3
Gamma (trend): 0.5

Accuracy Measures
MAPE:  1.8667
MAD:   4.2719
MSD:  23.9762
```

Row	Period	Forecast	Lower	Upper
1	13	314.652	304.186	325.118
2	14	325.976	314.108	337.843

The forecasts for the number of majors are 315 in 2000 and 326 in 2001. The lower and upper limits are 304 and 325 for 2000, and 314 and 338 for 2001.

Accuracy Summary for Education Majors

The last two examples illustrated the linear trend and double exponential trend forecasts. To find which model is the better fit to the time series, we compare accuracy measures.

	MAPE	MAD	MSD
Trend Analysis	1.37	3.13	13.78
Double Exponential Smoothing	1.87	4.27	23.98

Because the trend analysis model has smaller values for all three measures of accuracy, it provides a better fit for this time series. This conclusion may change if the weights for smoothing and trend are changed in the double exponential smoothing model.

14.4 FORECASTING MODELS WITH SEASONALITY AND TREND

Seasonality is often present in a quarterly or monthly time series. If a time series has significant seasonal effects and linear trend, a decomposition model or Winters' Method may provide useful forecasting methods.

DECOMPOSITION MODEL FOR TREND AND SEASONALITY

This model performs classical decomposition on a time series, using either a multiplicative or an additive model. Classical decomposition decomposes a time series into trend, seasonal, and residual components.

Stat ▸ Time Series ▸ Decomposition

%DECOMP *data* C	Does time series decomposition
MULTIPLICATIVE	Default model
ADDITIVE	Uses additive model
NOTREND	Does not include trend component
FORECASTS K	Generates forecasts
TREND C	Stores the trend component values
SEASONAL C	Stores seasonal component values
FITS C	Stores the fitted values
RESIDUALS C	Stores the residuals
FSTORE C	Stores the forecasts
NOPLOT	Does not draw the default plot
TABLE	Includes the table in the output
TITLE	Adds a title

■ **Example 5**   **Decomposition Model**

Satellite TV system sales have been growing dramatically in recent years. In one region, the quarterly satellite system sales for the years 1995 to 1999 were observed. Fit a multiplicative decomposition model to the time series. Forecast the quarterly sales for 2000.

Year	Quarter	Systems	Year	Quarter	Systems
1995	1	167	1997	3	234
1995	2	163	1997	4	257
1995	3	170	1998	1	269
1995	4	193	1998	2	258
1996	1	210	1998	3	261
1996	2	198	1998	4	291
1996	3	203	1999	1	302
1996	4	217	1999	2	296
1997	1	232	1999	3	300
1997	2	229	1999	4	322

Solution The data are saved in a file named **Satellite.mtp**. The three columns containing the data are named as above.

╢at ► Time Series ► Decomposition
Select Systems in **Variable:**
  Enter 4 in **Seasonal length:**
Click Generate forecasts
  Enter 4 in **Number of forecasts:**
Add a **Title: OK**

MTB > %Decomp 'Systems' 4;
SUBC>   Forecasts 4;
SUBC>   Title "Satellite TV System Sales".

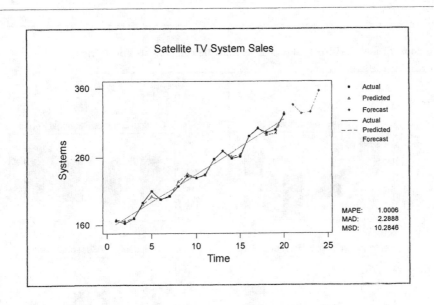

The Decomposition Fit display shows the linear trend line and the actual, fitted, and forecasted values.
The linear trend line has a positive slope; quarterly sales are increasing.

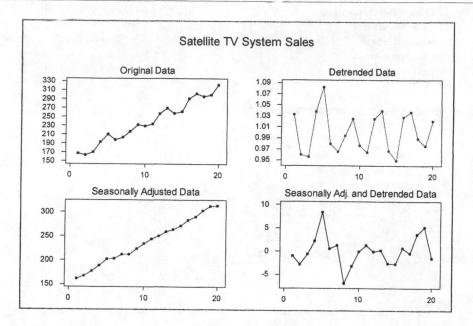

The component analysis display shows how removing components affects the time series.

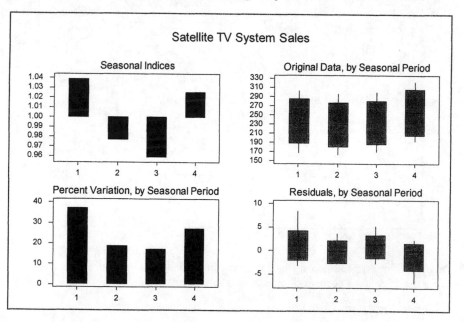

The seasonal analysis display provides information on the seasonal effect. The display shows the higher sales in the first and fourth quarters.

Time Series Decomposition

```
Data        Systems
Length      20.0000
NMissing    0
```

Trend Line Equation

$Yt = 153.621 + 8.09323*t$

Seasonal Indices

Period	Index
1	1.03867
2	0.976742
3	0.959110
4	1.02548

Accuracy of Model

```
MAPE:       1.0006
MAD:        2.2888
MSD:        10.2846
```

Forecasts

Row	Period	Forecast
1	21	336.092
2	22	323.958
3	23	325.872
4	24	356.721

The linear trend line is $Yt = 153.621 + 8.09323*t$. The slope of 8.09 shows that sales are increasing an average of about 8 systems per quarter. The seasonal index values indicate that sales in the first quarter are about 4% higher than the trend amount, in the second quarter about 2% lower than the trend, in the third quarter about 4% lower than the trend, and in the fourth quarter about 3% higher than the trend.

The sales forecasts for the next four quarters in 2000 are 336, 324, 326, and 357 satellite systems.

WINTERS' METHOD FOR TREND AND SEASONALITY

This method uses exponential smoothing to smooth data and forecast for time series that have significant seasonal effects and trend. It employs a leveling component, a trend component, and a seasonal component at each period. It uses three weights, or smoothing parameters, to update the components at each period.

Stat ▸ Time Series ▸ Winters' Method

%WINTMULT *data* C *season* K	Uses exponential smoothing
WEIGHTS K,K,K	Leveling, trend, and seasonality weights
FORECASTS K	Generates forecasts
TREND C	Stores the trend component values
SEASONAL C	Stores seasonal component values
FITS C	Stores the fits
RESIDUALS C	Stores the residuals
FSTORE C	Stores the forecasts
SMPLOT	Plots smoothed vs. actual values
NOPLOT	Does not draw the default plot
TABLE	Includes the table in the output
TITLE	Adds a title

■ **Example 6**   **Winters' Model**

Consider the satellite TV system sales given in Example 5. Use Winters' Method to smooth the time series. Forecast the quarterly sales for 2000.

Solution The data are saved in a file named **Satellite.mtp**; the three columns are named Year, Quarter, and Systems.

Stat ▸ Time Series ▸ Winters' Method
  Select Systems in **Variable:**
   Enter 4 in **Seasonal length:**
  Click **Generate forecasts**
   Enter 4 in **Number of forecasts:**
  Add a **Title. OK**

```
MTB > %Wintmult 'Systems' 4;
SUBC>   Weight 0.2 0.2 0.2;
SUBC>   Forecasts 4;
SUBC>   Title "Satellite TV System Sales".
```

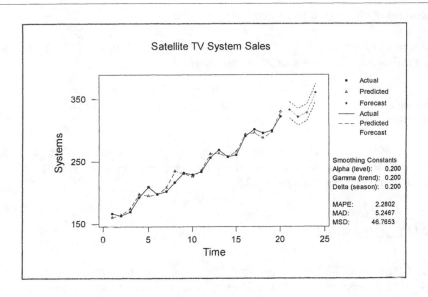

Winters' multiplicative model

```
Data           Systems
Length         20.0000
NMissing       0

Smoothing Constants
Alpha (level):      0.2
Gamma (trend):      0.2
Delta (seasonal):   0.2

Accuracy Measures
MAPE:   2.2802
MAD:    5.2467
MSD:    46.7653
```

Row	Period	Forecast	Lower	Upper
1	21	332.830	319.976	345.685
2	22	321.837	308.714	334.959
3	23	328.429	315.019	341.840
4	24	360.786	347.067	374.504

The plot shows the actual, predicted, and forecasted systems. The forecasts for the four quarters in 2000 are 333, 322, 328, and 361 satellite systems. Winters' model also provides lower and upper bounds on the forecasts.

Accuracy Summary for Satellite TV Systems

We have illustrated forecasts using decomposition and Winters' Method. To find which model is the better fit to the time series, we compare accuracy measures.

	MAPE	MAD	MSD
Decomposition	1.00	2.29	10.28
Winters' Method	2.28	5.25	46.77

The decomposition model provide a better fit for this time series; it has smaller values for all three measures of accuracy. However, this conclusion may change if the weights for leveling, trend, and seasonality are changed in the Winters' model.

14.5   AUTOCORRELATION

An important assumption of linear regression analysis is that the errors associated with any two observations are independent. This assumption is often violated with time series data because the residuals tend to be correlated with one another. This is frequently the case if there is a cyclical or seasonal component present in the time series. A plot of time series residuals versus time may show patterns in the residuals.

The correlation between adjacent time series residuals is called first-order autocorrelation. The test for first-order autocorrelation is

H_0: There is no first-order residual autocorrelation.
H_a: There is first-order residual autocorrelation.

The test statistic is the Durbin-Watson d statistic, which ranges from 0 to 4. The ideal value of d is 2, which means no first-order autocorrelation. If there is negative autocorrelation, in which adjacent errors are very different, d is significantly greater than 2. If there is positive autocorrelation, in which case the adjacent errors are similar, d is significantly less than 2. Use a table of critical values to determine if d indicates significant autocorrelation.

DURBIN-WATSON TEST FOR FIRST-ORDER AUTOCORRELATION

Stat ▸ Regression ▸ Regression

REGRESS C K *predictors* C ... C	Fits the least squares line
DW	Prints the Durbin-Watson test statistic

AUTOCORRELATION

This procedure computes and plots the autocorrelations, and provides *t*-test statistics and confidence intervals for checking for significant autocorrelation.

Stat ▸ Time Series ▸ Autocorrelation

%ACF *series* C	Computes autocorrelations
MAXLAG K	Indicates number of lags
CORR C	Stores autocorrelations
TSTATS C	Stores *t*-statistics
LBQ C	Stores Ljung-Box Q statistics
TITLE	Adds a title to the autocorrelations plot

■ **Example 7**   **Autocorrelations**

Refer to the satellite TV system sales data given in Example 5 of this chapter. Obtain and interpret the autocorrelations for the residuals for the decomposition model.

Solution   The data are saved in a file named **Satellite.mtp**; numbers of systems are in a column named Systems. We fit the decomposition model and store the residuals. The decomposition output is similar to that in Example 5 and is not printed.

Stat ▸ Time Series ▸ Decomposition
  Select Systems in **Variable:**
  Enter 4 in **Seasonal length:**
  Click **Storage**, choose **Residuals. OK**

```
MTB > Name C4 = 'RESI1'
MTB > %Decomp 'Systems' 4;
SUBC>   Residuals 'RESI1'.
```

Stat ▸ Time Series ▸ Time Series Plot
  Enter RESI1 in **Variable:**
  Click **Calendar**, choose **Quarter**;
  Click **Annotation**, choose **Title**, add a title;
  Click **Frame**, choose **Axis**,
    Enter Residuals in **Label 2. OK**

```
MTB > TSPlot 'RESI1';
SUBC>   Quarter;
SUBC>   TDisplay 11;
SUBC>   Symbol;
SUBC>   Connect;
SUBC>   Title "Residual Time Series";
SUBC>   Axis 11;
SUBC>   Axis 2;
SUBC>     Label "Residuals".
```

Stat ▸ Time Series ▸ Autocorrelations
  Select RESI1 in **Series. OK**

```
MTB > %ACF 'RESI1'
```

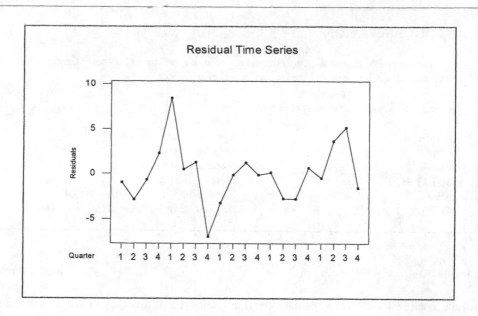

There does not appear to be a discernible pattern in the residuals.

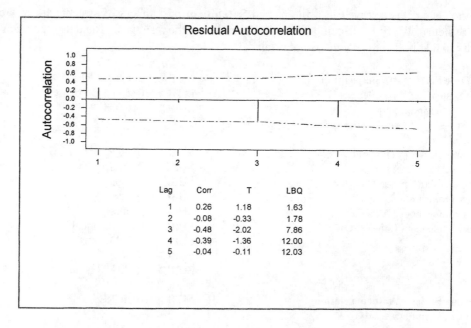

None of the autocorrelations shown on the plot extend beyond the confidence interval bands. There is not significant evidence of autocorrelation. The residuals appear to be independent.

EXERCISES

. Consider the average annual price of gold and silver for the years 1971 to 1999 given in Exercise 5 of Chapter 13. Both are measured in dollars per ounce. (Files: **Gold.mtp** and **Silver.mtp**)

   a. Calculate the 5-point moving average for both series for the years 1971 to 1999. Forecast the gold and silver prices for the next two years.
   b. Calculate the exponentially smoothed series for both series using $w = .3$. Forecast the gold and silver prices for the next two years.
   c. Compare MAPE, MAD, and MSD for both moving average and exponential smoothing forecasts for both series. Which is the better fit? Explain.

2. Consider the yearly income data of an anesthesiologist over the years 1973 to 1999 that are given in Exercise 3 of Chapter 13. (File: **RealIncome.mtp**)

   a. Calculate the 5-point moving average for the years 1973 to 1999. Forecast income for the next two years.
   b. Calculate the exponentially smoothed series using $w = .7$. Forecast income for the next two years.
   c. Perform a trend analysis on the data for the years 1973 to 1999. Forecast income for the next two years.
   d. Compare the forecasts determined in a-c. Which is the best fit? Explain.
   e. Use autocorrelation analysis on the trend model to determine if the residuals are independent.

3. Consider the baseball annual salary data for the years 1970 to 1999 that are given in Exercise 8 of Chapter 13. (File: **Baseball.mtp**)

   a. Perform a trend analysis on the data for the years 1970 to 1999. Forecast average baseball salary for the next three years.
   b. Fit a double exponential smoothing model to the data. Forecast average baseball salary for the next three years. Obtain and interpret the autocorrelations for the residuals for this model.
   c. Compare accuracy measures for the forecasts from parts a and b. Which is the better fit? Explain.

4. The following table gives the quarterly enrollment at St. Cloud State University for Fall 1985 through Summer 1998. (File: **SCSUEnroll.mtp**)

Year	Quarter	Male	Female	Total
1985-86	Fall	6,070	7,000	13,070
	Winter	5,876	6,527	12,403
	Spring	5,642	6,591	12,233
	Summer	2,162	3,245	5,407

Year	Quarter	Male	Female	Total
1986-87	Fall	6,591	7,629	14,220
	Winter	6,453	7,199	13,652
	Spring	6,050	7,348	13,398
	Summer	2,327	3,666	5,993
1987-88	Fall	7,109	8,411	15,520
	Winter	6,978	7,783	14,761
	Spring	6,666	7,779	14,445
	Summer	2,446	4,075	6,521
1988-89	Fall	7,296	8,956	16,252
	Winter	7,187	8,423	15,610
	Spring	7,026	8,465	15,491
	Summer	2,349	3,998	6,347
1989-90	Fall	7,514	9,037	16,551
	Winter	7,283	8,525	15,808
	Spring	7,276	8,895	16,171
	Summer	2,310	4,055	6,365
1990-91	Fall	7,862	9,214	17,076
	Winter	7,693	8,591	16,284
	Spring	7,359	8,729	16,088
	Summer	2,368	4,122	6,490
1991-92	Fall	7,599	8,726	16,325
	Winter	7,519	8,164	15,683
	Spring	7,260	8,182	15,442
	Summer	2,177	3,427	5,604
1992-93	Fall	7,509	8,538	16,047
	Winter	7,141	7,665	14,806
	Spring	6,900	7,501	14,401
	Summer	2,269	3,631	5,900
1993-94	Fall	7,161	7,957	15,118
	Winter	6,912	7,311	14,223
	Spring	6,730	7,130	13,860
	Summer	2,351	3,522	5,873
1994-95	Fall	6,978	7,695	14,673
	Winter	6,783	7,054	13,837
	Spring	6,367	6,891	13,258
	Summer	2,233	3,339	5,572
1995-96	Fall	6,697	7,411	14,108
	Winter	6,471	6,966	13,437
	Spring	6,150	6,832	12,982
	Summer	2,188	3,404	5,592
1996-97	Fall	6,537	7,457	13,994
	Winter	6,199	6,944	13,143
	Spring	5,948	6,847	12,795
	Summer	2,161	3,531	5,692
1997-98	Fall	6,396	7,656	14,052
	Winter	6,073	6,956	13,029
	Spring	5,914	7,070	12,984
	Summer	2,240	3,541	5,781

a. Plot the total enrollment time series.
b. Fit a decomposition model to the data. Forecast the enrollment for the next year.
c. Use Winters' Method to smooth the time series. Forecast the enrollment for the next year.
d. Compare accuracy measures for the forecasts from parts b and c. Which is the better fit? Explain.
e. Use autocorrelation analysis on the better model to determine if the residuals are independent.

5. Repeat the analysis of Exercise 4 using the male enrollment time series. Forecast the enrollment for male students for the next year. Discuss.

6. Repeat the analysis of Exercise 4 using the female enrollment time series. Forecast the enrollment for female students for the next year. Compare with the male enrollment forecasts.

7. The manager of Raymond Park Rink, an indoor skating rink, studied the daily attendance pattern in order to determine the number of full and part time employees to hire for each day of the week. About one employee is needed per ten skaters. The following table gives the November 1999 date, numbers of skaters, and day of the week for 21 consecutive days. (File: **Skaters.mtp**)

Date	Skaters	Day	Date	Skaters	Day
1	10	Monday	12	12	Friday
2	11	Tuesday	13	30	Saturday
3	13	Wednesday	14	20	Sunday
4	9	Thursday	15	13	Monday
5	13	Friday	16	13	Tuesday
6	32	Saturday	17	14	Wednesday
7	35	Sunday	18	11	Thursday
8	29	Monday	19	13	Friday
9	13	Tuesday	20	31	Saturday
10	20	Wednesday	21	33	Sunday
11	10	Thursday			

a. Plot the data. Based on the shape of the time series, fit two models that you think would be appropriate to describe the variation in the time series. Justify your choices.
b. Use the three measures of accuracy to decide which model provides a better fit.
c. Use autocorrelation analysis to determine if the residuals are independent.

8. Information on air travel and the number of flights resulting in accidents and fatalities in the United States beginning in 1938 is given in the Appendix. (File: **AirFatal.mtp**)

a. Plot the data. Based on the shape of the time series, fit two models that you think would be appropriate to describe the variation in the time series. Justify your choices.
b. Use the three measures of accuracy to decide which model provides a better fit.
c. Use autocorrelation analysis to determine if the residuals are independent.

9. Refer to Exercise 1 of Chapter 13. The Consumer Price Index (CPI), a weighted composite index of the prices of a "market basket" of goods and services purchased by the typical consumer, is

given for the years 1950 to 1999. The years 1982-84 are assigned the base and indices for othe
years are percentage changes from the base.   Based on the characteristics of the time series, f
two models that you think would be appropriate to describe the variation in both time serie
Justify your choices. Use the three measures of accuracy to decide which model provides a bette
fit. Conduct an autocorrelation analysis. (File: **CPI.mtp**)

CHAPTER 15

CATEGORICAL DATA ANALYSIS

This chapter illustrates Minitab commands to analyze one- or two-dimensional classification data. One-dimensional data, which are data classified on a single scale, are analyzed using a hypothesis test about multinomial probabilities. When data are classified on two dimensions, the result is a contingency table. The analysis is a test of independence.

NEW COMMAND

CHISQUARE

15.1 MULTINOMIAL DISTRIBUTION

A multinomial experiment is one in which a qualitative variable is classified into two or more distinct categories. The objective of the experiment is to make inferences on the probabilities, π_1, π_2, ..., π_k, that observations fall in k categories. Examples include consumer preference studies and opinion polls. The binomial experiment described in Chapter 5 is a special case of the multinomial experiment for $k = 2$ categories.

A test about multinomial probabilities determines whether the observed categorical data fit the hypothesized categorical probabilities. The test statistic χ^2 measures the amount of disagreement between the observed and the expected number of responses in each category. The formula for the test statistic is

$$\chi^2 = \sum_{i=1}^{k} \frac{(O_i - E_i)^2}{E_i}$$

where O_i and E_i are the observed and expected frequencies of category i. The expected frequency is

$$E_i = n\pi_i$$

where n is the number of observations. The hypotheses for a test on multinomial probabilities are

H_0: The category probabilities are π_1, π_2, ..., π_k
H_a: At least two category probabilities differ from π_1, π_2, ..., π_k

Under the null hypothesis, the sampling distribution of χ^2 is approximately a chi-square distribution with $(k - 1)$ degrees of freedom. The rejection region is located in the upper tail of the chi-square distribution.

Minitab does not have a command for a test on multinomial probabilities. However, you can use Minitab to calculate the expected frequencies and the *p*-value.

NOTE

*In this chapter, we show different graphs to study relationships. In Examples 2 and 4, we use the Minitab Editor to add text data to the line graphs. To add text, click on **Editor ▸ Show Tool Palette**; choose **T** for text; place the pointer on the graph where you want to add a text box for a name, and click. Enter the text in the dialog box. You can then click on the text box and move it anyplace on the graph. Click on **Editor ▸ View** to print or copy the graph.*

■ **Example 1**   **Multinomial Probabilities**

The Learning-Style Inventory (LSI) evaluates the way a person learns and deals with ideas and day-to-day situations. The LSI, based on several tested theories of thinking and creativity, indicates whether a person has one of four learning styles: Accomodator learns primarily from "hands-on" experience; Diverger learns best from viewing concrete situations and gathering information; Assimilator has interest in abstract ideas and concepts; and Converger finds practical uses for ideas and theories. The following table gives a distribution of the four learning styles found in a group of 200 educators at a workshop for teachers. Are there differences in the percentages of learning styles among educators? Test using $\alpha = .05$. Discuss.

Learning Style	Frequency
Accomodator	53
Diverger	60
Assimilator	44
Converger	<u>43</u>
	200

Solution If the percentages of learning styles are equal, we would expect 25% or 50 educators to fall in each group. The data are saved in a file named **LearningStyles.mtp**. Data are entered in three columns: learning styles, observed frequencies, and the expected frequencies if learning styles are equally likely to occur among educators.

First, we construct a bar graph of the observed and expected frequencies to explore possible differences. To construct this bar chart, we stack the data as printed below.

Manip ▸ Stack ▸ Stack Blocks of Columns
  Stack two or more blocks of columns on top...:
    Select Observed and Style
     and **select** Expected and Style;
  Store stacked data in:
    Click **Columns of current worksheet:**
     Enter 'Frequency' and 'LearningStyle'
    Enter 'Code' in **Store subscripts in:**
  Click **Use variable names in subscript column. OK**

```
MTB > Name C4 = 'Frequency'
MTB > Name C5 = 'LearningStyle' C6 = 'Code'
MTB > Stack ('Observed' 'Style')  &
CONT>  ('Expected' 'Style')  &
CONT>  ('Frequency' 'LearningStyle');
SUBC>  Subscripts 'Code';
SUBC>  UseNames.
```

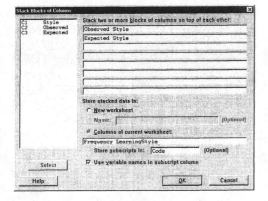

Manip ▸ Display Data
  Select Style - Code in **Display. OK**

MTB > Print 'Style' - 'Code'

Data Display

Row	Style	Observed	Expected	Frequency	LearningStyle	Code
1	Accomodator	53	50	53	Accomodator	Observed
2	Diverger	60	50	60	Diverger	Observed
3	Assimilator	44	50	44	Assimilator	Observed
4	Converger	43	50	43	Converger	Observed
5				50	Accomodator	Expected
6				50	Diverger	Expected
7				50	Assimilator	Expected
8				50	Converger	Expected

Graph ▸ Chart
  Select Frequency in **Graph 1 Y**;
   and LearningStyle in **Graph 1 X**;
  In **Data Display:** click **For each**, choose **Group**;
   Select Code in **Group variables**;
  Click **Annotation**, choose **Title**, add a title;
  Click **Frame**, click **Axis**, enter "Frequency" in **Label 2**;
  Click **Frame**, click **Min and Max**,
   Click **Y Minimum**, enter 20;
   Click **Y Maximum**, enter 70,
  Click **Options**, click **Cluster:**
   Select Code in **Cluster. OK**

MTB > Chart 'Frequency ' * 'Learning Style';
SUBC>   Cluster 'Code';
SUBC>   Bar 'Code';
SUBC>   Title "Learning Style Inventory";
SUBC>   Axis 1;
SUBC>   Axis 2;
SUBC>   Label "Frequency";
SUBC>   Minimum 2 20;
SUBC>   Maximum 2 70.

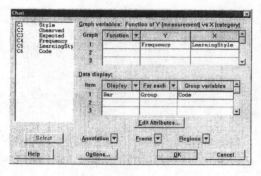
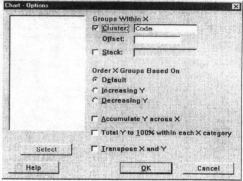

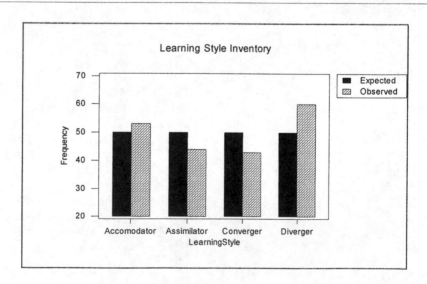

The chart shows that there are differences in observed and expected learning styles. For example, observed learning styles for accomodator and diverger occur more often than expected for educators.

The hypotheses to test whether the educators' learning styles differ are

H_0: $\pi_1 = .25$, $\pi_2 = .25$, $\pi_3 = .25$, $\pi_4 = .25$
H_a: At least two of the probabilities differ from .25

Calc ▸ Calculator
  Enter 'Obs-Exp' in **Store results in variable**:
  Enter Observed - Expected in **Expression. OK**

MTB > Name C7 = 'Obs-Exp'
MTB > Let 'Obs-Exp' = Observed - Expected

Calc ▸ Calculator
  Enter 'Value' in **Store results in variable:**
  Enter 'Obs-Exp'**2/Expected in **Expression. OK**

MTB > Name C8 = 'Value'
MTB > Let 'Value' = 'Obs-Exp'**2 / Expected

Calc ▸ Calculator
  Enter 'ChiSq' in **Store results in variable:**
  Enter Sum(Value) in **Expression. OK**

MTB > Name C9 = 'ChiSq'
MTB > Let 'ChiSq' = Sum(Value)

Calc ▸ Probability Distributions ▸ Chi-square
  Click **Cumulative probability**;
  Enter 3 in **Degrees of freedom:**
  Select ChiSq in **Input column:**
    Enter '1-pvalue' in **Optional storage. OK**

MTB > Name C10 = '1-pvalue'
MTB > CDF 'ChiSq' '1-pvalue';
SUBC>   Chisquare 3.

Calc ▸ Calculator
  Enter 'pvalue' in **Store results in variable:**
  Enter 1 - '1-pvalue' in **Expression. OK**

MTB > Name C11 = 'pvalue'
MTB > Let 'pvalue' = 1 - '1-pvalue'

Manip ▸ Display Data
  Select Style - Expected, Obs-Exp, ChiSq,
    and pvalue in **Display. OK**

MTB > Print C1-C3 C7 C9 C11

Data Display

Row	Style	Observed	Expected	Obs-Exp	ChiSq	pvalue
1	Accomodator	53	50	3	3.88	0.274717
2	Diverger	60	50	10		
3	Assimilator	44	50	-6		
4	Converger	43	50	-7		

Since the rejection region is the upper tail of the chi-square distribution, the *p*-value is the probability, assuming the null hypothesis is true, of obtaining $\chi^2 > 3.88$. The *p*-value = .27 is not less than $\alpha = .05$. There is not significant evidence to conclude that the learning styles differ among educators.

■ **Example 2**   **Multinomial Probabilitie**

Grade inflation is a concern of colleges and universities. The instructors of an Introduction t
Chemistry class have kept a record of the grade distribution for several years. The historical grad
distribution is as follows: A, 15%; B, 35%; C, 40%; and Other, 10%. A random sample of grades fo
120 students recorded this past year are given in the table. Has the grade distribution changed? Tes
using $\alpha = .05$.

Grade	Students
A	20
B	33
C	52
Other	15

Solution   We enter letter grades in a column named Grade, observed frequencies in Observed, and
historical proportions in 'p'.

Assuming the historical grade distribution is still accurate, we calculate the expected number of
students in each grade category by multiplying the historical proportions times the sample size 120.
We illustrate a multiple plot to graphically summarize the data.

Calc ▸ Calculator   MTB > Name C4 = 'Expected'
  Enter 'Expected' in **Store results in variable:**   MTB > Let 'Expected' = 'p' * Sum(Observed)
  Enter 'p' * Sum(Observed) in **Expression. OK**

Manip ▸ Display Data   MTB > Print 'Grade' - 'Expected'
  Select Grade - Expected in **Display. OK**

Data Display

Row	Grade	Observed	p	Expected
1	A	20	0.15	18
2	B	33	0.35	42
3	C	52	0.40	48
4	Other	15	0.10	12

Graph ▸ **Chart**
  Select Observed in **Graph 1 Y**
    and Grade in **Graph 1 X**;
  Select Expected in **Graph 2 Y**
    and Grade in **Graph 2 X**;
  Click **Display**, choose **Symbol**.
    Click **Display row 2**; choose **Connect** and **Graph**;
  Click **Frame** and **Axis**, Enter "Frequency" in **Label 2**;
  Click **Frame** and **Multiple Graph**,
    Choose **Overlay graphs on the same page**;
  Click **Frame**, click **Min and Max**,
    Click **Y Minimum**, enter 0;
    Click **Y Maximum**, enter 60.
  Click **Annotation**, choose **Title**, add a title. **OK**

```
MTB > Chart 'Observed' * 'Grade'  &
CONT> 'Expected' * 'Grade';
SUBC>  Symbol;
SUBC>  Title "Grade Distribution";
SUBC>  Overlay;
SUBC>  Connect;
SUBC>  Axis 1;
SUBC>  Axis 2;
SUBC>   Label "Frequency"
SUBC>  Minimum 2 0;
SUBC>  Maximum 2 60.
```

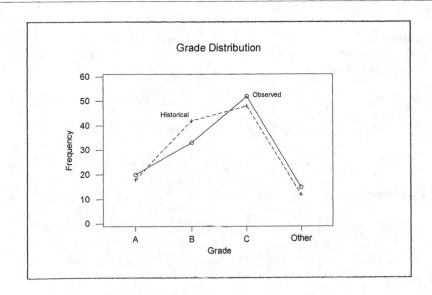

The display shows that there are some differences between the historical grade distribution and this year's grades. The differences could be due to random sampling error, or because the grade distribution has changed.

To test whether this year's grade distribution has changed, the hypotheses are

H_0: $\pi_1 = .15$, $\pi_2 = .35$, $\pi_3 = .40$, $\pi_4 = .10$
H_a: At least two of the probabilities differ from the hypothesized values.

Calc ▸ **Calculator**
   Enter 'Obs-Exp' in **Store results in variable:**
   Enter Observed - Expected in **Expression**. **OK**

Calc ▸ **Calculator**
   Enter 'Value' in **Store results in variable:**
   Enter 'Obs-Exp'**2/Expected in **Expression**. **OK**

Calc ▸ **Calculator**
   Enter 'ChiSq' in **Store results in variable:**
   Enter Sum(Value) in **Expression**. **OK**

Calc ▸ **Probability Distributions** ▸ **Chi-square**
   Click **Cumulative Probability**,
     Enter 3 in **Degrees of freedom:**
   Select 'ChiSq' in **Input column:**
     Enter '1-pvalue' in **Optional storage**. **OK**

Calc ▸ **Calculator**
   Enter 'pvalue' in **Store results in variable:**
   Enter 1 - '1-pvalue' in **Expression**. **OK**

Manip ▸ **Display Data**
   Select Grade, Observed, Expected,
   Obs-Exp, ChiSq, and pvalue in **Display**. **OK**

MTB > Name C5 = 'Obs-Exp'
MTB > Let 'Obs-Exp' = Observed - Expected

MTB > Name C6 = 'Value'
MTB > Let 'Value' = 'Obs-Exp'**2 / Expected

MTB > Name C7 = 'ChiSq'
MTB > Let 'ChiSq' = Sum(Value)

MTB > Name C8 = '1-pvalue'
MTB > CDF 'ChiSq' '1-pvalue';
SUBC>   Chisquare 3.

MTB > Name C9 = 'pvalue'
MTB > Let 'pvalue' = 1 - '1-pvalue'

MTB > Print C1-C2 C4-C5 C7 C9

Data Display

Row	Grade	Observed	Expected	Obs-Exp	ChiSq	pvalue
1	A	20	18	2	3.23413	0.356917
2	B	33	42	-9		
3	C	52	48	4		
4	Other	15	12	3		

Since the rejection region is the upper tail of the chi-square distribution, the p-value is the probability, assuming the null hypothesis is true, of obtaining $\chi^2 > 3.23$. The p-value = .36 is not less than $\alpha =$ .05. There is not significant evidence to conclude that this year's grade distribution differs from the historical grade distribution.

15.2 CONTINGENCY ANALYSIS

A contingency table contains data classified according to two categorical variables. An objective of a contingency table analysis is to test whether the variables are dependent. The general form of the hypothesis test is

H_0: The two classifications are independent.
H_a: The two classifications are dependent.

The formula for the test statistic for a contingency table of r rows and c columns is

$$\chi^2 = \sum_{i=1}^{r} \sum_{j=1}^{c} \frac{(O_{ij} - E_{ij})^2}{E_{ij}}$$

where O_{ij} and E_{ij} are the Observed and Expected frequencies of the cell in row i and column j. The expected frequency is defined $E_{ij} = R_i C_j / n$, , where R_i and C_j are corresponding total frequencies in row i and column j, for sample size n. Under the null hypothesis, the sampling distribution of χ^2 is approximately a chi-square distribution, with $(r-1)(c-1)$ degrees of freedom. The rejection region is located in the upper tail of the chi-square distribution.

CONTINGENCY TABLE ANALYSIS

This command does a chi-square test of independence for the table of frequencies given in the specified columns. The output includes a table of observed and expected frequencies, the calculations for the chi-square test statistic, degrees of freedom, and the *p*-value.

Stat ▸ Tables ▸ Chi-square Test

CHISQUARE *table* C ... C   Does a chi-square analysis for the table

---

■ **Example 3**   **Contingency Table Analysis**

A study concerning a type of sequential therapy treatment for small-cell lung cancer was conducted to determine whether male and female patients responded differently. Male and female patients were assigned the same combination of chemotherapeutic agents in each treatment cycle. Responses to the chemotherapy treatment are provided in the following table. Test whether the two classifications are dependent, using $\alpha = .05$.

Response	Male	Female
Progressive Disease	6	18
No Change	106	87
Partial Remission	71	55
Complete Remission	14	21

Solution   The data are saved in a file named **Chemo.mtp**. The bar chart that we illustrate for this example requires stacked data.

Manip ▸ Stack ▸ Stack Blocks of Columns
  Stack two or more blocks of columns on top...:
   Select Male and Response
    and **select** Female and Response;
  Store stacked data in:
   Click **Columns of current worksheet:**
    Enter 'Frequency' and 'Responses'
   Enter 'Gender' in **Store subscripts in:**
  Click **Use variable names in subscript column. OK**

MTB > Name C4 = 'Responses'
MTB > Name C5 = 'Frequency' C6 = 'Gender'
MTB > Stack ('Male' 'Response') &
CONT>   ('Female' 'Response')   &
CONT>   ('Frequency' 'Responses');
SUBC>   Subscripts 'Gender';
SUBC>   UseNames.

Manip ▸ Display Data
  Select Response - Gender in **Display. OK**

MTB > Print C1-C6

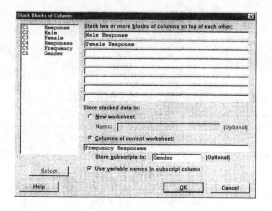

Data Display

```
Row  Response            Male  Female

  1  Progressive Disease    6      18
  2  No Change            106      87
  3  Partial Remission     71      55
  4  Complete Remission    14      21
```

Data Display

Row	Responses	Frequency	Gender
1	Progressive Disease	6	Male
2	No Change	106	Male
3	Partial Remission	71	Male
4	Complete Remission	14	Male
5	Progressive Disease	18	Female
6	No Change	87	Female
7	Partial Remission	55	Female
8	Complete Remission	21	Female

Graph ▶ Chart
  Select Frequency in **Graph 1 Y**
    and Responses in **Graph 1 X**;
  Click **For each**, choose **Group**;
    Select Gender in **Group variables:**
  Click **Options** and **Cluster: Select** Gender;
    Click **Total Y to 100% Within each X category**;
  Click **Frame** and **Axis**, enter "Percent" in **Label 2**;
  Click **Annotation** and **Title**; add a title. **OK**

```
MTB > Chart 'Frequency' * 'Responses';
SUBC>   Cluster 'Gender';
SUBC>   CPercent;
SUBC>   Bar 'Gender';
SUBC>   Title "Chemotherapy Response";
SUBC>   Axis 1;
SUBC>   Axis 2;
SUBC>     Label "Percent".
```

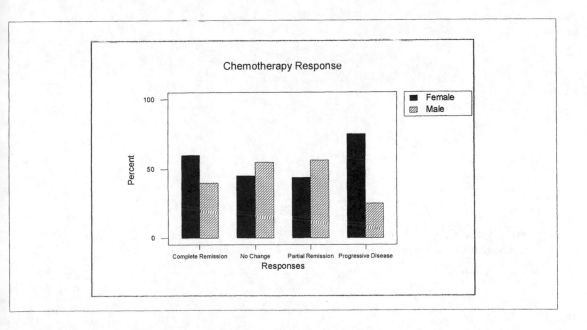

There are some differences in the effect that sequential therapy treatments have on male and female patients. It could be because of a very unusual set of sample data, or because the response is actually dependent on the gender of the patient.

The null and alternative hypotheses to do the test are

H_0: Chemotherapy response and gender are independent.
H_a: Chemotherapy response and gender are dependent.

Stat ▸ Tables ▸ Chi-square Test   MTB > ChiSquare 'Male' 'Female'
  Select Male Female
    in **Columns containing the table. OK**

Chi-Square Test: Male, Female

Expected counts are printed below observed counts

	Male	Female	Total
1	6	18	24
	12.51	11.49	
2	106	87	193
	100.58	92.42	
3	71	55	126
	65.67	60.33	
4	14	21	35
	18.24	16.76	
Total	197	181	378

Chi-Sq =   3.386 + 3.685 +
           0.292 + 0.317 +
           0.433 + 0.471 +
           0.986 + 1.073 = 10.644
DF = 3, P-Value = 0.014

The p-value =.014 is less than α = .05. There is sufficient evidence to conclude that sequential treatment response is dependent on gender.

◢ Example 4   **Contingency Table Analysis**

A bookstore classified books by type (childrens, fiction, nonfiction) and sales level (low, medium, high). The following table shows the results for random samples of 50 books from each type of book. Are sales levels related to types of books? Analyze using $\alpha = .05$.

Level	Childrens	Fiction	Nonfiction
Low Sales	15	10	25
Medium Sales	30	15	15
High Sales	5	25	10

Solution   The data are saved in a file named **BookSales.mtp**. In this example we illustrate a graph using proportion of sales. The Calculator command calculates the proportion of books sold in each category.

Calc ▸ Calculator
   Enter 'Childrensp' in **Store results in variable:**.
   Enter Childrens/Sum(Childrens) in **Expression. OK**

MTB > Name C5 = 'Childrens-p'
MTB > Let 'Childrensp' = &
CONT>   Childrens/Sum(Childrens)

Calc ▸ Calculator
   Enter 'Fictionp' in **Store results in variable:**
   Enter Fiction/Sum(Fiction) in **Expression. OK**

MTB > Name C6 = 'Fictionp'
MTB > Let 'Fictionp' = Fiction/Sum(Fiction)

Calc ▸ Calculator
   Enter 'Nonfictionp' in **Store results in variable:**.
   Enter Nonfiction/Sum(Nonfiction) in **Expression. OK**

MTB > Name C7 = 'Nonfictionp'
MTB > Let 'Nonfictionp' = &
CONT>   Nonfiction/Sum(Nonfiction)

Manip ▸ Display Data
   Select Level - Nonfictionp in **Display. OK**

MTB > Print 'Level'-'Nonfictionp'

Data Display

Row	Level	Childrens	Fiction	Nonfiction
1	Low	15	10	25
2	Medium	30	15	15
3	High	5	25	10

Data Display

Row	Level	Childrensp	Fictionp	Nonfictionp
1	Low	0.3	0.2	0.5
2	Medium	0.6	0.3	0.3
3	High	0.1	0.5	0.2

Graph ▸ Chart
  Select Childrensp in **Graph 1 Y**
    and Level in **Graph 1 X**;
  Select Fictionp in **Graph 2 Y**
    and Level in **Graph 2 X**;
  Select Nonfictionp in **Graph 3 Y**
    and Level in **Graph 3 X**;
  In **Display 1,** choose **Symbol** and **Graph** in **For each**;
    In **Display 2,** choose **Connect** and **Graph** in **For each**;
  Click **Frame** and **Multiple Graphs,**
    choose **Overlay graphs on same page**;
  Click **Frame** and **Axis**, enter "Sales" in **Label 2**;
  Click **Annotation** and **Title**; add a title. **OK**

```
MTB > Chart 'Childrensp'*'Level'  &
CONT>   'Fictionp'*'Level' 'Nonfictionp'*'Leve
SUBC>   Connect;
SUBC>   Symbol;
SUBC>   Title "Book Sales";
SUBC>   Overlay;
SUBC>   Axis 1;
SUBC>   Axis 2;
SUBC>    Label "Sales".
```

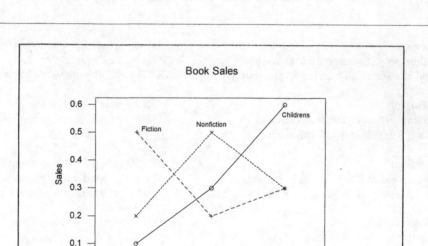

If there is no relationship between sales level and type of book, all three types of books would have the same distribution, and the lines on the graph would be parallel. The distributions from the samples differ substantially, indicating that there may be a relationship between the sales level of a book and the type of book.

The test to determine whether the two classifications are dependent is

H_0: Sales level and type of book are independent.
H_a: Sales level and type of book are dependent.

Stat ▸ Tables ▸ **Chi-square Test**
 Select Childrens Fiction Nonfiction
  in **Columns containing the table OK**

MTB > ChiSquare 'Children'-'NonFiction'

Chi-Square Test: Childrens, Fiction, Nonfiction

Expected counts are printed below observed counts

	Children	Fiction	Nonfiction	Total
1	15	10	25	50
	16.67	16.67	16.67	
2	30	15	15	60
	20.00	20.00	20.00	
3	5	25	10	40
	13.33	13.33	13.33	
Total	50	50	50	150

Chi-Sq = 0.167 + 2.667 + 4.167 +
         5.000 + 1.250 + 1.250 +
         5.208 + 10.208 + 0.833 = 30.750
DF = 4, P-Value = 0.000

The *p*-value of 0 is less than $\alpha = .05$. There is sufficient evidence to conclude that sales level is dependent on the type of book at this bookstore.

EXERCISES

1. A study concerning a type of sequential therapy treatment for small-cell lung cancer was reported in Example 3 of this chapter. A study was also conducted to determine whether male and female patients responded differently in an alternating therapy plan in which three different combinations of chemotherapy were given, alternating from cycle to cycle. Responses to the chemotherapy treatment are provided in the following table.

	Male	Female
Progressive Disease	4	11
No Change	12	33
Partial Remission	9	13
Complete Remission	16	12

    a. Graphically compare the response for male and female patients. Summarize.
    b. Do the data provide sufficient evidence that there is a difference in response for male and female patients in an alternating therapy plan? Test using $\alpha = .05$.

2. The Gallup Organization reported that the average American spends 21 minutes traveling to work each day. More specifically, interviews conducted with part-time or full-time workers showed that 14 percent traveled more than thirty minutes, 82 percent traveled less than thirty minutes, and 4 percent did not travel to work. A study of 200 part-time or full-time workers in Minneapolis revealed that 18 traveled more than thirty minutes, 176 traveled less than thirty minutes, and 6 did not travel.

    a. Graphically compare the Minneapolis data with the Gallup poll results. Summarize.
    b. Do the data provide sufficient evidence that the percentages of Minneapolis workers traveling to work differ from the percentages reported in the Gallup poll? Test using $\alpha = .05$.

3. If the sample sizes of a contingency table analysis are small, the sampling distribution of χ^2 may not approximate a chi-square distribution. Consider the following contingency table which gives the number of items sold, classified by size and color.

Color	Small	Large
Red	50	1
Blue	30	3
Green	10	6

    Use Minitab to test whether size and color are independent. Discuss the warning that is given on the computer output. Explain why this is a concern.

4. The U.S. Department of Labor compiles data on mean unemployment benefits and the percent of claims approved for each state. To study the relationship between the mean unemployment benefits and the percent of approved claims, a consultant used a random sample from 45 states. The following classifies the data by mean unemployment benefits and percent of approved claims.

Percent	Under $2,000	Over $2,000
50-65%	7	4
65-75%	9	6
75-95%	9	10

a. Graphically study the sample data.
b. Do the data provide sufficient evidence that mean unemployment benefit is dependent on the percent of approved claims? Test using $\alpha = .05$.

5. The manager of Rental Property in Phoenix, Arizona wants to determine whether rental prices within the city differ from prices in suburbs. A random sample of 200 rental prices of residential three bedroom homes, classified according to price and location, is given in the following table.

Prices	City	Suburb
Under $500	48	2
$500-$599	51	11
$600-$699	30	17
$700 and over	22	19

a. Graphically analyze the sample of rental properties.
b. Do the data provide sufficient evidence that rental prices and location are dependent? Test using $\alpha = .05$.

6. Consider the class data set given in the Appendix. Test whether the gender of students is related to whether the student owns an American car, owns a foreign car, or does not own a car. (File: **Classdata.mtp**)

7. During the summer of 2000, audits were made at four nursing homes to measure the quality of administering medication to the residents. Quality was divided into three categories: excellent - medication received within 15 minutes of scheduled time, acceptable - medication received between 15 and 30 minutes of scheduled time, poor - medication not received within 30 minutes of scheduled time. The auditor made two hundred observations at each nursing home.

	Nursing Home			
	A	B	C	D
Excellent	128	133	155	169
Acceptable	46	45	33	23
Poor	26	22	12	8

a. Graphically compare the quality of service at the four nursing homes.
b. Do the data provide sufficient evidence that the quality of service depends on the nursing home? Use $\alpha = .05$.

8. Consider the save rate statistics on heart attack victims given in the Appendix. Does whether or not a heart attack victim is saved depend on the location of the victim? (File: **Heart.mtp**)

CHAPTER 16

SURVEY ANALYSIS

In this chapter we describe a survey project that we generally assign near the end of a statistics course. The objectives of the project are to use Minitab to analyze a questionnaire and to provide a review of statistical methods covered in the course. The project illustrates a realistic approach to analyze a survey containing many variables. It is a survey for Fandels Department Store. The following questionnaire was distributed to 120 customers at the store. All or part of the data may be used for the project. The data file is on the computer diskette available with this guide.

QUESTIONNAIRE

We are interested in your opinion about Fandels Department Store. By completing this questionnaire, you will be providing information so that we can better serve your needs. Thank you for your cooperation.

1. Which of the following services, not now available at Fandels, would you most like to see offered? Check only one.

    1. __ Luncheon counter/restaurant
    2. __ Check cashing
    3. __ Child care
    4. __ Free gift wrapping

2. Overall, how would you rate the personnel at Fandels as compared to other department stores in the area?

    1. __ Definitely better
    2. __ Somewhat better
    3. __ No different
    4. __ Somewhat worse
    5. __ Definitely worse
    6. __ No opinion

3.   For each of the following, please check the blank which best describes your feelings about Fandel store.

                                        1 2 3 4 5 6
   a.   Poor Value   _ _ _ _ _ _   Good Value
   b.   Low Prices   _ _ _ _ _ _   High Prices
   c.   Unfriendly Atmosphere   _ _ _ _ _ _   Friendly Atmosphere
   d.   Old-Fashioned   _ _ _ _ _ _   Modern
   e.   Poor Selection   _ _ _ _ _ _   Good Selection
   f.   Poor Location   _ _ _ _ _ _   Good Location
   g.   Lower Class Clientele   _ _ _ _ _ _   Higher Class Clientele

4.   What is your age?

   1. _ 18-34
   2. _ 35-49
   3. _ 50-64
   4. _ 65 plus

5.   Gender

   1. _ Male
   2. _ Female

6.   Type of residence

   1. _ Own a home
   2. _ Rent an apartment
   3. _ Rent a home
   4. _ Other
   If Other, describe the type_____

7.   Annual income to the nearest one hundred dollars (If married, your household income)
   _____

8.   Approximately, how much did you spend in Fandels Department Store? _____

EXERCISES

1. Create a file containing the data set. Check the file for errors and make corrections if necessary. It is important that the data file be free of errors before beginning the analysis. Name the columns and save an error-free copy of the data set.

2. The questionnaire has been designed to provide answers to the following questions requested by Fandels Department Store.

    a. What percent of the customers would most like to have a child care service? A check cashing service? Which service not now available is most desired by Fandels customers?
    b. How does Fandels personnel rate when compared with other department stores?
    c. What is the overall feeling toward Fandels Department Store. If Fandels wanted to improve their image, where might they direct their efforts?
    d. Is there a relationship between the age of customers and the services desired but not now available?
    e. Is there a difference in the average amount spent for the four groups formed by the most desired service? Why is it important to know this?
    f. What are the average amounts spent by customers when they are cross-classified by sex and service desired? Discuss how this information can be used.
    g. What is the relationship, if any, between the amount spent and the two variables, annual income and age? How can this information be used?
    h. Estimate the average amount spent by all Fandels customers.
    i. Use regression to estimate the average amount spent by customers with income of $75,000.

    Outline the statistical procedure or procedures that you would use to answer each question. Hint: It is important to distinguish between qualitative or quantitative variables.

3. Use Minitab to obtain the output for the statistical procedures identified in Exercise 2.

4. Write a summary report of your survey analysis for Fandels Department Store.

APPENDIX

DESCRIPTION OF DATA SETS

The following data sets are used in examples and exercises in this guide. This Appendix gives a brief description of the data. A disk available with this guide contains all data sets. File names are provided in this Appendix and in the examples and exercises.

1. Background Information on Statistics Students
2. Class Project
3. Business and Education Professors
4. Heart Attack 911 Calls
5. Home Sales
6. How Safe Are The Skies?
7. Campus Crime
8. Residential Homes

DATA SETS

1. Background Information on Statistics Students

File name: **StudentInfo.mtp**
Source: Fall 1999 survey information was collected by 79 statistics students

Column	Name	Description
C1	Student	Student code
C2	Dept	Students' major department
C3	ReportedGPA	Grade point average reported by the student
C4	UnivGPA	Grade point average reported by the university
C5	AlgGrade	Grade in college algebra or equivalent course
C6	Windows?	Experience using windows on a PC: None, Some, Lots
C7	Gender	F = female, M = Male
C8	WorkHrs	Hours per week working on a job
C9	Credits	Number of credits this quarter

2.   Class Project

File: **Classdata.mtp**
Source: The class data set was created as a class project in a statistics course. To collect the data, questionnaire containing the following variables was given to 200 students enrolled in the course. Th codes used to create the Minitab worksheet are given with qualitative variables.

Column	Name	Description
C1	Gender	Gender M=0, F=1
C2	TotalCr	Number of credits earned prior to this quarter
C3	QtrCr	Number of credits this quarter
C4	Marital	Marital status: Single=0, Married=1, Other=2
C5	Age	Age
C6	Distance	Distance you live from class (in miles)
C7	HoursWork	Number of hours per week you work (on a job)
C8	GPA	Grade point average
C9	Car	Type of car: US=0, Foreign=1, No car=2
C10	Major	Major program: Business=0, Nonbusiness=1

3.   Business and Education Professors

File: **ProfStudy.mtp**
Source: Salary, degree, years of experience, and gender are recorded for 148 professors in the College of Business and College of Education in 1999.

Column	Name	Description
C1	Salary	Nine month salary
C2	Degree	Highest degree earned
C3	Experience	Years of teaching experience
C4	Gender	Gender
C5	College	Business or Education

4.   Heart Attack 911 Calls

File name: **Heart.mtp**
Source: An ambulance company servicing five counties collected data on 41 heart attack victims to determine what could be done to increase the chance that a patient is saved.

Column	Name	Description
C1	Patient	Patient number
C2	Age	Age of the heart attack victim
C3	Time	Ambulance response time in minutes

C4	Saved?	Whether or not the heart attack victim is saved
C5	SaveCode	Saved=1, Not saved=2
C6	Metro?	Whether or not the victim was in the metro area
C7	MetroCode	Metro area=1, Outside metro area=2

5. Home Sales

File name: **HomeSales.mtp**

This data set contains information on 36 home sales in two Minnesota communities. Since new homes do not follow the same pricing structure as existing homes, new homes were not considered. Two homes with unusually high prices are not typical of other homes in the data set. One was lake front property and the other had a five-acre lot with a creek running through it.

Column	Name	Description
C1	House	House code
C2	Price	Sale price of the home
C3	Bedrooms	Number of bedrooms
C4	SqFtArea	Finished area in the house in square feet
C5	Age	Age of the house in years
C6	Location	Community: Burnsville=0, Shakopee=1
C7	Style	Style of house: rambler=1, split level=2, two-story=3, other style=4

6. How Safe Are the Skies?

File name: **AirFatal.mtp**

Source: Air Transportation Association on World Wide Web (*www.air-transport.org*). Air travel in the United States is much safer today then it was many years ago. However there is a concern that the increase in the number of flights and airlines will result in more accidents and fatalities. Air travel statistics from 1938 to 1999 are provided in the data set.

Column	Name	Description
C1	Year	Year
C2	Passengers	Number of passengers carried
C3	Miles	Millions of aircraft miles flown
C4	Departs	Millions of aircraft departures
C5	Accidents	Number of aircraft accidents
C6	FatalAccid	Number of accidents resulting in fatalities
C7	Fatalities	Number of fatalities
C8	PassFatal	Number of passenger fatalities

7.   Campus Crime

File: **Crime.mtp**

Source: University Public Safety (UPS) collects campus crime information. Whenever a crime i
reported on campus, UPS officers are called to the scene before the city police and fire department ar
notified. The officers take reports of each incident that occurs on campus. This information i
compiled in annual reports that are made available to the public.

Column	Name	Description
C1	Semester	Time the crime occurred
C2	Crime	Type of crime
C3	CrimeCode	Alcohol arrest=1, sexual assault=2, non-forcible burglary=3 forcible burglary=4

8.   Residential Homes

File: **Homes.mtp**

Source: Minnesota Real Estate Research Center collected information on 200 residential homes sold
in a community.

Column	Name	Description
C1	Area	Location within the community: Area 1 is within the city, area 2 is suburbs, and area 3 is in the country
C2	Bedrooms	The number of bedrooms
C3	ListPrice	List price of homes
C4	SellingPrice	Price at which the home sold
C5	Finance	Type of financing: Assumed Seller's Financing=1, Cash=2, Contract for Deed=3, Conventional Loan=4, FHA Loan=5, VA Loan=6, Other type of Financing=7
C6	Days	Days on the marketing.
C7	MonthSold	Month sold (numbered)
C8	DaySold	Day of the month sold

INDEX

The Minitab session commands and subcommands are printed in capital letters in this index. Subcommands are listed with their respective commands. Menu commands are generally found on the same page.